CW01665508

BOOK MAKERS
British Publishing in the Twentieth Century

BOOK MAKERS

British Publishing in the Twentieth Century

IAIN STEVENSON

THE BRITISH LIBRARY
2010

First published 2010 by
The British Library
96 Euston Road
London NW1 2DB

© Iain Stevenson 2010

British Library
Cataloguing in Publication Data
A CIP record for this volume is
available from The British Library

ISBN 978 0 7123 0961 5

Designed by Ron Costley
Typeset by Norman Tilley Graphics Ltd
Printed by the MPG Books Group,
Bodmin and King's Lynn

JOHN HELM WILSHAW STEVENSON

1923-1983

A True Bibliophile

Contents

Illustrations

The author and publishers are grateful to all copyright owners who have given permission to reproduce illustrations in their book. We have used our best endeavours to obtain permissions where necessary, and will correct any errors or omissions in future editions.

Endpapers: *'After the Conference; the Penguin Editors'* (1955) by Rodrigo Moynihan (courtesy Penguin Books).

BETWEEN PAGES 190 AND 191

Preface

When I was a small boy, about eight years old, my father, a 'commercial gentleman' for the Newcastle soap-makers Thomas Hedley and Sons (part of the global Empire of Procter and Gamble), introduced me to the delights of books and reading that has lasted me a lifetime by taking me with him on his weekly excursion to the local library and giving me that key to the world – my very own library ticket. He had since his own childhood been a book enthusiast and despite coming from a decidedly non-bookish home (in working-class Scotland, 'books' were magazines) he was amazingly well-read and knowledgeable about authors, publishers and literature. Although he had little spare cash, he always managed to buy the latest 'six bob novel', and among my earliest memories are the yellow and claret jackets from the house of Gollancz, the blue and black artwork produced by Michael Joseph and the evocative coloured illustrations with which their various publishers embellished the outsides of works by Georgette Heyer, Denis Wheatley, Nancy Spain and Caryl Brahms and S.J. Simon. These he secreted in the glove compartment of his company-supplied Ford Anglia and they rarely appeared at home. My mother would not have approved of the household budget being diverted in such directions.

Later, when I was at secondary school, he would meet me after the closing bell (the Anglia had now become a Morris 1000) and we would drive off to some remote corner of the Clyde valley. Here we would devour our latest volumes, in the winter for a short time before the light faded and in those glorious, never-ending Scottish summers often till 9 or 10 in the evening. These excursions were explained to my mother as 'essential sales work' to the greater glory of Fairy Snow or Daz.

The magic that he wove for me since those days has never faded, and my lifelong attachment to books led inevitably to an academic career, a career as a publisher and back to academe again. Although he never said so, I think I had the kind of life chances that he would have coveted and his love of reading inspired me to seize the opportunities that he lacked. It was a cruel irony that he lost his sight in his fifties, robbing him of his greatest pleasure, and he died at the early age of sixty. Without his influence and example I would not have had the career I have had, nor would this book have been written. It is therefore dedicated to his memory with pride, gratitude and love.

Introduction

This is not a book about books, literary culture or authorship, although it is intimately concerned with all of these. It is primarily a history of the business structure of book publishing in Great Britain during the twentieth century and concentrates on the organizations, operations and personalities that characterized probably the most diverse, dramatic and productive period in the story of the British book business since William Caxton first set up his printing press in Westminster in 1476.

Book publishing is, however, a business like no other. It touches the lives of virtually everyone in their work, education and leisure, and in its goal of realizing, packaging and selling ideas, its raw materials are people. And those people are quirky, creative, unpredictable, exasperating, endearing, infuriating and gloriously diverse. This is what makes publishing of such wide interest compared to other large industries. I take as my starting point the creation of the regulatory environment of the Net Book Agreement in 1900 and close with its demise in 1995 as useful marker points in the development of publishing from a largely small-scale, family-run, inward looking business to the globally successful, mainly foreign-owned, multinational media conglomerates that dominate the British publishing industry at the beginning of the third millennium.

How this remarkable transformation came about is the principal theme of this history. In the space available it is not possible to provide an exhaustive chronological description of how the book industry grew and changed over the century, nor would such an approach be particularly useful to general readers who do not have extensive background knowledge. My aim has been to produce a readable and accessible account that anyone with an interest in books can enjoy, as well as providing a reliable overview for students and scholars. In any event, as book history develops rapidly into a major sub-discipline, large-scale collaborative projects like *The History of the Book in Scotland*, the *Cambridge History of the Book* and the forthcoming history of Oxford University Press will provide the interested reader with detailed scholarly accounts of the role of books and their creators, both authors and publishers, over the period. I have tried, therefore, to weave together a coherent account of how publishing companies large and small were organized, how they were managed and what the contributions were of the often colourful and idiosyncratic personalities who directed – and in some cases destroyed – them. I hope that the result provides a synoptic, coherent and entertaining sketch of how one of Britain's most successful and dynamic industries achieved its current position of being arguably the best and most productive of that newly fashionable rubric 'the creative industries'.

The method I have adopted is to divide the century more or less into decades and to examine the significant trends of publishing within those slices of time, mainly through the histories of selected companies whose activities seem to characterize the specific period under review. History, of course, does not neatly confine itself to decennial frames so the story will slip back and forth beyond the strict chronologies as the clarity of exposition demands. Nevertheless, it is remarkable how well a structuring of the history by decades fits the key trends and features of the industry at crucial points of its development. Each chapter uses the specifics of publishing house histories to exemplify the main issues and debates within the industry at the point in question.

The sources used have largely been the histories, personal accounts, autobiographies and memoirs produced by publishing houses and publishers themselves in the period. Since these tend to be celebratory, and indeed in some cases blatantly self-serving and blinkered, they are used with caution and corroborated against other sources. The literature produced by publishing about itself is actually surprisingly extensive, but there are some astonishing gaps. There is no history of Faber and Faber, for example, and only inadequate studies of John Murray, Chatto and Windus and Blackie. There are, however, a number of modern detailed studies of sometimes quite surprising publishing houses such as Joseph MacAteer's history of Mills and Boon and Jeremy Lewis's magisterial biography of Sir Allen Lane, *King Penguin*.

In the main I have not used manuscript or archival sources because there is such a richness of primary material (much of it never before mined) in the printed books detailed in the bibliography. There is, however, an enormous treasury of original source material relating to twentieth-century British publishing, much of it in the publishers' archives deposited in the University of Reading library, although there are also substantial holdings in the National Library of Scotland (relating to the now largely defunct but historically important Scottish publishing industry), the British Library and elsewhere. One of the aims of this history is to spark interest in the neglected history of twentieth-century publishing that these archives could document and to inspire their exploitation. Doctoral and post-doctoral research on specific companies, organizations and individuals making use of the archive material would be a most worthwhile and welcome development.

Throughout this book I have defined the term 'publishing' broadly. Previous historians have tended to concentrate on metropolitan publishing and especially the sector usually described as 'London trade fiction' or 'general' publishing. While the London literary houses have been vital to the shape and direction of twentieth-century publishing, and they are certainly not neglected here, I have striven to include the contributions of less fashionable and visible but nonetheless important publishing specialities such as educational, scientific and technical, and the whole gamut of book output gathered under the catch-all of 'non-fiction'. As befits a Scot, I have also tried to bear in mind that publishing, although dominated by London, was by no means exclusively carried out within five miles of Charing Cross. The other great publishing cities of Edinburgh, Glasgow, Oxford and Cambridge were significant in the twentieth century and their famous and vigorous houses, now sadly in many cases extinguished or only weakly flickering, played significant and even decisive roles in the way publishing developed in our period. It is also worth remembering that at various times publishing houses flourished and were influential from such unlikely geographical bases as Lutterworth, Welwyn Garden City, Newton Abbot, Norwich, Kingswood, Leicester, Loughborough and Stroud.

But it is, of course, the people who worked in publishing who created its history, and this prompted me to select the title *Book Makers* for their history. Many of those who were crucial to the successful realization of publishing have, however, proved frustratingly elusive to document. The memoirs and 'official histories' tended to be written by the directors and owners of the houses, naturally reflecting their preoccupations, prejudices and world views – and they, of course, tended to be men of a certain class, educational and cultural background (with many exceptions). For most of the century women are unjustifiably invisible in the sources, even though in their roles as secretaries, proof readers, editors, sales people and administrators they were important – and indeed essential – to the success of the industry. Where they do appear their roles are patronized and subtly downgraded. I have tried to evoke the environments in which the ordinary people of publishing worked, and to give a sense that the boardroom and the partners' desk was not the whole story. It is worthwhile recalling that the greatest symbol of publishing's transformation over the century is that at the time of writing four of the six largest British publishers now have female chief executives, and women directors are now the norm rather than the exception in every sector of the industry. Sue Bradley's wonderful compilation of oral history *The British Book Trade* (2008) allows many of the key people who worked in publishing at all levels of seniority in the last thirty years to speak eloquently about their lives. How I wish that we had such a similar rich archive for the first fifty years of the twentieth century!

Before returning to academic life, I was an active participant in publishing for over a quarter of a century, working mainly in the educational, academic, scientific and professional fields. I was only ever tangentially involved in trade publishing and never (knowingly at least) published fiction. I have in my active research gleaned my knowledge of how trade publishing works from observation and conversation with its protagonists, and my interpretation of its history should be read with that knowledge in mind. I have been lucky enough to know and talk with many of the history makers of the last three chapters of this book and have also shared their reminiscences of earlier key figures, events and trends. However, I have no knowledge and less sympathy with literary theory and cultural studies, and this history does not aspire to be a contribution to either. I have left it to others to trace the ontological impact of the books mentioned here and their contributions to patterns of thought, ideology and *Zeitgeist.*

This book is consequently a straightforward history of a unique form of business and the way in which its complicated and often convoluted progress over the last hundred years led to commercial models that – rather like books themselves – are enormously powerful, flexible, useful and important, but remain curiously under-regarded, poorly documented and misunderstood. This is not, therefore, a contribution to book history, but to the arguably greater and more rewarding field of publishing history.

1 'The Magna Charta of the Book Trade'

The beginning of modern publishing

As the nineteenth century drew to its close, British book publishing appeared debilitated and threatened. Its leading and old-established imprints, such as Longmans Green, John Murray and Thomas Nelson, despite flashes of innovation and originality in non-fiction and children's publishing, primarily concentrated on the increasingly old-fashioned, long-winded and convoluted novel published in three volumes (the 'three-decker') whose main (and in many cases only) purchasers were the subscription circulating libraries like Mudie's and W.H. Smith.

The typical one guinea annual subscription, plus an extra charge each time a volume was borrowed, was a significant barrier to access by less well-off readers to the libraries so the tastes of their buyers thus tended to reflect a conservative and unadventurous readership of the upper middle-class.[1] In effect the libraries dictated publishers' choices in the development of their lists. The circulating libraries clung to the system for purely mercenary reasons because it meant that they could charge their captive clientele three times for each novel. Readers were also ill-served by the system as they frequently found that the next volume in the sequence was unavailable when they wanted to continue the story. Royal Gettman's still unsurpassed meticulous study (1960) of the publishing history of the house of Bentley between 1829 and 1898 (when it was absorbed by Macmillan) documents in detail the rise and demise of the three-decker

1 The readership profile of the circulating libraries was to remain narrow and class-defined for decades to come. Laura Jesson, the guilt-ridden, cut-glass, would-be adulteress in Noel Coward's film *Brief Encounter* (1948) made her first fateful journey to Milford Junction in order to change her library books at Boots. Boots, who began life as manufacturing and dispensing chemists, was among the largest operators of subscription libraries in the middle decades of the twentieth century.

and its complicated impact on the businesses of publishers, circulating libraries and booksellers.

The market was therefore constrained and stagnant despite the growth of literacy following the Elementary Education Act of 1870 and increasing disposable income among readers. Even relative newcomers such as Macmillan and John Lane, despite dynamic starts, quickly fell into a business model that offered little prospect of expansion and competitive growth. Before 1900 fewer than 5000 new titles were published per year from about 120 publishers, most of whom were tightly concentrated in a few streets round St Paul's Cathedral in London, despite important outposts in Edinburgh and Oxford.[2] Even those like Cassell and Routledge, who had tried to serve the growing market of the newly literate produced by the Education Acts found their cheap editions and popular novels hard going to make profitable. Most publishers were content to fulfil the perceived literary wants of a relatively narrow social range of readers, serviced by the subscription libraries and increasingly querulous and quarrelsome booksellers.

In what will prove to be a recurrent theme in this history, the problems faced by *fin-de-siècle* publishing stemmed from the terms of supply from publishers to bookselling customers. This had been a perennial issue throughout the previous sixty years as some larger booksellers sought increased discounts from publishers in order to undercut their competitors' retail prices. Publishers had countered these claims by arguing that all booksellers should be treated equally and that, with the concession of an extra discount of 10 per cent for cash and the 'odd copy' system (thirteen copies supplied for the price of twelve), a fixed discount structure allowed for an orderly market. In an era of free trade, it proved increasingly difficult to maintain this position and, after a bellicose attack on literary protectionism orchestrated in the columns of *The Times* and by the entrepreneurial bookseller John Chapman, an arbitration by the leading jurist Lord Campbell led to a deregulation of book prices in 1852 (Ashton, 2006, pp.148-9). For the next forty years, publishers fought a rearguard action against 'underselling' by booksellers that put their profit margins under pressure and discouraged risk-taking. Ultimately booksellers suffered too in this free-for-all, and many went out of business during the recession of the 1880s. By 1890, calls were beginning to be made

2 This compares to over 120,000 titles published each year today from over 2000 publishers. In 1947, about 15,000 new titles were published (Stevenson, 2008, p.278).

to reconsider how books were priced and sold, and to widen the market by abandoning or modifying the established, rather elitist format of the three-decker and adopt other ways of packaging and marketing literature.

These new ideas and opportunities were seized on by (and in turn depended on) the emergence of a new type of publisher – one willing to break the mould of established structures, particularly the subscription libraries, with an entrepreneurial outlook and a sense of new markets beyond the middle and upper-class clienteles of traditional booksellers. Foremost among these was William Heinemann (Whyte, 1928, St John, 1990). Born in 1863 in Surbiton into a cultured family of Jewish antecedents with German connections (his father was from Hanover), he had early ambitions to become a musician, but his cosmopolitan education (he spoke French, Italian and German fluently) drew him ineluctably towards the world of books. His European outlook and travels gave him a sense of different models of publishing, particularly the competitively priced paperback reissues of copyright English novels for sale only on the Continent by Tauchnitz and others. This was put to good use when he was apprenticed to the first of the many European immigrants to transform the scope and range of British publishing, Nicholas Trübner, in 1879. Trübner was a both a shrewd businessman and an intellectual of wide interests and acquaintance. The list of his publishing company included not only fiction by Charles Reade and Samuel Butler's visionary fantasy *Erewhon*, but also philosophy, science and linguistics, with many translations including Hegel and Schopenhauer.

Heinemann learned from this mentor not only editorial skills, but also production, selling and negotiating, as well as the ability to build a wide network among European publishers largely ignored by his British contemporaries. Following Trübner's untimely death in 1884, Heinemann managed the business, but left in 1889 when the firm was acquired by Horatio Bottomley. Bottomley was later to be exposed as a fraudster and charlatan, and the business had to be rescued by a forced merger with Kegan Paul and Trench (Franklin, n.d. [1985] p.11).

Heinemann borrowed £500 from his father, who had built up a modest fortune as a director of Parr's Bank, and took the lease on some rooms in Bedford Street, Covent Garden in 1890 to set up his own publishing imprint. Even this location was a statement of his *avant-garde* approach. The traditional centre of the London book trade had been the district of Paternoster Row and Ludgate Hill, clustered round Stationers' Hall and the less salubrious 'Booksellers' Row' of Holywell Street at the west end of

Fleet Street, famed for pornography and sedition. Covent Garden, half a mile further west, in cheap but elegant Georgian accommodation in the shadow of the produce market – and much more convenient for the emerging booksellers of Charing Cross Road and the West End – was an inspired location.

It symbolized a break with the past and the creation of a distinctive profile for the future. Macmillan, the most innovative of the established publishers, was already here and in a decade they would be joined in Bedford Street or adjacent Henrietta Street by other members of publishing's new mould-breaking wave, including John Lane, Edward Arnold, Williams and Norgate, Gerald Duckworth, Hutchinson and Company, T. Fisher Unwin, J.M. Dent and Grant Richards (most of whom we will meet again later).

An early seasonal list of seventeen titles from Heinemann set out his distinctive stall as a new publisher of serious intent and great ambition and which incidentally was to establish the parameters of his firm's publishing specialities for most of the twentieth century (*The Bookseller*, 10 October 1890, p.1123). It comprised five translated novels or collections (including Tolstoy and de Maupassant) edited by Edmund Gosse (rather an establishment figure to be retained as an advisor by a revolutionary publisher, but Heinemann was nothing if not eclectic and surprising),[3] a couple of (imported) American history titles, two editions of De Quincey's letters, three practical science manuals (of American authorship and provenance), some miscellaneous *belles-lettres*, but only two original novels. This eccentric collection reflects in its essentials only what any new unknown publisher could get to start up by acquiring rights in Europe and the USA. The scientific books were bought in from their original American publisher as flat sheets and bound in Heinemann covers.

Nevertheless their presentation shows no lack of ambition and reveals the strength of his international network and grasp of wider markets. With no false modesty, the translations were billed as 'Heinemann's International Library' and the buy-ins as 'Heinemann's Scientific Handbooks' – as though they already had stature and reputation. Yet it was one of the novels (the other sank without trace) that was to establish Heinemann

3 Gosse was a literary critic, poet and man of letters who shared with Heinemann a knowledge and appreciation of European literature. He was the first to introduce Ibsen to England.

definitively as a powerful new publishing force and a breaker of established trade practice.

Hall Caine was a romantic historical novelist whose work is now largely forgotten, but who had an immense popular following in the 1890s. He had been published by Chatto and Windus, but they had declined to take his new medieval tale *The Bondsman*, as had Cassell. When it was offered to Heinemann during his first week of business he impulsively offered the author almost two-thirds of his entire capital (£300) for the rights. He printed three thousand copies conventionally in three-decker format for subscription library consumption at £1 11s 6d per set. Here most of his contemporary peers would have stopped or waited. Heinemann quickly announced that he would follow up with a cheap edition for the public at three shillings and sixpence barely six months after first publication. Most established publishers might have brought out a six shilling or seven shillings and sixpence edition after about a year, but presumably a stretched Heinemann needed the cash flow to replenish his depleted capital and was prepared to gamble on offending his library customers who had bought the first expensive edition. He was triumphantly vindicated and *The Bondsman* went on to sell 450,000 copies.

A second piece of luck came when, in negotiating the sale of the book to Mudie's, he met Sydney Pawling, the nephew of the library's founder. Initially the two men did not hit it off as they were opposites in character, tastes and outlook. Heinemann was a short, stout, dandyish *bon-viveur*, given to emotional outbursts and with exotic tastes in art and culture. He was friends with Whistler (whom he published) and Wilde (whom he did not), rejoiced in the ambiguous nickname 'TYV' ('The Young Voluptuary') and took pride in having a rich fish dish (Sole Heinemann) named in his honour.[4] Pawling was a tall, blond public school man (known as 'The Saxon' to Gosse), conservative in tastes and politics, an accomplished athlete who was a member of the Marylebone Cricket Club. Yet he had an excellent critical eye and a shrewd commercial sense. Heinemann cultivated him assiduously, and slowly a grudging friendship and mutual respect developed between the two. Pawling moonlighted from Mudie's by advising Heinemann on manuscripts (he warned against publishing a novel submitted by Shaw as he correctly and acutely divined it to be a recycled crude early work that the Irish critic was attempting to cash in on his growing reputation), and in 1893 Heinemann offered him a partner-

4 The dish was a staple of the menu of the Hotel Metropole in Brighton for many years.

ship of five-twelfths of the business on payment of £1908 (St John, pp.17-18). This was celebrated by dinner at the Conservative Club (doubtless Pawling's choice) and it was to endure successfully until Heinemann's sudden and early death in 1920. And it may have been in the elegant dining room in St James's that these two unlikely collaborators began to plot the assassination of the three-decker novel and the wholesale modernization of the British publishing industry.

Hall Caine was again their chosen weapon. Discontent with the circulating libraries' stranglehold on fiction formats had been growing, not least among authors, who felt that the expensive three-decker format excluded less well-off readers and that new types of writing that did not fit the moribund and rigid formula was discouraged. Most publishers complacently accepted that status quo and the solid but unadventurous benefits it brought their businesses. Heinemann decided to challenge this cosy cartel, all the more remarkably since his business partner was a scion of the Mudie clan. In July 1894 he announced that Hall Caine's forthcoming sequel to *The Bondsman*, *The Manxman*, was to be published immediately in one volume, priced six shillings, adding laconically 'There will be no edition in three vols' (St John, p.28). He had earlier announced his growing disillusion with three-deckers in a letter to the *Daily Chronicle*, but none of his peers actually believed he would go ahead and administer the killer blow.

Again, the results spoke for themselves: *The Manxman* sold 400,000 copies and the three-decker as a viable publishing model died virtually overnight. The 'six-shilling novel' – an original work of literature of up to 400 pages published immediately directly for sale to individual readers – was a flexible format that encouraged new writers and new types of writing. It endured more or less unchallenged and unchanged until the 1950s. The circulating libraries survived, of course, and even prospered, although they never again held such tyrannical sway as they had done over publishers'output or readers' choices.

Heinemann's reputation among his peers and the public soared. His business grew and by the turn of the century, a mere decade after its foundation, it was turning over £45,000 with a high net profit margin for the period of 7 per cent. His liberation of fiction from its triple corset brought him new and progressive authors such as H.G. Wells (of whose 'scientific romances' like *The Time Machine* he and rather surprisingly Pawling, given Wells's socialism, was an enthusiastic supporter), Joseph Conrad and D.H. Lawrence. He also attracted more traditional authors such as

Henry James and John Galsworthy, as well as notable writers in translation like Maxim Gorky, Peter Kropotkin and Alphonse Daudet. Heinemann kept the scope of his firm's interests wide, continuing to publish successfully science, philosophy and criticism while maintaining strong business and literary links with publishers in continental Europe and North America. Later he championed medical, educational and scholarly publishing, including the famous 'Loeb Classical Library' of ancient Greek and Latin texts and commentary. He was an early advocate of a regularized international copyright regime and he was influential in obtaining fairer legal treatment for foreign authors and publishers in the United States, ultimately resulting in the 1909 US Copyright Act.

In time Heinemann was to become a respected and trusted ambassador for British publishing in general. Although he suffered from a snobbish and spiteful anti-Semitism from Lytton Strachey and other disdainful members of the Bloomsbury Group, he had quickly become one of the most substantial and influential figures on the London literary scene and an important shaper of the course of literature. More importantly, he can be seen as the first modern publisher who set the structures, models and goals of the industry for most of the twentieth century and typified for many what a successful publisher should be.

While Heinemann was energetically reinventing and expanding the book market, the traditional tension between publishers and booksellers over their commercial relationship threatened to cancel any gains. Although it was booksellers who had agitated for the Campbell judgement of 1852 to deregulate book pricing, it had not produced the benefits that had been predicted. Booksellers pressured publishers for ever-increasing discounts on a limited range of popular titles and competed to 'undersell' each other below the publisher's recommended prices. Both publishers' and retailers' margins tightened and the range of titles stocked narrowed. Booksellers engaged in brutal pricing battles that materially harmed their businesses and in many cases drove them out of it. As we shall see in Chapter 9, many of these familiar circumstances surrounded the renewed deregulation of the book market a century later.

By 1890, Frederick Macmillan, who had entered publishing just as book price deregulation began,[5] identified this 'unsatisfactory state of things' as the 'greatest evil' hampering the growth of the book business (Macmillan,

5 His father and uncle had been booksellers in Cambridge. They set up their publishing firm in London in 1843, and Frederick entered in 1850 (Morgan 1943).

1924, p.4). In his famous letter of 6 March to the trade paper *The Bookseller* (then as now, despite its title, primarily supporting publishers' interests), he proposed the introduction of the 'net price' system. This would not allow selected titles to be retailed at less than the price set by the publisher, with copies supplied to all booksellers at a fixed discount. To test his contentions he proposed to publish an important new title, Alfred Marshall's *Principles of Economics*, at a fixed price of twelve shillings and sixpence net rather than a notional price of sixteen shillings. It was a brilliant *coup de theâtre* to use the work of the greatest economist of the age as the standard bearer for a new regime of fixed retail prices.

He hoped that his proposal, if generally adopted, would result in better value for the book buyer, an end of cut-throat price competition between retailers and a regulated market for publishers. Marshall readily assented to this high-profile experiment, although as he later admitted his understanding of Macmillan's arguments in making his book the first net title was fragmentary and he was not convinced of the economics (letter from Marshall to Macmillan, 17 November 1898, quoted in Kingsford, p.7).

Actually, despite his later claims, Macmillan's original 'net' scheme was neither particularly far-reaching nor immediately revolutionary in reforming publisher-bookseller relations. The number of 'net' published titles remained few; they were mainly confined to those which, like Marshall, would probably have not benefited in any case from price competition between retailers. Macmillan distinguished between 'net' and 'subject' titles: the latter were popular books 'subject to no regulations as regards price and [which] might be sold at a discount at the discretion of the dealer' (Macmillan, 1924, p.5). These 'subject' books comprised the bulk of his firm's output throughout the 1890s while 'net' titles (Table One) were confined to relatively expensive non-fiction or luxury books whose market was easily predictable and inelastic (to borrow a Marshallian term).

Despite this modest and rather tentative proposal, booksellers, although acutely conscious of the financial travails that deregulation had caused them, were hostile to and sceptical of net pricing. They described it to reporters from *The Pall Mall Gazette* as 'absurd', 'absolutely impractical' or 'muddled', and declared that 'the public will not stand [for it]' (quoted in Macmillan, *loc. cit.*, pp.10-12). Only John Bumpus, whose well-stocked and modern shop in Oxford Street had attracted a new middle-class clientele, expressed any support for the plan. A few established publishers, such as Methuen, Longmans, John Murray and Swann

TABLE ONE: Net books published by Macmillan 1890-97

Year	Titles
1890	16
1891	60
1892	68
1893	75
1894	107
1895	140
1896	122

Source: Macmillan, loc. cit., *p.17*

Sonnenschein (Karl Marx's publisher), tried out net price publishing on a few titles, but these were nothing more than cautious experiments. The first publisher to make a concerted and determined effort to impose net pricing was not one of the grandees of literary London but a small and thrusting newcomer, J.M. Dent.

Dent, a native of the decidedly unliterary town of Darlington, had begun his career as a journeyman bookbinder with a passion for self-improvement, good works and temperance (Dent, 1928). He was also a considerable entrepreneur who recognized the thirst for learning from the newly educated lower-middle class from which he had sprung. In 1867, at the age of eighteen, he moved to London. Within a few years he had married and owned a substantial bookbinding business in Great Eastern Street in Shoreditch. The death of his wife and a disastrous fire which destroyed his factory in 1888 nearly broke him, but the remnants of his insurance money and the support of his Evangelical friends enabled him to acquire the bankrupt business of the devotional publishers Suttaby. From this basis he expanded into reprinting out-of-copyright classics by Charles Lamb, Samuel Johnson, Henry Fielding, Jane Austen and Oliver Goldsmith, together with a few more contemporary writers whose rights could be cheaply obtained. These were gathered in a finely printed and nicely bound series, as befitted his indentured credentials, called 'The Temple Library'. They were priced at one shilling and sixpence or two shillings per volume and provided an influential model for later cheaply priced yet well produced classics (Dent, 1928, Chapter 4). As part of this development he conceived, with great flair but typical parsimony, the ambitious project of issuing the complete works of Shakespeare as individual plays in a pocket edition. He used Israel Gollancz, an unknown, 26-year-old scholar newly graduated from University College, London, as editor and the yet-to-be famous Walter Crane as illustrator. The 'Temple Shakespeare' began to appear in 1894 and it was complete in forty volumes by 1896. Priced at one shilling and sixpence each, they were good value and immediately popular. Dent fixed their prices as net, but the notorious 'cutting' bookseller Stoneham bypassed this restriction by obtaining supplies from the main trade wholesaler Simpkin Marshall and retailing them at one shilling and four pence. Stoneham had strongly resisted Macmillan's original proposals and as a major 'city and country' bookseller he was in a position to do so: larger publishers dared not confront him head-on because of the size of their business with them.

Dent was outraged when Simpkin told him they could do nothing, and he retaliated by threatening not to supply the wholesaler with any of his publications. This was an impulsive and possibly foolhardy move by a new and not very powerful publisher, but Simpkin buckled and told Stoneham they would not supply them any of Dent's publications without a guarantee to observe net terms.[6]

After attempts to source the books elsewhere, Stoneham capitulated and agreed to observe Dent's fixed price on all 'Temple' titles. Hugh Dent, in his edition of his father's memoirs (Dent, 1928, pp.64-6), could not resist pointing out it was only a couple of months *after* Dent had faced down Simpkin and Stoneham that Macmillan followed suit and imposed net terms on the wholesaler. Certainly, as Table One shows, it was only after 1894 that Macmillan began substantially to increase their output of net titles. Macmillan may have been the creator of net pricing, but Dent was the catalyst.

Whether it was Macmillan or Dent whose actions demonstrated the necessity for net pricing to stabilize publishing's commercial models, events now moved quickly in its favour. Most booksellers in 1890 had opposed the idea and continued to support the 1852 settlement. Trading conditions had actually improved, but price competition had worsened and many retailers feared that they might not survive a prolonged price war. Dent and Macmillan's forthright positions concentrated the retailers'

6 Simpkin posted a notice on their trade counter that the Stoneham 'runner' was not to be supplied with any Dent titles. This reputedly caused much hilarity among the notoriously rowdy and raucous bagmen who daily restocked central London bookshops from publishers and wholesalers, and was apparently a major factor in Stoneham's climb-down.

minds wonderfully.[7] In January 1895 a new trade organization called the Associated Booksellers of Great Britain and Ireland hurriedly and rather uncharacteristically united the fractious bookselling community. It endorsed a resolution to 'hereby approve the net system of publishing books ... and unanimously resolve to support it' (Macmillan, 1924, p.19). Rather disingenuously given the history, they called 'upon publishers to insist on all booksellers adhering to the published price of net books and ... [to] enforce this by more stringent regulations'. The society comprised the bulk of the London and provincial trade, and eventually even confessed agnostics such as Stoneham joined up.

This precipitate and unexpected conversion knocked the publishers onto their back feet. They were suddenly confronted by a united and clamorous trade demanding a reform that the publishers had themselves suggested but only tentatively supported. They needed to regain the initiative and take control. Publishers' individual efforts to suggest workable schemes, such as the fixing of wholesale prices enabling booksellers to discount by cutting their own margins, were rebuffed (Kingsland, p.8). Booksellers wanted net pricing and they wanted publishers to pay for it.

Publishers needed their own trade organization to represent their views and present a united front. Initially this was to be an *ad hoc* group of nine leading publishers (Longmans, Macmillan, Murray, Routledge, Sampson Low, Bentley, Blackwood, Smith Elder and Heinemann),[8] but it quickly became apparent that to be effective the organization needed to be permanent and more widely representative. Net books were the immediate problem, but plenty of other issues, including copyright, international relations, contracts and authors' terms, even the correct layout of title pages and bibliographical practice (the distinction between a 'new edition' and a 'reprint' was by no means consistent at this period) needed to be resolved. At the end of 1895 an open meeting of forty-nine publishers was held at Stationers' Hall. It drafted out the regulations for the creation of the Publishers' Association which came into being the

7 Interestingly, Macmillan does not mention Dent's action at all in his history of the Net Book Agreement and indeed he asserts that it was his influence that convinced Simpkin to impose net terms. He claims it was his closure of Stoneham's account that brought them to heel (Macmillan, *op. cit.*, pp.16-17).

8 Heinemann was the only one of the 'new wave' publishers included in the initial 1895 group, a measure of the respect that he had already earned from the old guard. It seems significant that others such as Dent (especially given his stand of the previous year), Unwin and Lane were excluded.

following January, with fifty-eight members under the chairmanship of the head of the senior British publishing company, Charles J. Longman (Table Two).[9]

The membership of the Association was representative, but by no means exhaustive. There were a number of surprising omissions and abstainers. William Collins, already a large and successful home and exporting publisher, was missing and did not join until 1906 (Kingsland, p.21). Cambridge University Press joined, but Oxford did not. Even more notably, significant trade publishers such as Batsford and Eyre & Spottiswoode were absent from the fledging Association. So, too, were specialist publishers whose business did not primarily depend on bookselling, such as Sir Isaac Pitman, mainly producing shorthand manuals, ready-reckoners and office stationery, the law publishers Butterworth and Shaw and Sons, and medical publishers J & A Churchill and E & S Livingstone.

Membership was overwhelmingly London-based, but included a few further-flung companies like Arrowsmith (Bristol), Jarrold (Norwich), Blackie (Glasgow) and Clark (Edinburgh). Interestingly for these provincial companies their businesses were primarily printing rather than publishing, and they may have felt it prudent to support their major customers. Simpkin Marshall's membership (although they did publish a little on their own account) was more controversial and they may have wished to back both horses (they were also members of Associated Booksellers). In the main, even large non-metropolitan publishers such as Oliver and Boyd, Chambers and the map publishers John Bartholomew, Gall and Inglis and Johnston of Edinburgh and McLehose of Glasgow University Press resiled, although the London cartographic publisher Stanford was a charter member and evidently thought membership worthwhile (Stevenson, 2007c, pp.337-41).

A further feature of the initial membership recalls that although the list included venerable, illustrious and considerable firms such as Longmans, Murray, Macmillan, Skeffington, Cassell and Chapman & Hall (who had been Dickens' publisher), the great majority of publishers of the era were small and financially weak with little clout if they acted individually. Of the fifty-eight founders only fourteen were large enough to justify limited-liability status, many of these only so because their businesses

9 Longmans was founded in London in 1724 and had under various combinations of imprints a distinguished publishing history from Samuel Johnson's Dictionary to Robert Louis Stevenson's *Dr Jekyll and Mr Hyde.* It was and remains the longest established commercial publishing company in Britain (see Briggs, 2008).

TABLE TWO: Founding member firms of the Publishers' Association, 1895[10]

George Allen
Edward Arnold
J.W. Arrowsmith
George Bell & Sons
Richard Bentley & Son
Adam & Charles Black
Blackie & Son, Ltd
William Blackwood & Sons
Bliss Sands & Co.
Burns & Oates Ltd
Cambridge University Press
Cassell & Co. Ltd
Chapman & Hall, Ltd
Chatto & Windus
T. & T. Clark
W.B. Clive
Archibald Constable & Co.
Dean & Son Ltd
J.M. Dent & Co.
Digby, Long & Co.
Wells, Gardner, Darton & Co.
Gay & Bird
Hachette & Co.
William Heinemann
H. Henry & Co. Ltd
Hodder & Stoughton
Houlston & Sons
Hurst & Blackett, Ltd
Hutchinson & Co.
A.D. Innes & Co.
Isbister & Co.
Jarrold & Sons
John Lane
Lawrence & Bullen
Crosby Lockwood & Son
Longmans, Green & Co.
Sampson Low, Marston & Co.
Macmillan & Co. Ltd
Methuen & Co.
John Murray
T. Nelson & Sons
J.C. Nimmo
Oliphant, Anderson & Ferrier
Osgood, McIlvaine & Co.
S.W. Partridge & Co.
Kegan Paul, Trench Trübner & Co. Ltd
Young J. Prentland
Rivington, Percival & Co.
George Routledge & Sons, Ltd
Simpkin, Marshall, Hamilton, Kent & Co. Ltd
Skeffington & Son
Smith, Elder & Co.
Swan, Sonnenschien & Co. Ltd
Edward Stanford
T. Fisher Unwin
J. S. Virtue & Co. Ltd
Ward, Lock & Bowden Ltd
F. Warne & Co.

Source: Kingsford, 1970, p.216

included interests other than publishing. For example, Hachette and Isbister were importers and distributors, Simpkin was a wholesaler and Virtue was a fine-art printer. Most of the others (including the mighty Longmans) were private, family-owned companies, recently established partnerships or even sole traders. The creation of the Association was

10 Firms' names are given exactly as recorded in the Publishers' Association minute book. They sometimes varied in their title-page imprint.

essential to give them a united and influential negotiating position with booksellers (and increasingly authors).

Although newer and smaller firms were welcomed into membership, the governing Council comprised almost exclusively representatives of the older and more powerful firms. Only Heinemann and T. Fisher Unwin of the new wave joined the Council and until 1904, when Heinemann became vice-president, the elected officers more or less rotated between Charles Longman, John Murray and Frederick Macmillan, despite an explicit constitutional clause to prevent one firm or individual dominating the organization. There is a distinct sense that the radical newcomers were merely tolerated and, although their support was important, the agenda was set by the 'big three'. The exception to this was Heinemann, who – regarded as a key link between the 'coming men' and the publishing graybeards – was quickly ushered into the Establishment. His judgment on trade matters was trusted and he was a natural ambassador, perhaps because of his languages, for international dealings on behalf of British publishing. He played a key role in setting up the International Congress of Publishers at whose Brussels meeting in 1897 he read a paper in French on '*droit d'auteur*', making it clear that such a dangerous continental concept was not appropriate to English-language publishing[11] (Kingsland, p.17).

Longman's initial presidential address set out a number of tasks for the new association, including managing imperial copyright, control of piracy and uniform bibliographical practice. However, the main objective was the creation of a workable Net Book Agreement.[12] Although publishers and booksellers alike now wanted the system, it took a remarkably long time for the details to be hammered out. The Associated Booksellers, whose Damascene conversion had made them zealots, initially demanded a rigid system fixing trade discount at 25 per cent to be applied to all books priced above seven shillings and sixpence, but publishers thought this was dangerously close to dictating at what prices they could publish and would thereby reduce competition.

It was not until July 1898 that proposals were sufficiently worked out

11 In fact, such 'moral rights' were not introduced into British copyright law until 1988. Even now such 'suspiciously foreign' concepts as '*droit de suite*' and 'parody right' are not available to British authors despite attempts at European harmonization (see Jones and Benson, 2002).

12 Price and discounts, copyright and piracy control still dominate the Association's agenda today. Bibliography has been replaced by digital concerns.

and agreed to be presented in a long and detailed speech by Frederick Macmillan during which he declared this 'momentous issue ... [is] of supreme importance to the trade ... [and] honestly and fearlessly carried out, it cannot fail to be successful' (Macmillan, 1924, pp.20 and 25).[13] Macmillan felt his scheme would meet everyone's approval and he took that of the Society of Authors for granted. He was wrong. The authors, led by the redoubtable Walter Besant and Bernard Shaw, suspected that the proposal was a Trojan Horse designed to cut their incomes. Publishers shied away from threatened concerted action by authors and dropped their support of the agreed scheme. The Associated Booksellers then produced a modified proposal that took authors' objections into account, but it was not until January 1899 that all sides reached agreement.

The principles of the Agreement were that all booksellers who signed up for the scheme were obliged to sell net books at the prices specified by the publishers, no matter what discount terms had been agreed. Apart from small discounts allowed to cash and certain account customers (usually 2d in the shilling), no bookseller could cut prices without permission – and any bookseller who did so would be penalized (usually by closure of his account). This, publishers contended, would disturb trade prices as little as possible. It could be adapted without serious difficulty to existing conditions, would simplify prices rather than complicate them and would not raise prices to the public '*more than necessary*' [my italics], thus to render assistance to the booksellers and enable them to keep a good stock (Macmillan, 1924, pp.28-9).

Actually the final agreed version of the Net Book Agreement (NBA), as it was now termed, was not as comprehensive as originally envisaged. It excluded school books, prize books, 'juvenile literature' and contract supplies to libraries and institutions. Generally net books were to be confined to literature and adult non-fiction retailing at more than six shillings per volume.

A further significant change was what seems in retrospect to have been an adroit sleight-of-hand played by the publishers on the booksellers. Retailers had taken the initiative in agitating for net prices when publishers had backed down in face of objections from authors, but the NBA was now to be the property of the Publishers' Association. Although booksellers and authors would be consulted, control would crucially

13 The entire speech is reproduced in Macmillan, 1924, pp.20-26. It is exceptionally tedious and includes one paragraph extending over three and a half pages.

remain with the publishers who fixed prices, determined discounts and meted out punishment to defaulters. It was an astonishing coup, but the retailers meekly accepted the shift of power and virtually all signed the new agreement. When it came into force on 1 January 1900, it was hailed as the 'Magna Charta of the book trade' (Macmillan, 1924, p.30). So it was to remain for ninety-five years, despite various challenges and modifications, until another seismic shift in publisher-retailer relations again overturned it dramatically (see Chapter 9) and redefined the power relations of the British book business.

As the NBA and the new century dawned, a new confidence had entered British publishing. The death of Queen Victoria just a year after the implementation of the historic concordat and the economic recovery that characterized the Edwardian decade symbolized a new beginning and a new optimism in the development of the book trade, both in home and overseas markets. In the last decade of the nineteenth century, new publishers in the mould of Heinemann such as Edward Arnold (1890), John Lane (1892) and Gerald Duckworth (1898) had emerged, but after 1900 the creation of new entrepreneurial publishers quickened.

Among them was George Harrap, who opened in the newly fashionable literary district of Covent Garden in 1901. He had learned his trade from Isbister and their educational import business gave him a taste for reference and academic publishing, including a range of foreign language dictionaries which were for many decades to be the foundation of his firm's prosperity, as well as cheap children's books. Other notable publishers who were founded during the 'long Edwardian summer' were T.N. Foulis (1904), Sidgwick and Jackson (1908), Mills and Boon (1908) and an array of specialist publishers such as the Architectural Press (1902), James Brodie of the famous *Notes* (1906), MacDonald and Evans (1907), Evans Brothers (no relation, 1908), The Medici Society (1908), Christopher (1906) and Ernest Benn (1909), although most were to make their most significant impacts during later decades. In many cases, the founders of these new publishers had followed similar career patterns. They had worked for more established houses – Mills and Boon for Methuen, Sidgwick for Lawrence and Bullen, Lee-Warner of the Medici Press with Chatto and Windus – but chafed at their old-fashioned and unenterprising attitudes. Consequently they set up on their own (often with minimal capital) to take advantage of the new and expanding book markets they perceived.

A publisher characteristic of the spirit and style of the first decade of the twentieth century was Grant Richards. Richards was born in Glasgow in 1872, nephew of the louche and glamorous *belle-lettriste* Charles Grant Allen who found him a place as assistant to W.T. Stead, the path-breaking editor of the famous *Review of Reviews* in 1890. Richards worked with Stead for six years and established himself as the centre of a literary and artistic network including the caricaturist Phil May, the art critic Robert Ross, the satirist Max Beerbohm, the essayist Richard la Gallienne, the dilettante Frank Harris and the artist Aubrey Beardsley. He placed an announcement in December 1896 in *The Athenaeum* that he was setting up in business as a publisher in Henrietta Street and, clearly with Heinemann's example in mind, told the world that 'Mr Grant Richards will always be glad to consider manuscripts on any subject'.

Richards had real flair for finding new authors and new publishing genres. His initial publishing list included poetry, novels, travel guides, children's books and *belles-lettres.* One of his earliest publications was A.E. Housman's *A Shropshire Lad* in 1896 and he published Samuel Butler's *The Way of All Flesh* (1903) to great acclaim. Among the other authors whose earliest books he published were Arnold Bennett, G.K. Chesterton, John Masefield, Alfred Noyes, H.H. Munro ('Saki') and Maurice Baring. Again like Heinemann he had an excellent eye and commercial taste, but he was impulsive and rather chaotic in his business. He lost many of these authors to better organized and more solvent houses, although Housman loyally remained throughout his career. His most famous discovery was James Joyce, whose *Dubliners* he published in 1912, although one senses from the correspondence that he was rather relieved to be rid of the mercurial Irish genius – not only because he ran up enormous proof correction bills, but also because Joyce's writing had scandalized some of Richards' trusted typesetters.

It was, however, in less exalted categories that Richards made his most significant innovations. In children's publishing, aided by his brilliant reader and editor E.V. Lucas (later to become chairman of Methuen and the publisher of Kenneth Grahame and A.A. Milne), he launched a series of colour 'Dumpy Books', including the now notorious but then unexceptional *Little Black Sambo* by Helen Bannerman. The format, presentation and pricing of these books were extremely influential elsewhere, including the colour story books of Beatrix Potter that were published by Frederick Warne a few years later. His limp bound, blue-cloth travel guides anticipated the later series from Macmillan that were the recognized format well into the 1920s. Most important of all, he created a cheaply priced hardback series of reprinted 'classic' fiction, criticism, history and philosophy under the title of the 'World's Classics' in 1900. Perhaps inspired by Dent's 'Temple Classics', he improved and standardized the format and promoted the idea of essential books that every educated person must read. This concept was emulated in similar sixpenny and shilling classics from Collins, Nelson and others. They clearly contributed to Dent's own perfection of the idea in the famous 'Everyman's Library' launched in 1905 and their influence can be traced to the 'Penguin revolution' of thirty-five years later.

Sadly Richards's editorial genius was not matched by his business acumen. Always generous with staff (if not with authors) and with a taste for luxurious living (he claimed to have his best ideas in the stylish but expensive Restaurant Frascati in the nearby Strand), he quickly over-reached his modest resources and, following a move to overly-plush offices in Leicester Square, he went bankrupt in 1903. This forced the sale of the 'World's Classics' series to Humphrey Milford; he eventually took them to Oxford University Press (who continue to publish them today). However, Richards quickly resurrected the company in his wife's name as E. Grant Richards. He experienced several further financial close shaves until he suffered a second crash in 1925, but he was always a publisher of style and consequence, with an eclectic and varied list ranging from books by Theodore Dreiser to Robert Tressall's *The Ragged-Trousered Philanthropists* (1914), as well as *The Boy's Book of Stamp Collecting* (1919) and music-hall comedian George Robey's collected after-dinner anecdotes (1923).

As publishing expanded and buzzed with entrepreneurial activity under the aegis of a newly regulated trade, the Net Book Agreement came under attack from an unexpected quarter which very nearly destroyed it. The 'Book War' of 1905-8 was a concerted attempt to destabilize the hard-won harmony between publishers and booksellers, and like any good war had more than its fair share of espionage, double-dealing, broken alliances and general skulduggery. It broke out in autumn 1905 when *The Times* newspaper announced that was establishing a book club for its readers. This would have been an innocuous enough event had it not been for the precarious condition of *The Times* as a business and the variously chequered motives of the protagonists.

The Times had entered the twentieth century as a shadow of its former eminent self. The Walter family who owned it had failed either to renovate its printing plant or its editorial content, especially in the face of the vigorous competition from new titles established by a new breed of aggressive press entrepreneur, most notably Alfred Harmsworth, Lord Northcliffe (Bourne, 1990, Chapter 2). Circulation had been declining for many years and the appointment of Charles Moberly Bell, a distinguished foreign correspondent, as business manger in 1890 was an attempt to recover declining markets. Moberly Bell initially made editorial improvements with more foreign news coverage, but the owners denied him capital and tasked him to increase the paper's earnings by other means. In 1898 he met a flamboyant American huckster, Horace Hooper, who proposed a money-making scheme to transform *The Times*' fortunes.

Hooper had previously obtained the rights, remaining sheets and stereotypes for his then employer, the Chicago bookseller Clarke and Company, of the 9th edition of the *Encyclopedia Britannica*, published in 1875, from the original publisher. A & C Black were glad to be rid of them, since the text, although authoritative, was badly out of date. Hooper moved to London and, although still nominally employed by Clarke, began to put his acquisition to commercial use. He suggested to Moberly Bell that the answer to his problems was to offer *The Times*'s readers a set of the fourteen-volume *Encyclopedia* at fifteen guineas as against the original selling price of £37. The terms were one pound down and the remainder in monthly instalments, a form of merchandizing never previously used to sell books. Hooper failed to tell Moberly Bell that his own profit would be a guinea for every set sold.

It might seem that what Hooper was proposing was an unlikely bait for the staid and conservative readership of *The Times*, but he was a persuasive talker and he quickly won Moberly Bell's confidence and agreement. The new associates proceeded to promote the premium offer in new and alarming ways. Described at the time as 'blatant', 'hysterical' and 'strongly suggestive of a transatlantic origin', Moberly Bell devoted entire pages of the paper to 'seductive conjurations' for the *Encyclopedia* which no home could be without – but unaccountably not mentioning its date of first publication (Bell, reprinted in Macmillan, 1924, pp.36-7). Lavish prospectuses were mailed 'to private homes' and additional offers made, including a mahogany revolving bookcase. Edward Bell,[14] president of the Publishers' Association during the 'Book War', tartly observed that the

14 One of the curiosities of this convoluted story is that the two major opposing contenders shared a surname. For clarity, *The Times* manager is referred to as 'Moberly Bell' throughout. They were, of course, no relation.

latter 'with the seldom-used volumes neatly stowed away in it ... [was] still an ornament of many a ... country-house library' (Macmillan, 1924, p.38).

Surprisingly these strident and hyperbolic appeals struck a responsive chord with *The Times* readership. Over 20,000 sets were sold, bringing the paper into profit for the first time in many years and making Hooper a personal fortune. During 1902-3 he went even further and obtained supplies of the new(er) 10th edition. He promptly sold 70,000 sets yielding a profit for *The Times*'s owners of £600,000 and a goodly portion for himself. Moberly Bell and his masters were beside themselves with glee. There was only one problem. *The Times*'s circulation was still declining.

The swashbuckling Hooper and his business partner Walter Montgomery Jackson saw a further opportunity to make even more money and turn the paper's fortunes definitively around. Moberly Bell was a book lover, and he knew that most of *The Times*'s readers were, too. He had convinced his miserly owners to launch *Literature* (which became the *Times Literary Supplement*), devoted entirely to book reviews, in 1902, and it had been remarkably successful. In 1904 Hooper and Jackson (who had by this time dumped their American business masters) were retained by *The Times* as 'advertising consultants', and Moberly Bell asked them to devise a scheme to increase circulation and revenue (Kingsford, 1970, p.23).

Hooper brought his aggressive marketing methods, the problem of declining circulation and the readers' demonstrated love of books together in one neat package. In 1905, *The Times* announced that those who committed to an annual subscription for the paper of £3 (compared to the prevailing rate of £3 18s) would receive, among other benefits, free membership of *The Times* Book Club. In reality, the Book Club was to be both a free lending library (thus challenging the circulating libraries), making all the latest books available to subscribers, and in addition a discounting bookseller. In its second role it gave members the option of buying books from the library stock at various stages from brand new to used, graded at intervals after publication at heavy but originally unspecified discounts (Kingsland, 1970, p.24).

Hooper told *The Times*'s proprietors that he expected to double circulation at a stroke and Moberly Bell that he was liberating literature. Moberly Bell was well aware of the discounting restrictions of the NBA, but *The Times* had a long history of denouncing what it saw as book trade exploitation of customers by price fixing, so his unreserved backing of

Hooper had venerable precedence. Besides, there was money to be made. A budget of £100,000 was allocated to launch the Book Club (nearly £5 million in today's terms) and plush premises in New Bond Street were leased from which the Club would operate by post and for passing subscribers.

Hooper was a self-assured showman and a confidence trickster, but he had enough caution to sound out certain publishers about his plan before going ahead. This is where the first of many devious and hypocritical diversions in this rollicking saga emerge. It later became apparent that he had spoken about what he had in mind to those two pillars of publishing rectitude C.J. Longman and John Murray, but they had failed to raise the alarm with other publishers – perhaps because Hooper had led them to believe they were being consulted on an exclusive basis and that the quantities of their books he would absorb were monumentally large (Bell, in Macmillan, 1924, p.37).

Hooper now played his hand with cool and exquisite shrewdness. During the first months of 1905 he approached publishers with the modest proposal that he be supplied with all new books 'at best trade terms' like any other bookseller for the Book Club. The only issue that made publishers uneasy was that as a condition of the Book Club order they were obliged to sign a five-year contract to place advertising in *The Times* equivalent to one-fifth of the value of the invoices (Hooper was on a commission for any advertising he sold). In return he would produce a catalogue of the books available through the Book Club in an edition of 100,000 copies. This would clearly increase book sales generally: he had no further territorial demands. More reassurance came in July when Moberly Bell signed the NBA on behalf of *The Times.*

When the Club opened in September 1905, the true extent of Hooper's real approach to pricing became shockingly clear. New (albeit non-net) books would be sold to members at a 25 per cent discount, but any circulated 'second hand' books, both net and non-net up to six months old, were to be sold, depending on their condition and age, at discounts of 20 to 50 per cent. The definition of 'second-hand' was merely a book that had been read by two subscribers and could no longer be sold as new. The established circulating libraries had agreed under the terms of the NBA not to sell their *ex-libris* copies of net titles until six months after publication. With superb aplomb, Hooper suavely offered 'clean uninjured copies ... virtually as good as new' at up to half net price. In reality the Club was already selling discounted new net titles to subscribers, including high-profile bestsellers such as Winston Churchill's biography of his father and ironically a new edition of *Lorna Doone* from Edward Bell's family firm, George Bell & Sons. Moberly Bell and Hooper were summoned, admittedly in a rather leisurely fashion, to the Publishers' Association to account for themselves on 9 May 1906, and the publishers rather meekly accepted their assurances that the Club was only shifting excess stock.

Hooper's reckless hyperbole (much of which he may have himself believed) and irresponsible financial management (he was selling many titles at below cost to inflate turnover) had seen the Book Club expand at a vertiginous rate. In April 1906 it claimed to be the 'largest buyer of books in the world' (Kingsland, p.25) and on 1 May (a full eight days before the bland assurances given to the Publishers' Association), it announced that it had moved to a new commodiously appointed building in Oxford Street to accommodate a stock of 600,000 new books for sale or loan. It also issued the following ringing *casus belli*:

> It is the opinion of *The Times* that books have always been sold at too high a figure, that if their prices were reduced to a scale more in correspondence for example, with the price of a newspaper, books would circulate in correspondingly larger numbers ... The cost of the paper, printing and binding ... [of a book priced at 21s net] ... may amount to 1s 6d. The enormous balance of its price goes in profits to the publisher, author and bookseller ... [a]t our great sale such books will be sold at 23 and 30 pence ... The books acquired from the publisher are of course entirely new. (*The Times*, 1 May 1906, quoted in Kingsland, p.26)

Kingsland is of the opinion that Edward Bell was being disingenuous in saying that when he met Moberly Bell and Hooper on 9 May he knew nothing of the public announcement of the sale of net books by the Club on 1 May, and did not become aware of the true state of affairs until 17 May. I tend to agree, although to be fair perhaps he was not a subscriber to *The Times* or habituated Oxford Street.

Whether or not the publishers or booksellers were genuinely unaware of what Hooper was up to, the public certainly knew. Immediately on opening the Oxford Street store was besieged by eager customers seeking bargains, and the doors had to be continually closed to regulate the crush. Tens of thousands of discounted books flew out, with biographies marked at 36 shillings net going for seven shillings and six shilling net novels for nine pence. Publishers had certainly connived at the Hooper circus by unloading vast quantities of new but slow selling titles on the Club at remainder prices (by that action themselves defying the NBA), but Hooper also orchestrated the excitement by buying books at ordinary terms and selling them at a dramatic low prices as loss leaders.[15]

Some of the more established publishers still rather guiltily dallied, but others – significantly mainly those who did not do much business with the Club – reacted with horror and demanded action. On 4 July John Lane put a motion to a hastily convened meeting demanding that net books, new or second hand, could not be legally sold at less than the published price within six months of publication and no books of any description, save school books, within the same period could be sold at discounts of more than 25 per cent. With qualifying modifications the motion was passed, and the Council of the Publishers' Association agreed to amend the NBA to specify these conditions. John Murray, perhaps still smarting from his earlier encounter with Hooper, suggested that publishers stop advertising in *The Times* until the paper came into line.

The amended NBA was due to come into force on 1 October 1906, but if its introduction was intended to strangle the Book Club, it failed miserably. Longmans and Simpkin Marshall, Hooper's two largest suppliers, discovered that they had signed binding five-year agreements with *The Times* to supply on previous terms and could not (or more probably would not) renege. Moberly Bell, although he had signed the old NBA, declined to sign the new one, saying he had to honour the commitment to his subscribers who had signed up for a year on advertised terms. Accusations of bad faith, hypocrisy and questionable practice were made on both sides.

Skirmishing burst into pitched battle on 25 September and the days following, when *The Times* used its columns to accuse the publishers openly of running a restrictive monopoly and of committing 'a real evil' by artificially inflating book prices to the public's detriment while fleecing booksellers with artificially low discounts. The economics that underpinned the paper's arguments were flawed (they ignored any payments to authors), but not for the last time in its history were the editorial columns of the 'Thunderer' used to promote shamelessly the commercial interests of its proprietors.

As 1906 drew to its close, there was an attempt at mediation led by

15 His tactics are not dissimilar to the aggressive pricing policies adopted by the supermarkets ASDA and Tesco that finally killed the NBA in 1995 (see Chapter 9).

authors who viewed an attack on book prices (quite correctly) as an onslaught on their income, but their intervention proved futile. Other observers found the war incomprehensible or risible. The weekly newspaper *Truth*, with its tongue lodged firmly in its cheek, proposed to set up The Truth Trousers Club. It would offer its subscribers an annual new pair of trousers, the right to change them as often as they liked at its office and to buy used trousers at great discounts depending on their condition even 'if they had become a bit baggy at the knee' (Kingsland, p.31 fn).

Despite such bemused satire, the struggle between *The Times* and the publishers became increasingly serious, bitter and vicious. Counsel were instructed and threats of injunctions on charges of conspiracy were exchanged. Simpkin Marshall was leant on to cease dealing with *The Times* by the threatened withdrawal of supply by major publishers and characteristically chose to comply, even though *The Times* claimed – with justification – breach of contract. Unaccountably Longmans, who had the same five-year contract, were not equally pressured, and apparently continued to supply *The Times* throughout the dispute.

Slowly, however, during the spring of 1907 supplies to the Book Club dried up and subscribers became disgruntled that they could not obtain the books they wanted at the kinds of prices they had been promised. Hooper continued to issue his monthly list and pitch the Club's advantages in the paper's columns and through mail shots, but *The Times* was by now losing both book sales and subscribers. The paper continued to publish letters and articles accusing publishers of making hidden profits and it attempted to enlist the support of authors. They obtained a major scalp when Bernard Shaw (contrarian as always) authorized an edition of *John Bull's Other Island* exclusively for sale by the Book Club, but the Society of Authors in general remained sceptical. *The Times Literary Supplement* continued to review the output of intransigent publishers, but appended a warning to these notices: 'The publishers of this book decline to supply *The Times* Book Club ... [S]ubscribers who would co-operate with *The Times*, to defeat the *Publishers' Trust* [my emphasis] may effectively do so by refraining from ordering the book ... until it is included in *The Times* monthly catalogue' (quoted in Macmillan, 1924, pp.32-3).

The defining engagement of the war occurred during autumn 1907. John Murray had become the regular target for excoriation by correspondents and columnists in the paper as an example of a publisher who was using the NBA to milk high prices from a suffering reading public and denying the Book Club. His firm was about to publish *The Letters of Queen Victoria* in three volumes at three guineas, and Hooper would dearly have loved to have got his hands on such a potential bestseller for his true-blue subscribers. He was only able to obtain a few lending copies, probably from a European source, and when *The Times Literary Supplement* reviewed the book it criticized its high price – unheard-of in reviews of the period. *The Times* then published under a pseudonym letters accusing Murray of 'simple extortion' and comparing him to Judas Iscariot. Murray sued *The Times* for libel, suspecting correctly that the review and the letters were inspired by Moberly Bell and Hooper, and eventually won damages of £7500 for harm to his reputation and his business.

Events now took on a surreally sinister atmosphere of secret diplomacy and conspiracy. Hooper had failed to meet his promises to the proprietors to increase circulation, the publishers' ban on advertising was hurting and shareholders outside the Walter family had grown increasingly disenchanted with their meagre dividends. Disaffected investors launched a legal action to demand the sale of *The Times*'s assets and it at first seemed likely that they would be acquired by C.A. Pearson, publisher of the *Standard*. Pearson was so confident of success that he actually approached the Publishers'Association with proposals to settle the Book Club dispute. However, it transpired that senior publishers had already been secretly talking with Lord Northcliffe who was laying his own plans to take the paper over.

Heinemann had been the go-between with Northcliffe. They had met at his Bedford Street office on 7 May 1908 to discuss the end of the Book War, with Northcliffe asserting it was losing *The Times* £40,000 a year. Heinemann urgently telephoned Macmillan to say that Northcliffe was walking over to his St Martin's Street office to discuss 'a matter of considerable importance ... which he would like [Macmillan] to promise to keep absolutely to [himself]' (Macmillan, 1924, p.67). When he arrived Northcliffe explained to Macmillan that he had formed a company to take *The Times* over, but since he did not have to register as owner of its shares for over a year he could keep his intentions hidden – ostensibly because he did not want to antagonize the unionized typesetters on his *Daily Mail* (*The Times* was a non-union shop and he planned to keep it that way). It seems more likely that secrecy was necessary to keep the eventual purchase price low.

Northcliffe wanted to keep the Book Club running, but he needed to make savings and by implication get rid of wasteful practices and staff. He sought to enlist publishers in the cause of peace and revealed that although Moberly Bell was aware of and approved his takeover plan, he still clung to the belief that publishers 'were a wicked race of men, who made outrageous profits and committed all sorts of crimes against the reading public' (Macmillan, 1924, p.68). Northcliffe asserted that to bring Moberly Bell and his staff round, *The Times* needed to lose the Murray libel suit and as new proprietor he would be happy to pay damages without challenge. He painted a picture of *The Times*'s staff as obsessive fanatics whose sole aim was to destroy British publishing. Even more sensationally, he confided that he had planted a trusted employee known only as under the *nom de guerre* 'Mr Bates' in the Book Club who could relay information and negotiate with the publishers on Northcliffe's behalf. He pledged that the NBA would be respected if minor cosmetic changes were made.

Heinemann and Macmillan agreed to support Northcliffe's audacious raid. They undertook to speak in favour of his plans to the other members of the Publishers' Association Council, but to keep his identity secret 'while assur[ing] them] ... that the person who had opened negotiations was in a position to carry them through' (Macmillan, 1924, p.69). Bell and Longman on behalf of the Association charged Macmillan with Heinemann's help to draft an agreement with 'Mr Bates' which the full Council approved without prejudice on 14 May. 'Mr Bates' proved more slippery than anticipated, perhaps because as well as representing Northcliffe he was also taking instruction from Moberly Bell,[16] but eventually an agreement for *The Times* to observe the NBA without reservation was hammered out during September 1908.

In the meantime on 30 June Hooper was sacked, barely three days after Northcliffe assumed his anonymous control of the paper, although this was not the end of his contribution to hostilities. It emerged that he, too, had been plotting to buy *The Times* and use its resources to fund yet another new edition of *Encyclopedia Britannica*. Moberly Bell had not trusted him enough to keep him in the picture and Northcliffe's sudden access of ownership must have come as a nasty shock. He attempted to recover his position by setting up an investment vehicle to wrest *The Times* from Northcliffe's grasp and develop the *Encyclopedia*, but before

16 Northcliffe told Macmillan that the legal judgement forcing the sale of *The Times* had 'saddled' him with Moberly Bell for at least five years as the paper's managing director (Macmillan, 1924, p.72).

he could swing into action he fell out acrimoniously with his partner Jackson over their respective shares in the venture. The two bitterly wrangled in the American and British courts over the next four years, and although Hooper eventually won in a landmark case for American corporate governance, his reputation for less than honest dealing was an enduring legacy. He returned permanently to New York where he died in 1922, aged 62.[17]

The concluding treaty of the 'Book War' was anticlimactic, partly because both sides agreed to make no public statement that hostilities were actually over. Its terms were that if the NBA was recognized by the operators of the Book Club as the absolute arbiter of how books were sold and its strictures embraced without demur then publishers would resume supply to *The Times* on 'best trade terms'. The peace was celebrated by a 'little dinner at the Savoy' hosted by Northcliffe, at which Moberly Bell grimly told Macmillan that he had wanted the war to continue. Macmillan remarked later that '[f]ortunately the proprietor of *The Times* did not consult Moberly Bell' (Macmillan, 1924, p.77).

The Times Book Club prospered under the new regime with over 30,000 members and remained an important element of the book market for decades. It continued to supply new and used books without discount (without members apparently much caring) and hysterical denunciations of publishing malpractice were replaced in the paper's columns by the long-absent publishers' advertisements. Bell noted with satisfaction that this proved that '*The Times*' case … [had been] a rotten one, in theory and practice, from first to last. The hypothesis that people can be bribed to buy what they will not buy spontaneously was unsound' (Bell, in Macmillan, 1924, p.66). Macmillan hailed the heroic outcome as having 'saved the Retail Book Trade throughout Great Britain from bankruptcy and the virtual extinction from which it was threatened, owing to the suicidal system of underselling' (Macmillan, 1924, p.77).

Although the NBA survived and was not to be seriously challenged again for nearly eighty years, the truth is that no-one comes out of the 'Book War' with much credit. Publishers behaved hypocritically and with selfishness. Macmillan was a bully, Longman and Murray were less than candid, Heinemann basked egregiously in the limelight and relished

17 There is an extremely guarded obituary of Hooper in *The New York Times* of 14 June 1922 headed 'Horace E. Hooper, Publisher, dies … LONG WITH LONDON TIMES/ American Disagreed With Former Partner Over Plans to Buy Paper Now Owned by Lord Northcliffe'.

the influence the affair brought him. The Associated Booksellers sat on the sidelines and were conspicuous by their absence at key moments. Moberly Bell was a swivel-eye obsessive with an irrational hatred of publishers, Hooper was a crook, albeit a charming one. Northcliffe used the whole affair as a stalking horse to grab *The Times* when it was weakened and its attention was distracted by a sideshow. Although the publishers had won, the reading public were left wondering whether book prices were in fact artificially inflated and whether there might be some justice in what *The Times* had claimed. The real legacy of the 'Book War' was a long, lingering suspicion among the book buying public that something was distinctly fishy about the way books were priced. Over a year after hostilities ended, *The Manchester Guardian*, the traditional keeper of the flame of Free Trade and no friend of *The Times*, mused in a leading article:

> The six-shilling novel has withstood several attacks ... and we seem to be entering upon an experimental period which may bring the solution of a considerable difficulty, MR WILLIAM HEINEMANN recently remarked on the inconsistency of paying precisely the same sum for long or short, good or bad, and he proposes now, in a letter which he has issued to the trade, to make certain distinctions. He will publish a series of novels in the autumn which will be either two shillings or three shillings net per volume, according to their size ... [H]ere we think Mr HEINEMANN is on dangerous ground ... Oddly enough, Mr HEINEMANN suggests that he has solved the problem of giving the buyer value for his money. The difficulty is, it seems to us, that it may be necessary to obtain the bigger prices for what are, from the publisher's point of view, the inferior novels.
>
> The uniform and comparatively high price of novels gives the chance to writers who could never hope for very large sales, though their books are of better quality than the ephemeral stuff that is bought by the thousands. Five hundred people might want a good, unpopular novel, and would pay a price that would give, say, a profit of sixpence to the publisher: but if this book be produced at a price that might give a penny profit there will not be three thousand readers for it.
>
> [Although] [i]t is consoling to remember that some popular books are good. (*Manchester Guardian*, 9 July 1909)

As the decade ended, publishing was a transformed business. The emergence of new houses with energetic owners willing to try out new ideas and cater for new markets among the middle and upper working classes followed the path beaten by Heinemann. Older models withered and, although the circulating libraries remained influential and would be an important part of the market for another forty years, many publishing houses that would not or could not adapt disappeared. Almost a quarter of the publishers who had joined the Publishers' Association in 1895 had ceased to exist by 1910. The Net Book Agreement seemed secure and a stable regime between publishers and booksellers was fixed.

Increasing prosperity saw demand increase not only for serious literature, but also for popular 'story-telling' and romances, enabling authors such as H.G. Wells, Arthur Conan Doyle, 'Saki' and John Buchan to achieve great popularity and large sales. Children's fiction, including *Wind in the Willows* by Kenneth Grahame (1908), reached new heights of sophistication and quality. Publishers felt confident enough to launch ambitious projects such as the collected *Pentland* edition of the works of R.L. Stevenson in 20 volumes, published in a limited edition of 1500 copied by Cassell in 1907. Publishing had successfully met the challenges from booksellers, *The Times* Book Club and the changing tastes of the public, but in so doing had in itself changed in a way that was not really understood at the time. Although the large firms that had dominated the second half of the nineteenth century – Longmans, Macmillan, Murray and Cassell – remained powerful, the way had been opened by Heinemann, Richards and others to show that small firms with flair, imagination, luck and judgement could make their mark dramatically and prosper. This set a pattern of the emergence of hopeful new publishing entrepreneurs with bright ideas and a drive to succeed but often with little money who were nevertheless able to compete effectively and sometimes, like Mills and Boon and later Penguin, achieve truly spectacular outcomes. This renewed pattern of business rebirth and reinvention created in the first decade of the century was a persistent feature of the publishing industry right up to the 1990s. The background stability created by the NBA was certainly a major factor in enabling this climate of confident entrepreneurship.

2 'Books by the million'

Publishing and the First World War

Although the 'Book War' was over, publishers had soon to contend with a real conflict that would transform much more profoundly their markets, structures, business relationships and products. Up until 1914, the long Edwardian economic golden afternoon persisted, and many publishers flourished in its light. The retail market was buoyant, and after the defeat of *The Times*'s challenge to net pricing in 1908 regulated prices kept it orderly. The blunting of price competition enabled new booksellers, such as W. & G. Foyle, founded in 1904, enthusiastically to pursue expansion by offering wide ranges and efficient service (Mountain and Foyle, 2004).

An example of a publisher whose books and outlook were characteristic of the enchanted lost land of publishing content immediately pre-1914 was the Edinburgh house of T.N. Foulis (Elfick and Harris, 1998). Thomas Noble Foulis, who shared the surname of one of Scotland's most eminent eighteenth-century publishers,[18] worked for publishers William Blackwood and Robert Grant and had travelled widely in Germany for business and pleasure. In 1904, at the age of thirty, he launched his own publishing company with capital of £2500 in Frederick Street, Edinburgh. He specialized in finely printed editions of poetry, classic tales and undemanding non-fiction aimed at the gift book market.

Foulis's output is distinctive because of the very high production quality of his titles. He used thick, often hand-made paper with deckle edges and with his Rose colophon incorporated as a watermark at least once in each section. His typography was carefully executed, eventually using an exclusively designed typeface. The books were lavishly illustrated

18 Robert and Andrew Foulis set up as University printer and publisher in Glasgow in the 1740s, producing finely printed editions of classical texts. It is not possible to demonstrate any familial links between them and Thomas Foulis.

in colour, with illustrations 'tipped in' on grey or chestnut mounts. Foulis used eminent artists, including many drawn from the 'Glasgow School' such as Sir John Lavery, Jessie M. King, Annie French and D.Y. Cameron, for illustrations and cover art. Bindings were often luxurious, employing vellum, suede leathers or textured cloth or silk cases, gilt edges and silk head and tail bands: buckram was standard as binding cloth even on cheaper editions. At the bottom end of the range, he produced smaller 'envelope books', effectively extended greetings cards containing a single poem or short story with exquisite colour illustrations and fine letter-press, ready to be posted.

Foulis was in effect bringing the quality of fine, private-press publishing to a mass audience. His delicate, colour-illustrated treatises on wild flowers, gardens, historic cities or musicians, or highly decorative presentations of popular poems like *The Ruba'iyat of Omar Khayyam* or Browning's collected verse, were just the thing to be read in the drawing room by the wives and daughters of an aspirational middle class on a long summer's afternoon. To be sure, much of Foulis's output was of small literary worth and cloyingly sentimental in tone,[19] but it was enormously popular and commercially successful during the decade leading up to the First World War.

In 1906 his business had grown to the extent that a London office was opened, inevitably in Bedford Street, but this soon proved inadequate to meet the high demand from booksellers. In 1911, after a brief sojourn in Paternoster Square, he took the lease of a substantial Georgian house in Great Russell Street by the British Museum.[20] In the meantime he had joined the Publishers' Association and brought his brother Douglas into partnership as production manager.

Part of Foulis's success was explained by the incredible cheapness of his publications in the light of their quality. In 1913 a 320-page extended Crown hardback edition of Izaak Walton's *The Compleat Angler*, featuring

19 Although he did occasionally issue more challenging works, such as the poems of Heine in the original German, the muscular illustrations of Frank Brangwyn, or the pioneering *photographie verité* of Charles Reid of Wishaw. He even published political works right across the spectrum, from the extreme right-wing anti-statism of Hilaire Belloc to the radical socialism of Ramsay MacDonald, later to be Britain's first Labour prime minister. He also published the complete works of Frederick Nietzsche as well as a commentary on German philosophy.

20 This later became a famous publishing address as the offices of Hamish Hamilton in the 1930s.

a frontispiece and twelve tipped-in colour plates, was priced at five shillings net in buckram or seven shillings and sixpence net in full leather. 'Friendship booklets' printed in two-colour letterpress on deckle-edged paper of popular poems were priced at sixpence each in paper covers or two shillings and sixpence bound in 'Rich Tyrian Silk with marker'. He was unsparing in his insistence on the highest quality of materials, and this became heightened when he employed the distinguished French designer and typographer George Auriol in 1911 to produce a display and text font for his exclusive use.

Thomas Foulis had sublime disregard for budgets and balance sheets (much to his brother's consternation), but his firm remained buoyant as the economy and his leisured middle-class market continued to prosper. The outbreak of the First World War initially did little to cramp his style, but as bleak reality took hold the demand for pretty books on sundials, dogs or the hunting field plummeted. There was still less taste for Germanic philosophy or poetry. Quality materials became harder to source and economic perturbation put pressure on book prices. Foulis's readers were now in the forces or had become female factory workers; they wanted reading more in tune with the times. At the same time other publishers, such as T.C. and E.C. Jack, attempted to ape the Foulis style with similar titles produced to cheaper specifications, doubtless eroding such of the market that had survived. It was becoming increasingly clear that the taste for this kind of insubstantial, frivolous Edwardian publishing had perished in the brutal realties of modern mechanized warfare. The firm published 75 new titles in 1913. This dropped to thirty-five in 1914, but only eight new titles appeared in 1915, ten in 1916, sixteen in 1917 and twelve in 1918.

Thomas's blithe disregard for cost control came home to roost during the later stages of the war, and although the company struggled on for a few years after the armistice it was a pathetic shadow of its pre-1914 incarnation, mired in debt and rudderless due to Thomas's growing alcoholism.[21] It did manage a few significant publications, such as the debut work of the Scots poet Christopher M. Grieve (Hugh McDiarmid),

21 Douglas had joined the Royal Scots in 1914, and was later commissioned into the Cameronian Rifles, eventually becoming Colonel in 1918. With his watchful eye on his brother's finances missing, Thomas became uncontrollably extravagant and many printers refused to accept new orders from him because of unpaid bills. Douglas resigned from the partnership in 1921, later becoming a successful director of the Edinburgh bookbinder Hunter and Foulis.

but by 1924 Thomas was apparently no longer associated with his eponymous imprint and his Edinburgh headquarters had been taken over by Hodder & Stoughton. Bound copies and sheet stock were acquired by Peter Davies (reputedly J.M. Barrie's model for Peter Pan) who had worked for Foulis during and after the war, but he was never successful and later tragically committed suicide. Thomas Foulis himself, lonely and alcoholic, lived on to see another war and died in 1943.

Another distinctive feature that contributed to the gilded prosperity of British publishing immediately prior to 1914 was the steady growth and high profitability of book exports and overseas publishing by British-owned subsidiaries. Exports had begun to assume importance since the 1860s when steamships and an efficient global postal service enabled books to be easily sent round the world. Naturally, British publishers looked firstly to markets within the British Empire and the United States to expand their book sales. India was a major target for book exports, both for general literature and educational titles. Local offices had been established in the late nineteenth century by companies such as Longmans and Nelson, acting both as agents to distribute home-produced titles and increasingly publishing on their own account. Most publishing houses produced 'colonial editions' (mainly for India, but often also available in Australia, New Zealand and Canada) of their most popular titles with their distribution restricted to their designated territory; they were often priced cheaper than home market versions.[22]

Macmillan had been trading successfully with India since the mid 1860s. In 1901 it opened a publishing office in Bombay (Mumbai); five further branches were operating throughout the subcontinent by 1914 (Morgan, 1943, p.186). Their business was mainly educational and comprised three classes of publication: direct imports of British published titles including 'colonial editions'; British books specially modified for Indian conditions but produced in the UK; and books entirely edited, printed and published in India, sometimes in local languages. No statistics are available for the size of the export market in this early period, but there is little doubt that the 'colonial business' of most British publishers between 1900 and 1914 grew substantially and contributed

22 Publishers' abuse of colonial markets and the issue of cheap colonial editions had been a bone of contention with *The Times* in its justification of its assault on the Net Book Agreement in the 'Book War' of 1905-8. Colonial editions were often described as 'dumping', and this in many cases was not far from the truth.

healthily to domestic balance sheets.[23] In fact, it was a common complaint from incipient nationalist commentators that the dominating presence of British publishers in imperial territories poisonously inhibited the development of a domestically-owned publishing industry, despite the eventual emergence of companies such as Thacker and Co in India (Kipling's original publishers), Angus and Robertson in Australia and William Briggs, later the Ryerson Press, in Canada.

The United States was, however, the largest and most attractive potential market for British book exports, but also one of the most intractable. British publishers had no political clout there, and the American reluctance to sign up for the international copyright treaty the Berne Convention made publishers' rights vulnerable.[24] The United States held a traditionally protectionist attitude to imports as well as displaying something of a 'cultural cringe' to European literature. America had a well-established domestic publishing industry of its own, with firms such as Scribners, Lippincott, Houghton Mifflin, Holt and Wiley feeding domestic demand. The indigenous publishers were mainly concentrated in Boston, so when British publishers decided to set up shop in the USA they tended to settle in New York.

The Macmillan Company of New York was set up in 1896 and under the direction of G.P. Brett, a native Yankee, it quickly became a considerable publishing house on its own account, with revenues approaching $1 million by 1914. Harold S. Latham, a New Yorker educated at Columbia University, was typical of the kind of local staff that the overseas subsidiaries employed. He joined Macmillan in 1909 and has left an entertaining account of his time there as marketing man and editor over the following half-century (Latham, 1966).[25] Similar American ventures were launched by Longmans, Nelson and Collins, and even small companies

23 It is curious that most company histories dealing with this period are largely silent on the export business, despite its evident importance. Morgan on Macmillan is a notable exception.

24 The Berne Convention was established in 1886 to provide mutual protection for copyrights in signatory countries under 'national treatment'. The USA remained outside the Treaty until 1969, and the attitude of their publishers to foreign copyrights in the 1900s finds present-day echoes in the cavalier attitude of American corporations such as Google and Microsoft to contemporary copyright issues.

25 Latham later gained fame as the editor who discovered Margaret Mitchell's *Gone with the Wind* in 1935. He rather modestly claims that his major contribution to the book was convincing the author to change the heroine's name from Pansy to Scarlett O'Hara (Latham, p.53).

such as Ward Lock operated successful subsidiary houses in New York. (Liveing, 1954, pp.62-3). The American branches of British publishers tended to operate semi-autonomously and few of their domestically published titles came into the British market. There was a certain resentment felt towards these interlopers by both American publishers and readers, but their impact was undeniably important. They may not have exported books to the old country, but they did export significant profits which added to their parents' pre-war prosperity.

By contrast, British publishers showed little interest in the potential of continental European markets. Despite the efforts of cosmopolitans such as Heinemann and even Foulis, British book sales in Europe were small and there was little attempt to set up publishing branches in France, Germany or Italy or publish directly in local languages.[26] This was partly due to the overwhelming dominance of the German Tauchnitz company. Tauchnitz had an enormous business selling licensed copyright editions of English-language books, mainly novels and undemanding non-fiction, in paperback to itinerant British tourists and English-reading locals alike through a vast network of railway bookstalls from Portugal to Russia. The company survived the First World War, but they never again regained their absolute dominance of the market for English books in Europe. However, they did later collaborate with Albatross to produce a successful paperback German-language series in the 1920s, often seen as the model for Penguin Books (see Chapter 4). Nevertheless British publishers never filled that void.

Perhaps the most important and lasting publishing event of the immediately pre-1914 era was the arrival of a Bill for a new Copyright Law in 1911. The previous Acts of 1842 and 1862 were badly out of date and the advance of new technology, particularly cinematography and sound recording, meant that important areas were unprotected by legislation. The Berne Convention required that British law be regularized if its provision for 'national treatment' was to be met.[27] Heinemann, by now president of the Publishers' Association and ever sensitive to international issues, lobbied for new legislation, including the controversial provision that the legal term of copyright be fixed at fifty years from the date of

26 Nelson was one of the few British companies to set up in France.

27 Berne provides that a copyright work published in one country is treated exactly the same as if it been a locally produced book when it is published in any other signatory state. This is 'national treatment'.

death of the author or creator.[28] A particularly contentious issue was whether the new law could be extended to colonial administrations and given, as we have seen, that there was some resentment within the Empire towards British publishers' expansion there, there was doubt whether governments in the Dominions, in particular, would accept the new provisions.

In the event the new Copyright Act came into force in July 1912 and was to govern the intellectual property regime of British publishing until 1956. It introduced the 'life plus 50 years' duration of copyright and abolished the venerable system of the necessity to register copyright at Stationers' Hall. The act of publication now automatically gave copyright protection. The Act's writ was to run in all British imperial possessions, except Australia, Canada, Newfoundland, New Zealand and South Africa whose local legislatures were invited to approve similar legislation.[29] Most crucially, the Act applied to British India, thereby securing for British publishers a protected status in that huge and lucrative market that would persist until independence in 1947 and beyond.

The initial impact of the outbreak of the First World War in August 1914 on British publishing was rather muted. To begin with, there was little disruption in the book trade and indeed publishers saw the opportunity for new markets, busying themselves with patriotic tracts and accounts of German brutality. Arthur Waugh, writing of the impact of the war on Chapman & Hall, recorded 'business as usual', although he noted that some publishers had used the outbreak of hostilities as a pretext to cancel contracts and prune forward publishing lists (Waugh, 1930, p.266). Edmund Gosse sounded an alarmist note, fearing that all literature would be extinguished by the war, but most publishers faced the emergency with stoicism rather than panic (Mumby, 1930, p.370). The fact that continental Europe had never been a particularly significant market for British

28 It was argued that this would allow two generations of the author's descendants to benefit from income, but the proposal to tie copyright protection to the life of the author, rather than the date of publication, was highly controversial – not least among publishers who saw this as the thin end of the wedge of that dangerously foreign conception of authorial 'moral rights'.

29 In the event all but Canada did so, which meant that for many years authors did not enjoy a 'life plus fifty' protection there – although they did in Newfoundland, producing an anomalous situation when the latter joined Canada in 1947. This legislation is the origin of the 'British Publishers' Traditional Market' (BPTM) which was until the 1990s the exclusive market area demanded by British publishers in authors' contracts.

books doubtless cushioned the initial impact of the sudden loss of trade with the Central Powers.

Inevitably, however, as it became clear that the war would not 'be over by Christmas', publishing began to experience ever more serious problems in staffing, access to materials, economic disruption and changing tastes among readers. In the first flush of patriotic enthusiasm many younger publishing staff (then almost exclusively male) joined the forces, and as the carnage on the Western Front became evident, it was clear that many would not return. Waugh sadly noted that his trade department was now staffed by 'men ... who looked as if they had been at school with Charles Dickens ... who could not under any circumstances be of use for military service' (Waugh, 1930, pp.267-8).

Paper quickly became in short supply as imports from Canada and Scandinavia were blockaded and freighters were sunk by German submarines. Certain special high-quality papers, made from esparto grass imported from North Africa, became virtually unobtainable. The government exercised priority over access to paper stocks – and increasingly printing – for the enormous quantity of documents war administration demanded, and publishers found that their manufacturing orders were delayed or cancelled at short notice. After three decades of economic stability, prices of raw materials began to increase dramatically. Reprints were especially problematic as ironically the public's expectation of fixed retail prices arising from the Book War made it difficult to increase prices to meet increased costs. The price straitjacket of new net novels at six shillings and cheap reprints at sixpence or seven pence came close to bursting. The cheap quality series such as 'Everyman's Library' and 'World's Classics' had their prices doubled by degrees from one shilling in 1914 to two shillings in 1916, and so lost much of their appeal (Mumby, 1930, p.371).

Paradoxically the first years of the war saw the issue of lavishly produced, large-format illustrated volumes celebrating patriotism and the civilized cultural values of the Allies. Although raw materials were becoming scarce and expensive, books were seen by the government and publishers as an important part of the war effort to keep up morale. Typical of these was *King Albert's Book* (1915), produced by Hodder and Stoughton for *The Daily Telegraph* and edited by Hall Caine. Bound in white buckram, it contained almost two hundred pages of text and colour tipped-in illustrations by eminent artists extolling the suffering of overrun Belgium. A similar venture, also from Hodder, *Princess Mary's Gift*

Book (1914), sold over 600,000 copies in two years and the patriotic publisher donated all their profits to charity (Attenborough, 1975, p.78). Most lavish of all was *Edmund Dulac's Picture-Book for the French Red Cross* (n.d. but probably 1916). It showcased the exquisite artwork of the French designer in the style of his famous Christmas annuals, which in strictly limited editions had graced the Edwardian list of Hodder and Stoughton. With a huge print run of 50,000 it sold rapidly and well, and Hodder pledged to donate 25 per cent of revenue received from all their titles during Red Cross week in May 1916 to the charity.

The government provided special allocations of paper and machining for these publications, but elsewhere shortages were increasingly serious. By 1916 the Board of Trade was proposing paper rationing and a Royal Commission was established to work out the principles of distribution. Frederick Macmillan represented the publishers on the Commission, and he argued that supplies should be secured in order of priority for educational and scientific books, cheap reprints for leisure reading by troops and war workers and exports. He was particularly worried that American publishers were raiding overseas markets that British publishers were unable to supply through shortages (Kingsford, 1960, p.530). This, of course, had an element of special pleading for his own business interests.

Lack of materials and manpower, increasing costs and a changing and uncertain market had a direct negative impact on the output of the industry. Interestingly, it may have been that publishing had reached its high-water mark just before the outbreak of war. In September 1913, traditionally the key month in the 'publishing season', a total of 1203 new titles were published in all categories, but only 853 in September 1914 although these must have been planned and put into production well before war became imminent (Mumby, 1930, p.371). However, book production steadily declined throughout the war (Table Three).

TABLE THREE: Book output 1914-18

Year	New books	New editions	Total
1914	8863	2674	11,537
1915	8499	2166	10,665
1916	7537	1612	9149
1917	6606	1525	8131
1918	6750	966	7716

Source: compiled by Mumby (p.371) from listings in the Publishers' Circular

Although new titles were showing signs of recovery as the war was coming to a conclusion, new editions (at this point, the term also included reprints) had suffered a precipitous decline of almost two-thirds. While production and pricing problems, as we have seen, doubtless contributed to this, the major cause seems to have been a seismic shift in taste among the reading public that increasingly rejected the moribund publishing stock in trade of Victorian classics, light novellas and complacent tales of imperial derring-do that had dominated pre-war lists. They were not reprinted because they were no longer wanted. Instead, an edgy and increasingly war-weary public wanted reading matter that reflected their woes, worries and emerging aspirations for an improved postwar world. How individual publishers recognized and reacted to this new mood determined their fortunes during this time of accelerating social change.

Not all picked up successfully on the shift in the prevailing taste, but it was remarkable how quickly even some of the most conservative publishers made the transition. The Edinburgh publisher William Blackwood, stolid and respectable, quickly added realistic graphic accounts of battlefield action to its list, many of which were tried out in the pages of its famous *Magazine*. It scored notable bestsellers with the first-hand descriptions of soldiering from the light romantic novelist Ian Hay, writing as the 'Junior Sub'. His *The First Hundred Thousand* and its sequels sold tens of thousands of copies in shilling editions, as did the battle reminiscences of serving writers better known for other genres such as Neil Munro.

Non-combatants also met the demand for realistic contemporary fiction from Blackwood, most famously John Buchan,[30] whose *Thirty-Nine Steps* (1915) provided a model for an action-led spy story playing on fears of German infiltration in British society – although its plot and characterization was highly derivative of Erskine Childers's *The Riddle of the Sands* (1903) which founded the genre of German invasion scare literature. When *Blackwood's Magazine* celebrated its centenary in 1917 its pages were dominated by war stories, despatches from the Front and heartfelt if rather maudlin battlefield poetry. '*Maga*' (as it was familiarly referred to) was widely circulated in the trenches and its combatant readers kept up a lively correspondence on literature and the

30 Buchan was intimately involved in publishing as he became a director of Thomas Nelson in 1906 at the invitation of his friend 'Tommy' Nelson, killed on the Somme in 1916. Interestingly Blackwood rather than Nelson was often his publisher of choice, although his literary advice shaped much of Nelson's output during and after the war.

war with its editor which even now reads with immediacy and power (Tredrey, 1954, pp.205-11).

Blackwood's Magazine flourished during the war (and was to continue publication until 1980), but other publishers' periodicals experienced more chequered careers. Odhams Press, founded in 1890, produced a large number of special interest magazines, but many foundered during the war as paper shortages played havoc with periodical schedules. Newnes's *Strand Magazine*, in which Arthur Conan Doyle and P.G. Wodehouse began their writing careers, first appeared in 1891 and was popular for light diversion among wartime troops.[31] A number of book publishers had set up their own magazines during the late Victorian era as forcing houses for new literary talent and showcases for their lists. Many successful writers scored their first successes in their columns and established authors such as Stevenson, Conrad and Wells used them to try out their skills in shorter compass. Even before the outbreak of war, some of them had begun to seem old-fashioned and backward-looking with a distinctly retrospective air of the country-house library and the shooting weekend. Longmans closed their magazine in 1905 and *Macmillan's Magazine* followed in 1907.

Typically moving against the trend, Heinemann was an enthusiast for periodicals as an adjunct to a book programme. He had bought *East and West* shortly after he set up and he took over *The New Review*, edited by W.H. Henley, in 1894. Both lost money and he quickly relinquished them. He even purchased *The Badminton Magazine of Sports and Pastimes* from Longmans in 1900, but quickly sold it on to *The Sphere and Tatler*, who published it until 1914.[32] These setbacks did not extinguish his liking for magazines, and in 1902 he acquired an interest in *The World's Work*, published in the United States by Doubleday. He launched it in Britain as 'A new illustrated magazine of national efficiency and social progress' and its rather incongruous combination of earnest improving articles, cash prizes for readers' competitions and high quality and imaginative use of half-tone illustration was surprisingly successful. In 1913 he floated it as a separate company, clearly in anticipation of continued growth, but it

31 Although not as long-lived as *Blackwood's*, *The Strand Magazine* continued to publish until 1950. Both Odhams Press and George Newnes (today incorporated into magazine publisher IPC) were considerable book publishers as well, often offering titles as premiums to magazine subscribers.

32 Longmans had launched this in 1895 as a support for their long-running and highly successful 'Badminton Library' of aristocratic sporting books.

faltered during the war, especially since its appeal depended largely on the printing of large photographs on nearly-unobtainable art paper. It revived a little in the 1920s, but was to close in 1930, a victim of the reverberations of the Wall Street Crash.[33]

Even worse timing marked his *Gazette du Bon Ton*, which had been launched in Paris in 1911. Shamelessly billed as 'the most expensive magazine ever published', it featured articles on art, fashion and luxury and priced at an unbelievable ten shillings per monthly number. Heinemann took over British distribution in January 1914, but despite extensive promotion he failed to sell more than a handful of copies. He gave it up before the end of the year, although it continued its lavish publication from Paris until 1925.

Right from the outbreak of war, there had been a concerted effort to provide a supply of books to serving troops. The British War Library, organized by Mrs H. Gaskell from Surrey House in London's West End, appealed for donations of books to be sent to France and the Middle East. The public responded generously with used books, but soon the programme began to purchase new titles, provoking a shortage in the domestic market. Eventually the War Library confined its activities to supplying books to wounded and convalescing soldiers away from the Front, ultimately distributing over six million volumes (Mumby, 1930, p.376).

A network of Camp Libraries met the reading needs of frontline soldiers with similar organizations supplying reading matter to active servicemen in the Royal Navy and Royal Flying Corps. 'Books by the million' were literally supplied, with Oxford University Press alone printing almost four and a half million New Testaments for use in the field. A group of publishers organized 'National Book Fortnights' in 1915 and 1916 to 'quicken public interest in the use of books for reading, solace, and instruction' (Mumby, 1930, pp.374-5). Its main aim was to encourage members of the public to 'buy books very freely' to send to troops overseas. When the United States entered the war on the side of the Allies in 1917, similar book drives were organized under the direction of the London office of the American publisher Putnam to supply US troops. Initially ten million publications were obtained in the States for distribution, but these proved insufficient and were quickly supplemented by books sourced in Britain.

33 'The World's Work (1913) Ltd' was occasionally used as an imprint later for Heinemann books on improving or domestic subjects.

Among publishers who rallied to the call for 'books by the million' to sustain military and civilian morale were Hodder and Stoughton, Dent and Chapman & Hall. Hodder rebranded some of their novels as 'action stories' with vivid yellow paper wrappers (Attenborough, 1975, p.82). Dent struggled to keep 'Everyman's Library' afloat, although uncertain raw material supplies meant frequent lack of stock. He had lost his two eldest sons in the fighting and was determined that his firm should survive, partly as a memorial to them (Dent, 1926, pp.197-8). Arthur Waugh recorded that 'in those days almost everything that ... [Chapman and Hall] published got sold' although he noted regretfully that '[t]hey look[ed] shabby enough ... printed on a sallow, rough paper, and lettered in an imitation-gold foil, which has long since faded to brown, and become almost illegible'. He describes how despite rising prices, declining quality, lack of new publications and intermittent supply, there was strong demand for any old books from which publishers might reap the benefit of sales:

> But they were bought by somebody, especially the cheap novels; perhaps because everybody was earning money, rushing to and fro in Tube railways, and in desperate need of something to read upon the journey. And vast parcels of fiction went out to the trenches by every mail. (Waugh, 1930, p.286)

Such uninspired publishing proved embarrassingly lucrative for some. Waugh admitted the last two years of the war 'were among the most profitable in the firm's history and 1918 was a record year all round' (Waugh, 1930, p.286). Financial results were, however, patchy across publishing. Dividends fell at Hodder and many other publishers saw their profits decline. Several well-established firms faltered or collapsed, among them Smith, Elder which failed to survive the death of its principal in 1916 and was merged with John Murray.

Among the publishing *avant-garde*, Heinemann suffered mixed fortunes during the war. At the outbreak he had actually been in Germany, managing the British presence at the Leipzig Book Fair, and he endured a difficult journey home across Germany and through (neutral) Holland. His German name attracted opprobrium and his Bedford Street offices were pelted with refuse and horse dung. He toyed with the idea of anglicizing his name, but felt that would betray his antecedents and all he had achieved. It seems likely that his publishing – strong as always in social criticism and radical writing – attracted the attention of official censors and perhaps even the Secret Service, but his output during the war was impeccably patriotic, although by issuing intelligent critiques such as Philip Gibbs's *The Soul of War* (1915) and *The Battles of the Somme* (1917) he challenged the mindless chauvinism of British militarists.[34] John Masefield, future poet laureate, served in the Dardanelles campaign in Turkey, and his *Gallipoli*, which Heinemann published in 1916, did not minimize the bloody horror of the Allied landing. It was criticized for being too explicit, but was also widely perceived as positively influencing American opinion in favour of the Allies. Heinemann also produced practical titles of which Charles Richet's *War Nursing* (1918) was widely used in military hospitals.

Literature was not neglected and Heinemann recognized the qualities of the war poets Robert Graves and Siegfried Sassoon, whose first collections he published. Perhaps identifying with the dilemma of a patriotic Englishman with a German name, he developed a special friendship with Sassoon, visiting him in hospital and publishing two further volumes of his poems before the war's end.

Heinemann was not immune from the shortages and privations of wartime publishing. Sales dipped for the first time in 1915, and he recorded his first trading loss. He was forced to increase the price of novels from six shillings to seven shillings and sixpence, and he discontinued or failed to reprint several less remunerative titles. By careful husbandry, as well as typically brilliant publishing, the firm's fortunes were rebuilt; by 1918 it had recovered sufficiently to post profits equivalent to those pre-war, although turnover was still down. Heinemann remained proud of his German heritage and the humane values he had absorbed during his continental education, but he was unforgiving of the atrocities the Prussian military machine had visited on European books and learning, such as the wanton destruction of the great medieval library at Louvain in Belgium.[35] He remained convinced of the

34 Philip Gibbs wrote several thoughtful and unflinching analyses of battles and campaigns for Heinemann, culminating in his *Realities of War* (1920) – intended as a warning for the future of the dangers of militarism. He was an official war correspondent on the Western Front and eventually knighted for his services, so his work cannot have been total anathema to the establishment (St John, 1990, p.156).

35 When the Germans invaded Belgium in August 1914 they encountered little resistance. On 15 August they deliberately set fire to the famous fifteenth-century University Library in Louvain, destroying an irreplaceable collection of manuscripts, incunabula and books amounting to 210,000 items. There was no military or strategic

redeeming value of scholarship and books in overcoming the brutalities of war. Perhaps this is expressed most clearly in the *Plea for Books* that prefaced his autumn list for 1918 (although the words are almost certainly those of Edmund Gosse):

> If you do not intend to allow the tension of the war to harass your spirits beyond all endurance, temper that distress by the sedative of reading. At this moment, whatever is stinted and discouraged, the production and dissemination of literature ought to be directly protected by the State. What will be the profit to us if we gain the whole world and lose our own souls? So far from placing vain and tiresome obstacles in the way of publication of literature, our rulers would be wise to take it under their special guardianship. There is no weakening of the national effort, there is no vain expenditure of material and of energy in keeping alive the generation of books. It is a national benefit to pour oil into the lamp by which the hunted spirit of Man may trace its path over the dark moorland to victory. (Quoted in St John, 1990, pp.161-2)

While the war certainly brought mental exhaustion, financial hardship and spiritual impoverishment to British publishers, it also caused real physical damage and loss. As we have seen, senior people such as Dent, Nelson, Hodder-Williams and Macmillan lost sons and close relatives to the bloodbaths of trench warfare, and promising young publishers like R.C. Jackson – who with his partner Frank Sidgwick had issued the poems of Rupert Brooke – were killed before they could fulfil their promise. The almost exclusively male publishing workforce of clerks, warehousemen. packers, bagmen, travellers and salesmen was decimated as the insatiable demand for cannon fodder continued, leaving many houses severely understaffed and crippled. Casualties were even sustained on the home front, for although air warfare was in its infancy and there was no destruction comparable to the blitzing of the British book trade in the 1940s, silent Zeppelins frequently succeeded in penetrating as far as London to drop bombs. During one raid in 1915, the publishing offices of Covent Garden sustained considerable damage to premises and book stocks.

Labour shortage was the most intractable physical problem that publishers faced. Many had lost key personnel in the first enthusiasm to

---

reason for the destruction – it was simple vandalism. The library, also a major scholarly publisher, was rebuilt following the original design after the war.

volunteer in 1914, but after the introduction of conscription, deep and disabling inroads were made into staff resources at all levels. By 1917, publishers only had 'old men, young boys and women' to operate their businesses. There were representations to the government to exempt publishers from conscription as a 'trade of national importance', but although there was sympathy for the trade's plight, it was not until July 1918, with the end of the war only a few weeks away, that publishers gained reserved occupation status. By then, the employment demographics of the industry had been transformed. In 1914 publishing had employed 2891 men and 658 women – but by 1918 its workforce comprised 1559 men and 1522 women and boys under eighteen (Kingsland, 1960, p.58).[36] As in many other industries, women had entered employment to release men for military service, but their access into publishing was not easy nor universally welcomed.

Waugh recorded that Chapman & Hall had only employed one woman, Miss Muriel Silk, the managing director's secretary, from a staff of over fifty in 1914, and it was not until 1918 that she was joined by two other female employees. A man of his time and, as befits the father of the curmudgeonly and misogynistic Evelyn, he rather patronizingly writes:

> [T]he first women to break down the male monopoly in the house of 'Pickwick, London' ... they are still, to the firm's continual advantage, to be found at their busy desks.
>
> The years that lie between have added appreciably to their number: and now, in the early hour of morning, before the business of the day has properly begun, the big glass cage that bears the label 'Enquiries' is full of cheerful noise, with the typewriter ticking, the telephone buzzing, the whole place alive with gossip, gaiety, and laughter: until suddenly, like the shadow of a hawk, the figure of the Sales Manager looms in the doorway: and lo! – the rest is silence. (Waugh, 1930, p.277)

Despite entrenched sexist attitudes, women did of necessity appear in greater numbers in the publishing workforce in the last years of the war, although invariably in lowly positions as stenographers or clerks. It would be almost thirty years before women would be entrusted with the tasks

36 These figures were calculated by W.M. Meredith of Constable for the Publishers' Association. He contacted eighty-two firms of whom sixty-two responded, so the figures are underestimates of the entire publishing workforce. He found that in 1918, 429 men in publishing employment were over fifty-one years of age and there were 101 working directors or partners (Kingsland, 1960, p.58).

of editing or be offered boardroom seats, but even the likes of pioneer female executives Eunice Frost of Penguin and Norah Smallwood of Chatto and Windus began their illustrious editorial careers as secretaries.

One woman who was entrusted with the running of a publishing company during the war was not a notable success. Mills and Boon was founded in 1908 as a broadly based general publisher with a strong educational list and had made good progress up to and beyond the outbreak of war. With authors such as Jack London, E.F. Benson and Hugh Walpole they had quickly achieved renown and commercial rewards as serious literary publishers, admired by G.K. Chesterton and Arthur Quiller Couch (McAleer, 1999). A small part of their list comprised romantic novels in the Elinor Glyn mould, but these were seen as mere-potboilers of no significance.

Gerald Mills and Charles Boon were in their late thirties as war broke out, but they eventually decided they had to do their national duty in 1916, with Mills joining the Royal Navy and Boon working for the Ministry of Munitions. They entrusted the running of their firm to Boon's sister Margaret, who had been employed as a general office help since the firm had set up. She was evidently a kind and generous woman with an occasional sharp tongue, but she had little business acumen and possessed a vague and unfocussed management style. Even worse, she had no understanding of money management and cash flow. When the founding partners returned from war work, they found that although the firm had continued to publish and even grow, Margaret had laid in massive problems for the future by her erratic decision-making and failure to plan.

She had reprinted titles that had stopped selling and there were over a million un-saleable books in stock. She had not signed up many new authors and made unwise advances to old ones. In a scandalous scenario that would not disgrace one of her firm's racier titles, she was even conducting an affair with the brother-in-law of one of the firm's best-selling authors, Sophie Cole, who went to another publisher in consequence. In a later book, not published by Mills and Boon, Cole caricatured Margaret as a lovelorn incompetent spinster barely disguised as 'Madge' (McAleer, 1990, p.39).

Margaret Boon's chaotic management took some time to come home to roost. As other firms reacted to the end of paper rationing and a booming postwar market in 1919 by issuing a flood of new titles and new authors, Mills and Boon found that they had nothing but a mountain of unwanted old books that Margaret had stockpiled and little in the way of new publishing in the pipeline. Their sales of new fiction peaked at just over 40,000 units in 1919 and fell steadily to under 25,000 units in 1926. Where Margaret had made publishing acquisitions, they were bizarrely un-commercial. A lavish 'hunting diary', which she had produced at a time of materials shortage during the war, regularly sold only one copy a year in the early 1920s 'at Christmas'.

Largely as a result of the overstocks, the firm plunged into loss in 1923 and took four years to return to profit. Margaret's mistakes were written off eventually, but they very nearly sank the firm. She continued to work for the house and even once again briefly took control following Charles' unexpected death in 1943, but, perhaps chastened by her First World War experience, she decided not to stockpile reprints during this new conflict in the expectation of post-war plenty. To be fair to her, Margaret had been asked to take over the company at short notice without any training, and she probably felt severely out of her depth. It is important to recall that she was by no means unique in creating overstocks on unrealistic sales expectations, and that male publishers were by no means immune from similar miscalculations. Some seventy years later, a monumental over-optimistic provision of stock sank the illustrated reference publisher Dorling Kindersley, who ironically occupied the same offices as had Mills and Boon in Margaret's time (Davis, 2009).

The First World War transformed British publishing as it had so much of the rest of society. The old settled certainties had been swept away. Women who had worked outside the home were reluctant to return to the old roles of housewife or mother, although many had no choice but to resume their former domestic positions. Nevertheless, their horizons had widened and they had new aspirations. At long last they had obtained (an albeit limited) franchise, and with it the prospect of greater political influence. Returned servicemen had the expectation of secure jobs, sanitary housing, good wages and new prospects. These would largely not be fulfilled, but the hope was there. Most of all, no section of the population had been untouched by the consequences of death and destruction on an industrial scale. There was a new realism, perhaps a new cynicism but also optimism and the hope that a rigid class-bound society could now become fluid and open. Books were to play their part in the new postwar settlement, and although the challenges were great and changes would not come smoothly, publishing was about to enter a new decade in which new firms, new ideas and new markets would dominate the scene.

3 'Books fit for heroes'

Reconstruction and renewal in British book publishing between the Armistice and the Great Depression

Although there was a great deal of continuity between prewar publishing and the trade in the 1920s, there was also a sense of a new beginning that fostered new structures and allowed new ways of doing business to emerge. The great, old-established houses like Longmans, Macmillan and Murray operated in much the same way as they had always done, with family directors and deep backlists which they continued to mine, particularly in the educational and colonial markets.[37] For smaller firms, the war had proved transformational and, as they sought to recover from the consequences of lost staff and publishing programmes in disarray, many restructured and set out in new directions.

A typical example is Frederick Warne (King and Stuart, 1965). Founded in 1865, Warne was a modest family firm, organized for the first forty-five years of its existence as a simple partnership and managed until 1918 by the sons of the founder. They operated from a small office in Bedford Street in Covent Garden and specialized in middle-brow fiction, travel and *belles-lettres* and most of all illustrated children's books. They published the iconic artworks of Randolph Caldecott, Kate Greenaway and Beatrix Potter, who in fact became engaged to marry the youngest Warne brother, Norman, before he died unexpectedly of pernicious anaemia in 1905.[38]

37 Longmans, for example, had first published Kennedy's *Latin Primer* in 1884, and it has remained in print continuously since then. The latest edition is 2007.

38 The story of Norman Warne and Beatrix Potter is the subject of the feature film *Miss Potter* (2006), directed by Chris Noonan and starring Renée Zellwegger and Ewan Macgregor. It gives a very accurate picture of a small publisher at the beginning of the century, even if its evocation of an Edwardian publishing office is rather romanticized and its portrait of Fruing and Harold Warne is a trifle unkind.

Wartime conditions had left the firm short of capital and although it still held its lucrative children's copyrights, it had very little in its forward list to suit post-war tastes and markets. It became incorporated as a limited company in May 1919, its board now for the first time made up mainly of non-family members. The eldest brother, Harold Warne, left the company altogether, and his younger sibling Fruing Warne became Managing Director. New external shareholders brought in much needed cash, but required strange innovations such as board meetings and dividends. The children's list was strongly developed and a new successful venture was a series of full colour annuals or 'Bumper Books'. A major new publishing strand was natural history and landscape titles which eventually became the famous 'Observer' series that set the standard for the authoritative, finely printed, pocket-sized hardbacks that were essential purchases for readers interested in the outdoors. Along with Potter's *Peter Rabbit* books, they were the foundation of the firm's prosperity right up until it was absorbed by Penguin in 1983.[39]

Another firm, very different in scope and outlook from Warne, that also re-organized at the end of the war was George Allen and Unwin. This house had its origins in 1871 when, mistrustful of publishers, the art critic and philosopher John Ruskin decided to set up his own publishing imprint and asked his assistant, George Allen, to manage the operation. Allen had a printing background and he set up a press in Orpington, Kent from which he began to issue his master's earnest tracts and criticism. As Ruskin's popularity waned, Allen added other authors to the list which always maintained a serious, liberal tone.

After Ruskin died in 1900, George Allen expanded his publishing further. From 'Ruskin House'[40] in Charing Cross Road issued a stream of new titles, concentrating on art history, socialism and criticism. Allen died in 1907 and the business passed to his children who embarked on an ambitious but ill-advised series of takeovers. They acquired the publishing list of the printers Bemrose in 1907 and Swan Sonnenschein, publishers of Karl Marx and Sydney and Beatrice Webb, in 1911. However, the public taste for the kind of messianic visionary writing that typified these lists was disappearing, and sales declined rapidly. By 1912, the firm

39 The very first book I ever purchased was Warne's *Observer's Book of British Railway Locomotives* in 1958. It cost five shillings and needed months of hard saving. I still have it.

40 This would always remain the formal name of the publishing house and its successors until its takeover by Robin Hyman in 1986. It would occasionally appear as an imprint on title pages.

was in serious financial difficulties and by 1914 it was in receivership. There then appeared a pushy young publishing entrepreneur, Stanley Unwin, who had fallen out with his step-uncle T. Fisher Unwin, from whom he had learned the publishing trade, and with a mind to acquire the insolvent business.

Stanley Unwin, slight, bearded and much given to *pince-nez* and plus fours, cuts a rather Pooterish figure in his photographs, but his benign exterior concealed a razor-sharp financial brain and a powerful streak of ruthlessness. In his autobiography he made no bones about his intentions towards his new firm: '[m]y plan was to find a bankrupt concern and buy the assets so as to have something to sell to cover the immediate overheads' (Unwin, *The Truth about a Publisher*, 1960, p.126). He wrangled for months with the Receiver over the price and terms; eventually on 4 August, the actual day of the outbreak of the First World War, the new firm of George Allen and Unwin was registered with Unwin as managing director.

To his horror, Unwin discovered that despite their high-minded socialism the Allen directors had treated their staff very badly, whilst themselves drawing excessive salaries from the firm. Although the total weekly wage bill for the dozen staff was less than £20 there was frequently not enough cash available to pay them at the end of the week. Although the terms of his acquisition meant he could not in the short term get rid of the three Allen directors, he proceeded to make life very difficult for them. He limited annual directors' emoluments (his own included) to £300 and closed the extravagant offices in Rathbone Place in Fitzrovia, moving to the cheaper (and he thought intellectually more bracing) environs of Museum Street. These were later to become a major publishing quarter to rival Covent Garden and Paternoster Row.

The war brought immediate problems of shortages and business disruption, but, as he noted sardonically '... there is no evil out of which some good cannot be extracted if you look for it. Our competitors all had capital locked up in autumn lists of publications produced for quite other conditions. We had no such commitments or preoccupations. We could concentrate our attention upon what changed circumstances called for' (Unwin, 1960, p.131). Wartime enthusiasm for salvage also brought a major historical disaster as all the papers of Swan Sonnenschein were pulped, including manuscripts and letters by Marx, Engels and George Moore. Unwin, who only learned of this after it was too late, mused sorrowfully and characteristically: '[i]t is almost painful to contemplate the amount the Bolsheviks would have paid for all those ... letters' (Unwin, 1960, p.132).

Although the new firm did publish some titles during the war, including works by the young philosopher and mathematician Bertrand Russell, Unwin spent the conflict mainly treading water – realizing the stock assets he had inherited by remaindering and chafing under what he saw as pettiness, incompetence and laziness from the other directors he had been saddled with on his acquisition of the firm. By his account, they were an intolerable lot, none more so than the company secretary C.A. Reynolds who had sent the Marx correspondence for salvage and whom Unwin referred to as 'indeed a strange person'. Reynolds fancied himself as a literary man, but his taste was old-fashioned and prudish, despite decorating his desk with statuettes of 'little bronze nude ladies' (Unwin, 1960, p.137). When the firm was offered a novel with homosexuality as its major theme, Reynolds reacted with outrage, demanding it be rejected, and his squeamishness also cost the firm Marie Stopes' famous and revolutionary sex manual *Married Love* which Unwin wished to publish and of which, he ruefully observed, 'more than a million copies were soon sold by another publisher', the little-known house of A.C. Fifield in 1918 (Unwin, 1960, p.138).

As the war progressed, circumstances played to Unwin's advantage. Two of the troublesome directors were conscripted and although Reynolds remained until 1917 when he was eventually called up, Unwin steadily isolated him from publishing decisions. Unwin himself was declared medically unfit for military service, although he was a keen tennis player and walker in the Shavian mould. He declared himself a pacifist but without registering as a conscientious objector which would have meant a prison term. He did volunteer for the London VAD (Voluntary Aid Detachment) of nursing auxiliaries and he often attended the publishing office in uniform.

By the time the war ended the firm was in healthy financial shape, and Unwin was ready to seize total control. When the other pre-war directors returned, they behaved incredibly stupidly, denying Unwin a bonus for his work in their absence. Reynolds was eventually persuaded to sell out to Unwin, giving him a majority of the shares and removing an irksome thorn in his side. The others proved more recalcitrant although he persuaded most of them to retire to benefit from their admittedly generous dividends. The most difficult to dislodge was E.L. Skinner, a conservative Welsh solicitor, who had bought a slice of the ailing George

Allen in 1912 despite its publishing being diametrically opposed to his political and social views, and he clung on determinedly.[41] Stanley Unwin paints a picture of Skinner as an unpleasant schemer, but his nephew Philip Unwin, who joined the firm at the end of the war, is more sympathetic and reveals a soft spot for the chain-smoking, bespoke-suited, cricket-loving Welshman (P. Unwin, *The Publishing Unwins*, 1972, p.75). Whatever the truth of the relationship, Skinner remained to irritate and frustrate Stanley until 1934 when, finally to get rid of him, he sold him the serious philosophical imprint Williams and Norgate which Stanley had bought as a 'derelict concern' in 1928 and turned around (S. Unwin, 1960, p.215).

Stanley Unwin was by nature a spiky outsider with little patience for the concept of publishing as a profession for gentlemen of leisure with long lunches and generous expense accounts. He ran his firm with strict economy and an almost ascetic sense of personal abstemiousness, verging on parsimony. Philip recalled on the unusual occasion when he was taken to lunch by his uncle, Stanley ordered without consultation '[a]pple pie for two and *one* portion of cream' (P. Unwin, 1972 , p.79). There is some suggestion that Stanley's prickly and self-righteous nature alienated publishing colleagues and competitors. His first application to join the Publishers' Association had been blocked, ironically by G.S. Williams of Williams and Norgate whose bankrupt firm he later rescued, and although he later rose to be Publishers' Association president and received a knighthood for 'services to publishing', it seems that he was viewed with cool respect rather than affection by his contemporaries.[42] Certainly, as his memoirs clearly show, he, Bourbon-like, never forgot a slight nor forgave anyone who ever crossed him. *The Truth about a Publisher* inadvertently reveals much more about Stanley's problematic personality that he intended.

No matter his personal shortcomings, Stanley was a publisher of flair,

41 Skinner was an Old Etonian who always read the ultra-conservative *Morning Post* and entertained lavishly at the Travellers' Club. Why he should have wanted to be a director of a firm known for its left-wing publishing is baffling, although the shares he bought in 1912 were very cheap.

42 There is a doubtless apocryphal story that when on a Saturday morning his publishing neighbour Hamish Hamilton noticed that Unwin's premises were on fire and the workaholic Stanley was untypically absent, Hamilton waited until the fire had taken a good hold and then telephoned Stanley at home to announce curtly: 'Unwin, your office is on fire. I do not intend to call the fire brigade.'

vision and commercial acumen. As soon as he could in 1919 he re-organized his firm as a limited company, and with at long last a compliant board of directors he embarked on the 1920s with a clear plan of becoming the leading serious publisher in London. He not only personally acquired new titles and series, but also made himself familiar with every stage of production, sales and distribution, as ever with his customary zeal for shaving costs and watching cash flow. He summarized his approach in his famous manual *The Truth about Publishing* in 1926 which, for all its tedious concern with balance sheets and denying rapacious booksellers longer discounts, contains much good sense about how to run a publishing house. It became a primer for succeeding generations of aspiring publishers, remaining in print until 1995.

Although he always maintained a respectable literary list (ultimately crowned two decades later by J.R.R. Tolkien's *Lord of the Rings* sequence), it was his philosophy, current affairs, politics and social science titles that made his publishing so distinctive and influential in the Britain of the 1920s. Fired by a mission to explain great social change to the public and perhaps seeing himself as a latter-day Ruskin, he commissioned authors such as Arthur Ransome to report on Bolshevik Russia and Beatrice Webb to comment on social questions at home. He secured the rights to publish Trotsky and Lenin in translation in 1919. Later he nurtured the great socialist historian R.H. Tawney, whom he had acquired as publisher for the London School of Economics. He re-issued the works of Sigmund Freud which George Allen had published before the war and built up a considerable list in psychology and psychoanalysis.

Unwin deliberately courted controversy by insisting on publishing *A Young Girl's Diary* to which he had been introduced by Freud himself, but which the Director of Public Prosecutions, Sir Archibald Bodkin, dismissed as '[f]ilth, my dear Sir, filth' (S. Unwin, *The Truth about a Publisher*, 1960, p.171). To protect the public, Bodkin insisted that every invoice for the book bore a printed label declaring '[t]his psychological study is intended for the use of the members of the educational, medical and legal professions only' (Unwin, 1960, p172). If this condition was met, he would refrain from prosecuting Unwin for obscenity. Nothing, of course, inspires interest like a restricted book, and the title became a bestseller, with Unwin innocently assuring the DPP that he had done everything he could to stop booksellers selling it to the public.

By the end of the 1920s, through shrewd acquisition and careful management, Allen and Unwin had achieved Stanley's goal to become not just a leading commercial publisher but also an important influence on current affairs and serious thought. As well as Williams and Norgate it had acquired the Dublin imprint Maunsell, publisher of J.M. Synge and many other Irish playwrights. He was the proud publisher of the memoirs of Jan Masaryk, the founder of Czechoslovakia (who decorated him with the Czech Order of the White Lion),[43] and Spengler's *Decline of the West* while equally proudly declining Hitler's *Mein Kampf.* Although his firm's true glory days were yet to come, Stanley's dynamic leadership exemplified the new spirit of postwar publishing, energetic risk-taking and, above all, of commercial awareness.

Another firm which had been semi-dormant during and immediately prior to the war but which came to life spectacularly during the 1920s was Hutchinson and Company. Its renaissance was due to the autocratic, or some might say monomaniacal, leadership of Walter Hutchinson, a man who made the penny-pinching and hard-nosed Stanley Unwin seem like Saint Nicholas by comparison. Hutchinson & Co was yet another late-Victorian firm that had lost its way, and despite producing a successful flurry of part-works on natural history, architecture and royalty, its list was firmly stuck in the past with writers such as Jerome K. Jerome and Anthony Hope of *Prisoner of Zenda* fame. Walter, the son of the founder, had worked in the firm during the war, balancing his role with a day job as superintendent of publications at the War Office. Whether it was his experience as a military civil servant or simply his nature when he became a partner in 1919 he immediately assumed a reckless, overbearing and bullying style that profoundly shook up the sleepy family firm. His father had been ultra-cautious and despite receiving a knighthood for 'services to literature' in 1912 (the first publisher to be so honoured), he never knowingly took a risk nor borrowed a penny.

Walter was a shocking contrast. His first step was to acquire a small Essex printer, Anchor Press at Tiptree, where he erected a new building and refitted with new presses, informing his fellow directors later. His father, who was habituated to pay printers in advance with cash on hand, was dubious but acquiescent. He then set up a fleet of story magazines aimed at the bottom of the middle market and featuring gory crime, adventure or detective yarns, partly to make use of the printing capacity

43 Stanley was very proud of the decorations he amassed during his career. As well as his KBE and the Czech medal, he received the Gold Palm of the Belgian Order of the Crown, the Order of Orange Nassau (Holland) and was an officer of the *Académie Française* (see Hampden, 1957, p.271).

he had just created. None of them ever really kept their heads above water and their increasing costs nearly capsized the company. He opened new branch offices in Australia and South Africa and embarked on a spree of company acquisitions, buying a block maker, another printer (William Brendon of Plymouth) and a paper manufacturer, together with a heterogenous fleet of small, mainly badly run-down publishers. These included Rider, specialists in the occult, Geographia the cartographers, the Norwich-based Jarrold, John Long with its list of mystery stories, Stanley Paul, publishers on sports and pastimes, and Popular Dogs, among several others.

His interests were not confined to books and during his tenure he also bought a racing stable, a small airport, a cosmetics concern and a sausage manufacturing company. His fellow directors were aghast at his reckless spending, but since he had progressively acquired control of all the shares, there was little they could do. If they dared to argue, they tended to find themselves summarily dismissed. His father, probably in despair, retired in 1926 and left Walter to it. The company expanded vertiginously. In 1926 it published 211 new titles, but the following year almost five hundred new books were issued. Despite, or perhaps because of, this hyperactivity, Hutchinson during the 1920s published much original and bestselling literature, ranging from the works of the critic Frank Swinnerton to Richmal Crompton, author of the *Just William* books.

Everything the house published was marked by the bizarre opinions and outlandish self-aggrandizement of Mr Walter (as he was universally known). His books bore no publication date, in defiance of the law, because 'books with dates in don't sell'. He insisted that all his firm's advertisements bear the strap line 'The Largest Publisher in the World'. This caused Edmond Segrave, punctilious editor of the trade paper *The Bookseller* to refuse them on the grounds the claim was nonsense, provoking a bitter feud that was to last until Walter's death in 1950. *The Bookseller* never carried any Hutchinson advertising while Walter lived. He had a very short attention span and his career is littered with half-baked projects and publishing initiatives that absorbed cash but never produced any worthwhile output. Some of his ideas, had he given them the patience, resources or attention they deserved, would have been very successful. For example, during the 1920s he conceived a series of paper-covered cheap reprints that look very much like the Penguin Books of a decade later, but after a few were published he lost interest and the series withered.

Walter Hutchinson inspired a kind of horrified, desperate affection among his staff (to whom he could very occasionally be impulsively generous) and colleagues, but his competitors regarded him as a dangerous unrestrained monster, a living incarnation of the raging bull colophon he had adopted in a moment of rare self-awareness. Alone among the principals of the leading publishers, he was never elected to office in the Publishers' Association and to some his unpredictable, fickle and quixotic style was not unlike that of another later publishing monster, Robert Maxwell, although without the dishonesty but certainly his equal in megalomania.

It is impossible to write about Walter Hutchinson without straining for superlatives and expletives. He was the ultimate contradiction in terms, a genius and a fool, a madman and a clear thinker, a bully and kind-hearted patriarch – in Robert Lusty's memorable phrase, a man of 'benevolent malevolence' (Lusty, 1975, p.46). Lusty's summing up of his character is probably the most judicious assessment that can be made of him:

> But he was certainly not a villain, nor even a tycoon in the sense of today. He was not even ruthless in the attainment of his own aims; he hardly knew what these were. He did not exploit, in the modern sense, those who worked for him. He simply bullied, shouted, threatened, raved, and ranted to so absurd an extent that it succeeded in rallying a certain obtuse loyalty. He simply did not know about people or understand the realities of any life other than his own … Mr Walter could deride and ridicule a request from a senior employee for an additional five or ten shillings a week with a contemptuous 'Don't you know it costs me three pounds a week to feed one of my horses?' The reaction would not be one of contempt or hate but rather 'what a story to go the rounds': a sort of oneupmanship boost to morale. Some of those treated most abominably never ceased in loyalty and even a certain affection. (Lusty, 1975, p.47)

While a new generation of young men such as Unwin and Hutchinson were shaking up the old-fashioned businesses over which they had taken control, an older generation of publishers began to depart the scene. The most important loss was Heinemann, who died unexpectedly in 1920 of a heart attack at the age of fifty-seven. He had energetically continued to expand his firm during the war, but when his cousin John Heinemann, whom he had been grooming as his successor, was killed at Ypres in 1916 he lost heart and most of his characteristic *brio*. His health, probably psychosomatically, began to trouble him and he experienced failing eyesight. His last years were miserable with panic attacks and what would today be described as clinical depression. There were the occasional flashes of the old Heinemann, witty and urbane, when he met a favoured author or hosted a dinner party, but, like many non-combatants of the war, knowledge of the carnage and sacrifice endured by those who had fought had affected him deeply with feelings of guilt.

His death inspired warm obituaries and genuine sorrow from the publishing and literary communities, but it quickly became apparent that he had made no provision for the future of his firm. In his will, he left funding to create a literary prize,[44] but no clear instructions on how his business should be taken forward. His business partner Pawling had an option to buy Heinemann's shares on his death, but did not have the money. Rescue came from the American publisher F.N. Doubleday, who had actually come to London to have dinner with Heinemann and was horrified to find he had died. He immediately offered Pawling a financial lifeline, buying Heinemann's shares for £25,000 but leaving Pawling to run the business as a partner (St John, 1990, p.168).

There was concern that Doubleday would introduce alien business methods, provoking Kipling to half-jokingly dub him 'Effendi', but he was shrewd enough to know that what worked in North America would not necessarily run in Britain. Pawling did all he could to reassure the Heinemann authors that all would continue as usual, but many expressed doubts. The strain began to tell and Pawling's health declined. He died just before Christmas 1922, leaving the firm once again rudderless.

Pawling had, in fact, been more provident than Heinemann. Shortly before his death, he had converted the firm into a limited company with an authorized shareholding of £80,000. Of these, Doubleday's company owned £40,500, with £18,000 in preference shares. After Pawling's death, Doubleday acquired his holding of £18,000 preference shares which now gave him total overall control.

Heinemann was thus the first major British publisher to become American-owned and although Doubleday's proprietorship was usually benign, the remote management control that the new owners obliged took away much of the creative energy and immediacy that had marked the firm in its first quarter century. Charles Evans, a seasoned publisher, was put in day-to-day charge, but overall responsibility for the firm was

44 The Heinemann prize is still awarded by the Royal Society of Literature.

given to Theodore Byard, whom Doubleday named as 'Resident Chairman' – a rather dilettante art-lover with no experience of publishing. Real control was, however, firmly with Doubleday who identified that the profligate habits of the founder had made the house financially 'shaky and by no means conservatively managed' (St John, 1990, p.174). He had to invest $140,000 to keep the business afloat and introduce up-to-date accounting practices to ensure stability. For the first time unsaleable and slow moving stock was written off the balance sheet, thereby releasing funds for investment. Staff were offered performance bonuses and, despite initial suspicion of such an un-English practice, this was grudgingly accepted and seemed to produce results. The firm began to revive, and despite discovering that Heinemann had been cheating Loeb, the editor of the 'Classical Library', by wrongly charging him expenses (duly paid back), finances were at last open and accountable. Title output had decreased to 91 new books in 1921, but eventually grew again with a slight downturn during the economically difficult years of 1925-6 and had more than doubled to 226 titles by 1929.

Elsewhere, other prominent figures who had shaped the publishing world during the first quarter of the twentieth century died or retired. Algernon Methuen, whose eponymous firm[45] had seen meteoric growth by publishing Ibsen, Wilde, Marie Corelli and Kipling – as well as the English translation of Albert Einstein's *Relativity* and Edgar Rice Burrough's *Tarzan of the Apes* – died in 1924. Methuen's list was always wide-ranging and adventurous, but they probably overstepped themselves when they published 'the monstrous wilderness of phallicism', D.H. Lawrence's *The Rainbow*, in 1915 (Duffy, 1989, p.55). Although mild by modern and indeed by Lawrence's own later standards, *The Rainbow* initiated the first of the author's and his various publishers' brushes with the law. The Director of Public Prosecutions tried the book for obscenity and Methuen offered no defence, agreeing to destroy the remaining stock, amounting to 1011 copies. Duffy (1989, pp.55-61) contends that Lawrence was pursued more because he was thought 'unpatriotic' for having

45 'Eponymous' is an interesting observation as Methuen actually bore by birth the surname Stedman, but he had named the firm he founded Methuen & Co in 1889, selecting one of his middle names as perhaps a more memorable and distinctive imprint. He always wrote under the *nom-de-plume* A.W.S. Methuen, and he formally adopted the surname in 1899 – a unique case, surely, of a founder naming himself after his publishing house rather than vice-versa. When he was raised to the baronetcy he styled himself Sir Algernon Methuen Bart (Duffy, 1989, p.27).

married a German than the depravity of his writing. She finds it odd that Methuen, who had bravely kept all Oscar Wilde's work in print at the height of his opprobrium, caved in to official prudery and offered Lawrence no support. Lawrence simply called Sir Algernon 'a skunk'. When, forty-five years later, the more famous, and for publishing law much more important, case of Lawrence's *Lady Chatterley's Lover* was prosecuted, the precedent of Methuen's spineless abandonment of his author may have inspired its publisher, Sir Allen Lane of Penguin Books, to fight harder then (see Chapter 7). One key to Methuen's attitude may be that Lawrence, as always oblivious to the consequences of his occasional mean-spiritedness, had written an unkind caricature of the brother of the firm's chief editor, who had recently been killed in France.

Methuen, unusually among publishers, was also a considerable author himself, writing books on current affairs and gardening as well as editing a very successful anthology of verse (Duffy, 1989). It was, however, children's books that sustained the firm's success, guided by the sure hand of E.V. Lucas who had built such an innovative list of juvenile literature for Grant Richards (see p.17). Lucas signed up A.A. Milne and Kenneth Grahame, and fostered the work of illustrators such as Ernest Shepard, W. Heath Robinson and H.M. Bateman. When Sir Algernon died, Lucas succeeded him as chairman and he led the firm very successfully until his own death in 1928. He combined his executive role uniquely with that of chief reader (for which he was paid a separate salary) and his sharp eye and shrewd commercial judgement brought authors as diverse as P.G. Wodehouse, Pearl S. Buck, Maurice Maeterlinck and Enid Blyton to the list. Sellar and Yeatman's great parody of English history and its teaching, *1066 and All That* (published in 1930 but taken on by Lucas before he died) was an inspired acquisition that sold enormously and epitomizes his commissioning style. It is still in print and has sold hundreds of thousands of copies in the past eighty years.

Others of the old guard who gave way to new blood during the 1920s were Charles J. Longman, Sir Frederick Macmillan and John Murray IV.[46] Longman had presided over his firm since becoming a partner in 1877 and over trade affairs since his formative role in the foundation of the Publishers' Association in 1895. Under his guidance, the house of

46 All the heads of the House of Murray have been named 'John' since its foundation in 1768 and they are conventionally given regnal numbers. The current Murray is John VII (John Richmond Grey Murray). See Carpenter, 2008.

Longmans[47] had seen solid if unspectacular growth, with its fortunes riding mainly on its educational and export business rather than literary or publishing innovation. Charles had become progressively more conservative and cautious as a businessman, and when Longmans celebrated its bi-centenary in 1924, his eulogy is backward-looking, rather than anticipating the future (Cox and Chandler, 1924, pp.66-70). Alone among the great firms after the First World War, Longmans remained organized as an old-fashioned partnership which limited its resources to family capital. It eventually became a limited company in 1926 and Charles retired two years later, dying in 1934. Even in the judgement of Philip Wallis, the official Longmans chronicler, who was trying to be kind, Charles had failed to keep up with the times and left his firm unprepared to face the challenges of the modern world, causing it almost to founder during the 1930s. He was one of 'the old men (who) had stayed too long' (Wallis, 1974, p.32).

Frederick Macmillan had been more circumspect and progressive in yielding control of his company to younger and more energetic members of his family. In 1920 he was about to turn seventy and had already passed a great deal of the day-to-day running of the business to his younger brother Maurice and his nephew, Harold, although the latter became steadily more involved in politics, elected as a Conservative MP in 1924 and eventually, of course, becoming Prime Minister in 1956.[48] By 1925 Sir Frederick had more or less disengaged himself from the company, although he would occasionally still entertain favoured authors such as Kipling and Hardy and offer advice on new projects. He lived on until 1936, but sensibly spent the last fifteen years of his life in bookish purdah, rarely visiting the elegant offices in St Martins Street that his business skills had built and paid for (see Barker, in James, 2002).

John Murray IV died in 1928, after remaining active in trade politics and the book world until the end of his life. His firm still occupied its

47 The company has had many imprints during its almost three hundred-year history. See Wallis (1974, p.40) for a list. During most of the twentieth century it was 'Longmans, Green & Company (Ltd)', then became 'Longmans' (1959) and finally 'Longman' (1969). However, for anyone who worked there since the 1950s, including myself, it was and always will be 'Longmans'. In this book, when I write 'Longmans', the firm rather than an individual is intended.

48 Harold always remained closely involved with the firm until his death in 1986 and was frequently seen around the company's offices where he was invariably referred to as 'H.M'.

historic home at 50 Albemarle Street opposite the Royal Institution which remained its headquarters until it sold out to Hodder in 2001. His son John V ('Jack') had been taking over more of the firm's operations since he had returned from the war with rank of lieutenant-colonel in 1918. According to Carpenter (2008, p.239), he was 'temperamentally ill-suited to being a publisher'. He certainly lacked his father's energy and taste for book-trade gossip and intrigue, but I find this judgement harsh, probably reflecting its author's bias towards the literary and the louche. Jack had a canny eye for commercial opportunities which saw him diversify his publishing to include lucrative lists in education and non-fiction to supplement the poetry, *belles-lettres* and fiction on which its reputation among the literary public rested.[49] He may not have been a literary *flâneur* in the mould of his nephew John VI ('Jock'), whom he brought into the firm in 1930.[50] Nevertheless it was his business shrewdness and clever exploitation of markets that others did not see or disdained that kept his house independent and thriving much longer than any of his competitors. Although he was a good strategist, however, his individual editorial judgement could be questionable. He published a laudatory account of the British Union of Fascists by James Drennan and was unenthusiastic about taking on the work of John Betjeman.[51]

The economic and social background against which these changes within publishing were played out was turbulent. The war had wrought profound transformation in the roles and rights of women as well as the relations between the classes, bringing pressure for educational reform, the full extension of the franchise and an opening up of new economic opportunities. Expectations were high that the 'war to end all wars' had

49 Although it should be remembered that Murray was one of the premier scientific publishers of the nineteenth and early twentieth centuries with Charles Darwin and David Livingstone among its authors, as well as producing many scientific journals, such as the *Journal of the Royal Geographical Society.*

50 Jack and his wife were childless, so Jock, as his sister's son, became the heir, eventually succeeding as John Murray VI although his birth name was John Arnaud Robin Grey. He changed his surname to Murray by deed poll when he joined the firm at the age of twenty-one.

51 He may have, initially at least, been right. Jock and Betjeman had been friends at Oxford and the former was keen to publish his playful and rather immature collection *Continual Dew;* Jack was uncertain and would only agree if his nephew would underwrite the book against loss. In the event it did not sell as well as predicted and Jock had to make up its losses by £53 (Carpenter, 2008, p.249). Betjeman eventually, of course, became a major earner for Murray.

altered the lives of ordinary people for ever, and that everyone would share in a new age of prosperity. Publishing played its part in firing this mood and the catalogues issued during and after the war are filled with hopeful tracts about the new bright world of the Peace. Other writers were more circumspect, however, for example Nobel peace prize winner Norman Angell, whose *Fruits of Victory*, published by Collins in 1921, warned that post-war life would not necessarily be easy or bountiful.

And so it proved. The influenza pandemic of 1918 cost many lives among those who survived the fighting, and almost immediately the economy at home and abroad, stretched to breaking point by the war effort, encountered problems of inflation and low productivity. There were material shortages and restrictions on foreign trade, while once stable currencies like the Latin Union, based on the French franc, succumbed to devaluation and fiscal chaos. Returning soldiers discovered that the promised well-paid jobs were chimerical and unemployment soared. Housing stocks were depleted and dilapidated. Food prices rose and wages fell. Marxist revolutions in Russia and Hungary terrified the bourgeoisie and presaged a new order of a kind that had not been imagined by the prophets of postwar utopia. In Italy, Mussolini's aggressive nationalistic fascism toppled a government and brought totalitarian rule. Trades unions became more militant and strikes became common, ultimately leading to the nationwide stoppages of the General Strike of 1926.

The impact of such disruption and uncertainty on publishing was direct. Books were discretionary purchases from constrained budgets, and sales declined with many publishers recording losses. Relatively few houses actually went out of business, but many had to cut back severely their staffs and forward lists. There were a few bright interludes. The founding of the British Broadcasting Company (later Corporation) in 1923 created a new medium that would be an avid consumer of publishing's products for use on radio. Stanley Unwin, with characteristic vision, grasped the potential of this new fledgling and offered to publish for them. He hammered out a lucrative exclusive arrangement that less opportunistic competitors loudly and bitterly bemoaned. He would also provide authors for that quintessential BBC form of the inter-war years, the ten-minute 'talk', often contributing himself on bookish matters. Cinema, a sideshow curiosity before the war, had expanded enormously to become the preferred leisure activity of the masses escaping from everyday hardships; it plundered publishing for storylines for treatment and production. 'Film rights' as a source of income for authors and publishers suddenly assumed importance, and although the payments were generally individually small, they mounted up and were pure profit.

Overall, however, the prospects facing publishers in the 1920s were problematic to say the least. Established firms were struggling to meet new markets, to find new authors and new forms of literature to fit changing tastes, while economic circumstances increased costs and put pressure on prices. Competition intensified and the traditional export markets in the Empire and the United States deteriorated in the face of overvalued sterling and local importing restrictions. It was hardly the most propitious time for new publishing ventures to start up from scratch. Yet not all postwar optimism had been totally extinguished, and one of the most remarkable aspects of British publishing in this period was precisely the emergence of new publishing firms. They were created by a group of young and hopeful entrepreneurs prepared to brave adverse circumstances and confident that their new approaches would find favour with the reading and book buying public.

The first of these was Jonathan Cape.[52] Cape had been born in 1879 and entered publishing in 1904 as a salesman for Gerald Duckworth, a small, Covent Garden-based publisher. He quickly progressed and by 1919 was running the business as general manager. Duckworth, half-brother of Virginia Woolf, was a snob, and although he knew that Cape was the reason his business was flourishing he despised Cape's lower-middle class origins (his father had been a builder and his grandfather a sub-postmaster) and refused him a directorship.

This slight convinced Cape that he should set up on his own and in 1919 he placed a classified advertisement in *The Times* requesting a partner for a new publishing venture (Howard, 1971, p.21). The only reply came from Geoffrey Faber who, as we shall see, was thinking along the same lines. When they met, they discovered that neither had sufficient capital and each was looking to the other to provide it. They parted on good terms, wishing each other luck in their plans.

Cape briefly took a job with the Medici Society to supervise the rebuilding of its export trade in fine-art prints after the war, and as a side-line set up a small reprint house in partnership with Olyve James. This

52 Cape's full name was actually Herbert Jonathan Cape and for most his career he signed himself 'H.J. Cape'. Olyve James, who became his second wife in 1927 after many years as his secretary, convinced him to use the more distinguished 'Jonathan' in his imprint.

company he named Jonathan Page & Co using his middle name and his mother's maiden name. He wished partly to disguise what he was doing from his former employer, although rather cheekily he obtained reprint rights (using Olyve as a go-between) from Duckworth for the racy novels of Elinor Glyn which he issued in paperback format to retail at one shilling each. He gambled on large print runs of 25,000 and was delighted when Simpkin Marshall bought the entire stock for wholesale supply. Further reprinting ventures were also underwritten by the wholesaler buying the entire run, and by the end of 1920 his sideline venture had turned a respectable profit of £2000. He used this to acquire the sole agency for Medici Society publications.

This early successful venture has many of the features that would mark his later publishing. Cape was primarily a salesman with a sharp eye for evolving markets and an ability to measure risks and take them. He knew that Glyn's heady mixture of exotic sex and purple prose would appeal in cheap editions to a large new postwar market which would never have bought the expensive hardback editions issued by Duckworth.[53] He was a firm believer in giving the market what it wanted rather than, unlike some of his contemporaries, what they thought it needed.

He also knew that he was not a strong judge of good writing or a discoverer of original talent. Still less was he accomplished in book design or production. He understood how the book trade worked and how to take commercial advantage of its sometimes arcane practices, but he needed a partner to find authors and develop a new-look publishing list with a distinctive typographic style. At the Medici Society he had worked with a young, bookish, public school and Cambridge graduate named George Wren Howard who understood design and production as well as literature. Howard was twenty-seven and anxious to make his way in the book world. He and Cape agreed to form a partnership, with Cape as the senior partner and pledging the assets of Page & Co. Howard brought £5000 that he had borrowed from his father, an electrical engineer and mayor of Hampstead.

On 1 January 1921 the new house of Jonathan Cape (Publisher) opened at 11 Gower Street, initiating another new London publishing district on the western fringes of Bloomsbury. Over the next fifty years it would progressively become the centre of gravity of the city's literary publishing.

53 A contemporary doggerel 'Oh to sin on a tiger skin with Elinor Glyn' sums up her rather overheated appeal.

It seems contentious and unfair that the new firm was not Cape and Howard, since much of its subsequent success was due to Wren's efforts, but Cape's personality was overbearing and he insisted that the firm bear his name alone.[54] Howard commissioned a friend, Eric Lucas, to design the 'Capapot' – the distinctive fruit bowl colophon with the flanking letters 'J.C.' that would adorn all subsequent Cape publications. His fine typographic eye and exquisite taste in marrying sharp letterpress to good paper and fine binding gave their books the feel of quality and importance that set the new imprint apart.

Two early pieces of luck gave the firm a head start. The first was to be able to take on Edward Garnett as literary adviser. Garnett, almost as unassuming as Wren Howard, had worked for Heinemann and later for Duckworth, where he had known Cape. When Cape opened for business he was languishing at the Bodley Head, where he found the principal John Lane unsympathetic. Cape invited him to join him just three weeks after the firm began. Garnett was a gentle, rather unworldly and troubled character, but he had an instinctive nose for good writing and possessed brilliant literary taste and judgement. Cape never paid him well, certainly not what he deserved, and he nearly sacked him in 1925 when he felt he was not getting enough value for money from him, but he eventually rather grudgingly agreed that '[w]e can count Edward Garnett as one of the main contributors to our present position in the publishing world' (written in 1936, Howard, 1971, p.41). Garnett nurtured authors as varied as Ernest Hemingway, Hugh Lofting (author of the Dr Dolittle books), Christopher Isherwood and Henry Williamson, although in an uncharacteristic false step he did advise against publishing Samuel Beckett.

The second piece of luck that helped Cape and Howard to make rapid initial progress was the decision to publish a lavish and expensive edition of C.M. Doughty's *Travels in Arabia Deserta* as their very first publication, and to acquire the enigmatic and romantic T.E. Lawrence ('of Arabia') to edit it. This project had in fact been discussed at Duckworth when both the partners were there, but its cost was felt to be prohibitive and its market difficult. It took guts and determination for the fledging firm to take this on as its introduction to the literary world, but its timing was

54 Wren's son, Michael, later to be Cape's Chairman, who wrote the official company history in 1971 discreetly skirts around this issue. Wren was a mild-mannered man who loved books and editing while Cape was vain, capricious and, in Rupert Hart-Davis's memorable judgement, 'one of the tightest-fisted old bastards I ever encountered', so it seems likely that Wren was acquiescent.

brilliant. Lawrence was a war hero and an intriguing figure, and the Middle East, with the collapse of the Ottoman Empire and Britain taking the mandate in Palestine, was newsworthy. Cape ensured wide press coverage by promising review editors a free set of the book which retailed at nine guineas (then the equivalent of a month's wages for a working man) if they guaranteed to publish a notice.

The book was a great success despite the warnings of booksellers and other publishers. Had it failed, so would have the new company. Howard spared no pains and expense to produce a truly beautiful two-volume set of books with a large folding coloured map, lavish illustrations and fine binding, setting the standard for the imprint's future. Still it took nerve to continue: when the proofs were completed, advance orders had only reached fifty copies. Cape's energetic sales campaign then began to work. Orders poured in from individuals and libraries, including many from the United States, where Cape had shrewdly established an agency.[55] Many copies were sold directly by mail order, thereby avoiding bookseller discount. The title was published in January 1921, and by summer a reprint was needed. The firm's investment was handsomely returned and its future secure.

Cape was innovative in many directions. He saw the opportunity to acquire rights of American publishers' titles and regularly travelled to North America to buy and sell licences, creating a trade model that still dominates Anglo-American publishing commerce. Garnett spotted authors such as H.E. Bates, who would develop a loyal following who would anxiously await the next new book in a form of celebrity worship *avant de la marque*. High-quality literature went alongside well-presented reprints exemplified by the 'Travellers Library', which included classics of exploration and reportage. Turnover grew rapidly from £10,000 per year in 1921 to over £50,000 in 1926. On the way it had become a limited company and moved to more spacious accommodation nearby in elegant Bedford Square.

Not all was plain sailing in the firm's first decade. Capital was always short and Cape was occasionally frustrated when Howard would not compromise on production quality. A new director, P.G. Thompson,

55 The imprint on the title page reads: 'Lee Warner, Publisher to the Medici Society. Ltd., and Jonathan Cape, London: And at Boston, U.S.A. 1921'. The spine reads: 'Lee Warner & Jonathan Cape'. My copy is an *ex-libris* from the Library of 'The Episcopal Theological School' in Maryland, from which it was apparently only issued once in 1960. This was a fairly typical purchaser of this expensive and rather arcane work.

arrived in 1924, bringing a capital injection of £4000 which enabled the company to pay higher advances so as to acquire the notoriously avaricious and promiscuous (in several senses) H.G. Wells and, significantly for the imprint's future prosperity, Ernest Hemingway.

In 1928, the firm published *The Well of Loneliness* by Radclyffe Hall, a daringly explicit (for the time) novel about lesbianism. Cape knew exactly what he had and the controversy it would cause. He paid Hall a £500 advance, enormous by the standards of the time, and asked the sexologist Havelock Ellis to provide an introduction. He printed 1500 copies 'in plain wrappers' and awaited developments. Although reviews were generally good, predictably *The Sunday Express* exploded with bile and outrage, demanding that the book be banned and the publisher prosecuted. Cape obligingly sent the home secretary, William Joynson-Hicks, a copy of the offending book and offered to follow his advice.

Joynson-Hicks declared the book obscene and told Cape it must be withdrawn. He apparently compliantly did so, but then began to play a very devious game. He sold a licence to publish an English edition of the book to Pegasus Press in Paris (in which he had an interest) and shipped them 'flongs' (*papier-mâché* casts of the letterpress) to make stereotypes to reprint the books. Copies were duly smuggled back into Britain for sale and were seized by the police. Cape was charged with obscenity and unwisely chose the bumbling barrister Norman Birkett QC to defend him. Birkett presented a laughable defence, claiming that the book portrayed only 'normal friendship between women' (with which the author publicly and vehemently disagreed), and it was judged obscene with all copies ordered to be destroyed. Cape was ever afterwards very careful of any book that had sex as a central theme, rejecting works by Samuel Beckett and Naomi Mitchison on those grounds. He would even occasionally expurgate Hemingway if he felt that the great man's language was offensive.

Nevertheless Cape survived and continued to prosper. Jonathan had created in a remarkably short time an enduring image of what a modern literary publisher should be and what its books should look like. The popular public perception of a publisher as a tall, pipe-smoking, bow-tied and bespoke-suited literary gentleman working from behind an antique desk on the first floor of a bow-fronted Georgian house on a Bloomsbury Square is Jonathan Cape and his famous editorial address of 30 Bedford Square to the life – or at least the image he liked to project. In reality, he could be disloyal, mean, foul-mouthed, ruthless and unpleasant, with his bonhomie masking a selfish, petty and rather vicious streak. As we have hinted, he often claimed credit for what his associates achieved, not least from the long-suffering Wren Howard. Nevertheless, he was incontestably astute, sensitive to what the public wanted to read and buy and genuinely creative and original in his conception of a new kind of publishing. Without him, British publishing in the 1920s would have been duller, less adventurous and much more parochial.

Another new arrival in the 1920s, very different in business terms from Cape but quite similar in spirit, was the Hogarth Press. This had its origins in a private press operated by Leonard and Virginia Woolf from their home at Hogarth House in Richmond in Surrey where they produced small editions of stories and poems written by themselves and their friends including the US poet T.S. Eliot. As key members of what would become the Bloomsbury Group, they had no shortage of writers and readers. When they moved to Tavistock Square near University College London in 1924, they decided to expand their amateur dabbling into a commercial publishing operation. They divided the tall Georgian terrace house into living quarters above and offices and storage below, employed a junior and set out to publish finely printed and cheaply priced poetry and essays which reflected their *avant-garde* taste.

Richard Kennedy's wry and frequently hilarious memoir of working at the Press provides a portrait of a chaotic, self-consciously high-minded and well-connected enterprise that was quintessentially Bloomsbury (Kennedy, 1972). He memorably sums up Virginia Woolf as '[r]ather cruel in spite of the kind, rather dreamy way she looks at you' (Kennedy, 1972, p.9). Whether the Press would have survived without their personal wealth and the patronage of their friends such as the Duchess of Wellington is very doubtful. It remained a rather dilettante operation until the arrival of John Lehmann in 1931, who introduced a much-needed dose of professionalism. Nevertheless, it provided a publishing outlet for many young writers, particularly poets who probably would not have been taken on elsewhere such as Cecil Day Lewis, W.H. Auden and Stephen Spender. It also made available in translation important works in psychoanalysis by Sigmund Freud and his Viennese circle. Later, as we shall see, Hogarth Press would make more substantial contributions.

The third new arrival of the 1920s, and arguably the most important, was Faber and Faber (Pregnall, 2001). Geoffrey Faber was a classical scholar who joined Oxford University Press directly from university in 1913. Following war service he was elected a Fellow of All Souls and was made a director of his family brewery, Strong and Company of Yorkshire, in 1920. As we have seen, he had been thinking of setting up as an independent publisher and had briefly discussed partnership with Jonathan Cape. His plans were delayed by legal studies (he was called to the Bar in 1921 but never practised). In 1924 he gave up his brewery directorship and invested the proceeds with his Oxford colleague Maurice Gwyer in a publishing partnership. Gwyer already owned a successful publishing house The Scientific Press, specializing in medical books and journals, including *Nursing Mirror*, which his wife, Alsina, had inherited from her father, Sir Henry Burdett. What Faber had in mind was publishing of a very different character, and when Faber and Gwyer Ltd, as the successor to the Scientific Press, opened its doors at 24 Russell Square near the British Museum in 1925, the scene was set for the creation of probably the most influential literary publisher of the twentieth century.

Faber described his motivation and goals in a speech to booksellers:

> … I began my business career in a publisher's office [i.e. OUP] (but) I spent three years of it in a far more lucrative form of business. For those three years I was a managing director in a big brewery … (b)ut I have never been so bored in my life … (s)o I had the best of all reasons – personal experience – for saying … (I) would rather be making a competence out of books than a fortune (elsewhere) … to me, at least, books are better. (Faber, 1934, p.51)

He went on to explain his publishing credo:

> Conditions have altered very much since (the nineteenth century). Lending libraries, book societies, newspaper stunts, the enormous increase of published books, the standardization of business methods – these things have taken a lot of the individuality out of the book trade … The old moral earnestness has largely gone, and though there is a far bigger potential reading public than there used to be, it takes no serious interest in books … On the face of things, the conditions for bookselling – and for publishing too – are about as unpropitious as they could well be.
>
> … (However) we may be about to see an increase of serious interest and real revival of the more solid and important form of bookselling … The principal reason for this is that … we are undoubtedly in for a bad time … (there is) the perception that things are already seriously wrong, with the world as a whole and with

> ourselves in particular, and the consequence will, I think be that numbers and numbers of people will begin to ask themselves all sorts of questions which only books can answer. (Faber, 1934, pp.54-6)

Although he spoke the above in 1931 when the depth of the recession was already clear, Faber's view that serious books could enlighten, shape, warn and rescue as well as entertain was the guiding principle of his new publishing house from the beginning. To realize this, he decided to build on the core of nursing and medical titles (which would remain a feature of the Faber list for decades afterwards) by creating a literary and non-fiction list of the highest quality. He recruited T.S. Eliot, who had recently given up his humdrum job at Lloyds Bank and shared Faber's vision of the importance of good publishing, as his literary adviser. Fellow directors included Richard De La Mare, son of the popular poet Walter, Frank Morley, C.W. Stewart and Morley Kennerley. Faber embarked on a wide-ranging programme, from science to music and poetry, and created a very distinctive high-quality list, that like Cape, had a distinctive typographic elegance.[56] More importantly, the publisher married commercial and literary judgement in an unique and highly original mixture. Such a strategy continues to underlie its publishing approach today as one of the few successful imprints to maintain its independence from corporate ownership.

Gwyer retired from the company in 1929 and sold his share to Faber, who used the proceeds from the sale of *Nursing Mirror* to finance the arrangement, and the house was renamed Faber and Faber. This was a typically quirky development as there was never more than one Faber involved in the firm at any one time. Company legend insists that the idea was suggested by De La Mare who thought the new name more euphonious.

As the decade of the 1920s came to a close, British publishing seemed to have survived a storm and was in good shape to meet the future. New houses had been successfully established, and older ones had modernized. The challenges of new media like radio and the cinema had been met, and to an extent co-opted. Arthur Waugh, writing in 1930 in elegiac mood, found the new publishing world rather distasteful:

56 Although not without its foibles, one of which was the insistence on printing the publication date in Roman rather than conventional Arabic figures. This aberration lasted well into the 1950s. It has been suggested that this was a ploy, worthy of Walter Hutchinson, to disguise the date of publication.

> The business of the book-trade is only one very small fraction of the importunate work of the world; but, like every other form of energy, it bears its witness to the overpowering saturnalia of noise, clamour, struggle, all but cut-throat competition. Noise at work, noise at play, noise in the street, noise in the air: to look back, out of the thick of all this hurly-burly, into the quiet beginnings of a hundred years ago, is to be rapt into a day-dream of urbanity and peace. (Waugh, 1930, p.309)

Waugh may have yearned for the certainties and simplicity of a quieter and easier age, but, even as he wrote, the resurgent publishing world was about to face new economic problems and social and political stresses. The Wall Street Crash of 1929 ushered in a frightening new world that would make even heavier demands on the enterprise, imagination and energy of its practitioners. Yet the bleak combination of global recession and financial uncertainty, mass unemployment and the rise of totalitarianism in Europe would actually inspire publishing to its greatest levels of innovation.

4 'The Penguins are coming!'

British publishing in the 1930s

One figure so completely dominates British book publishing in the 1930s that it would be tempting to devote this entire chapter to Allen Lane and his creation of Penguin Books. Lane's great invention will be given its due consideration later on in the chapter (and indeed throughout the remainder of this book), but I would like first to consider other companies and trends before dealing with the 'paperback revolution'. This is for several reasons. Firstly, Lane did not launch Penguin until 1935 when the economy had actually began to recover from the economic recession following the Wall Street Crash of 1929, and the first five years of the decade did provide a very different publishing environment. Secondly, I would contend that the real 'Penguin decade' was the 1940s when the list came of age and reached the status of a national institution comparable to the role played by the BBC. Thirdly, it should be remembered that Lane was a considerable, perhaps even a great publisher, before he founded Penguin. He was also a man of his time whose outlook and ideas were shaped long before he had his great insight into how the market for books could be changed. His invention of Penguin Books was partly a response to the economic and social conditions he perceived as Britain emerged from global recession and confronted an uncertain future. No matter how profound and transformational, his impact did only refer to one sector of the market. Elsewhere, other publishers saw the 1930s differently.

So far, I have only considered educational, academic and professional publishing tangentially as part of wider lists. For many of the publishers discussed, such as Longmans, Macmillan, Nelson, Methuen or Heinemann, books in those areas may have been unglamorous, but they provided a solid bedrock of guaranteed revenue and predictable profit that supported their more risky literary or 'trade' non-fiction publications. As we have seen, educational titles were 'non-net' so they attracted only short discounts of about 10 per cent, and they were to a large extent supplied to their ultimate users by educational contractors who had negotiated substantial, steady arrangements with local authority education departments to supply books for schools. While educational publishing was never as absolutely centralized and closed as in, say, France,[57] the concept of the textbook as a long-lived repeated sales channel was understood clearly both by their creators and consumers.

Typical of the companies who supplied school books to local authorities was E.J. Arnold of Leeds. E.J. Arnold, a printer and stationer (and no relation to the London publisher Edward Arnold), founded the company in 1863 in Barnstaple. In 1870 he moved to Leeds where he set up as a printer, stationer, publisher and supplier of materials to local schools. This latter business expanded rapidly when the passing of the 1902 Education Act gave free education to all and quickly began to eclipse other sectors. Four generations of the Arnold family expanded the business, and by the 1980s the company employed over 1000 staff and served all the UK and a wide overseas market, particularly in Africa. The deregulation of state education during the 1980s saw the abrupt end of 'central buying' which, coupled with changes and problems in export markets, drove many contractors, including E.J. Arnold, out of business.

Until the 1930s, educational publishing was conservative and rooted in a fossilized curriculum and old-fashioned ideas of pedagogy. To be fair, this was because schools and their teachers were tied to tried-and-true methods that had evolved in the nineteenth century and derived in part, particularly in the grammar schools, from an uncritical admiration of and aspiration to what the public schools provided. The vast majority of pupils only completed elementary education and left school at the ages of twelve to fourteen, having used books which were often very old and uninspiring. Even candidates for School Certificate, regarded as potential white-collar and professional workers, found their classroom texts often ancient and outmoded.

Publishers, of course, gave the market what it wanted and reprinted their established titles over many decades, often with minimal revision. Kennedy's *Latin Primer* may have been an extreme and understandable example, but even in subjects that were more contemporary such as

57 Famously, Guizot, the French education minister, opened a textbook in the 1840s to show some guests and remarked, '*Messieurs*, at this very moment every schoolchild of fourteen years in France is looking at that page.'

geography, textbooks enjoyed incredibly long lives (Walford, 2001). The *Modern Geography* series written by D.M. Preece, a geography mistress from Crewe and chief examiner for the Oxford School Certificate, and H.R.B. Wood, director of education for Wallasey, was first published by the small specialist schools publisher, University Tutorial Press, during the 1930s. It survived through many reprints right until the mid-1950s or even later, but some of the content was dated even when it was first issued. As late as the third edition of 1946, all the statistics quoted refer to the 1920s or early 1930s, and it is as if the Second World War had never happened, apart from a brief reference to the German occupation of the Channel Islands (Preece and Wood, 1946).

Although it was proud of the longevity of Kennedy, its publisher Longmans was one of the first to attempt to rejuvenate its schools publishing from the early 1930s (Briggs, 2008, pp.391-4). It was perhaps more urgent for them than most since under the regime of Charles Longman the house had rested on its educational laurels far too long – even by the standards of the time, its list looked threadbare and out-of-touch. It was lucky that it could call on the considerable creative talents of two remarkable individuals, Ernest W. Parker for the 'home schools' market and C.S.S. Higham for what was still thought of as 'the imperial and colonial educational' market.

Parker had joined Longmans in 1911 straight from school and after war service, for which he was awarded a Military Cross, he devoted his time to developing the firm's publishing for British schools. He was sent on the road as a 'schools traveller' during the 1920s, and he learned first-hand from teachers and educational bureaucrats that his products would no longer cut the mustard (Wallis, 1974, p.55). Following Charles Longman's death the company's fortunes were at a low ebb, and it looked for a short time in the wake of the Great Crash of 1929 that it might founder. Parker realized that if he could rebuild Longmans' schools publishing he could recover their dwindling share of the only guaranteed market available to publishers in a time of recession, and help secure the company's future.

He identified the public and grammar schools as the most potentially remunerative markets and during the 1930s built up a revolutionary list that served generations of senior pupils with their fundamental textbooks well into the 1960s and beyond; in many cases they also crossed-over into university teaching. Parker's range was wide: he commissioned the innovative history texts of R.H. Rayner; the systematic approach to geography (structured by 'topic' rather than discussing regions) by Dudley Stamp and Stanley Beaver[58] that was revolutionary for its time; as well as scientific texts such as the manuals of chemical analysis from Arnold Vogel. His two most important contributions were W.F.H. Whitmarsh's *School Certificate French Course* of 1935, which was absolutely to dominate language teaching in schools for forty years, and *The Heritage of Literature* series founded in 1934. Designed to 'provide interesting reading matter for children at school', this was the first educational series to include modern as well as classic authors in a series of English readers (Briggs, 2008, pp.392-3).

Higham, to whom Parker reported, had joined Longmans in 1926 from the staff of the history department at Manchester University. He began his publishing career with the home educational list, but he quickly passed this over to Parker and developed an increasing interest in the overseas educational market. A visit to Egypt (self-funded, so precarious were Longmans' finances at that time) convinced him of the potential of such emerging markets, and he oversaw the adaptation of Michael West's *New Method Readers* (originated by Longmans' Indian subsidiary) there (Wallis, 1974, p.53). This was the beginning of the teaching of English as a foreign language publishing later to become the foundation of Longmans' development into the largest and most profitable British publisher.

Higham proved a shrewd and intuitive judge of sales and markets. According to Dudley Stamp, an equally cunning literary entrepreneur, his approach was '[t]his book is needed, it must not cost more than 5*s*, we will publish it' (quoted in Wallis, 1974, p.54). Although funds were tight, he insisted that his new educational titles should be well printed, strongly bound, competitively priced and written by the best authors. His university teaching background stood him in good stead as he knew many of the best young scholars personally and could persuade them to write. His greatest coup was to convince G.M. Trevelyan that there was such a thing as 'social history' and to write the best-selling *A Social History of England*. First published by Longmans' Canadian branch because of wartime restrictions on materials in 1944, it was still selling strongly over fifty years later. Despite his scholarly background, Higham did not disdain more

58 Professor Beaver who was still active as an editor and adviser when I took the list over forty years later had particularly vivid and fond memories of Parker as a supportive editor. When the geography title *The British Isles* which Parker had commissioned from him and Stamp celebrated its fiftieth anniversary in 1984, I had a special commemorative edition bound in red morocco to be presented to him. He died the following year.

practical subjects studied at technical and craft level, and Longmans developed strong publishing lists in areas such as office practice, principles of accounts, electronics and eventually hairdressing, catering and retailing.[59] Higham was made a director rather grudgingly in 1940 when the family directors were off on war service, but his health had suffered from his extensive foreign travel. He began to pass more publishing decisions over to Parker and concentrated on building the sales infrastructure in key overseas markets, particularly India. He died in 1958 and his son Adrian joined the firm, in what was to become a recurrent pattern of sons following fathers at Longmans. Adrian eventually became managing director of the University Division, and later chief executive of the British subsidiary of the American academic publisher John Wiley.[60]

Much of what we would today describe as academic publishing was in the 1930s and earlier classified as 'general' on the lists of trade publishers. 'Serious' houses such as Macmillan, Allen and Unwin or Methuen would regularly issue treatises by academic authors – the economists Alfred Marshall or John Maynard Keynes, for example, or the historian Louis Namier, or scientists such as Patrick Geddes, J. Arthur Thompson or Archibald Geikie – as part of their general non-fiction lists. These kinds of books were staple items for public and circulating libraries and the reading lists of the relatively few universities and university colleges, but just how much they were bought by the general public is questionable. Publishers regarded them as worthwhile and prestigious rather than money-makers. A few houses did however develop high-level specialized academic lists, the most surprising of which was perhaps the Glasgow-based firm of Blackie and Sons (Stevenson, 2007c).

Blackie was founded in 1809 and had built its reputation on school-level educational titles, finely printed 'toy' and 'reward' books – intended for presentation as prizes to pupils in day and Sunday schools – and

59 The publisher of the 'further education and craft list' which Higham founded was in the 1970s a fascinating character called Basil Wilby. He vividly recalled to me the trials of commissioning books from – and selling them to – the formidable 'commercial ladies' who ruled the world of office practice.

60 Longmans had a grand tradition of long service among its employees. Robert Coombs, for example, spent a lifetime with the firm developing publishing in the Middle East markets, commissioning works from the great scholar Edward Said and actively sponsoring the 'York Notes' series. His father had been the company accountant in the 1920s. David Lea began as a warehouse hand in the 1950s, retiring as a much respected head of contracts in the 1990s, an example of employment longevity almost unimaginable today.

children's stories, including the 'Flower Fairy' series written and illustrated by Cicely May Barker. It had occasionally included scientific titles on its general list, but from 1920 on it embarked on a world-class list of scientific books at the cutting edge of research that eventually became the strongest British publishing list in the area from a commercial publisher. This was due to the work of Frederick Bisacre, who in 1918 married Jean Blackie, grand-daughter of the chairman Walter Blackie, and was consequently taken into the firm as a partner.

Bisacre had trained as a mechanical engineer and a mathematician at Cambridge and had a strong interest in theoretical physics. He had very strong international connections and was able to attract to the list leading figures such as the Italian mathematician Tullio Levi-Civitá and the German Nobel laureate for physics, Max Born. He was later able to help the latter, a refugee from the Nazis, obtain the physics chair at Edinburgh. Bisacre eventually became managing director, but he maintained a strong interest in scientific research and writing, and himself produced an admired textbook on applied calculus.

More specialized academic and scholarly publishing was the province in the main of the two University Presses at Oxford and Cambridge. Both had long and distinguished histories, but had rather decayed by the twentieth century.[61] They had been granted the 'letters patent' which gave them the exclusive rights to publish the King James version of the Bible and the Prayer Book,[62] and much of their revenue came from this solid and undemanding market. Of the two, Oxford was the more commercially-minded, although the publishing policy of both was (and remains) determined by a ruling committee of university academics, the 'Syndics' at Cambridge and the 'Delegates' at Oxford. As university departments the Presses were free of the usual financial constraints faced by commercial publishers, and were thus able to invest in projects that consumed large amounts of capital and paid back only slowly. Oxford had begun its great English dictionary during the 1880s, only publishing

61 Cambridge University Press was founded by a declaration of Henry VIII in 1534, while the first books printed under the auspices of Oxford University date to 1478. It was not until the eighteenth century that either press emerged as a publishing house in anything like the modern sense.

62 This was a special form of copyright that restricted the publication of the 'authorised versions' to designated publishers. Apart from the University Presses, the letters patent were also held by the King's Printers, Eyre & Spottiswoode, and in Scotland by William Collins and Sons.

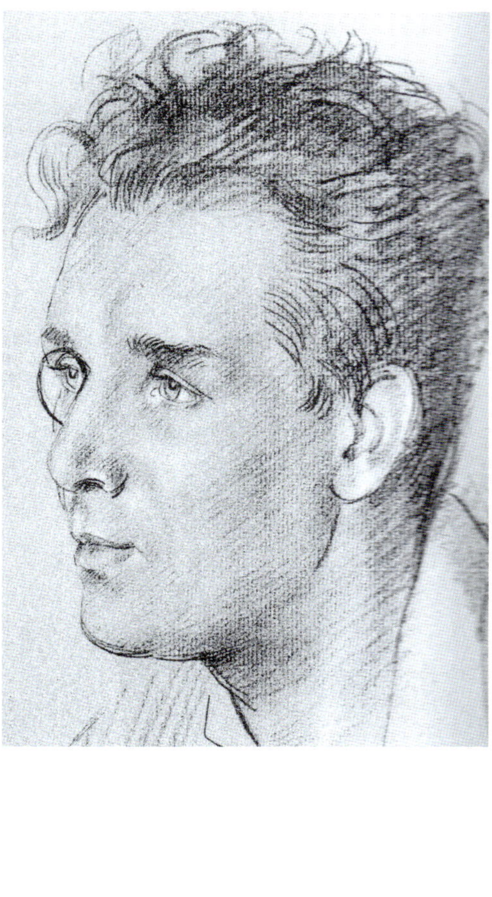

1 William Heinemann circa 1900 as 'The Young Voluptuary'.

2 The original Heinemann office at 21 Bedford Street, Covent Garden, remarkably unchanged in 2009 from its original appearance in 1900.

3 Grant Richards circa 1903, sporting his characteristic monocle.

4 The building at 29-32 Bedford Street, Covent Garden by the west entrance to St Paul's Church was until 1897 the offices of Macmillan and Company, and then occupied by J.M. Dent until 1913.

5 The new Dent building, Aldine House, at the corner of Bedford Street and Chandos Place, designed by E. Keynes Purchase. Opened in 1913, it still dominates the site in 2009 with its original ground-floor wooden panelling and corner lookout tower intact.

6 J.M. Dent in later middle age, circa 1909.

7 A selection of 'pocket classics' in finely-printed editions, bound in leather and gold stamped with gilt edges from Dent and Longman, circa 1904. These were intended to serve the luxury end of the 'everyman' market and retailed for six shillings. Note the influence of Art Nouveau on the presentation of the binding.

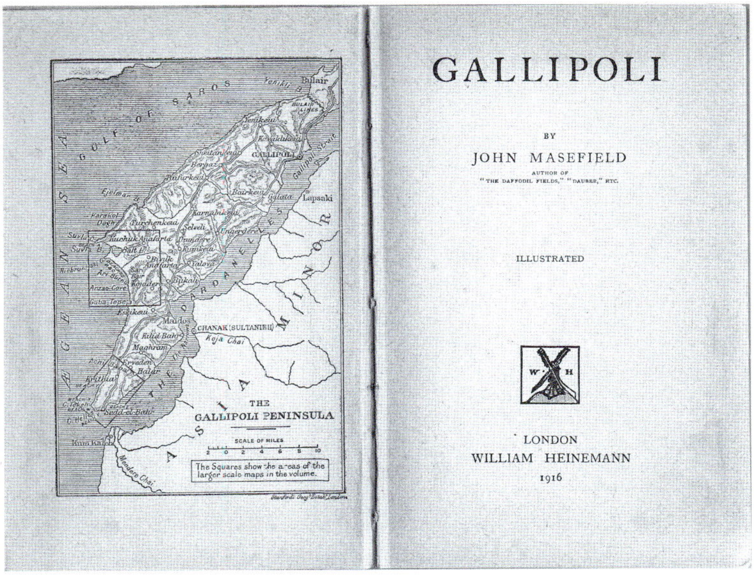

8 Title page opening of *Gallipoli* by John Masefield, Heinemann, London, 1916.

9 The two volumes of the first title published by Jonathan Cape in 1921, *Arabia Deserta* by C.M. Doughty, shown against the map included in a pocket of volume one. Retailing at 9 guineas, it included an introduction by T.E. Lawrence.

11 30 Bedford Square, Bloomsbury, London, the former offices of Jonathan Cape, 2009.

10 Jonathan Cape in the 1920s.

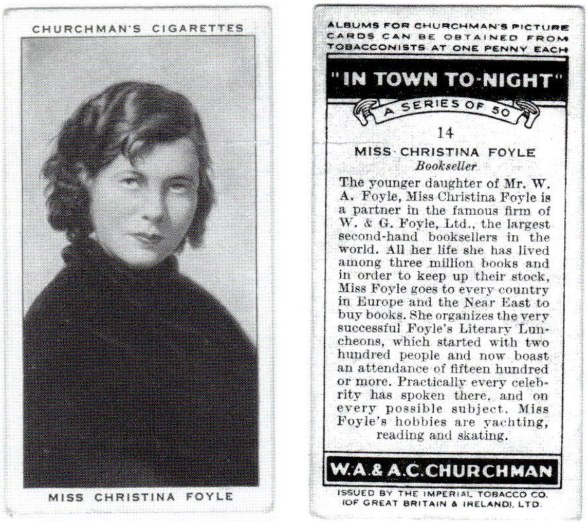

12 Obverse and reverse of a cigarette card issued by Churchmans in 1932 from the series 'In Town Tonight' picturing the glamorous bookseller Christina Foyle. Interestingly Miss Foyle was the only publishing or literary celebrity included in this series of fifty London celebrities.

13 Sir Geoffrey Faber, 1947.

14 The Faber building, 24 Russell Square, Bloomsbury, 2009.

15 T.S. Eliot on his way to work at Faber and Gwyer, 1926.

16 Leonard and Virginia Woolf by Gisèle Freund, 1939.

17 The Heinemann warehouse, print works and administrative offices at Kingswood, Surrey from the air, circa 1932.

18 The first ten Penguin titles published in 1935.

19 Sir Sydney C. Roberts.

20 The London office of Cambridge University Press, Bentley House, Euston Road, London, 2009.

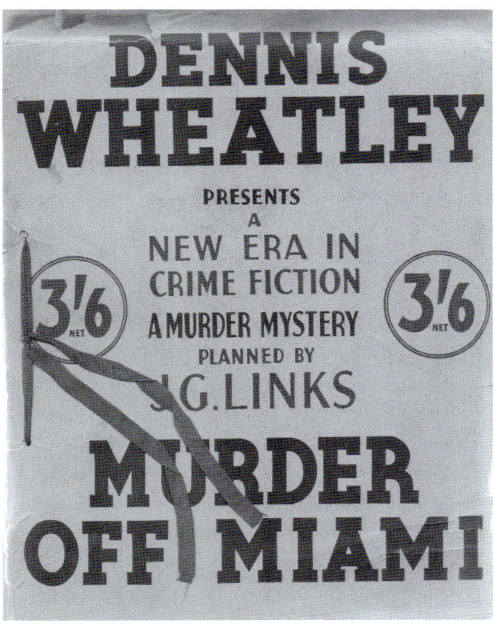

21 The front cover of the 'murder mystery dossier'. *Murder off Miami*. planned by Dennis Wheatley and J.G. Links, and published by Hutchinson in 1936 which included 'real clues', including documents, letters, photographs, hair, cigarette ends and a 'bloodstain'. Four similar dossiers, each increasingly complex, were published up to 1939.

22 Charles Fry, memorably described by John Betjeman as a 'phallus with a business sense' in the antiquarian bookshop of Batsford, South Audley Street, Mayfair.

23 A selection of the 'Britain in Pictures' series produced by Adprint for William Collins during the Second World War. This was the first 'packaged' series and was intended to be a patriotic contribution to the war effort. It eventually included over one hundred titles, celebrating British culture, education, science, history, art and institutions.

24 The quintessential British publishing house, a five-storey (including attic, basement and area) Georgian house at 40 Bedford Square, Bloomsbury, last occupied by Edward Arnold (Publishers).

25 The former Methuen building in Essex Street, Temple, London. The arch in the background which leads to Temple Steps was used by the house as its colophon.

the first 'fascicle' in 1928 (Winchester, 1998). Although Cambridge never commissioned anything so large or ambitious, it produced a steady flow of academically important if sometimes obscure monographs and dissertations that would have never found commercial outlets otherwise. Merit rather than money was their guiding principle.

The key figure in Cambridge publishing in the 1930s was the Secretary to the Syndics (in plain language, managing director), Sir Sydney Roberts (Roberts, 1966). He was born in 1887 and, after taking a classics and history double-first at Pembroke College, looked destined for an academic career. Instead he joined the university press in 1911, taking over as Secretary in 1922 to become the youngest head in the house's history. Although Roberts remained an academic at heart (he would eventually become Master of Pembroke and university Vice-Chancellor), he was a shrewd businessman and an astute publisher. His donnish and witty persona[63] (he was a renowned and feared mimic) served him well in charming authors and winning over reluctant Syndics to his projects, and under his stewardship Cambridge modernized both its manufacturing facilities and its publishing operation.[64]

He was a plain speaker and a clear thinker. He described his approach to book commissioning as follows:

> Broadly speaking, manuscripts offered to the Press were in three classes [in the 1930s]: first, there were those which were rejected out of hand either because they were rubbish or because they were wholly unsuited to the Press catalogue; I never ceased to marvel at the persistent optimism of those authors who submitted work so remote from the standards of a university publishing house. Secondly, there were manuscripts of serious intention in every kind of subject; for these, the first thing to do was to choose the most competent referee, or, if the choice were not obvious, to ask one of the Syndics for advice.

63 He had a habit of writing spoofs and pastiches, of which the funniest is *Zuleika in Cambridge*, a novella in which Max Beerbohm's *femme fatale*, having caused mayhem in Oxford by her lightly-bestowed charms, passes almost unnoticed in Cambridge. It may be significant that they were published not by the University Press, but the bookseller Heffer.

64 Cambridge remains the only British publisher to maintain its own printing works, although at the time writing its future may be doubtful. Uniquely now in the world, Cambridge maintains its editorial offices, its printing house and its warehouse on a single campus site near Cambridge railway station. Oxford closed its Printing House in 1987.

> Lastly, there was the manuscript of general interest, or of what the author thought would be of general interest. It was this class which held a special interest for me … (Roberts, 1966, p.63)

The Cambridge University Press (CUP) list expanded with authors from far beyond the Fens and a particular interest was expansion in the United States. Macmillan had looked after Cambridge publishing there (Oxford had established its own New York branch in 1896), and in 1931 Roberts negotiated a 'Cambridge department' to be set up within Macmillan to be in sole charge of ordering and selling their titles. Macmillan disliked the idea, but Roberts threatened to take the agency away and they eventually agreed, appointing F.R. Mansbridge as the cuckoo in the nest, with CUP contributing half his salary. He eventually became president of the independent branch established by CUP on Madison Avenue in 1948. Mansbridge added American authors to the list from Harvard, Yale and other Ivy League schools, although many had Cambridge connections.

Nearer to home Roberts oversaw expansion in London. CUP had long had a ramshackle and inconvenient office in Fetter Lane off Fleet Street to supply the requirements of London booksellers, but by 1935 it was clearly too small and verminous. Roberts commissioned the architect W. Curtis Green to design a grand new building, 'a rare opportunity of planning and building a publishing house *ab initio*' (Roberts, 1966, p.163). This was Bentley House, named for a former distinguished Cambridge printer of the seventeenth century on a new freehold site on Euston Road, handy for King's Cross station and the Great Northern railway line to Cambridge. It was opened in May 1938 and was a brave investment in the prevailing financial conditions, although it proved highly successful and very lucrative when CUP eventually sold the building in the 1980s. 'The only criticism of this designation', Roberts wryly remarked, 'was that "Bentley House, Euston Road" might suggest trade in motor-cars rather than books' (Roberts, 1966, p.163).

Although never approaching Oxford in size, range or scope, CUP reconstructed its publishing most successfully in the 1930s, particularly in science, literature and history, reflecting the university's growing dominance in those fields. A.S. Eddington and J.H. Jeans produced major bestselling works in astronomy and physics, prompting comparisons with Newton whom CUP had published two centuries before. Under the guidance of J.H. Clapham, a Syndic until 1938, multi-volume histories were planned which took several decades to execute, with occasional excursions into popular history publishing such as the bestselling biography of Samuel Pepys, written by Arthur Bryant in the late 1930s. Literature was served by Arthur Quiller-Couch, the long-established professor of English Literature who, under the pen-name of 'Q', wrote criticism, *belles-lettres* and short stories, both for CUP and other publishers. However, newer and more contentious Cambridge critics were emerging whom the Press would also publish. Roberts had been the examiner of the PhD thesis of one F.R. Leavis (Chainey, 1985, Chapter 22).

Other smaller university presses existed at Liverpool, Manchester, Edinburgh and Glasgow. They had mainly insignificant outputs, although Glasgow, with a distinguished history stretching back as far as 1638, did produce some important titles in science and mathematics (MacLehose, 1931). The University of London had attempted to create its own press as early as 1909, but unwisely entrusted its development to 'a gentleman, ignorant of publishing, who had astutely registered the title earlier' (Harte, 1966, p.180). Hampered by its federal structure of the University, which tended to encourage in-fighting, there were numerous abortive attempts to create a university press in London throughout the twentieth century. All of them ended in collapse and failure, with the wreckage being sold off to commercial publishers such as Hodder[65] (Attenborough, 1975, pp.68-9, 178-9).

Publishing for professionals such as lawyers, medical doctors and architects was generally in the hands of highly focussed commercial firms who knew the subject intimately and often employed practitioners to oversee their output and ensure its quality and accuracy. Medical publishing was mainly carried out by three firms, John Wright of Bristol, J & A Churchill of London and E & S Livingstone of Edinburgh, although some larger publishers did include major medical titles on their lists, such as Longmans with *Gray's Anatomy* and the *Medical* and *Veterinary Dictionaries* published by A & C Black (Stevenson, 2007c). A number of tiny firms, like Christopher Johnson, catered for the mysteriously strong demand among medical practitioners for reading and writing clinical

65 An entertaining history could be written about how – and why – London never got a real University Press. After the failure of the University of London Press Ltd there was a renewed attempt in the 1940s to create another one with the Athlone Press, in its turn sold to the private sector. University College established its own Press in 1988, and it has had at least three owners since then. Imperial College Press is a trading name licensed to a publisher of scientific books from Singapore.

anecdotes and reminiscence like *Goodbye Harley Street* by R. Scott Stevenson.[66]

Law publishing, partly catered for by a number of small specialists such as Wildy, Simmonds and Hill who were stationers and booksellers as well as publishers, was dominated by two firms: Sweet and Maxwell, and Butterworth and Company, of which the latter was by far the largest. Henry Butterworth had set up shop in Fleet Street in 1818 to service the book needs of the denizens of the nearby Inns of Court. When his last descendant died without heirs in 1895, the business was acquired by the law stationers Shaw and Sons, owned by the brothers Charles and Richard Bond (Kay Jones, 1980). They and Charles's son Stanley, who eventually took over the company, overhauled and energetically expanded it by creating major reference works indispensable to every law practice in the country. These included the *Encyclopedia of Forms and Precedents* and, the jewel in its crown, the multi-volume *Laws of England* edited by the Earl of Halsbury, the Lord Chancellor – one of the few books, like Gray, Whitaker or Bradshaw, to be universally identified by the name of its author alone. *Halsbury*, which was first published in 1911, has remained continuously in print and the current edition, last revised in 2008, runs to 61 (loose-leaf) volumes.

Stanley Bond was both a visionary publisher and a hard-driving monomaniac, probably deserving Kay Jones' judgement that he 'owned people rather than employed them' (Kay Jones, 1980, p.92). He worked long hours and expected the same of everyone else; unmarried until the age of sixty-one,[67] he did not understand the demands of family life. His entrepreneurship had made him rich and his firm prosperous, but despite this he continued to work himself and employees relentlessly. He could be brutally frank in criticizing the perceived shortcomings of staff, and had an almost pathological need to be absolutely in charge of everything to do with the company's business. He demanded (and received) total loyalty and obedience. Comparisons can be drawn with Walter Hutchinson,

66 Christopher Johnson, set up in the 1940s, was actually the name of the publisher's small son. Johnson junior later became an eminent economist, Editor of *Lloyds' Bank Review* and the bank's chief economic adviser.

67 He eventually married Violet Fletcher, thirty-one years his junior, in 1938. She produced two sons in quick succession, and there is a suggestion that he only married to obtain 'an heir and a spare' for his company. This, as we shall see, caused great problems for the survival of his firm after his death.

although Bond was much more tightly controlled and possibly even more frightening.

Although a limited company with some outside shareholders, by the 1930s Butterworth & Co had become an absolute despotism totally ruled by Bond. It had expanded successfully to set up companies in India, Australia and Canada, and had established subsidiaries to publish professional journals – one of the first commercial organizations to identify the potential of this lucrative branch of publishing. In 1936 it had moved into medical publishing by applying the successful encyclopedia format in that field. In 1937 Bond decided that he needed to reorganize the company and called a board meeting to inform the other directors of his plans. These involved the humiliating downgrading of his managing director George Bellew, who had faithfully served Bond for over thirty years, in a coup that effectively made Bond both chairman and managing director. Bellew considered his position and resigned a few months later. On the day he left he called the Butterworths staff together to an extraordinarily emotional meeting where, amid tears and recriminations, he wished them '[g]oodbye and good luck' (Kay Jones, 1980, p.105). In later decades abrupt dismissals or 'resignations' (usually characterized as the departee wishing to pursue 'other interests') became commonplace in publishing, as elsewhere in business, but in the 1930s Bellew's shameful treatment was shocking and extremely unusual.

Bond was, however, unrepentant and now totally in the ascendant. Never short of self-regard, he made the following immodest claim in a letter to the director of his Australian company a couple of days after Bellew's departure:

> To speak quite plainly, the driving power, whereby the business has progressed to its present size, from quite a small beginning, has emanated from me personally – the creative ideas have also come from me.
>
> I have an endless number of ideas: they come to me out of the blue. (Kay Jones, 1980, pp.105-6)

Neville Cusworth, Butterworths chairman five decades later, sees Bond as resembling the protagonist of a Greek tragedy, his hubris planting the seeds of the destruction of all he had built (Cusworth, in Graham 2006, pp.vii-viii). Another successor, Gordon Graham, makes a less dramatic but more balanced judgement, recognizing Bond's extraordinary energy, determination and creativity without shirking his more unattractive characteristics (Graham, 2006). Whether or not we believe in poetic justice, Bond died unexpectedly (perhaps from overwork) in 1943, with all the reins of power in his hands and in the expectation of even greater triumphs. He left a net estate worth over half a million pounds, probably the greatest personal fortune ever created by publishing up to that point, and two infant sons whom he had hoped would eventually inherit his business. As we shall see later, this was not to occur, and his obsessively created law publishing powerhouse came close to destruction.

Books for schools, academics and professionals were relatively isolated from the economic problems of the decade, leaving their publishers reasonably secure in markets where books were necessary purchases. Elsewhere, book sales were seriously affected as the recession took hold. Exports fell, unemployment increased to almost three million and in 1931 Britain had to abandon the gold standard of the currency, causing the exchange rate to collapse. Stanley Unwin, ever the optimist, made a relatively upbeat assessment in 1935 as President of the Publishers' Association:

> Economic recovery has, we are told, to some extent been achieved in this country, but whether this be or not the book trade would be ungrateful to complain of its position. The trade has not suffered to anything like the same extent as have many others, and during the year under review a definitely optimistic note was sounded, particularly towards the close of 1934. Such progress as has been made, however, has been confined to the home trade, and unfortunately has to some extent been offset by the fact that export business has become increasingly difficult. Exchange restrictions, tariffs, certificates of origin, piracies and so on involve an ever increasing expenditure of time. (quoted in Kingsford, 1970, pp.113-14)

Whether many of his competitors, surveying reduced print runs, rising manufacturing costs and clamorous demands from booksellers for longer discounts and payment terms would have agreed with Unwin is uncertain. The home trade market may not have collapsed, but it was certainly stagnant. Many publishers became risk-averse, particularly when launching new authors or new publishing genres. One unpleasant facet of the recession economy was the creation of the trade practice of publishers supplying booksellers on 'see-safe' terms – effectively sale or return – which yet bedevils the book economy (Stevenson, 2007a, p.322).

Unwin was, however, certainly right about the mayhem the recession had visited on exports. Devaluation did not improve matters as its beneficial effect on export book prices was more than cancelled out by sudden massive increases in imported raw materials, particularly paper and binding cloth. Even gold leaf for title blocking and spine brassing rocketed in price and cheaper substitutes were of obviously poor quality.[68] Import tariffs were applied to books in the United States and in Canada, despite the policy of 'imperial preference' established at the Ottawa conference in 1932 which created protected markets between British Empire countries. Exchange controls were introduced by Britain and most other countries, making the remission of revenue generated overseas difficult and thereby causing cash flow problems for many publishers. Once-closed imperial markets were challenged as cheaper American – and sometimes European – editions of books for which British publishers thought they had exclusive rights leaked not only into Canada, but also into Australia, New Zealand and South Africa.

Piracy, that is the unauthorized reprinting in foreign markets of copyright editions without royalty payment (often from plates created from photographed pages), had once been an irritating but minor annoyance. It suddenly became rife. Egypt and India were the main offending countries but pirates were also active in Japan, China and Argentina. Educational titles, then as now, were the main targets, but novels, reference books and children's titles were also illegally copied. An amendment to the Berne Convention protecting copyright in 'typographical arrangement', approved in 1928 and coming into force in 1931, provided a little protection. However, it did not help in countries such as Egypt, which had not signed the treaty.

The creation of the British Council in 1935 was a direct attempt by the government to promote British culture overseas and win back some lost markets for British cultural products, although its budget (only £5000 per year to begin with) was very limited. Books were high on the Council's agenda, and it established libraries of British titles in many foreign cities and supported book sales by exhibitions and local promotion. Unwin characteristically devoted great energy to supporting the Council and its book activities (see Unwin, 1960, Chapter 23) and Longmans were enthusiastic publishers of a number of titles it commissioned for overseas.

68 Many hardback books published in the 1930s have not worn well as their publishers tried to economise on materials. Poor quality cloth and foil blocking in particular are now often very obviously deteriorated compared to books decades older.

These included the 'Writers and their Work' series and the handbook intended for overseas students, *Higher Education in the United Kingdom*, first published in 1936.[69]

There were a number of imaginative schemes to inject some life into the stagnant home market. One of the most original was the introduction of Book Tokens. These were invented by Harold Raymond, publisher at Chatto and Windus in 1932, to encourage the giving of books as gifts, allowing the recipient to select their preferred titles themselves in exchange for the token. Tokens comprised a gift card priced at three pence in which were placed adhesive stamps to the value selected by the donor so they could be easily posted. Publishers were enthusiastic, but booksellers needed convincing that the fiddly business of selling cards and accounting for stamps of various denominations would be worth the trouble. Despite some booksellers refusing to co-operate with the scheme (Newcastle-upon-Tyne was a hotbed of scepticism), the first Christmas the tokens were available, despite minimal advertising, was very successful, and the idea slowly gained ground. It was not until 1940 that Book Tokens became universally accepted by the book trade, and only then after booksellers were bribed with additional discounts on the books for which they were redeemed. Eventually, partly to avoid problems with income tax, an independent company – Book Tokens Ltd – was set up to operate the scheme and continues to this day.

Part of the antipathy towards Book Tokens from booksellers arose from confusion with the gift vouchers provided by the tobacco manufacturers Wix and Sons with Kensitas cigarettes. Originally conceived as a promotional alternative to the free cigarette cards most tobacco firms of the period provided in their packs, Wix provided a list of gifts that could be saved for by means of the vouchers included with their cigarettes. This was an obviously attractive offer during a recession when spending cash was tight but cigarettes were regarded as a necessity in an era when 'everyone smoked'. Among Wix's gifts was a list of 450 book titles

69 I revived this title in its final edition in 1984, by which time the Council's interest in books was in serious decline. Its subsidy for the title was withdrawn and I replaced it by selling advertising for university courses which – although a commonplace today – caused much consternation at the time. At around the same time the Council axed its highly successful and influential English Language Book Society (ELBS) scheme which provided cheap tertiary textbooks in developing countries. Today the Council has virtually no interest in books and publishing, and like many quasi-official bodies seems to believe that the answer lies in the digital. We shall see.

published by fifteen publishers. Booksellers pointed out that the purchase price of the cigarettes necessary to obtain the books was in many cases less than the net price of the books. They also argued that smoking one's way to literature was 'derogatory to the standing of books' (Kingsford, 1970, p.146). Publishers were torn between expanding their market and offending their primary customers. Wix solved the problem at the end of 1933 by withdrawing the gift tokens at the behest of the Tobacco Trade Association, which condemned the scheme as unfair competition to other cigarette manufacturers.

During the decade various newspapers and periodicals, including the *Daily Mail* and the *Daily Herald*, offered books as premiums by printing vouchers for readers to save and redeem. The latter had arranged in 1934 with Bernard Shaw, always cavalier with the niceties of book trade etiquette, to offer its readers a complete edition of his plays for six coupons and three shillings and nine pence. Constable, his publishers, and booksellers complained, but Shaw was characteristically unrepentant:

> [T]his particular transaction will increase the business of every bookseller in the country by adding to the book-reading public many thousands of customers to whom 12*s* 6*d* books are as inaccessible as Rolls-Royce cars. I must not, however, suggest that there is anything outside the ordinary and inevitable routine of business in my dealings with the Odhams Press [the publishers of the *Daily Herald*]. The field is open to all distributors … [including] the most modest single bookshop … If the Woolworth firm sends me an order of sufficient magnitude to enable it to sell copies at its stores for 6*d* and yet give me a better return for my labour than I can obtain through prices that are prohibitive for nine-tenths of the population, I shall execute the order joyfully. And let the bookseller who would do otherwise cast the first stone at me. (Statement published in *The Bookseller*, October 1934, quoted by Kingsford, 1970, p.147)

As we shall see shortly, Shaw – not for the first or last time – was being uncannily prophetic if not emollient.

Less contentious were the creation of promotional events to foster book sales and awareness as public exhibitions. *The Sunday Times* was very active in organizing book events and sponsored a National Book Fair at Earl's Court in 1933 attended by many thousands of people. The work of the recently founded National Book Council was influential in providing travelling exhibits, and they even produced two of those quintessential 1930s art-forms, short documentary films for cinema distribution, *Cover to Cover* and *Chapter and Verse* in 1936. Books played an important role in the last great national festival of the pre-war years, the Empire Exhibition Scotland of 1938. It was held at Bellahouston Park in Glasgow and the major Scottish publishers – Collins, Nelson and Blackie among several others – had stands. They produced commemorative volumes, including a finely printed facsimile of the Kilmarnock edition of the poems of Robert Burns (Crampsey, 1988).

Another device intended to increase the book market in a time of economic recession was the re-invention of the book club. Although *The Times* had continued to run its operation in a low-key way since the end of the 'Book War', many publishers and booksellers nursed their resentment of reduced priced subscription clubs until failing economic conditions forced them to reconsider. The Book Society, founded in 1929, was a rather upmarket literary association which chose a 'book of the month' by a committee including Hugh Walpole and J.B. Priestley but sold its selections to its members by post at full net price so was not controversial. However, in 1937 John Baker founded the Readers Union, the first general club to offer reprints of recently published titles at discounts of up to five-sixths of the net price provided members undertook to select a minimum number of books per year (usually four). Twenty-one years later Baker described the context of his plan to 'lower the cost of book loving':

> To project yourself into the world of 1937 calls for a feat of imagination. You must picture an England slowly pulling itself from a trading depression and still with a million and a half unemployed, with the nightmare of Fascism mounting in Europe and in Britain 'Three Kings in One Year'. It was also the world of 'Underneath the Arches' and 'The Lambeth Walk'. You could live well off £500 a year, but you were lucky to get it. People interested in books had a wide selection at prices ranging from the classics at 2s, to near contemporary works at 3s 6d … Culture was everywhere but you could barely afford it …
>
> Among much resounding sales material written by [this] author was a phrase which perhaps recalls our approach to those times. 'At any time, in any mood, when you are fresh or weary, in winter's gloom or summer's sun, you may, by turning to your own resources,

> find at slightest cost, the highest kind of pleasure and the liveliest type of enjoyment. It is no exaggeration to say as long as you devote to *self-improvement only a two pence a day* [italics in original] you need never lack interest in living and *a sense of moving on* ... [B]ooks wait on you: not you on your books. You buy your books at borrowing rates' ... Note the ringing tones, the earnest evangelism: note the emphasis on self-improvement, the last legacy of the days of log cabin to White House. (Baker, 1958, pp.1-2)

Baker had judged the realities of the demand for books well. Within weeks his Club had recruited over 17,000 members and he was selling many thousands of licensed reprints from publishers such as Cape, Dent, Heinemann, Faber, Longmans and Murray. Baker's initiative was popular with publishers since it extended print-runs and gave them the benefits of 'run-on' costs to spread their initial investment. However, it was less welcomed by authors who were paid royalties on the reduced prices and booksellers who saw the Net Book Agreement being undermined yet again by its supposed guardians.

There was much wrangling within and between the Publishers' Association and the Associated Booksellers and it took some time to reach an agreement. The Associated Booksellers in 1937 called for book club sales to be made through booksellers (one of the most successful book club operators was in fact the London retailer W. & G. Foyle) and requested that if a book was to be sold at a discounted price in a club this should be disclosed to the retailer when the book was subscribed to them before publication – clearly an impossible condition. In 1939 regulations were agreed between publishers and booksellers that brought about an uneasy acceptance of book clubs, although many booksellers and some publishers felt that they were a breach of the NBA.

Nevertheless book clubs were set to become a permanent fixture in the publishing landscape. They arose genuinely out of the economic adversity of the 1930s and in succeeding decades substantially extended the market for books, probably without eroding the core retail market very much.[70] Readers Union[71] was undoubtedly successful; by 1958 it had sold almost

70 Proponents of book clubs always maintain that club buyers are different customers from bookshop buyers. The book clubs that survive today mainly serve specialist interests like history, railways or children's literature, although there has been a renewed success of 'party-plan' bookselling by travelling booksellers like the Book People.

71 Readers Union never takes an apostrophe for an obscure reason.

eight million books spread across 417 titles from 64 publishers (Baker, 1958, p.11). Other clubs founded in the 1930s, such as the Reprint Society which was a consortium of publishers, were also successful.

The 1930s was a decade not only of economic but also political crisis. The rise of Fascism in Italy and Germany, the growing power of Soviet Russia, the demands for home rule in the European colonial empires and the rise of Japan as a militaristic imperial power in the Far East – as well as poverty and social unrest at home – all led to growing awareness of the importance of understanding how world politics were changing. Economic hardship had radicalized workers and intellectuals, creating an insistent demand for ideologically informed publishing to explain and support new political positions. Demand came from all points of the political compass, but in Britain it was the Left that produced the most influential and prominent publishing. Many publishers shared in this movement, but it was the house of Victor Gollancz, which borrowed the Readers Union model to create the Left Book Club, that led the way.

Gollancz, nephew of the Shakespearian scholar who had launched Dent's 'Temple Classics', established his own publishing house in 1927. He had worked for Benn Brothers and he had very successfully created for them the imprint Ernest Benn Ltd which specialized in reference and art books, although it also had a successful list in popular fiction including the detective novels of Dorothy L. Sayers. His relationship with Benn was ambivalent: they were politically poles apart,[72] and although Benn admired Gollancz's energy and judgment there is a lingering impression that he did not completely trust him, possibly tinged by some fashionably upper-class anti-Semitism. Despite the offer of a board appointment Gollancz judged that Benn was not prepared to pay him what he thought he was worth, so he left to set up on his own in a cramped and dilapidated office in Henrietta Street in Covent Garden.

The earliest lists were solid and literary, with Gollancz discovering novelists like A.J. Cronin and Elizabeth Bowen whom he published to critical acclaim and modest financial success. Gollancz may have continued as a rather insipid version of Jonathan Cape had not the juxtaposition of his own political views, his intuitive grasp of the power of publishing brands and the value of distinctive design and image come

72 Benn was fervently right-wing, and it is a great irony that his great-nephew, Anthony ('Tony') Benn became a noted left-wing politician and a minister in a Labour Government, as indeed has his great-grand-nephew, Hilary.

together at just the right time in the mid 1930s to create the most emblematic publisher of the period. The key figure in forming the Gollancz 'look' which was so critical to the imprint's success was the typographer Stanley Morison, who had worked with him at Benn as a designer. Collaborating with Gollancz's wife Ruth, who was a gifted artist, Morison drew upon dis-tinctive letter forms and bright colours for his jackets, producing the famous maroon and yellow combination that made the imprint's books unmistakeable even from a distance. They were supported by innovative advertising – Gollancz invented the 'jacket blurb' in its modern form – and a very slick publicity operation (Hodges, 1978). From the very beginning Gollancz advertisements were typographically exciting; their eye-catching use of display types, rules and line images had a modernistic Art Deco look which made other publishers' announcements appear staid.

Gollancz was a natural salesman who understood the importance of keen pricing in a difficult market. 'Highest Price 8/6' blared his front full-page advertisement in the *Observer*'s Christmas supplement for 1931. He pioneered the concept of omnibus volumes, in which he issued books for which he had already paid the typesetting in sharply priced collections at five or six shillings for over 600 pages. (Both author and publisher were thus given a second bite at sales.) The announcement of a new Gollancz title was an event eagerly anticipated and impossible to miss. And the quality of what he published was always excellent, even if sales were sometimes patchy.[73] He had a normally unerring eye for what would please the public and fit the taste of the times, be it the darkly melodramatic tales of Daphne du Maurier with *Rebecca* and *Jamaica Inn* or the snobbish if witty novels of Ivy Compton-Burnett (which he must have disliked for their right-wing presumption although he could clearly see their commercial potential).[74] His commercial judgment was matched only by his own fine literary taste, and by his good sense in employing people such as Norman Collins who, Gollancz noted in 1932, 'is the man for the job, as he seems to me that very rare thing – a *young* man … (who) will be able to get on with

73 He published the works of Colette and Franz Kafka in translation, and despite promoting them very hard he failed to make them sell successfully. Perhaps the former was after her time, and the latter before.

74 One of the paradoxical mysteries of Gollancz's character is the genuine warmth and affection he felt for Compton-Burnett which although she was loyal to his house she hardly reciprocated.

me: and there are not many men who can get on with me in an office' (Hodges, 1978, p.102).

For, as he himself was well aware, Gollancz was a difficult man. Brilliant, mercurial and inspirational, he was also temperamental, given to rages and grandiosity, and would brook no contradiction or insubordination, as well as being perhaps troubled by his sexuality. There is a well documented incident when he was once seen at his office window examining his genitalia in full view of the actresses' dressing-room in the theatre opposite, after which the cast sent him a note warning him to take more care in future (Dudley Edwards, 1987, p.388). He certainly had a fear of contracting syphilis, and in 1943 suffered a severe mental breakdown accompanied by alarming sexual symptoms and debilitating anxiety (probably brought on by overwork and guilt over his affairs).

Yet he was a publisher with unique flair and honesty fired by genuine passion and a commitment to using books to improve the world. He was also an engaging, sociable and witty man who could be charming and extremely good company. Ruth Dudley Edwards, in her affectionate but searching biography, portrays him as an honest, generous and kindly man, who despite being occasionally naïve and petulant, was absolutely genuine in his concern for humanity (Dudley Edwards, 1987). Although he enjoyed the social whirl of literary London and being lionized by society hostesses as the publisher of the latest fashionable novelist or witty dissector of modern morals, it was his political books that mattered most to him and made his greatest impact.

From his earliest days Gollancz had been a man of the Left. He had been sacked in 1918 from his first job as a master at the public school Repton for teaching 'civics', a thinly disguised class in socialism, and he never afterwards lost his radical political edge. His publishing always included free thinkers and political reformers, mainly but not always from the Left, and he saw the potential before many others of the socialist reportage of George Orwell, whom he published throughout the 1930s. He did nevertheless reject *Animal Farm*, Orwell's biting and barely concealed satire of Stalinist Russia in 1944. This was not on ideological grounds, but because he thought it would be difficult to publish an open criticism of an ally at a time when they were bearing the brunt of the Nazi onslaught (Hodges, 1978, p.111).

As the power and aggression of Fascism at home and abroad, and particularly the brutalities of the Spanish Civil War, mounted during the 1930s, Gollancz took the view that books could galvanize and mobilize left-leaning opinion and provoke action to attack and neutralize the threats the Fascists posed. Accordingly on Leap Year's Day in 1936 he announced the creation of the Left Book Club in the pages of the *New Stateman and Nation*. Basing the concept on the as yet unlaunched but widely discussed Readers Union, or indeed more closely on the Crime Club run by William Collins and Son, club members 'who desire to play an intelligent part in the struggle *for* World Peace and *against* Fascism' would receive every month a new book selected from the Gollancz list for half the price or less of the published trade edition. Titles were selected by a committee consisting of Gollancz. Harold Laski of the London School of Economics and John Strachey, both leading left-wing intellectuals. The themes of the books would be unrelentingly serious and earnest, dealing with topics like slum clearance, educational reform, industrial management and foreign politics. A major inspiration and source were the books of Tom Harrisson and his Mass Observation movement which Gollancz published and rather unwillingly provided finance for Harrisson's sociological experiments. A magazine, *Left Book News* (later simply *Left News*), was also published and widely distributed free of charge.

It was at once both a brilliant marketing strategy and a deeply moral attempt to influence the course of world events. Gollancz was convinced of his own rectitude in setting up the Club, but he was widely criticized both by opponents on the Right and the more extreme Left. A competing Right Book Club was created, but never proved very successful. There is no doubt that Gollancz's motivation was based on honest conviction: he had, after all, suspended trading with Germany and Japan long before any other publisher did so. However, the fact that the Club only sold Gollancz titles did increase his firm's turnover enormously, as well as bringing him authors who might have gone elsewhere.

The Club was instantly successful. Within a few weeks it had 10,000 members, all eager to pay their half-crowns for the latest radical treatise. Branches were set up in Europe and by the outbreak of the Second World War in 1939 its global membership was 50,000 strong (Hodges, 1978, Chapter 6). The Club organized meetings, rallies and events, and under its slogan 'Knowledge, Unity, Responsibility' it became a considerable political force in its own right ('a genuine *movement of the masses*', Gollancz would write), campaigning not only against Fascism but also espousing radical causes such as prison reform and the abolition of the death penalty. Gollancz was its centre, and he found that the Club began to take up most of his time. Even with his legendary capacity for hard work and attention to detail, he had to pass over the day-to-day publishing work to Norman Collins, although he continued to receive regular reports of contracts signed and manuscripts received.

At its height, the Left Book Club (LBC) was a broad socialist grass-roots movement that embraced politicians as diverse as David Lloyd George, George Lansbury, Ellen Wilkinson and Aneurin Bevan in its support. It could fill venues as large as the Albert Hall and the Queen's Hall, and on one famous occasion in 1939 the Empress Stadium reached its capacity for a rally. The distinctive orange or red limp cloth bindings of Club selections became familiar on the bookshelves of miners, steel men, railway workers and farmhands throughout the country, as well as on the desks of intellectuals, students and journalists. Its activities were not confined to books: it organized the Left Book Club Theatre Guild, which presented the plays of many emerging radical playwrights and supported the activities of over 250 Left Wing amateur dramatic societies. It even effectively had its own Member of Parliament in Vernon Bartlett, who won the Bridgwater constituency from the Conservatives in 1938 on an Independent Progressive ticket, upsetting a majority of over 10,000. Bartlett was widely recognized as the 'Left Book Club Man' (Hodges, 1978, p.134).

Gollancz quickly became a hate figure of the reactionary and even moderate Right. The *Daily Telegraph* and *Morning Post* denounced him as a crypto-communist and the Catholic press was particularly hysterical, its ardour doubtless fired by his Jewishness. One Catholic priest denounced the books as 'responsible for the Red Terror in Spain' and causing 'the animal existence which is being led in our pagan schools and pagan homes' (quoted in Hodges, 1978, p.139). The most common accusation was that its 1200 local branches, its theatre groups, its reading circles, its field organizers, even its badges and regalia were funded not by selling thousands of copies of half-crown books, but by paymasters in Moscow. Although the Club ran trips to the Soviet Union there is absolutely no evidence that there was any funding, clandestine or otherwise, from the Russians. Indeed many of the Club's titles were openly critical of Soviet policy and Gollancz was on record as an anti-Stalinist. Strachey was undoubtedly close to the Communist Party of Great Britain, although never a member, and Communist writers and intellectuals certainly contributed to the list. However, the Club was a success *sui generis* because it tapped into a real sense of political need for books with a Left perspective that would interpret a frightening and alienating world for ordinary people. That Gollancz spotted this need and met it is to his enduring credit, both as a publisher and as a believer in the human spirit. It is often said that had Hitler successfully invaded Britain, Victor Gollancz was on the list of the first hundred public figures to be arrested and shot, along with Winston Churchill, Bernard Shaw and Sigmund Freud. Although he always reacted to this claim with scepticism, the sheer fact that in less than three years between founding the Club and the outbreak of war he had been able to sell over three million books on Left Wing politics does qualify him as one of the most significant political figures of the decade.

For many people, however, the 1930s was not a decade of political activism, economic privation and fear of total annihilation in a *Blitzkreig*. For the wealthy and the professional middle classes it was a time of prosperity and pleasure. More new houses for private purchase were constructed in the decade than in any other until the 1970s, a network of new motor roads was being constructed and motoring was increasingly an affordable pastime even for those on modest salaries with mass-produced Ford, Austin and Morris cars. For the better-off, passenger aircraft flights and luxury cruises on iconic liners, like the *Queen Mary* and *Empress of Britain*, were popular.[75] For these fortunate individuals, the serious-minded activism of the LBC was of no interest. They wanted to read books that would entertain, lightly inform and reflect their conservative if blinkered view of a settled and untroubled polity where political and social threats were invisible.

Much of this need was met by publications from the house of Batsford (Bolitho, 1943). For almost a century, Batsford had operated mainly as a bookseller, maintaining a bit of publishing on the side. In 1930 it moved to North Audley Street in the heart of Mayfair and fitted out a large shop to be devoted to the sale of fine editions and rare books. The recession almost immediately dried up this market so Harry Batsford and his partner Charles Fry decided to turn their talents to publishing what Fry described as:

> ... an entirely new kind of book. The writing to be on subjects akin to our own ... Britain, its churches, its houses and its landscape. But we planned to put more than a hundred illustrations in each book, to present them with ... attractive wrappers, and in editions so big that

75 It is ironic that these liners, fitted out with great luxury, were commissioned to alleviate unemployment on Clydeside or Belfast.

> we could afford to sell the books for as little as seven shillings and sixpence each. (Bolitho, 1943, pp. 65-6)

Despite Fry's claims, the genre of the undemanding, nostalgic, highly illustrated travelogue in which an upper-crust motorist meanders across the country and comments wryly or romantically on the foibles of solid yeomen and the glories of stone-built churches was not new. Methuen and H.V. Morton had enjoyed great success in the 1920s with the 'In Search of' series. *In Search of England*, published in 1927, was reprinted sixteen times by the end of 1931. Longmans produced an 'English Heritage' series priced at three shillings and sixpence, with authors such as Edmund Blunden and Neville Cardus, adding introductions by the Conservative politician Stanley Baldwin, soon to be Prime Minister, to make the political colours of its intended readers absolutely clear.

Batsford began their series by commissioning the usual suspects – H.J. Massingham, S.P.B. Mais, Gertrude Jekyll and A.E. Richards – to write dreamy, backward-looking, adjective-heavy prose steeped in the values of the squirearchy and avoiding the modern, the industrial and the squalid. The rich man may have been in the castle, but the poor man had discreetly disappeared from his gate.

The sunlit contrasty photographs that they chose to illustrate their books are notable for their lack of inhabitants, and when people do appear they are stolid honest peasants in gaiters and waistcoats herding cattle or ploughing with heavy horses. The first series was entitled 'English Life', to be followed by 'British Heritage' and finally 'The Face of Britain', eventually running to almost sixty titles published between 1932 and 1953. The topics covered included churches, country houses, public schools, fox hunting, gardens and inns, and the regions were covered in traditional form, as 'Shakespeare's Country' or 'Wessex'. Where cities were treated they were York, Salisbury or Cheltenham, and not Liverpool, Birmingham or Leeds. This was a mythic, safe Britain where workers knew their place, the old values ruled and it was always sunny on the open road before the diamond-paned windows of the rustic thatched cottage. Such a reassuring world had enormous appeal to conservative readers seeking to avoid the real looming landscape of poverty and industrial and political unrest.

Out-of-touch and self-deluding they might have been, but Batsford's 'Heritage' books were undoubtedly successful, selling many thousands of copies. No first printing was below ten thousand copies, and virtually every title reprinted (Bolitho, 1943, p.66). What set them apart were two distinctive features. The first was that early on Harry Batsford and Charles Fry decided that to save money they could dispense with authors. In 1935 they bought 'an elderly Austin' and motored all over the country, making notes and taking photographs which they would put together as books under their own names. They were an unlikely couple, with Batsford a bluff, red-faced John Bull figure and Fry a lean, saturnine and rather elegant man with a widow's peak and a perpetual Turkish cigarette between the fingers. Jeremy Lewis describes Fry as a 'demonic character' and a 'drunk and lecher of satanic proportions', quoting John Betjeman's memorable description of him as 'a phallus with a business sense' (Lewis, 2008, p.32). He would punctuate their trips with monumental drinking bouts, sexual orgies with both sexes and 'indelicate boasting' about his conquests, none of which is evident from his yearning, nostalgic writing in *The Cathedrals of England* (1934) or *The English Cottage* (1938), which doubtless charmed many a maiden aunt or Surrey stockbroker of blameless morals.

The second feature that made Batsford books distinctive and successful was their dramatically striking jackets. Bold use of slab colour and wraparound images gave them unique presence and appeal. Although their subjects – churches, villages, inns, farmyards and downland views – were traditional, their treatment was up-to-the-minute, and in the manner of the modernist graphic art of contemporary posters and ceramic design. They were the work of Brian Cook, Harry's nephew and one of the best and most innovative artists ever to work on jacket design (Cook, 1987).

Cook's vision of Britain was vivid with blue hills, purple trees, red-tiled roofs and blue-grey church towers. He took advantage of the little-known Jean Berté process which used interlocking rubber printing plates to create his effects from original oil, watercolour or ink and wash drawings. His images are immediately recognizable and make the books he worked on still widely collected today. Cook eventually became a partner in the firm, took the surname 'Batsford' and became chairman in succession to Harry in 1952. He also became a Conservative Member of Parliament and was knighted in 1974.

Another publisher who catered for the undemanding tastes of the middle and upper-class reader of the 1930s with at least a section of his list was Hamish Hamilton. 'Jamie' Hamilton had worked at Cape for two years in the early 1920s, where Jonathan, with his customary meanness, had not paid him a salary for the first year 'as he was learning the job'. Hamilton left to take over the London office of New York publishers Harper Brothers. Hamilton was a clubbable, witty man with some private means and a shrewd eye for commercial literature. In 1931 he leased the grand but by now decrepit office that had once housed T.N. Foulis. He began to build a highly sellable if intellectually middling list which included authors like Denis Brogan, James Thurber and Nancy Mitford. Hamilton had an American mother and his association with Harpers enabled him to acquire rights to the works of American authors. Norrie suggests that a guiding principle of his publishing was to improve Anglo-American relations (Norrie, 1982, p.65), but a glance at his catalogue from the mid-1930s shows he was mainly concerned with publishing novels appealing to middle-class sensibility, spiced with the occasional popular reference or current affairs title. As his publishing matured he did include a range of more challenging titles, but he never approached the moral earnestness of his near neighbour Stanley Unwin, whom he cordially loathed.

A number of other publishers like Michael Joseph (1935) and Secker and Warburg (1934) set up during the 1930s, but their real impact came later and they are looked at in detail in Chapters 5 and 6. It is remarkable that despite the economic problems and upheaval of the decade it saw the emergence of so many new publishers, and despite vicissitudes very few actually went out of business. This in part reflects the industry's flexibility and relatively low fixed capital requirements compared to other forms of business. Publishers were, and always had been, good at cheese-paring and finely calculating risks to adjust their print runs and office costs. There was even the odd burst of spending as the decade neared its end, perhaps none more so than the elaborate 'Crime Dossiers' planned for Walter Hutchinson by the thriller writers Dennis Wheatley and J.G. Links.

These compilations such as *Murder Off Miami* (1936) included 'real' police files, documents and clues like torn photographs, spent matches, 'blood-stained' fabric and human hair (reputedly donated by some of Walter's blonde female staff). The reader was invited to sift the evidence, name the culprit and compare their answer with the actual solution sealed in an envelope at the end. They were popular, retailed for three shillings and sixpence and each sold over 100,000 copies, although they were a nightmare to produce. In part they drew their inspiration from the stylish *films noirs* that were just beginning to enthral cinema audiences seeking escapist entertainment.

And so to Allen Lane and his epoch-defining invention of Penguin books (Morpurgo, 1979, Hare, 1995, Lewis, 2005). Lane, born in Bristol in 1902, can fairly be claimed as the most important British publisher of the century – not only for his creation of a new type of book and the identification of a new reading market, but also for his influence on others, his contribution to the overall shaping of the book business and his bravery (and occasional arrogance and foolhardiness) in fighting for the freedom to publish and read. He originally bore the surname 'Williams', but as a *quid pro quo* for being employed by his uncle John Lane at the Bodley Head in 1919, he, his brothers, his sister and his parents had to agree to take the cognomen of his benefactor. Allen learned about publishing the hard way, working as a packer and a bagman. He learned quickly, never losing his understanding and appreciation of the nuts and bolts of the warehouse and the trade counter as well as developing a keen sense of what things cost and how savings might be made. John Lane died in 1925 and Allen joined the board of his company. He was already a dapper, well-dressed figure who liked fine wines and good restaurants although he was still living in insalubrious 'digs' in the remote and obscure south London suburb of Worcester Park.

Shortly after joining the Bodley Head board he took on a book that very nearly ended his career and has echoes of the later, more famous confrontations at Penguin over *Lady Chatterley's Lover* and *The Satanic Verses*. This was *The Whispering Gallery*, a scurrilous scandal diary purporting to be the memoirs of a retired diplomat and 'edited' by a ne'er-do-well hack journalist called Hesketh Pearson. This contained intimate and less than flattering portraits of prominent dead or living personalities such as Winston Churchill, Herbert Asquith, Lord Kitchener, David Lloyd George, V.I. Lenin, Benito Mussolini, Henry James and Cecil Rhodes.

It was published in November 1926 and the first printing of 5000 copies quickly sold out, as did an immediate reprint. 'Young Lane', as he was thought of by his fellow directors, basked in their admiration until they saw the headlines of the *Daily Mail* on publication morning. 'A SCANDALOUS FAKE EXPOSED', they screamed in thirty-six point type. Lord Rothermere, owner of the *Mail*, objected to the way the book had caricatured his brother Northcliffe and exacted revenge in his time-honoured fashion. Other newspapers like the *Observer* joined the fun, delighting in pointing out discrepancies, inconsistencies and errors in the diary entries. Doubts were raised over the identity of the mysterious diplomat (which Lane, despite trying, had never been able to obtain from

Pearson before publication). The *Mail* then turned its fire directly on the Bodley Head, excoriating them as 'a disreputable publisher'. In its traditional fashion it also invoked a Red scare: 'it is a hoax or plot of a Bolshevist emissary' (*The Daily Mail*, 20 November 1926, p.10).

Pearson named the anonymous diarist as Sir Rennell Rodd, a distinguished ex-ambassador, but Rodd told Lane when he called to see him that he had had nothing to do with the book. The Bodley Head directors, except Lane, decided that they either had to sue the *Mail* or withdraw the book, and they capitulated. The *Mail* was jubilant: 'Daily Mail Exposure Succeeds. Faked Book Withdrawn' (ran the headlines); 'The greatest literary scandal of recent times reached a dramatic climax last evening' as it reported the withdrawal of the title from sale in the face of 'strong public indignation' (quoted in Lewis, 2005, p.43).

The Bodley Head directors publicly humiliated Lane. Basil Willett, the chairman, wrote as their spokesman to all the daily and literary newspapers, including the *Mail*, apologizing for publishing the book and blaming it all on the inexperience of 'our junior director' (despite the fact that they had been keen enough on the book when Lane proposed it). Willett also stopped the cheque for the remainder of Pearson's advance and decided to sue him for obtaining money under false pretences. Despite advice from Bernard Shaw and other eminent *literati* that the case was hopeless, Pearson decided to fight, declaring that we would prefer serving three to six years in prison rather than caving in to 'a pack of cads, cowards and humbugs like the Lanes' (Lewis, 2005, p.45). Pearson relished his day in court and made the Bodley Head directors look foolish, credulous and greedy, provoking as the *Mail* gleefully reported 'much laughter in Court'. He taunted Allen Lane for his neglectful failure to verify the source of the diary and, while not admitting that he was himself the author of the anonymous work, neatly placed the blame on 'the dirty little rats' of publishers who 'daren't look their own publications in the face'. The jury, who evidently had enjoyed his performance, found him not guilty, congratulating him on his bravery when they met him for a drink in the pub afterwards.

Pearson then decided to sue the Bodley Head for the 'pain and suffering' they had caused him, but despite making brave noises they had no stomach for further legal battle and settled out of court. The whole affair had made them the laughing stock of literary London and they became known as 'John Lane The Badly Had'. Allen Lane kept his job and he seemed to bear no ill-will towards Pearson, publishing his books as

Penguins later, but he was badly hurt by the way his fellow directors had set him up and allowed him to be publicly crucified. Fate gave him his revenge as John Lane's widow died during the trial and left her shares in the house to Allen and his brothers, giving them control. Allen became Managing Director and several fellow board members, including Willett who had cravenly thrown him to the wolves, were summarily 'persuaded' to leave. His brother Richard ('Dick') joined him as financial adviser. Nevertheless the incident left lasting scars which moulded Allen Lane's combative character and convinced him that he needed to control his own destiny entirely.

Despite their being in nominal charge, the atmosphere at the Bodley Head between Allen and Dick and the other directors was never again comfortable. Staid and disapproving, the other Bodley Head managers resented that the Lanes were now living in some style with a butler and servants in a Bayswater flat and decorating their walls with paintings 'borrowed' from the publishing office. Allen was a handsome, debonair figure who featured regularly in the gossip columns for his extravagant partying, often with a glamorous young woman such as the beautiful bookseller and socialite Christina Foyle on his arm.[76] Worse, he would take publishing decisions without reference to the board, and although the results were generally remunerative they were sometimes felt to be tacky and inappropriate. One such venture that would have important repercussions was his importation of coloured 'pop up' books featuring the characters of the newly popular cinema cartoonist Walt Disney to be sold through the high-street retailer F.W. Woolworth, famous for its price threshold of 'everything costs sixpence'. It was suggested by their fellow directors that the Lane brothers might like to underwrite the risk of such investments from their own resources while using the company to provide publishing services, which was in fact exactly the arrangement used to launch Penguin Books.

There are many legends surrounding how Allen Lane had the idea that became Penguin Books (Lewis, 2005, pp.71-6). As we have seen, the

76 Christina was the younger daughter of William Foyle, the founder of the bookshop. She took over the management of the shop in the 1930s and organized highly popular 'literary lunches' at which leading authors and personalities would speak. She was a prominent woman in a world dominated by male managers and became a highly visible figure on the London social scene – so much so that she was the sole literary personality featured on a series of cigarette cards portraying metropolitan celebrities.

concept of a uniform series of cheap reprints was hardly new; many publishers including Dent, Oxford, Nelson, Collins and Macmillan among others had established such series successfully over the previous fifty years. What made Lane's insight unique was the creation of a brand that combined accessibility with quality, cheapness with worth, and most of all the identification of a new market that would buy paper-backed books 'for the price of a packet of cigarettes'. Other publishers' series shared some of these elements, but they tended to confine their markets to established readers whom they reached through conventional bookshops. Lane, while gathering in this clientele, went beyond into the wider non-book-buying public, who would avidly join the reading circle for the first time by buying a book for sixpence in their local Woolworths.

Lane nursed his scheme while the Bodley Head's fortunes deteriorated, only avoiding bankruptcy by the skin of its teeth.[77] He reputedly crystallized the idea at the beginning of 1934 when returning from a weekend in the west country, at the house of the mystery writer Agatha Christie. On changing trains at Exeter, the publisher could find nothing to read on the platform bookstall. Although he later liked to propagate the myth of that moment of inspiration, it is clear that he had been thinking about a cheap reprint series for some time, at least since the *Whispering Gallery* fiasco (Lewis, 2005, Chapter 5).

By the end of 1934, Lane was ready to make his move. In September he attended a conference of publishers and booksellers at Oxford organized by Stanley Unwin and Basil Blackwell, the Oxford bookseller, to discuss how the market for books could be extended. Lane both shocked and intrigued the assembly by announcing that from within the Bodley Head he was about to launch a series of sixpenny paperbacks to be sold at Woolworths and other chain stores like Boots or Timothy Whites as well as bookshops (cf. the account in Unwin, 1960, p.389 which does not mention Lane's intervention at all[78]).

Booksellers and other publishers reacted with rage and incomprehension. A Glaswegian trader roared that he would have 'naething' to do

77 In 1934, the company may have actually been technically insolvent and it was only some financial sleight of hand that kept it afloat. Eventually it went into receivership and was bought by an old adversary, Stanley Unwin. Allen departed with his shares worthless although Penguin was well up and running by this time. However, for long afterwards he nursed the ambition to buy his ancestral firm back (see Lewis, 2005, pp.67-70).

78 Lane is not mentioned at all in Unwin's memoirs, nor is Penguin Books. Surely the sainted Stanley could not have been jealous of Allen's achievement?

with such a travesty and he prophesized disaster. The chief buyer at W.H. Smith, David Roy, an implacable opponent of book clubs and cheap books, was incensed. As Lane spoke, Roy became more flushed and rudely interrupted several times, in the end having to be restrained from physical assault. Lane was undaunted and continued to prepare for his launch.

He took his influences from several sources: after several attempts the name was suggested by the cheap paperback editions of English copyright books for sale only on the Continent from German publisher Albatross Verlag, begun in 1932;[79] also adapted was their practice of publishing titles in monthly batches. The typographic look and the colour coding of the covers most likely was borrowed from Gollancz: certainly Stanley Morison knew Lane well and later became his typographic adviser. Pricing and range of titles came from his own experience at the Bodley Head, and observing the cheap series at other publishers. But his unique contribution was to bring all these diverse factors together and recognize that the time was ripe. So on 30 July 1935 the first ten Penguin titles were released, including books by Ernest Hemingway, Compton MacKenzie, Agatha Christie, Beverley Nichols and Eric Linklater.

Although the legend suggests otherwise, the path to Penguin success was not easy nor was Lane always totally confident of the viability of his enterprise. Writing in *The Bookseller* of 22 May 1935 in an article entitled 'All about the Penguin books', he was candid and downbeat:

> I would be the first to admit that there is no fortune in this series for anyone concerned, but if my premises are correct and these Penguins are the means of converting book-borrowers into book-buyers, I shall feel that I have perhaps added some small quota to the sum of those who during the last few years have worked for the popularization of the book-shop and the increased sale of books. (Quoted in Hare, 1995, p.3)

His fellow-publishers were hostile or censorious but he needed their cooperation. An essential element of his plan was to buy paperback rights from a wide range of publishers rather than issuing cheap editions from

79 The name was actually suggested by Lane's secretary, Joan Coles, as she overhead an inconclusive discussion over the title of the new imprint when typing some letters. Lane immediately was struck by its aptness and sent his assistant Edward Young off to London Zoo to sketch a Penguin from life, later to become the famous colophon (Lewis, 2005, p.91).

only one list, as had been the previous practice. Newman Flower at Cassell refused point-blank to sell Lane reprint rights (not the last time, as we shall see, that a member of that publishing dynasty made a wrong decision of monumental proportions), and even Harold Raymond from Chatto and Windus, the inventor of Book Tokens, thought that sixpenny paperbacks were a step too far and although he later recanted was publicly sceptical. Unwin, Heinemann and Gollancz, all mould-breakers in their day, were reluctant to sell Lane rights and privately canvassed non-cooperation with the new venture. The first list was dominated by titles leased from Cape, and Jonathan later confided to Lane that he had only done so because 'I thought you were bound to go bust and I thought I'd take 400 quid off you before you did' (Lewis, 2005, p.97). Just before the launch Lane had an attack of the jitters and considered cutting the first print runs from twenty to ten thousand for each title, since subscription orders from booksellers had trickled in so slowly with barely seven thousand orders per title committed weeks before publication. Since break-even was between seventeen and eighteen thousand sales, so tight were the margins, this would have been an act of suicide.

It was Woolworths who came to Lane's rescue, but even their participation was initially doubtful. Lane used all his charm and showmanship to sell his new idea to the retailer's chief haberdashery buyer, Clifford Prescot, who looked after books. Prescot was very doubtful the books would sell in his shops, even at sixpence, because they 'had no pictures on the front' compared to the Collins 'Reader's Library' at a similar price. The story goes that Prescot's mind was changed by his wife who, anxious to be taken to lunch, had dropped in on her husband. She was immediately impressed both by the Penguins and the good-looking Lane, and showing great foresight she convinced Prescot over lunch to take the books on. The buyer nevertheless remained cautious and placed an order for 60,000 copies 'on consignment'.

Lane later claimed he had no idea what this meant, but he was happy to have the numbers. When he learned that if the books failed to sell they would all come back and he would bear the loss, it was too late for he had already printed Woolworth's quantities. Lewis casts some doubt on this story and concludes it was a piece of heroic mythmaking on Lane's part, noting that he would hardly have gone ahead without clear support from Woolworth much earlier on and an experienced publisher must have known what consignment sales were (Lewis, 2005, pp.99-100). Wherever the truth lies, the rest is history. Penguins were an instant hit, and on

1 January 1936 a new company called Penguin Books Ltd, with the Lane brothers as directors, was set up, albeit initially as an imprint of the Bodley Head.

For the remainder of the decade Penguin was a lively and successful company, but there were only a very few indications that it would grow into the great cultural institution that was to come. Its premises were rudimentary. Lane took over the cold, damp and eerie crypt of the Holy Trinity Church at the top of Great Portland Street near Regent's Park as his warehouse, and conditions there were notoriously squalid.[80] His editorial offices were a couple of rooms above a car showroom across the road. Lane preferred to spend his meagre funds on imaginative promotion and advertising, including the coin-in-the slot 'Penguincubator' machine that dispensed new sixpenny paperbacks at all hours from the pavement on Charing Cross Road.

Lane had begun his list with decidedly middlebrow titles, placing detective fiction and biographies to the fore, but as he became certain that his formula worked his list building grew more ambitious. He was never a particularly intellectual or even bookish man, but he firmly believed that reading was the key to improving the minds and morals of ordinary people. In August 1936 he initiated the Pelican imprint 'similar to Penguins only a little more serious in tone ... the true everyman's library of the twentieth century, covering a whole range of the Arts and Sciences, and bringing the finest products of modern thought and art to the people' (letter to Cecil Franklin of Routledge, quoted by Lewis, 2005, p.113). He engaged the temperamental Indian intellectual Krishna Menon to edit the series, perhaps itself a rather daring and radical gesture since Menon was closely associated with the Indian Congress Party who were agitating for independence from Britain. Pelicans in the early years had a distinctly Left-Wing tone, perhaps more because Lane had observed Gollancz's success with the LBC rather than from any political conviction on his part. However, this enabled him to attract eminent authors to his imprint from among leftish intellectuals like R.H. Tawney and Julian Huxley.

It is difficult to pin down Lane's personal political views. He was probably Left-leaning, but never allowed his convictions (if he had any) to get in the way of commissioning a good book (by which he meant one that

80 The church had no toilet so each morning Lane would give every employee four pennies to enable them to use the public convenience at the Underground station across the road. How he arrived at the calculation that four visits were required in the working day is unrecorded.

would sell), a clubland dinner or champagne with a duchess. What he did have was an unerringly accurate sense of what would work and sell well in the climate of opinion at the time, combined with a rather altruistic view that people would want what was good for them. As the outbreak of war approached in the late summer of 1939, this sense of *Zeitgeist*, a curious mixture of patriotism, intelligence, duty and moral rectitude spiced with a good dash of mischief, commercial savvy and good luck, prepared Penguin to assume the role of the people's publisher in the face of one of the greatest threats the country would ever encounter. It was a mantle that, as we shall see in the next chapter, Lane was ready to accept with relish and aplomb.

5 'Winning on the Book Front'

British book publishing in the Second World War and its aftermath

Publishers were much better prepared for the outbreak of the Second World War than the First. It had been clear from the expansionist policies of Hitler's regime in Germany that armed conflict would sooner or later become inevitable, and that Chamberlain's brief respite of 'peace in our time', gained at Munich in 1938, would only temporarily avert a war that would involve destruction on the home front of an unprecedented scale as well as battlefield engagement. Publishers' lists of 1938-9 featured sober dissections of international politics and escapist literature in great and probably equal profusion. Both genres were products of the impending sense that war was imminent and that readers both needed to understand it and try and put it from their minds.

Valerie Holman (2008) observes that most publishers' memoirs tend to skip over the period of the Second World War, dismissing it as a time of sterile retrenchment, privation and difficulty separating periods of great creative energy and innovation. Her history *Print for Victory* shows otherwise. Perhaps the protagonists were too close to the events they described, for I tend to agree with Holman that for publishing the war was an essential catalyst, crystallizing and fixing the new directions made in the previous years and preparing the way for the great changes that were to follow. Publishers not only played a pivotal role in the war effort, but the war also was crucial in creating new conditions. Most of all, it provided a clean slate that enabled the book business successfully to reinvent itself yet again.

The most obvious shared assumption among publishers was that 'this time' everyone would be at risk, and that air attack and *Blitzkrieg* would bring the battle to the heart of their operations. Even before war was declared air raid precautions were put in place, and drills, shelters and black-out procedures were instituted. Some firms considered whether London locations would be too dangerous to maintain; evacuation of offices was discussed and in some cases actually carried out. Gollancz moved a large proportion of their staff to a 'hut' in the garden of Victor's country home at Brimpton near Newbury (Hodges, 1978, pp.144-5). Batsford decamped to Malvern Wells in deepest rural Worcestershire. Heinemann already had an extensive country print works at Kingswood in Surrey and most publishing functions were removed there. Stanley Bond moved most of the Butterworth staff to his country home at West Dean near Chichester, although the transfer may have had more to do with asserting his control over them than ensuring their safety.[81] Hodder and Stoughton moved their editorial and accounts staff to an old school in Bickley in Kent – ironically destroyed by a wandering V1 rocket in 1944 (Attenborough, 1975, p.138).

Most London publishers, however, stayed put and prepared to brave the expected onslaught from the *Luftwaffe*. Stanley Unwin (1960, p.253) proudly records that he only spent a few days out of London during the whole of the war when an unexploded bomb in his garden obliged him to seek refuge with friends in Bishop's Stortford.[82] He also noted – perhaps with po-faced irony (it is difficult to tell with Unwin) – that the first thing he saw when he returned was Geoffrey Faber stumble and fall into the bomb crater outside his house.

For the first few months following the outbreak of war, an uneasy anticipation pervaded the publishing community. The expected air raids did not come and although the full panoply of Emergency Regulations, Controls and Restrictions was in place, business continued more or less as normal, or indeed was improved. Book sales increased as people stocked up with reading matter for long nights in air raid shelters. Demand for books explaining the causes of the war was high. Allen Lane commissioned Harold Nicolson to write *Why Britain is at War* as one of the first of the Penguin Specials a few days after the declaration on 3 September 1939, taking delivery of the manuscript three weeks later and publishing in November (Lewis, 2005, p.150). It immediately sold 100,000 copies. Unwin diverted his production resources from the autumn 1939 fiction list to revive a series of aeroplane spotters' handbooks and updated

81 Bond had actually had a 'dry-run' for evacuation in September 1938 during the Munich crisis when he moved publishing staff to Graffham near West Dean in Sussex.
82 Although he does not say so, these were probably the Longmans who had a country home in the village of Braughing nearby.

them with silhouettes of the latest German war planes (Unwin, 1960, p.251). Over at Gollancz Dorothy L. Sayers temporarily suspended her writing of stylish thrillers and detective stories to compose, at Victor's invitation, a Christmas message booklet to express 'that the fight is worthwhile and must be stuck out cheerfully because of the particular values for which we are fighting' (Hodges, 1968, p.145). Methuen, whose aging list had not been thriving, convinced a patriotic A.A. Milne to cut his advance on his autobiography by more than half 'because of the war', but even they managed to benefit from the buoyant market of the 'phoney war' by producing *French War Aims* by Denis Saurat and books of cartoons by the quintessential war humorist Fougasse (Duffy, 1989, pp.114-15).

One by-play of the unreal atmosphere of the war's beginning was the resentment publishers felt over the imposition of War Risks Insurance (WRI) (Kingsford, 1960, pp.160-1; Holman, 2008, pp.15-17). This had been introduced a few weeks before the war broke out, requiring that all traders carrying stock worth over £1000 must insure it against enemy action. The Act introducing compulsory insurance specified a premium of 1.5 per cent for the first three months and 0.5 per cent thereafter. Because the stock turn of books was slow compared to other traders, for example food producers or manufacturers of radios, publishers faced very high bills. Methuen, by no means the largest holder of stock, faced a premium of £12,000 per year which would have been likely enough to wipe it out before a bomb had been dropped (Duffy, 1989, p.116). The ever-cantankerous Stanley Unwin complained that it 'penalized the provident and endowed the improvident' (Unwin, 1960, p.253).

Within a few days of the outbreak of the war, the Publishers' Association called an emergency meeting to determine whether, as the Act allowed, publishing should be exempted from the scheme as its products were 'uninsurable'. Opinion was hotly contested and divided. Small publishers in particular felt that they could not afford the premiums. Worries were expressed that the cost of the insurance would force book prices up just at the time when the trade was experiencing something of a recovery. A suggestion that a special insurance levy be applied to book prices was supported by educational and professional publishers, who judged they could pass it on, while trade and general publishers, mindful of the impending Christmas season, felt such a levy would kill their reviving market stone dead. In the event, a resolution that publishers should not seek exemption was passed by the narrowest of margins. The Associated Booksellers in their traditional fashion dithered, but eventually decided that they must be covered. Kingsford (1960, p.160), active in the Association at the time, feels that given the differences of opinion clearly expressed within publishing and between publishers and booksellers that the Board of Trade as regulator would have been unlikely to grant exemption to the book trade in any case. And perhaps it was just as well, for very soon, publishers would be very glad of the insurance.

As the Battle of Britain was waged overhead in the sunny summer of 1940, publishers enjoyed a last glorious market boom. Paper rationing had been introduced on 3 March 1940, but had yet to have significant impact; paper mills, printers, block makers and binders were operating at full stretch to supply a seemingly inexhaustible demand for books on the home front, and overseas, both as exports and for serving troops. Lane energetically expanded the Penguin list and 'Specials' poured from his new base at Harmondsworth near Heath Row Aerodrome on aspects of the war. Unwin broadcast on the BBC on book topics and endorsed the advice of a bishop on how the deal with composing oneself before going to bed in wartime: 'To commend themselves to God. To read a book. To go to sleep' (Unwin, 1960, p.255).

Gollancz, bullish that the struggle against Fascism was now real and seemed to be uniting the country behind his values, was cheerful and optimistic as he wrote to an American publisher just before Christmas 1940:

> The book business has been in a bad way here at various times since the war. Last Christmas [1939] was shocking, and we reached the lowest possible ebb just after the fall of France. [10 June 1940]. But things have been picking up remarkably well (they began picking up, in fact, in mid-July), and we are really having the best Christmas we have had for about five or six years. (quoted in Lodge, 1978, p.147)

A few days later this indian summer of prosperity was shattered. On 29 December German bombers launched a *Blitzkrieg* of high explosives and fire bombs on the City of London. The historic publishing district round St Paul's Cathedral was devastated, although the church itself miraculously escaped serious damage. Longmans' warehouse and offices took a direct hit and were levelled to piles of rubble, and most of their neighbours in Paternoster Row were set alight. Books that the fire did not consume were destroyed by water from the fire-fighters' hoses. Thomas Nelson, J. Whitaker and Sons (publishers of the trade paper *The Bookseller*), Bagster, Sheed and Ward and Hodder and Stoughton lost their bases and stocks, and the historic Stationers' Hall was badly damaged. Worst of all, the entire stock of the wholesaler Simpkin Marshall, amounting to three million books, was reduced to charred pulp. An eye-witness[83] vividly described the scene:

> The hub of the English book trade lies in a smoking ruin. Such a scene of destruction I have never seen or imagined. For sheer formless desolation it can hardly have been surpassed in Warsaw, Rotterdam or Coventry. With many others Simpkins, Whitaker, Longman, Nelson, Hutchinson, Sandle and further afield, Collins and Eyre & Spottiswoode are gutted shells. In their basements glowed and shuddered the remnants of a million books …
>
> This would have been bad enough by itself. But these famous houses, and the streets in which they stood, marked only the boundaries of a scene of destruction so complete, so utterly irretrievable that it held me spellbound. Nowhere were pavements or road surfaces to be seen. From Warwick Square in the West to Ivy Lane in the East, from the [Paternoster] Row nearly to Newgate Street there lies now an undulating sea of broken yellow bricks. I looked round Paternoster Square and recognised nothing but a pillar box, the top beneath my feet; there was nothing left to recognize … In the distance water hissed and rafters crackled, but near me the silence was almost absolute. London, silent, is always rather strange and unnatural: but London dead, burnt and buried with such staggering completeness, I found weird, oppressive and uncanny in the extreme. Later, as I peered down side streets cluttered with debris, I began to look into the future with a questioning eye. For here, I realised, was the great opportunity. The rabbit warrens of the Row are no more; and with them dies, perforce, a distributive organisation as old, as out-of-date, as uneconomic as the buildings which housed it. For the moment, we have to carry on somehow. But with peace will come reconstruction and there at last is the great opportunity. (*The Bookseller*, 2 January 1941).

This observer gets the impact of the blitz exactly right. Although its immediate effects were devastating and tragic, in the medium and long-term it was a blessing in disguise. It broke Simpkin Marshall's

83 This was Hubert Wilson (writing in *The Bookseller* as 'Petrel') who owned a bookshop in Ship Tavern Passage just off Gracechurch Street, north of St Paul's.

stranglehold on book distribution, which along with the only other book wholesaler of the period, W.H. Smith and Sons, dictated how and on what terms retailers should be supplied. It was quickly reformed and reconfigured as a cooperative, non-profit making company, but never again would achieve an unhealthy dominance in book supply.[84] A common estimate is that in this attack and subsequent bombings, the British publishing business lost 20 million books. A tragedy doubtless, except that many of these books were unsaleable and their insurance value provided their owners with cash flow that they had not anticipated. In fact, for some it was so abundant that it threatened to place some in a position of paying excess profits tax (Kingsford, 1960, p.161).

Unwin might harrumph, but he did not refuse the payments from the hated WRI when his binders or printers were bombed or his exported books were sunk by U-boats. Enemy action provided publishers with perfect excuses to wriggle out of commitments that new conditions made them think better of.[85] Apart from Cassell, who lost their historic *La Belle Sauvage* premises on Ludgate Hill during the last mass bomber raid on London in May 1941, most other publishers who had remained in London sustained surprisingly very little damage from bombs or the later rocket attacks. Covent Garden was virtually untouched.[86] Apart from a few broken windows, Methuen and Geoffrey Bles's offices at the other end of Fleet Street carried on as before. In Bloomsbury and around the British Museum, Cape, Allen and Unwin, Hamish Hamilton, Michael Joseph and Heinemann (who had moved to Great Russell Street in 1928) all suffered near misses but survived intact. 'Business as usual' was a wartime mantra that was remarkably true of publishing.

Longmans recovered remarkably quickly from their loss, impelled by the prompt payment of insurance money (Briggs, 2008, pp.400-8). Actually they had prepared for the eventuality of the destruction of their

84 This new firm was Simpkin Marshall (1941) Ltd, owned by a consortium of publishers, including Cape, Harrap, Allen and Unwin, and Oxford University Press, and managed on their behalf by Sir Isaac Pitman and Company Ltd, the technical and commercial publisher. As we shall see, it would later become the bridgehead for a perhaps more subtle invasion from Eastern Europe after the war had ended.

85 I recall being shown a sumptuous armchair covered in red leather at Macmillan's Essex Street office and being told that it was upholstered with the binding leather for a luxury edition of Kipling, planned in 1939 but never published.

86 Although it was said that Gollancz's office in Henrietta Street with most of the staff away in the country *looked* as if it had been bombed, as under Victor's insouciant care it became so untidy.

central London office by leasing as early as spring 1939 an evacuated school – Ambleside in Albert Drive, Wimbledon, overlooking the All-England Lawn Tennis Club. Half of the staff and some stock had been transferred to south-west London during the weekend before the war broke out, and after the blitz destruction, all of the employees moved there. Chairman William Longman had resisted the renting of the Wimbledon building, but he was a mild-mannered man and he had allowed himself to be persuaded by his manager, Noel Brack.[87] After the loss of Paternoster Row, Brack supervised the removal of what could be salvaged to Albert Drive, including the fireproof tin box containing 'Mr Willie's secrets' (contracts and mortgages) and some leather-bound ledgers.[88] Brack recorded in a letter to Longmans' New York manager that 'a vast quantity of material has perished. It will mean that a great number of books will have to go out of print – many dear old friends, slow, steady sellers – but not commercial propositions as reprints' (quoted in Briggs, 2008, p.402).

A few titles that had been stored as flat sheets at printers or binders were swiftly located and a few caches of undamaged bestsellers uncovered, including 613 copies of Stella Gibbons' *Cold Comfort Farm*. From the five thousand or so titles in Longmans' pre-war catalogue, only twelve were available immediately for supply but, despite paper rationing and the destruction experienced by suppliers, the list was quickly rebuilt and the 'dear old friends' quickly forgotten. Life at Ambleside was peaceful and busy, if vigilant. John Dracott, Longmans' home trade sales manager in the 1970s, recalled to me that as a young apprentice his main job was to watch for flying bombs from the glass walled eyrie at the top of the building's tower and to blow a whistle if it looked as if one was coming close.[89] C.S.S. Higham, the head of educational publishing, planned with Brack the campaign of reprints and new editions and realized that the destruction had given them an unique opportunity to secure the firm's

87 'Mr Willie' was famous for his meekness. My late assistant Pam Troughton, who worked for him in the war, recalled that when she entered his room he would often cower under his kneehole desk. Although Pam was formidable, she was not *that* fierce. In her out of duty hours she drove 'Green Goddess' fire engines for the WRVS.

88 Some of which remained in use until the mid 1980s. I was responsible for the 'probate book' in which was recorded the value of deceased authors' copyrights and it was one of the business records rescued from the ruins of Paternoster Row and remained in remarkably good condition, considering its adventures.

89 A couple dropped in the garden and on one occasion Dracott blew his whistle and ran 'like hell' down the spiral staircase as the glass-enclosed room exploded behind him.

fortunes without the dead legacy of past publishing mistakes. More than any other factor, it was the destruction of the 'old' Longmans at Christmas 1940 that enabled it to rise as a completely born-again modern publisher. It sowed the seeds of the company's dominance of the home and overseas educational market that would last until the last decade of the century.

Other publishers also benefitted from the wiping out of their pasts, William Collins and Sons among them (Keir, 1952, Stevenson, 2007c). Founded in Glasgow in 1789, Collins had been ruled over for its first century by generations of strict Calvinist divines who combined moral uprightness with careful Caledonian attention to the cash-book. Their business was dominated by bibles, stationery (including the famous diaries and account books) and a gigantic print works among the slums of Glasgow's East End. However, in the early twentieth century, a recessive gene perhaps became apparent and the company was inherited by William Collins III, a rather racy and louche character who moved the literary end of the business to London and pioneered cheap sixpenny editions that kept his Glasgow presses running and widened his house's profile. He was killed, somehow fittingly, after falling down a lift-shaft in his block of flats after a long publishing lunch in 1906. His grandson William A. Roy Collins (William V but always known as 'Billy') was to prove almost his equal in energy and vision. He entered the company in 1932, taking over publishing duties from his uncle Godfrey who had been made Secretary of State for Scotland in Ramsay MacDonald's National Government of 1931-5. Billy was in charge when the Bridewell Place warehouse and trade counter was flattened in the Christmas raid of 1940, and within days they were operating again out of temporary offices in Bow Street, near the Royal Opera House in Covent Garden. Luckily much of their stock and all their printing plant was in Glasgow and, despite the heavy attacks on Clydeside, the factory survived the war unscathed and maintained full production. Collins would later also lose their London editorial office in Pall Mall during a raid in February 1944, but Billy's inspired direction maintained a constant and lucrative flow of new books throughout the war.

Early in the war, Collins commissioned the popular historian Arthur Bryant to write a series of stirring patriotic accounts of the nation's past, like *English Saga* – a kind of literary equivalent to Laurence Olivier's famously bracing film of Shakespeare's *Henry V* and likewise designed to strengthen morale among the people. Another inspirational series of publications was *Britain in Pictures*, launched in 1941 and including full colour illustrations of the British landscape, heritage sites and artefacts to remind readers what they were fighting for. It eventually extended to over one hundred titles. This series is significant because it was put together by a new kind of publishing organization, the packager, in this case Adprint. The company was founded in 1937 by Wolfgang Foges, a refugee from the Austrian *Anschluss*, and it included Walter Neurath (later to go on to found Thames and Hudson). Adprint was engaged to compile and oversee the production of the books which were then sold to the nominal publisher for onward sale and distribution. This arrangement arose from publishers' wartime need to get books quickly on the market and overcome material and manpower shortages, but, as we shall see, it was to become much more a feature of the publishing scene during the following decade.

Other Collins ventures envisioned by Billy found their inspiration in the atmosphere of renewal and intellectual excitement that accompanied the turning of the war's fortunes in 1944 after D-Day and the prospect of a democratic and well-educated future. One of the most important of these was the *New Naturalist* series, conceived at the height of the war by the scientist James Fisher as a contribution to bringing the latest scientific knowledge in an accessible form to the layman (Marren, 2005, Stevenson, 2007c). Illustrated by high-quality colour photographs and written by the most distinguished scientists, the series comprises over one hundred titles and continues today as the major popular series in natural history.

While demand remained high, the main problem facing publishers was obtaining enough paper to reprint destroyed stocks and produce new titles. Plans for paper rationing had been put in place well before the war broke out, with the Ministry of Supply placed in charge of determining how the scarce resource should be allocated by a complicated and controversial formula. A paper controller was appointed, and when the system came into force in March 1940 publishers were taken by surprise that their allocation, by company, was to be only 60 per cent of their verified consumption in the year from August 1938. An optimistic few had hoped that publishing would be exempted from rationing altogether since the government had continually endorsed the view that books were essential for morale. This was never going to happen since most book papers needed imported softwood pulp from the increasingly isolated Scandinavia[90] or dangerously imported across an Atlantic infested with U-boats

90 Finland was an ally of Germany in the war and Norway was occupied, so these traditional sources were cut off. Neutral Sweden continued to supply pulp, but the Germans blockaded Swedish ports and sank ships trading with Britain.

from Canada. Nevertheless, publishing did not do well out of the Ministry of Supply's formula. The bulk of the allocation, some 250,000 tons, went to newspapers while government requirements, managed by His Majesty's Stationery Office (HMSO), were assessed at 100,000 tons. Magazines and periodicals received 50,000 tons while books only got 22,000 tons. Unwin was a doughty fighter in trying to badger more supplies out of the controller; even twenty years later he was still bitter that publishing had been short-changed: 'It is a tragedy that for the lack of another 8000 tons we were compelled to hand over many of our export markets to America, to deprive students of necessary text-books, and to be unable to supply the liberated countries with the books they needed immediately the war was over' (Unwin, 1960, p.258).

Despite the fact he had only set up a mere three years before, Lane was not disadvantaged by the formula; Penguin's massive growth meant that among publishers he had been second only to Collins in the amount of paper used in the reference year. Nevertheless, he wanted to get a larger slice of the paper cake for his ambitious expansion plan. Instead of loudly protesting like Unwin or making a nuisance of himself to the controller as Gollancz did (although Victor actually received a better ration than many other publishers of a similar size because of the vast size of LBC output in the reference year), Lane suavely and quietly charmed his powerful friends in decision-making circles, particularly Brendan Bracken as Minister of Information. He convinced them, because of Penguin's special role in providing books of an ideal size and price for troops, he should receive a larger paper ration than the formula delivered.

This argument worked well and Lane received more than his due (competitors would have argued 'his fair share') of paper. This provided the foundation for the transition of his business from just another publisher to a household word (Lewis, 2005, pp.162-3). He was undoubtedly sincere in his patriotic fervour in producing 'books for the troops', but it also gave him an inestimably valuable business advantage. Penguin was seen by Ministers and the general public as 'doing its bit', and the books from early in the war carried a note advising the reader to drop the finished book off at a local Post Office where it would be transmitted free to serving troops. Lane was also adept at arguing for special allocations for particularly important titles. Early in 1941 he applied to the paper controller for additional material to produce *Aircraft Recognition* by R.A. Saville-Sneath and was awarded 240 hundredweight, although he had requested 400 hundredweight (Holman, 2008, p.88). Nevertheless, this allowed 150,000 copies to be printed which were immediately sold out.

As imports became more difficult and losses by enemy action increased, paper rationing became more restrictive, even for Penguin. During 1941 the allocation figure based on each publisher's consumption in 1938-9 was progressively reduced from 50 per cent to 42 per cent, and finally to 37.5 per cent, and even less for those who had not signed the War Economy Agreement (Kingsford, 1960, p.172). Even books in demand, like Chambers' *Dictionary*, could not be reprinted and booksellers' orders were restricted. The Publishers' Association managed to get the consent of the Ministry of Supply to provide an additional 'pool' of 250 tons which could be allocated to books of special importance by the decision of a committee. Known as the 'Moberly Pool', this was controversial right throughout the war and until paper rationing was discontinued in 1949. Gollancz was particularly cutting: 'What is more important', he asked, 'a Roman Catholic breviary or the works of Karl Marx?' (Kingsford, 1960, p.173). The independent chairman of the committee, Sir Walter Moberly, was Vice-Chancellor of Manchester University and his publishing advisory committee, including Kingsford of CUP, came from firms representing educational, academic and professional publishing. Although they did not neglect general and trade publishing, they tended to favour their own sectors (Table Four).[91]

TABLE FOUR: Allocation of additional paper supplies in the Moberly Pool between 1941 and 1945

Category of Book	Percentage Allocation
Educational	24.5
Medical	17.5
Scientific and Technical	15.8
Religious	15.2
General	13.1
Dictionaries	10.0
Legal	3.1

Source: Kingsford, 1960, p.174

91 A persistent divide in the Publishers' Association was that between 'general and trade' publishers and the 'rest', with the former regarding themselves as 'real publishers'. Academic and educational publishers until 1994 had to pay an additional subscription, while trade publishers did not. This anomaly was not resolved until the 1990s with the setting up the general books division of the PA when the levy was abolished.

The Moberly Pool remained a source of disaffection and disagreement, but it did produce some sort of order in the rationing system. There were avenues of abuse whereby printers could under licence obtain 'free' paper allocations, in theory to be used for miscellaneous printing requirements like brochures and stationery. This obviously favoured publishers who owned their own printers like Blackie, Collins, Dent, Nelson, Heinemann and the University Presses. Rationing also had to be introduced in other areas affecting book production. Binding cloth for hardback editions was in short supply (another factor which favoured Lane and his paper covers) and poor quality substitutes were increasingly used. A National Book Recovery Appeal was launched to get books for salvage and recycling, mainly to obtain material for cover boards. This was notably successful and by the middle of 1943 almost 8 million books had been salvaged from the public. Over three quarters of a million of these were sent to libraries and the forces with the remainder being pulped (Kingsford, 1960, p.175).

Type metal became scarce as publishers and printers responded to the call for recyclable material for weapons and other essential war manufacturing. Much standing type (which would normally be held for eventual reprints) was taken down and melted. Zinc, copper and brass, used for block-making and cover stamping, became almost unobtainable and illustrated books consequently became more difficult to produce, particularly those incorporating screened half-tone photographs. This is the reason that many wartime books are illustrated by line blocks, which used less metal, where half-tones would normally have been used. Kingsford estimates that publishers contributed over 5000 tons of metal to the war effort, thereby destroying the printing plant of over 10,000 titles (Kingsford, 1960, p.177).

Apart from official control and various private salvage initiatives, publishers also set up a voluntary War Economy Agreement with the Ministry of Supply in January 1942 (*see* Holman, 2008, Appendix 11, pp.268-71 for full text of the specification and terms). This imposed on its adherents the obligation to observe designated standards as regards layout, margins, typography, binding and use of space normally unprinted, with the aim of reducing the quantity of paper and materials in new books. For example, type area was not to be less than 55 per cent of the printed page (sometimes a problem to carry out with children's books and poetry) and a greater number of words than usual were to be set on each page. Reprints were, of course, exempt from the typographic standards although the preliminaries[92] were to be reset to meet the general requirement of no more than four introductory pages. This meant that long-held typographic convention which dictated that contents pages were always printed on a *recto* (right-hand) page was abandoned.

Limits for paper bulk were established for fixed categories of books with no text or plate section paper to exceed 120 pounds per quad crown ream (516 sheets). Most books were to be printed on paper of 70 pounds weight or less. This on average meant that the weight of books of similar length was reduced by about one-fifth compared to pre-war. The weight of binding boards was also reduced. Books produced under this Agreement were to bear the statement '[t]his book is produced in complete conformity with the authorised economy standards' and a colophon picturing a recumbent, Landseer-esque lion surmounting an open book inscribed 'BOOK PRODUCTION WAR ECONOMY STANDARD'.

By February 1943, 750 publishers, printers and other organizations had subscribed to the agreement, representing virtually all British book production. It remained in place until after the end of the war and had a lasting effect on the look of British books, giving them a lean and spare aspect that actually was quite elegant although the 'show-through' of the bulk reduced papers of the period is notorious. An amendment to the scheme suggested later was the abolition of book jackets, but this proved a step too far. However, it was agreed that the flaps of jackets should be used to promote patriotic activities, like the overseas broadcasts of the BBC or salvage drives.

We have already seen that a much larger element of the paper ration went to government printing and publishing than commercial book publishing. This area was the responsibility of His Majesty's Stationery Office (HMSO) which had co-ordinated all the State's publishing requirements since 1786 (Barty-King, 1986). HMSO was in fact the country's largest publisher, producing annually between four and six thousand new

92 The 'prelims' at the beginning of a book comprise the half-title page, the title page, the imprint page (containing bibliographic information), the lists of contents, illustrations, tables and the preface, as well as sometimes dedications and epigraphs. They are traditionally numbered in roman numerals so as not to disturb the Arabic-numbered pages of the main text which follows if added to or compressed. To reduce all this information tidily to four pages was a great challenge. Half-title pages and prefaces were frequently discarded, and table or figure lists were often combined and pushed on to contents pages.

titles. It had sales to the public exceeding £200,000 per year, as well as providing Ministries and other official bodies like Parliament, the Post Office and Royal Commissions with their essential printing requirements. As early as 1938, HMSO had anticipated the coming conflict by giving its secure press at Harrow over to the secret production of over 79 million ration books for food and clothing, as well as millions of petrol coupons. After the outbreak of war, these items, as well as identity cards and billions of official forms, continued to form the bulk of the output of HMSO, but they also produced thousands of books to support the war effort including air raid precaution manuals and recipe books extolling the new austere rationed diet of the era such as the infamous 'Woolton Pie'.[93]

The destruction by bombing of the central London press of HMSO interrupted some production although *Hansard*, the daily record of parliamentary debates, never faltered nor did the Government's official newspaper, the *London Gazette*.[94] Book publishing continued with official records of major battles and campaigns like *The Battle of Britain* (1941) which were intended to raise morale. Most of HMSO's publishing comprised dull but necessary official reports and documents, but many of these were politically and socially important. The *Beveridge Report* of 1942, for example, which laid the foundations of the Welfare State, sold many thousands of copies to the public in a remarkable testimony to the firm faith of a better life once the war had been won. Norman Scorgie assumed the title of Controller of HMSO in the middle of the war in 1943; he streamlined the organization and absorbed a number of commercial printers to augment its infrastructure. As the war ended HMSO prepared and issued a number of publications for popular consumption outlining the contribution that government departments had made to the war effort, such as *The Post Office Went to War* by the well-known light novelist Ian Hay (1946). Arrangements were also made to prepare and publish the multi-volume *Official History of the Second World War*, which still remains to be completed. It is now being produced under the auspices of the Cabinet Office, and is handled by a commercial publisher.

93 Named for the Minister of Food, Lord Woolton, this was a meatless dish, featuring diced potato, carrot and cauliflower, flavoured with Marmite and doused in Bisto gravy which apparently overcomes people of a certain age with yearning nostalgia.
94 Published every day since 1655, the *London Gazette* with its sister titles the *Edinburgh* and *Belfast Gazettes* is not a real newspaper but a record of official notices which do not have legal force until they are published in the Gazettes. This is the origin of the expression 'to be gazetted.'

One major series of books produced in wartime was never intended to be seen by the public. These were the *Naval Handbooks*, in-depth geographical studies of most European and many other countries, intended for the use of military personnel who might be called upon to invade or even administer them (Clout and Gosme, 2005). Writing, editing and printing these was a major operation carried out in secret by a group of mainly university academics and cartographers based in Cambridge and Oxford under the direction of a young geography lecturer, Henry Clifford Darby.[95] Eventually the series, uniformly bound in blue cloth, ran to almost one hundred titles, covering places as diverse as Corsica and Tonga and setting the very highest standards of up-to-date information, including maps, diagrams and photographs. Based on a similar series produced in the First World War, they were much improved in scope, accuracy and content. The Director of Naval Intelligence, J.H. Godfrey, described the thinking that had inspired them in 1942:

> The purpose of the books is primarily naval. They are designed first to provide, for the use of Commanding Officers, information in a convenient and comprehensive form about countries which they may be called upon to visit, not only in war, but in peace-time; secondly, to maintain the high standard of education in the Navy and, by supplying officers with material for lectures to naval personnel ashore and afloat, to ensure for all ranks that visits to a new country shall be both interesting and profitable.
>
> Their contents are, however, by no means confined to matters of purely naval interest. For many purposes (e.g. history, administration, resources communications etc) countries must necessarily be treated as a whole, and no attempt is made to limit their treatment exclusively to coastal zones. It is hoped therefore that the Army, the Royal Air Force, and other Government Departments (many of whom have given great assistance in the production of the series) will find these Handbooks even more valuable than their predecessors proved to be both during and after the last war. (*From the series preface: the odd orthography and punctuation is reproduced exactly as in the original.*)

95 Darby, who was an authority on the draining of the Fens and the Domesday Book, had just completed the first PhD in geography awarded at Cambridge. After the war he obtained an academic post at Liverpool and was thereafter Professor of Geography at UCL and at Cambridge. Even when I knew him, thirty years after the event, he was very reticent about his work on the *Naval Handbooks*.

The books often contained large, full-colour folding maps of the territories described, produced under security conditions by the Edinburgh cartographic publisher John Bartholomew and Sons and folded in a pocket at the back. During the war these were classified documents and HMSO received secret paper allocations to produce them, but they were derestricted after 1945 and were then sold to the public. Other organs of government produced similar classified books like the RAF's enigmatically titled *Works* (1939) – actually a detailed manual of how to construct an airfield or convert a civil aerodrome to military use.[96]

The other difficulties to be overcome by publishers in the war included the shortage of staff, disruption to export markets and distribution problems at home. Women as well as men were now subject to conscription so female substitution was not as easy or as automatic as it had been previously, but in general women took over many publishing roles and functions. In a staid and traditional house like Methuen the arrival of lively 'girls from the Ministry of Labour' was disconcerting to the older male staff, and by the end of the war they out-numbered men in the company by eight to one (Duffy, 1989, p.120).

Even so, the workforce was severely overworked and overstretched. Fewer than half as many people worked in publishing and allied trades in 1945 as had done in 1939, and of the 173,000 people employed at the end of the war almost 77,000 were women. (Holman, 2008, p.251). As the war ended, demobbed servicemen returned to take up their old positions, but although, as at Methuen, this 'necessitated dispensing with the services of a number of young women who have been of considerable help in the war years' (quoted in Duffy, 1989, p.124), many women who had entered publishing before or during the war in secretarial positions, such as Eunice Frost at Penguin or Norah Smallwood at Chatto and Windus, had proved themselves in ability and potential. They achieved managerial or editorial positions and in some cases denied their returning male colleagues their previous positions.

Exports of books had naturally been adversely affected by attacks on shipping and the priority that other essential materials took over print in being allocated cargo space. The overseas branches of companies like Longmans, Macmillan, Nelson and Oxford seized the opportunity of 'difficulty of supply from home' and, particularly in the United States,

96 I actually reissued *Works* in association with the Air Historical Branch of the RAF when I was publishing director of the (then) Stationery Office in 1997 as a 'collector's edition'. It sold out in less than a month.

Canada and India, developed free-standing publishing programmes. The Macmillan Company of New York had already pursued a markedly independent line (Latham, 1965) and under George Platt Brett, grandson of the manager that Frederick Macmillan had installed to found the company in 1896, had built up a business turning over $12 million a year by 1947. This made it almost five times larger than its English parent at the then-current exchange rate (James, 2002, p.170).

During the war, they had made their publishing even more distinctively American and the home-based Macmillans found it increasingly difficult to understand. The division led to Harold Macmillan eventually selling the company to Brett (including the name) in 1951, apparently in the belief that his company's future did not lie in America. The split was amicable, but, as we shall see, it was to prove a decision of monumental ineptitude, creating problems that would haunt both companies almost to the end of the century.

Despite these difficulties, British publishers did manage to maintain substantial overseas sales of books throughout the war. On average about a third of British book sales by value had been exported in the five years up to the outbreak. By 1941, this had dropped to under 29 per cent, but this was still worth almost £4 million. Books destined for export received special paper allocations, so publishers were keen to keep export channels open as it would help them to keep titles in print domestically as well. The British Council, highly active in neutral countries such as Portugal, as well as South America, set up a Book Export Scheme. This eventually became an independent book exporting company that would be of great importance in providing British books to the newly liberated countries of Europe in the aftermath of the war.

Distribution to booksellers in the home market was fraught with difficulties. Because of paper shortages, supply was erratic and publishers provided bookshops with allocations of what they had available rather than what had been ordered. This is one of the reasons that the so-called temporary system of 'see-safe' supply, allowing booksellers to return unsold books for full credit, was not abandoned, although it had been introduced to allay booksellers' financial difficulties in the recession of the 1930s. It continues to be a bugbear of the trade today.[97] Petrol rationing

97 The returns system, whereby booksellers are effectively shielded from risk by virtually never buying their stock 'firm', has been the most notable bone of contention between publishers and booksellers from the 1930s to the present day. It is one of the main causes of remaindering (where unsold books are disposed of very cheaply) since

meant that van deliveries were unpredictable and the old trade counter system, where roving booksellers' bagmen would visit London publishers in turn to collect replacement stock on a daily basis, began to break down. For once, publishers were experiencing an almost unlimited demand for their products and were frustrated that they could not meet it.

Nevertheless and in spite of all these problems, publishing prospered during the war. Heinemann saw its turnover grow steadily between 1940 and 1945 from £170,247 to £251,294 (St John, 1990, p.297). Apart from 1940, their net profits were never less than 10 per cent and in 1945 they nudged 20 per cent. Indeed, some publishers were accused of profiteering and the Excess Profits Tax (EPT) introduced early in the war was felt to bear unfairly on publishers (Holman, 2008, pp.238-9).[98] Geoffrey Faber campaigned vociferously against it as an unjustified imposition,[99] and the directors of Methuen were worried that the huge margins they were making would 'make authors dissatisfied with their royalties' (Duffy, 1989, p.123).

Smaller and newer publishers found that the war years allowed them to establish their rather precarious imprints and gave them the necessary base to expand after the end of hostilities. Michael Joseph was founded in 1936 when the former journalist, literary agent and advertising man decided to strike out on his own as a publisher, reputedly inspired by Allen Lane's example (Joseph, 1986). Initially he operated with funding and accommodation provided by Gollancz, but like many others he found working with Victor impossible. In 1938 he severed the link with Gollancz and, with Robert Lusty and Charles Pick as his editor and sales director, made his fledgling house completely independent. Joseph was

---

returned books are often unsaleable through damage and publishers' reprint decisions – based on initial orders – are often wrong. It was also open to fraud as until the 1970s at least the bookseller had only to return a torn-out title page to obtain credit, and many books without title pages were sold without being paid for by the retailer. As booksellers have clamoured for higher discounts from publishers, the *quid pro quo* has often been an end to return for full credit, but at the end of the first decade of the twenty-first century the issue remains unresolved. However, a number of publishers, most notably Hodder Headline, have attempted to reduce the practice, most recently on environmental as well as business grounds.

98 Law Publishers even benefited from the EPT by publishing manuals on how to decipher its tortuous rules, such as A.G. McBain, *Concise EPT and NDC*, Sweet and Maxwell, 1944.

99 As always, he argued that publishing was 'special' unlike other businesses and deserved exemption. He cited the NBA in support of this.

mainly interested in publishing fiction, and he was able to use his contacts and knowledge from his time as an agent to identify and acquire outstanding authors, such as Daphne du Maurier and Monica Dickens. He established an elegant office in Bloomsbury Street under the sign of the Mermaid which he had chosen as his colophon. With his tall, rather military figure, his pencil moustache and his beloved Persian cat on his lap, he exemplified, like Cape, the popular image of the 'gentleman publisher'. He was lucky in his acquisition of the historical novelist C.S. Forester, until then rather unsuccessful; his 'Hornblower' sequence of Napoleonic naval yarns exactly hit the taste of the early war years for patriotic morale-builders, and they became bestsellers. His greatest discovery was the Welsh writer Richard Llewellyn. *How Green was My Valley*, with its rather mystical portrayal of working life in the Welsh Valleys, was published in 1939, also capturing the mood of 'this is what we are fighting for'.

Joseph, although approaching middle-age, volunteered for military service and left the running of the company to Lusty, who was ruled unfit to join the forces. This was extremely fortuitous since Lusty was a better judge of commercial fiction than Joseph,[100] and, although they conferred on new manuscripts, it was Lusty who really built the company's lists in the crucial early war years with significant new authors such as H.E. Bates (Lusty, 1975). Joseph was invalided out of the forces in 1941, and he retired to rural Gloucestershire to regain his health. Pick had meantime joined the Army Pay Corps, leaving Lusty in overall charge. Joseph and Lusty would later fall out, but for the moment the founder was reasonably content to leave his company in the latter's hands. However, he was not necessarily happy with the prospects for the future – as witness a memorandum for fellow directors that he wrote at the close of the war:

> I think the time has come to take stock of our position.
>
> The abnormal prosperity which all publishers have enjoyed in coming rapidly to an end if it has not already ended. [We] have had more than our fair share of this prosperity partly (I like to think) because of our own good judgment and the efficiency of our office team. But it would be foolish to pretend that we do not owe much of our success to sheer good luck.

100 This may be a controversial opinion, but I believe Lusty, who was not a modest man, can be fairly credited in these terms. Richard Joseph, who wrote his uncle's biography, naturally does not agree.

> We have indeed enjoyed one of those prolonged runs of luck which the way of some publishers and our present position is perhaps comparable to that of Heinemann twenty years ago [ie. 1925]. I think it is especially true in publishing that nothing succeeds like success … For some time past I have increasingly felt that we are all inclined to be too complacent and too ready to believe that our run of luck will continue. [We] have received a great deal of praise from the trade and I recognise that our Sales Department has earned it by tact and efficiency during difficult years …
>
> For all these reasons I think we should stiffen our policy. In the trade we must always be on our guard against overselling the market. It is far better to be frank with buyers about our books and our expectations: in the long run this policy will pay good dividends. On the editorial side we must keep a careful eye on contract renewals and be more attentive to authors … Inside the office itself there must be much closer co-operation and co-ordination. In the past there has been a lamentable reluctance to pass on information which ought to be shared … I therefore propose to tighten up office organisation in this respect.
>
> To sum up, war-time conditions … have inevitably had an unhealthy effect. We have had too much praise and not enough criticism. Publishing is a highly competitive business and competitive conditions are fast returning. We must not be smug about our past success and we must not assume it will continue. (Quoted in Joseph, 1986, pp.168-70)

There is more than a hint here of Joseph's resentment about being side-lined, but his assessment of the post-war market for publishing is accurate. Nevertheless, for a company barely a decade old when he wrote this note, he does acknowledge the extraordinary success the war had brought him.

The Hogarth Press in the 1930s was still close to a cottage industry, with Leonard Woolf obsessing over the price of postage and Virginia Woolf serenely hand-typesetting the works on her poetic friends in Bodoni old-style (Kennedy, 1972). By 1945 the Press was barely functioning with only four new titles published, although it had enjoyed a brilliant and productive swansong earlier in the war years. Virginia had sold her shares in 1938 and committed suicide by drowning in March 1941. Hogarth Press itself was one of the few Bloomsbury-based publishing houses to be bombed out. It was flattened during a daylight raid very early in the war in September 1940, and it moved its operation to Letchworth in Hertfordshire.[101] Its publishing was now directed by the brilliant editor John Lehmann (he would later set up his own imprint in 1946) who conceived the *New Hogarth Library* of poets and, probably his greatest achievement, *New Writing and Daylight*. This quarterly hardback periodical introduced the work of many notable new writers in prose and poetry, including William Sansom, Cecil Day Lewis (eventually to become Poet Laureate) and Raymond Williams. Lehmann also pioneered the use of documentary photography, and especially the use of film stills and stage shots from theatre productions. Given the difficulty of block-making at the height of the war this was a major achievement. Lehmann eventually grew tired and impatient with Leonard Woolf's moaning and penny-pinching, offering to buy him out in 1946. Woolf instead bought Lehmann's shares and promptly sold the entire company to Chatto and Windus. Lehmann also produced a successful 'New Writers' series for Penguin (Hare, 1995).

Perhaps not surprisingly, the publisher who experienced most prosperity and who benefited to the greatest extent from the war was Allen Lane and Penguin Books (Lewis, 2005). We have seen how he had transformed his already robust fledgling into a cultural institution by clever promotion, excellent publishing, cunning manipulation of paper rationing and all-round charm when making use of his influential contacts. He was both brave in trying out new ideas (like the colour-illustrated mini-hardbacks, the *King Penguins*) and enjoyed more than his fair share of luck. Penguin had begun life as a reprint house, but, while that remained the mainstay of the business, the war enabled it to publish its own original editions as the famous 'Specials'. Building on the Pelicans, it now published in most non-fiction subjects as well as providing an enormous range of fiction, all at the magic price of sixpence per volume. By 1945 Penguin was undoubtedly the best known, if not yet the biggest, British publisher,[102] already strong in the United States[103] and poised to expand in Australia. In ten years, Allen Lane had created his legend.

101 Bizarrely, Hogarth Press kept its imprint as '37 Mecklenburgh Square' throughout the war although the house was nothing more than an overgrown bomb site for most of it. How its post was delivered remains a mystery. The books enigmatically note 'All communications should be addressed to John Lehmann at the Hogarth Press.' *How?*

102 Probably Collins held that title, although Nelson with their enormous export business were close.

103 Penguin Books Inc. was incorporated in 1939 (see Hare, 1995, pp.148-55).

As Joseph predicted, post-war publishing did not become easier: in many respects it faced worse market conditions than it had experienced during the war. Rationing and restrictions continued, and although exports were easier it took time to rebuild disrupted networks of agents and distributors. Exchange controls caused great problems with revenue flows and books were no longer a priority for Attlee's new Labour government elected in 1945. Grappling with railway, mining and steel nationalization and the establishment of the National Health Service, it had bigger fish to fry.

Nevertheless, publishing shared in the ethos of rebuilding, and in particular there was a desire to help in the reconstruction of the European publishing industry. The Nazi regime had absolutely controlled the output of German publishers and restricted their publications to politically approved, ideologically pure content. Some companies such as Bertelsmann and Springer had controversially been compliant and served the Hitler State, while others – particularly those with Jewish connections such as Ullstein and Schiffren – had been all but destroyed in Germany and the occupied territories of the Greater Reich. Defeated Germany was divided into separate zones administered by the Americans, Russians, French and British. In the British zone – which included the publishing centres of Stuttgart and Hamburg as well as the western sector of Berlin – the Control Commission, which operated until 1949, embarked on a programme of 'denazification' in which publishing was planned to play a vital role. A major element of this initiative was the creation, less than a month after the surrender had been signed in May 1945, of German Educational Reconstruction (GER) to provide replacement textbooks for the corrupted Nazi books used in German schools since 1933 (Holman, 2008, pp.229-31). Humphrey Milford from OUP and Gollancz were supportive of the need for books for Germany, but other publishers were less willing to help. The British public contributed generously – and perhaps surprisingly – to an appeal launched by Gollancz for 'good English novels' for German schools, but supplies were patchy at best.

At home, the publishing community was reinforced and reinvigorated by the immigration of innovative new blood from Eastern Europe. Some were here already, such as Walter Neurath, who had fled from Austria before the war. He used the skills and contacts he had built up working for Adprint to create the revolutionary fine-art publisher Thames and Hudson in 1949, with help from the Norwich printer Jarrolds – one of the few manufacturers to possess the advanced colour reproduction technology the books demanded.[104]

In the next Chapter, we shall look at the profound effects that a remarkable group of publishers from Eastern Europe had on British publishing in the 1950s and 1960s, but this Chapter closes with consideration of two forerunners, each very different in style, impact and reputation. The first of these was André Deutsch (Athill, 2001). Deutsch was born in Hungary in 1917, the son of a Jewish dentist. He fled Hungary as war broke out, fearful that the puppet regime of Admiral Horthy would arrest and imprison him. When he arrived in Britain he was promptly interned as an enemy alien. When eventually released he obtained a publishing job with Nicolson and Watson, a firm that would later metamorphose into another house led by a great European *émigré*, Weidenfield and Nicolson. Deutsch found publishing much to his taste and when he met a gifted editor from the BBC, Diana Athill, he decided to set up his own company in 1944. The pair had a brief romantic affair, but for the remainder of Deutsch's life they maintained a highly effective professional relationship – bracingly described by Athill in her memoir *Stet* – that was among the most productive and creative in post-war publishing. He chose 'Allan Wingate' as the name of his new venture since he judged that his own name would be 'too German' to thrive in the aftermath of the war.[105] Deutsch operated on a shoestring, and while he was a shrewd and canny businessman he had a blind spot in trusting the honour and probity of the English gentleman. He ill-advisedly admitted a couple as directors; proving to be both lazy and venal, they quickly caused the nascent house real harm. In the end they ejected Deutsch and Athill from the company they had founded.

Allan Wingate made a real impact when Deutsch was in charge and its early books included Norman Mailer's *The Naked and the Dead* (1949). He also made a speciality of books about publishing, including

104 It is often mistakenly thought that Neurath's house was named from the surnames of two (mythical) partners – they are, of course, the rivers that flow through London and New York. He chose the name partly to disguise his own Germanic origin and to signal his focus on international co-editions on which his business would depend.

105 No person called Allan Wingate ever existed and no-one seems to know where Deutsch got the name. The imprint had a chequered history and after André and Diana were unceremoniously dumped out of the company in 1950, it staggered on for a few years, falling into receivership in 1959. The imprint was revived between 1970 and 1984, but the books produced then are pathetic shadows of what was earlier published and are best forgotten.

Michael Joseph's *The Adventure of Publishing* (1949). Within weeks of his defenestration in 1950 he had set up a new company, this time under his own name, that was to become one of the legendary publishers of the next two decades.

The other East European who arrived in the late 1940s casts a much longer and much more sinister shadow. This was Ian Robert Maxwell, arguably both one of the most brilliant and most villainous characters ever to grace and disgrace British publishing. Maxwell was born Abraham (later renamed Ludvik) Hoch in Szlatina on the Romanian–Czechoslovakian border in 1923, where he attended synagogue school and reputedly was destined for the life of a rabbi. The invading Germans deported most of his family to Auschwitz where they were murdered, but the young Hoch escaped to France, where he joined the Czech army in exile in 1940.

After the fall of France, he fled to England and enlisted in the British army under the name Leslie du Maurier, apparently after the cigarette brand rather than the novelist. He participated in the D-Day landings in 1944, by which time he had become the less aristocratic Leslie Jones, and displayed considerable personal bravery, being awarded the Military Cross and receiving a field commission to captain.[106] Finally in 1946 he became Ian Robert Maxwell (some say appropriating the name of a fellow officer from a Scottish regiment who had been killed) and became a naturalized British subject. Because of his fluency in German, Czech, French and Russian he was appointed to the Allied Control Commission and was ominously given responsibility for films, books, newspapers and the theatre. This brought him into close collaboration with the resurgent German scientific publishers, primarily Ferdinand Springer, as well as – many believe – the Soviet Intelligence Service, the KGB.

Meanwhile in Britain, there was concern that because of its isolation from European research during the war British science had fallen behind. In time-honoured fashion the remedy was entrusted to a committee of the great and the good which determined that unfortunately the task of re-inventing scientific and technical publishing should be given to Butterworth and Company. As we have already seen, Butterworth's megalomaniac owner Stanley Bond had died early in the war, leaving his company to his infant sons (pp.83-4). While they were minors, his trustees had given the direction of the company to a lazy, not-very-bright, vain,

106 Thereby becoming, in *Private Eye's* memorable coinage, the piratical 'Cap'n Bob'.

pompous and mendacious City solicitor named Hugh Quennell who was more interested in film starlets and the turf than the intricacies of professional publishing.[107] Quennell convinced the grandees of the committee that a partnership between Springer and Butterworth was the formula for rebuilding British scientific excellence.

Maxwell had arrived in London in 1947 and had set up a company to import German periodicals and newspapers. He got wind of the Butterworth proposal and represented himself as Springer's representative. Impressed, the Butterworth people agreed to work with Maxwell and a 'joint' publisher named Butterworth-Springer was set up, as well as another company with Maxwell and Herr Lange (the Nazi-approved Ayran who had managed Springer while the Jewish owners, Julius and Ferdinand Springer, had sheltered in Switzerland) as directors (Kay Jones, 1980, pp.130-1). In a pattern that would become familiar, Maxwell ran rings round his Butterworth partners and although a new scientific journal, *Research*, was launched in 1949 by the joint company, most of the financial benefits fell to Maxwell and Lange. Although Butterworth-Springer was a wholly owned subsidiary of Butterworth and Company, it was clear who was really in charge.

In 1950, Quennell – in the judgement of the distinguished American scientific publisher Maurits Dekker of Interscience 'the only man genuinely feared by Robert Maxwell' (quoted by Kay Jones, 1986, p.129) – abruptly left Butterworths. This was apparently because of some financial irregularities, and Maxwell saw his chance. He began to freeze Butterworths out of their own subsidiary, and by the end of 1950 he had convinced them to give up. He bought the company for £36,547, persuading Butterworths to agree to waive a debt of £23,547, and renamed it 'Pergamon Press'. He took over the stock and the staff, including Dr Paul Rosbaud, a distinguished nuclear scientist who was the founding editor of *Research*. Rosbaud, a German academic who had concealed his Jewish antecedents from the Nazis, had almost certainly been a British spy during the war and was possibly also a double-agent for the Russians. He is believed to have smuggled the details of Hitler's atomic bomb programme out of Germany.

In his deal with Butterworths, Maxwell bought for a trifle one of the

107 I base my interpretation of Quennell on Graham (2006) and some personal reminiscences from contemporary witnesses. Graham is much more restrained about Quennell than I am, but he clearly did not think much of him (pp.27-8).

most potentially valuable publishing properties it is possible to imagine, along with a clutch of key scientific journals and books. On this foundation he would go on to launch, as the 1950s dawned, a publishing career that proved to be uniquely brilliant, uniquely profitable and uniquely dishonest.

6 'A Tonic for the Nation'

British publishing in the 1950s

In 1951, the post-war British Labour government organized a great exhibition on the South Bank of the Thames in London, with related events taking place throughout the country.[108] The 'Festival of Britain' was intended to mark the centenary of the world's first Great Exhibition held in London in 1851, and also to provide 'a tonic for the nation' whose citizens were emerging from more than a decade of conflict, austerity, rationing, shortages and economic torpor (Kynaston, 2007). The main exhibition featured modernistic and forward-looking architecture such as the Festival Hall, the 'Skylon' and the Dome of Discovery, and was intended to showcase Britain's new place and role in a world that was becoming post-imperial, ideologically divided and driven by technology. There was also a more light-hearted side to the Festival, with a fun fair, rides on Rowland Emmett's surrealistic 'Far Tottering and Oyster Creek Railway' and a Mississippi-style showboat at the end of Battersea Pier.[109] As we shall see, the cultural and social influence of American images and practices was to become a keynote of the 1950s.

There were many publications linked to the Festival, but a particularly interesting group was the thirteen-volume series of 'About Britain' guides, published by Collins for the Festival of Britain Office and sponsored by the Brewers' Society. These are small octavo hardbacks with full-colour printed-paper cases featuring relief maps of each region covered and the famous Festival symbol of Britannia designed by Abram Games. Each

108 Simner and Tonkin (2001) provide a graphic overview of the images of the Festival.

109 The Festival itself did not fare as well in its legacy. There had been plans to keep it as a semi-permanent installation, but Labour lost the 1952 election and the incoming Conservative government suspected it as being dangerously socialist. It was abruptly closed and most of its buildings removed, with only the Festival Hall remaining today.

featured a full-colour painting on the title page by a noted artist such as E.W. Fenton and contained several colour plates. 'Each volume contains several illustrations in full colour and approximately 50 illustrations in black and white, two relief maps and about 14 pages of strip maps,' explained a blurb printed on the inside back cover. The books were a uniform ninety-two pages in extent and the texts were provided by rather *avant-garde* writers such as Leo Walmsley, novelist (Lancashire and Yorkshire), W.G. Hoskins, landscape historian (East Midlands and the Peak) and Sid Chaplin, essayist and screen-writer (Lakes to Tyneside), each of whom had strong local connections with the 'portrait' they were contributing. Obvious antecedents to these books were the hardback King Penguins that Lane had launched in association with Foges and Neurath's Adprint in 1939.

Yet they were very different in content, aim and ideology from the King Penguins which were largely historical and nostalgic in their subject-matter, including Redouté's *Roses* and views of historic Oxford and Cambridge colleges. 'About Britain' were witty, well-written, modern accounts of British regions looking forward to industrial and social prosperity. They would as often feature photographs of factories and 'New Towns' as of natural landscapes and cathedrals. A vital component of each was a selection of a dozen 'motor tours' which a newly-emergent, car-owning middle-class could negotiate in their Ford Populars or Triumph Vanguards, the guides safely to hand in the glove compartment. Each book sold for three shillings and sixpence, and they were very popular.

The series was edited by the poet Geoffrey Grigson and supervised by an editorial board comprising, as chairman, Gerald Barry, chief administrator of the Festival, along with a brace of geography professors, Eva Taylor and Sydney Wooldridge, the explorer and founder of *Geographical Magazine* Michael Huxley, the novelist and travel writer Peter Stucley, the topographer and folk historian Gerald Millar and the astronomer Penrose Angwin.

The books set features that would become characteristic of non-fiction publishing during the 1950s. These included the relatively lavish use of colour printing, the recognition among publishers of a new consumer market beyond traditional book-buyers, the value of commercial sponsorship and the bringing together of high quality literary writing with the rather earnest anticipation of a better future for all. Books were seen as tools of social and economic transformation in the brave new world of what would shortly become known as the 'New Elizabethan Age'.

There were two names among the creators of this series who are important for the history of post-war publishing. The first of these is their production editor, Ruari McLean, born in 1917 and the leading typographer of his generation (see his autobiography, *True to Type*, McLean, 2000). He had begun to learn book production before the war at the Shakespeare Head Press, a private press operated by Bernard Newdigate in Stratford-upon-Avon and funded by the Oxford bookseller Basil Blackwell who sent him to Germany to sharpen his skills. There McLean was introduced to the work of Jan Tschichold, later to have so much influence on the look of Penguins and other publishers' books during the 1950s (p.160). He joined the Royal Navy during the Second World War and served in naval intelligence. On demobilization he was offered a job at Penguin, introduced by a shipmate, Edward Young, who had designed the Penguin colophon. McLean admired Lane and found him congenial if erratic company (Lewis, 2005, pp.226, 232), but when Vivian Ridler, the new Printer at Oxford University Press,[110] offered him freelance design work he left Penguin to set up on his own in 1949. He wrote *Modern Book Design* in 1951 at the invitation of the British Council for their Longmans series.

The other executive member of the 'About Britain' editorial board was George Rainbird. He had been a book salesman from Essex and had observed how Adprint had packaged books for Collins and Penguin. In 1951 he was working in advertising when he was asked to supervise the 'About Britain' series on behalf of the Brewers' Society. This gave him a taste for publishing and, as he recalls in his autobiography, 'I decided to ... throw my cap over the moon and make or lose my name with the publishing imprint' (Rainbird, 1985, p.xiii). Very different in personality from McLean, who was rather serious, scholarly and Scottish, Rainbird was a *bon-viveur* who enjoyed social gatherings, art and the theatre. He was something of a wine connoisseur and he wrote knowledgeably about the subject, eventually publishing one of the earliest colour guides to wine. The Festival of Britain commission from Collins brought this rather unlikely pair together, and after it was completed they set up in business as the first real book packager in the sense understood today – a business

110 In perhaps typical Oxbridge style, the 'Printer' at both the ancient University Presses was in fact a senior manager, equivalent to Chief Executive of the manufacturing divisions.

producing fine, full-colour editions from conception to final form for a number of publishers. The range of subjects was wide, from food, wine, and art to fine limited editions of literature by writers such as the Irish novelist Arthur Joyce Cary. Rainbird McLean Ltd (as the company was first incorporated) was a pioneer in the international co-edition market where the colour sheets using the technology of 'four back one'[111] could be sold to many publishers, producing sales revenue as well as licence income.

The company became rather sidetracked by McLean's obsession with fine printing and design, resulting in their production of volumes that were undoubtedly beautiful but not particularly cost-efficient, considering the time they took and the overhead they consumed. These included the morocco-bound, slip-cased album *Heads, Figures and Ideas* by the artist and sculptor Henry Moore, published in a limited edition of 150 copies in 1958. At last, in 1958, they parted company amicably, with McLean joining Shenval Press, the noted fine printer, and Rainbird continuing to package distinctive, colour-printed books for non-fiction publishers. He was eventually to publish under the imprint George Rainbird Ltd, until he sold the company to International Thomson in 1966. Rainbird remained involved in book design and production until his death in 1986 (Rainbird, 1984).

Rainbird had, however, shown what could be done, and it was left to one of the East European emigrés who came to prominence in the immediate post-war years to take his idea and create from it an entirely new publishing business, ultimately to become one of the dominant genres of the second half-century. This was Paul Hamlyn, born in Germany in 1926 to a cultured and bookish Jewish paediatrician. His family, actually

111 This printing technique meant that one side of the printing sheet (normally containing thirty-two pages, sixteen on each side) was printed in colour, with the other in black only. The costs of colour printing were thereby substantially reduced, but when the pages were folded up, the impression was given of a book printed in colour throughout. This would later become a widely used and lucrative technique for selling 'flat sheets' to overseas publishers, either with the (black) text space blank so a foreign-language translation could be dropped in or 'integral', that is with the English remaining in place so an overseas English-language publisher could tip in their own title page and bind them up in their own binding. The reason for doing this was to extend the print run, reduce the unit cost and underwrite the cost of colour origination. It would be the mainstay of the business of a number of colour-illustrated publishers such as Thames and Hudson, Phaidon, Studio Vista, Dorling Kindersley and, most of all, as we shall shortly see, Octopus. See Owen (2006) for a technical discussion of the procedure.

named Hamburger, fled Nazi persecution in 1933 to settle in London where the young Paul, having been teased as 'sausage' at school, adopted the less culinary-sounding Hamlyn. During the Second World War he worked as a Bevin boy in the mines of South Wales – interestingly a milieu that shaped the career of another innovative and creative publisher with an east European Jewish heritage, Frank Cass.[112]

After returning from National Service, Hamlyn took a clerical job with the publisher of theatre scripts Samuel French and then, or so the legend attests, sold books from a barrow. He proceeded to work as an assistant in Zwemmers bookshop in London. Zwemmers was one of the traditional book retailers of the Charing Cross Road in London; it carried a mixed stock of new, remaindered and second-hand and antiquarian books, concentrating on fine art and scholarly books. It is probable that the young Hamlyn got the sense of the market for cheap, handsome books while serving in the shop. He usually claimed that is where the idea came from.

Hamlyn eventually got enough capital together to launch Books for Pleasure (BfP) in 1949. BfP was an entirely new concept in publishing, book marketing and distribution, created by a natural entrepreneur with a flair for design and an instinctive sense of what the public wanted. He ignored established book trade channels and mainly sold his books through 'non-traditional' outlets such as department stores and food retailers. Hamlyn pioneered the concept of point-of-sale merchandizing, providing his retailers with custom-designed stands and 'spinners' which his sales representatives would fill with new and established titles without waiting for the seller to order. Initially he had sold second-hand and

112 Cass, born in the Jewish east end of London in 1930, was evacuated to Merthyr Tydfil in 1939, and he recalled the mining community and its reverence for education as a formative influence. He became a bookseller in 1949, pioneering specialist academic bookselling with his shop in Woburn Walk in the shadow of the University of London. He began to publish reprints of out-of-print academic classics which his customers were seeking to purchase in the early 1960s, and later published scholarly journals and original books in emerging academic fields such as black studies and sports studies. Cass's greatest publishing achievement was the mammoth edition of British Parliamentary Papers, which he produced under the imprint Irish Academic Press. Shortly before his death in 2007 he disposed of the bulk of his business to Taylor and Francis for almost £12 million, but he retained the Irish Academic Press imprint and the Jewish interest publisher Vallentine Mitchell, which his children, Stewart and Hayley, continue to run with flair (Black, 2008).

remaindered titles, but, noting Rainbird's success with packaged titles, he set up his own BfP imprint and using cheap colour printing in Czechoslovakia began to produce hundreds of keenly priced, beautifully produced colour books on good quality paper that were unlike anything that had ever appeared on the British market before. They were an instant success, and the newly acquired coffee-tables of 1950s Britain groaned[113] with recipe, lifestyle, art and travel titles published by Hamlyn from his (unfashionably located but undoubtedly stylish) white-washed brick warehouse in Kentish Town in north London.[114]

Despite, or perhaps because of, his success, Hamlyn was ignored, deplored or patronized by the publishing establishment. When Allen and Unwin published *The Book World Today*, edited by John Hampden in 1957, entire chapters were devoted to 'provincial book-selling' and 'the National Book League'. However, Hamlyn and his non-fiction revolution of bringing books to people who were, in his words, 'terrified and intimidated by bookshops' receives no mention.[115] Sydney T. Hyde, who had graduated from selling shorthand manuals for Sir Isaac Pitman to become publicity manager for W.H. Smith in 1948, contributed a notably po-faced chapter to this book on 'sales promotion'. He dully recounts the usual means of promoting books, including jackets, catalogues, window displays, exhibitions and even, daringly, the promotion of books on television by 'advertizing' (*sic*). However, he says nothing about Hamlyn-style merchandizing, although it may have occurred to him as he excused himself by the following classic concluding paragraph to his chapter:

113 As did the equally newly-acquired radiograms since Hamlyn, a music-lover from youth, created the first budget record label, 'Music for Pleasure', in 1965, in association with EMI. Hamlyn was a noted philanthropist in later life, establishing the charitable Paul Hamlyn Foundation which supports good causes in the arts, educational and development fields. He made enormous donations to the Royal Opera House and the British Museum, filling the empty and redundant Reading Room with books for free access when the British Library moved to its new premises in 1998.

114 Most publishers of the period were concentrated in Covent Garden, Bloomsbury or Mayfair.

115 Allen Lane does get an entire chapter on 'paper-covered books', but is rather dismissively biographed as having 'joined John Lane The Bodley Head Ltd as an apprentice in 1919. He is managing director of Penguin Books Ltd., which he founded in 1935', compared to the very fulsome biographies provided for the other now mostly very obscure contributors, such as Lionel McColvin, who merits fifteen lines to Lane's three. I suspect this is Lane being mischievously ironic at the expense of his old adversary Unwin by supplying a terse biography. Unwin, of course, gets seventeen lines.

> It is impossible to do more here than review the general lines of sales promotion in the book trade. With more space one might have said something of experiments that have been made from time to time to confirm or influence and suggest lines on which further experiments might be attempted in the future. As these would call for lengthy argument and justification, they would also require space which is not, unhappily, available. One might like also to have drawn attention to some notable campaigns that have reflected great credit on their authorship. An apology for omission is coupled with the plea that space did not permit. (Hampden, 1957, p.197)

Nevertheless Hamlyn pursued his restless and relentless construction of a publishing empire by giving his customers what they wanted. He bought up failing or moribund imprints and applied his energetic brand of market understanding to their ailing lists. While never as self-consciously devoted to 'improvement' as Lane, and given to some personal indulgences of great bad taste such as his famous pink Rolls-Royce, Hamlyn was a figure of genuine cultural importance. Although his name will forever be associated with the (truly useful and high-quality) books on cookery, gardening, needlework and interior decoration that bear his imprint, he also successfully brought words and, most importantly, pictures of art, architecture, music and theatre to readers who had never been able to own – or even see – such lavishly produced books before.

When he was joined by the marketing man from Boots the Chemist, Philip Jarvis, in 1959 (who proceeded to outrage decent cultural opinion by claiming he could 'sell books like soap'), Hamlyn had created a mass-market for books that was totally new. A mercurial, rather elfin figure, slight in build and with a large head and a perpetual smile, he had also made publishing fun, and earned on the way a great deal of money.[116] When he sold out to the International Publishing Corporation in 1964 he was paid over £2 million – a record for a publishing company by that date. He remained to build an even bigger publishing empire there and

116 A lively and affectionate short biography of Hamlyn can be found in Ian Norrie's limited-edition reminiscences *Mentors and Friends* (n.d. 2006). With only 210 copies produced for subscribers it is difficult to find, but well worth the hunt. Norrie makes the point that Hamlyn loved to surround himself with mavericks such as Lionel Leventhal who would not have fitted into more conventional publishing structures and who often went on to build notable publishing enterprises. Hamlyn is surely a figure who for his cultural and business importance deserves a full-scale biography.

a few years later, as we shall see in the next chapter, he bought back his original company for much less than he had sold it for.[117]

While Hamlyn was revolutionizing trade publishing by inventing the new, rather disturbing category of consumer publishing, another emigrant from Eastern Europe was continuing to wreak havoc on the settled niceties of trade practice and inventing new markets and new ways of selling books. When we left Robert Maxwell, he had just outwitted Butterworths to acquire their science publishing for peanuts and had set up Pergamon Press (p.131). In the meantime he had also bought up the weakened and effete book wholesaling co-operative Simpkin Marshall, which even by 1950 had not recovered much more than a shred of its former size or importance since its destruction in the Blitz in 1940. Maxwell used his charm and chutzpah to delude, bamboozle and deceive its gentlemanly owners; once he had disposed of them he shamelessly asset-stripped the company, exploiting its cash-flow to fund other business ventures in a pattern that was to become depressingly familiar in his future publishing operations.

By 1954 Simpkin Marshall was insolvent, and it collapsed in a welter of bad debts and recriminations. The Board of Trade investigated, but amazingly accepted Maxwell's assurances that *he* had been the victim of fraud, and he was exonerated. There was much gossip and complaint among publishers and booksellers, but Maxwell was already notoriously litigious so in the published comment of the time, at least, open criticism of his behaviour is muted. There is, however, little doubt, based on private reminiscences of the time, that Maxwell dishonestly appropriated Simpkin Marshall's funds and perpetrated the first of the serial frauds that marked his career. In the process he destroyed one of the great historic names of British publishing and caused distribution problems that would beset the book trade for more than two decades. Eventually new wholesalers such as Bertrams (founded in Norwich in 1968) and Gardners in Eastbourne would emerge, but none would ever enjoy the hegemony over book supply exercised by Simpkin Marshall.[118] A few

117 When I first met Hamlyn at the Frankfurt Book Fair, perhaps in 1986, he was rather crassly introduced to me as 'the most powerful man in British publishing'. He smiled modestly and demurred. '*One* of the most powerful …,' he corrected.

118 Elsie Bertram, born in 1912, established the company in disused chicken sheds on the former ground of Norwich City FC with her son Christopher (Kip). She was a noted bookselling personality and one of the first women to emerge as a business leader in the book trade. In an era when book orders would often take a month or more, she

smaller intermediaries such as William Dawson of Folkestone concentrated on library supply, although they briefly and unsuccessfully set up a publishing arm in the 1970s.

Pergamon Press, on the surface at least, was an eminently respectable publishing operation. In Maxwell's own immodest estimation it was 'the achievement for which Bob Maxwell is least-known, but will be best-remembered' (Maxwell, 1988, p.1). In this, ironically, he was uncannily accurate. Despite all we know about his dubious moral character, his self-deluding grandiosity, his petty meanness, his bullying and his breath-taking dishonesty, it must be admitted that with Pergamon Press he created the first modern Science, Technology and Medicine (STM) English-language publisher, and he evolved the grammar and syntax of the modern scientific journal that has been successfully followed by publishers up to the present. In this field at least, he was a publisher of genius showing great vision and insight. His shrewd ability to make commercial judgements about specialized and often arcane subjects was to prove most remunerative, at least to him and his shareholders if not to the authors and editors he used. It is not an exaggeration to claim that Maxwell invented scientific publishing in its modern form and, while making an intemperate profit on the way, he provided forums and channels for scientific communication in many fields from physics to medicine that would not otherwise have existed, and without a doubt contributed greatly to scientific progress.

In his extraordinarily hubristic and unintentionally revealing 886-page *Festschrift*, published in 1988 to mark Pergamon's 40th anniversary and his own 65th birthday, Maxwell described how he set up and operated this

—

promised (and gave) 'next day delivery'. She built her business partly by recognizing, before almost anyone else, the value of what Hamlyn (whom she admired) was doing, and she promoted his books strongly. Elsie was sometimes described as 'formidable' or 'a dragon' (particularly by misogynistic and less efficient male competitors), but she was in reality focussed, efficient and, not suffering fools gladly, prone to speaking her mind. Many smaller booksellers trusted her taste and service implicitly, and when she retired she received the warmest of tributes from all sectors of the book business. Her company was eventually sold in 1999 for £50 million and became part of the distribution arm of Woolworths, whose collapse in 2008 brought widespread supply problems to booksellers. One can imagine what Elsie's assessment of the situation would have been. See Bradley, 2008, pp.126-28 for Elsie's own account of her career, including a memorable confrontation with Robert Maxwell).

new kind of publishing business (Maxwell, 1988).[119] He skates delicately over the Butterworth saga, merely noting that the venture required more capital than was available. He correctly divined that the existing method of communicating scientific research – by which learned societies published papers in their own journals for their own members – was restrictive and led to bottlenecks in publishing. Few papers were peer-reviewed and quality was variable. Maxwell borrowed the model of blind peer-review from German scientific journals as well as the structure of editorial boards, regional editors and book review teams. He foresaw the coming great expansion in universities and research institutes that would shortly inundate the world with research papers, and he realized that the greatest market for his product would be the very people who produced it. Effectively he would sell back to scientists (or more correctly to their libraries and grant-givers) their own work at high prices. What was more, they would provide the papers and the editing labour for free 'for the good of science'. It was a commercial model made in Maxwellian heaven.

In 1951 Maxwell launched his enterprise with five periodical series (annual books reviewing specific scientific fields) and three journals. This had increased to forty journal titles by 1959. Eventually he would publish over 400 journals across the fields of medicine and life sciences, earth, engineering and physical sciences, chemistry, and social and behavioural sciences, as well as having published over 4000 book titles. He was able to move his operation to Oxford, where he rented the gracious mansion

119 Although unsigned it is clear that Maxwell himself wrote 'Pergamon Press; a short history' (pp.1-28). His distinctive gravel tones and sonorous phraseology can be heard as you read the text. The remaining 850 pages of the book are comprised of glowing tributes to Maxwell from hundreds of distinguished scientists, including many Nobel Laureates, Fellows of the Royal Society and Academicians of many nationalities. Most of these mention his charm, his determination, his amazing grasp of their subject and his enthusiasm for education and science. None mention the fact that he rarely paid them. They include Sir Derek Barton and Sir George Porter, Nobel prize-winners in Chemistry, Sir Hermann Bondi, Alex Comfort, Denis Noble and Sir Denys Wilkinson, among many others. Perhaps the oddest tribute in the book comes from Harold Baum, renowned author of the 'Biochemist's Songbook' who penned a Gilbertian ballad (to the tune of 'the Duke of Plaza Toro' from *The Gondoliers*) in Maxwell's honour, containing the immortal lines: 'But it is in his publishing/ That his fame rests eternal/ Like Mol. Aspects of Medicine/ That most distinguished journal/ With songbook authors who play coy/ He's known to interact well/ That celebrated, cultivated, elevated, birthday boy/ Dear Captain Robert Maxwell' (p.258). Perhaps the most poignant in the light of later events is 'The Contribution of Robert Maxwell to Maritime Communication' by Captain Fred Weeks (pp.237-9).

Headington Hill Hall, overlooking the City and Colleges as his business base and family home.[120] He gathered round him a loyal and talented staff, many of whom, like Brian Cox and Richard Charkin, later to become head of Macmillan, maintained a sneaking affection for 'the monster' and his unorthodox ways, which included folding five and ten pound notes into staff Christmas cards.[121] In the mid 1950s Maxwell cut a slim, debonair, almost beautiful figure, with jet-black hair, a pencil moustache and expensive bespoke suiting – unrecognizable from the later obese, beetle-browed bully of popular recollection. He travelled widely to the United States and behind the Iron Curtain to attend scientific meetings and seminars and sign up distinguished scientists, both young and older, to his programme. By this time other publishers such as Marcel Dekker at Interscience and the old-established Dutch academic house of Elsevier had seen the potential of his model and had begun to copy it, but he had a head start and had cherry-picked the best titles and subject areas.[122]

As his empire grew, Maxwell refined his money-making machine to produce even greater profits. Since his market was not individuals but libraries and institutions, he knew that they were not price-sensitive and that, particularly in the United States, deep in Cold War anxiety, there was an almost infinite market for science – particularly that produced in the USSR and other Soviet satellites. He used his multi-language fluency to obtain translation rights from Russian, Polish, Czech, Hungarian and Romanian Academies, and published their journals in English translation. It has to be admitted that the quality of some of this work was dubious, and Maxwell would later publish some very questionable East European science such as the 'chemical research' of the wife of the Romanian dictator, Elena Ceaucescu. Nonetheless, they were all essential purchases for any university library which needed to keep its community

120 He would without an iota of self-awareness or irony describe it 'as the largest council house in England' since his landlord was Oxford City Council. He charged the rent, rates and running costs to his company, so he and his large family of seven children lived there free in considerable style and luxury. It is now owned by Oxford Brookes University.

121 Apparently you could gauge your position in the pecking order by just how much you received in your tax-free Christmas bonus. If your prospects were particularly poor you would receive nothing but a job advertisement cut from *The Bookseller*, which staff were not normally allowed to see.

122 Elsevier would eventually absorb Pergamon and today, as the Anglo-Dutch behemoth Reed-Elsevier, it is the largest publisher in the world – with gigantic revenues based almost entirely on scientific journal and reference publishing.

abreast of new developments. Maxwell introduced differential pricing, so that American libraries paid more: he was the first publisher to quote list prices in dollars only, so he was immune from exchange rate swings (and he used a notional exchange rate that was much weighted in his favour). He also invented the trick of re-publishing 'special thematic issues' of journals a year or so after their appearance as expensive hardback books with different titles, so that librarians would innocently buy what they already had.

Maxwell certainly behaved with characteristic lack of probity, but if one reads the tributes in his *Festschrift* it is undeniable that his editors and authors regarded him with admiration, gratitude, affection and even love. These were among the brightest minds on the planet, so it is disingenuous to dismiss them all as simple dupes, easy prey for Maxwell's scheming and double-dealing. The uncomfortable truth is that they probably all understood very well what he was doing in publishing, if not in business terms, but that he was in return giving them what they wanted and needed. He left them alone to edit and write what they wanted, he did not interfere with editorial decisions (this is a repeated mantra in the tributes), his journals gave its contributors, editors, referees and board members high professional status and assured them promotion, grants and foreign travel. The authors and editors all had their salaries paid by their institutions who regarded this work as valid professional activity, so they did not need payments or royalties.

Maxwell's journals did, let it be said, genuinely advance science and human knowledge enormously. They led, particularly in the medical and life sciences, to important breakthroughs that alleviated human suffering. In the recesses of his dark heart Maxwell was proud of what he was doing for science, and somewhere there was, or at least had once been, a spark of idealism. He loved to be pictured with Nobel laureates or to address plenary sessions of scientific congresses. The money that was flowing relentlessly into his coffers came from the tax-payer, so who was being hurt? It would only have been wasted on military hardware if it had not been spent on Pergamon journals (one can imagine the reasoning). And the profits were enormous. Maxwell's financial affairs were always murky, but by 1960 he was making at least £500,000 in declared annual net profit, with probably a lot more being siphoned off into trusts, shell companies and other vehicles in secretive Liechtenstein.

It is an interesting speculation what would have happened had Maxwell been content with his academic publishing cash machine and remained simply the leading scientific publisher of his day. Would he now be honourably retired, loaded with international scientific honours and feted as a major figure in world publishing, perhaps with a knighthood or even a peerage? Certainly one could imagine him as a chancellor of a mid-range university. However, he was too restless and ambitious to settle for what he had created, and he took the fateful decision to take Pergamon public in 1964 as the basis for further publishing adventures. As we shall see in the next and later chapters, this was to sow the seeds of his eventual downfall, disgrace and controversial death.

While the new generation of entrepreneurs from Eastern Europe such as Deutsch, Hamlyn, Maxwell and others (for example Paul Elek who had built an admired trade books list) were for good or ill energetically creating new markets and new publishing categories, the 1950s also saw the creation of more traditional companies. They built on the older models of literary fiction acquired by editorial flair leavened with serious non-fiction. The most important of these was Rupert Hart-Davis, probably the last of the trade publishers built on a pre-war scale and style (Garnett, 2004). Hart-Davis, a bookish, clubbable ex-Guards officer of vaguely cultural leanings (he had been briefly married to the actress Peggy Ashcroft) had before the war worked for Jonathan Cape and actually held a substantial shareholding in the company. As he approached demobilization he wrote to Cape asking if he could return and participate more in the equity. Cape brusquely rejected the request, suspecting (incorrectly as it happened) that Hart-Davis had received an offer from another publisher and was hoping to up the ante. In fact, Hart-Davis was naively over-estimating his value and skills and, as we shall see, indulging a life-long propensity for laziness and dilettantism coupled with the arrogance that only family money and a private education can provide. Cape extended the olive branch by writing to invite him to return, but not to make unreasonable demands for salary and shares:

> It is a good maxim I think not to throw away dirty water before you have clean ... the first requisite I should say was to get back to harness and settle down to the collar ... I have taken out the figures of what you received from [us] ... during the past eleven years ... They don't strike me as either meagre or inadequate ... [Your] progression could have been counted on to continue as your capacity to *earn* instead of to *receive* became increasingly manifest. (Howard 1971, pp.197-8)

With typical shrewdness Cape had summed up his former employee's character, and although he later expressed regret that Hart-Davis had not returned, he was probably well rid of him.

Hart-Davis did not trouble to reply to Cape, but instead sold him back his shares at a tidy profit and used the proceeds of £3000 to set up on his own with David Garnett, son of Cape's reader Edward Garnett. David pledged £10,000 of his family's money to the new venture, which opened for business in May 1946 in a bombed-out bakery just off the Edgware Road in west London. Problems with paper rationing (which continued until the late 1940s) caused initial delay, but the first books, reprints of editions of Henry James and Rupert Brooke, appeared in 1947. Hart-Davis disdained the War Economy Standard (which was still in force) and produced his books very lavishly (often ill-advisedly so), with wide margins and thick paper. He made a somewhat dubious arrangement with a greetings card manufacturer, the Classic Card Company, in order to make use of their paper allocation.

Hart-Davis was lucky in his partners and authors. The former worked hard and made up for his own management and financial deficiencies, and the latter fell into his lap, often coming through his social and artistic contacts. Early on he acquired Stephen Potter whose 'Gamesmanship' books became something of a cult in the early 1950s. An interest in cricket (he was a member of the MCC) brought him the cricket columnist of the *Manchester Guardian*, Nevile Cardus, and his taste for yachting encouraged him to launch a series of sailing books, eventually to become the best publishing in the subject. By 1950 the imprint was well-established in pleasant offices in Soho Square with a striking colophon of a fox designed by the noted graphic artist Reynolds Stone and a strong list of middle-brow fiction (such as Eric Linklater's *Mr Byculla)*, popular non-fiction (J.H. Williams's *Elephant Bill)* and a rather eclectic clutch of books on cricket, yachting, cookery and poetry not unlike that of Grant Richards in his prime. Hart-Davis's social contacts and not inconsiderable charm brought him authors that the small size of his firm and the tiny royalties he was able to offer would have otherwise denied him. His theatrical friends introduced him to the journalist and broadcaster Alistair Cooke[123] (he rather than the BBC published the famous *Letters from America*). The American science-fiction writer Ray Bradbury, whose metaphor-heavy, allusive style appealed to the literary stylist in Rupert, was taken on

123 Cooke was an accomplished amateur actor before he emigrated to the USA. He had been close friends with Peggy Ashcroft, who is thought to have introduced him to her ex-husband.

through a chance dinner-table conversation with the author's agent. Rupert was very much at home in a publishing environment where the wishes of the author were paramount. Although small (and chaotic) he was congenial, and would keep books in print when strictly in accountant's terms they were dead. With increasing conglomeration, the 1950s was probably the last decade when this could be the publishing norm.

Hart-Davis's heart was really in the scholarly literary editions, poetry and classic reprints that he produced to modest or no profit, and he was content to leave the better-selling fiction and travel memoirs to his partner David's son Richard Garnett, who had joined the firm as production editor. Again, he was very fortunate here. Reputedly when the firm signed up the wildly popular zoologist and explorer Gerald Durrell, whose *Three Singles to Adventure* was published to great commercial success in 1953, Rupert thought he was getting Gerald's much more literary and much less-lucrative brother, Laurence. By 1957 the house was annually publishing 53 new titles in hardback in editions of between 2000 and 10,000 copies, with authors ranging over Eric Linklater, Ray Bradbury, Joseph Conrad (*Sea Stories* in the Mariner's Library), Paul Verlaine and Cardinal Newman. Although still very small compared to Collins or Macmillan, it competed respectably in size and influence with houses such as Secker and Warburg or Hamish Hamilton, and was not far short of Cape.

This style of books, literate, quirky, nostalgic, and beautifully produced, using illustrators such as John Piper, Joan Hassall and Faith Jacques, appealed strongly to the English middle-class market who voted Conservative, had enjoyed 'a good war' and had the spare income to lay out a guinea on a book of not-too-demanding poetry. In short – the kind of 1950s' settled bourgeois who were famously told by another publisher, by then the Prime Minister, that they 'had never had it so good'.

So Hart-Davis flourished although its finances, chiefly through Rupert's financial illiteracy, were always precarious.[124] It provided him and his other directors with a comfortable living. Rupert had installed his mistress, Ruth Simon, in the flat above the editorial office and employed her as an editor for which she had a natural gift, showing great accomplishment in acquiring and developing authors. In 1955 Heinemann, recently taken over by the transport-based combine Thomas Tilling,

124 Apparently during the company's entire independent existence only two board meetings were ever held, and no trading accounts were ever filed with Companies House.

approached Rupert with an offer to buy his company and promised to allow him to continue to run the business in his own way. This was an irresistible inducement and he signed the shares over to them in 1956.

The arrangement proved not to be as attractive as it first appeared. Heinemann by now had its management base at the remote, if picturesque, woodland printing factory at Kingswood in Surrey. Rupert hated making the long and tedious railway journey to attend board meetings there, so he did not often go and was kept out of the loop. Heinemann poached his gifted and energetic sales director, Harry Townshend, to oversee sales for the whole group, and Hart-Davis's own sales suffered. Although in his memoir, *Halfway to Heaven* (1998), he recalls that he read every manuscript and rewrote and edited many, Richard Garnett rather kindly demurs. Garnett's view is that Hart-Davis only looked at the titles that interested him while the bulk of the editing, production and design work fell on himself (Garnett, 2004, pp.32-3). It is clear that by the time of the Tilling purchase Rupert had lost interest in the day-to-day business of the firm. He was devoting most of his languid energy to compiling scholarly editions of the letters of Oscar Wilde and Charles Dickens, as well as keeping up a voluminous correspondence with the Etonian schoolmaster George Lyttelton, father of the jazz trumpeter and wit, Humphrey. In 1961, in a final bizarre twist, Rupert convinced William Jovanovich, the hard-nosed and hard-talking American publisher of Montenegrin extraction, now head of the educational publisher Harcourt, Brace and World, that his firm was the ideal means of selling US college textbooks in Europe. A casual glance at the list would have confirmed this as unlikely in the extreme, but Jovanovich approached Tilling with an offer to buy the firm out of Heinemann. This they agreed to, with surprising reluctance, in 1962.

Although there was initial enthusiasm and new investment, including the appointment of new editors such as Michael Wace to build an educational list, the impatient Jovanovich very quickly realized the extent of his error. The break-point was Rupert's refusal to publish Mary McCarthy's novel *The Group*, which Jovanovich liked and Rupert found distasteful. Coupled with the unsurprising poor results from sales of college texts, Jovanovich – true to his hot-headed Balkan ancestry – ordered Hart-Davis to be got rid of at any price.

Rupert did not help matters by sending his truculent owner affable and incomprehensibly whimsical telegrams, and eventually the firm was sold off at a knockdown price to the television mogul Sidney Bernstein, who was busily investing his immense advertising profits in building a publishing empire for Granada. Although Rupert remained on the holding company board until 1968 he had no influence; the imprint itself disappeared in November 1963, with the very last title of the 637 books published since October 1947 being Christopher Devlin's *Hamlet's Divinity*.

More established traditional firms also had varying fortunes in the rapidly changing postwar world. One of the more cautionary examples is provided by Cassell (Nowell-Smith, 1958, Flower, 1991). The company had its origins in a temperance grocery business founded in the 1840s, which had diversified into publishing almanacs and anti-alcohol tracts. By the end of the nineteenth century it had become Cassell, Petter and Galpin, and was a major producer of cheap improving literature, including magazines and self-educators. It had been very good at spotting authorial talent, including buying rights to *Treasure Island* by the then largely unknown R.L. Stevenson and employing Oscar Wilde in the role of editor of the 'intellectual and cultured magazine' *The Woman's World* in 1887 – before he achieved fame as a playwright and *belle-lettrist*.

By the end of the nineteenth century, Cassell occupied the ancient coaching Inn *La Belle Sauvage* at the foot of Ludgate Hill, below the historic publishing district around St Paul's Cathedral, and adopted the rather risqué colophon of a bare-breasted Amazon drawing a bow. It enjoyed great success with popular writers such as H. Rider Haggard and most of all R.L. Stevenson, who had become a literary superstar following the spectacular success of *Treasure Island*. The company was purchased by Sir Newman Flower in 1927, and he groomed his son Desmond eventually to take the firm over and develop it as a leading publisher of popular literature.

Newman Flower was an irascible iconoclast described by his rather sensitive and shy only son as 'a workaholic, very temperamental, with a very slight sadistic streak' (Flower, 1991, p.11). He had violently disapproved of Lane's paperback revolution and had refused to licence any of his copyrights to him, but his son wrote a paean of praise to Lane's invention (Flower, 1959). Sir Newman insisted that his son learn the business from the ground up, and by the time Desmond left on military service in 1940 to join the Argyll and Sutherland Highlanders he had worked in every department. He had also begun to edit his own authors, having become the company's literary director (a uniquely-titled and rather forward-looking appointment for the time) in 1938.

Desmond was a cultured and sensitive, rather dreamy young man who collected antiquarian books and china and displayed a passion for golf (he wrote a history of the game) and poetry. He had a conventionally 'good war', winning a Military Cross and being mentioned in dispatches. While he was away the firm's historic coaching inn was razed by German bombers (p.112). The staff were dispersed to a number of temporary offices round Holborn underground station, including the premises of Crittalls, the manufacturers of metal window frames; they eventually settled in St Andrew's Hill in the City near the offices of the *Observer* newspaper. Desmond returned in November 1945 and found waiting for him what was literally a licence to print money. Winston Churchill, smarting from his ousting at the hands of the electorate, determined to write his self-justificatory history of the Second World War. He chose Cassell as the publishers since they had treated him well when he had been out of office in the 1930s.[125]

Churchill's history eventually ran to six volumes. After the author had reputedly asked for, and received, the largest advance on royalties ever paid to that date, it was published at intervals between 1948 and 1954. The project racked up enormous sales which became astronomical as soon as paper rationing was lifted and the apparently infinite demand for the books could be fully satisfied.[126] Cassell added collections of Churchill's speeches and reprints of his earlier books in uniform bindings which sold in tens of thousands. The initial subscription order from the British book trade alone for the first volume, *The Gathering Storm*, was an unprecedented 90,000 copies. To circumvent paper control, cast *papier-mâché* 'flongs' of the typesetting were air-freighted to Australia, so that supplies could be printed there for distribution in the southern hemisphere. Suddenly Cassell were awash with money.

And what did they do with it? The answer is, sadly and chasteningly, they did not invest it in new books or new publishing ventures. Instead they built a rather vainglorious office block, designed by John Osborne in the brutalist style of modernism at 35 Red Lion Square. Churchill laid the

125 Churchill famously remarked in 1946 that he was going to be treated kindly by history, since he intended to write it. He did not, of course, anticipate doing it quite so soon.

126 Virtually every home had at least a copy of the first volume, *The Gathering Storm*. I can recall my grandfather, an ex-miner and no friend of Churchill cherishing his copy with its black spine label, red cloth binding with Churchill's signature brassed in gold on the front. I believe it was the first real hardback book I ever saw.

foundation stone in 1956 and the building opened a year later. They did have some successes with other publishing, including Nicholas Monsaratt's *The Cruel Sea* in 1950, which did eventually sell over a million copies, but this was not typical of a list that becoming old-fashioned, unadventurous and moribund.

On Churchill's profits alone, Cassell could have bought any other British publisher and invested in its development. Indeed, they could have afforded a string of them. That they chose instead to build an anonymous, eight-storey concrete monstrosity speaks volumes for the lack of vision of the Cassell directors. Even as they celebrated their 110th anniversary in 1958, the cracks in their strategy were beginning to show. In the end they bought only the small nursing and veterinary publisher Baillière, Tindall and Cox in 1964, and by that time they were themselves being eyed up as potential acquisition material. In the same year Newman Flower died.

Desmond is frank in his autobiography *Fellows in Foolscap* (1991) about his own increasing alcoholism and the pressures of trying to keep his firm afloat. His judgment became more and more erratic, and he agreed in 1968 to publish *The Story of PQ17* by David Irving, later to gain notoriety as a Holocaust denier. This was an account of the Murmansk convoys in the Second World War which libelled one of the commanders of the ships. He won his case and large damages were awarded against Cassell. This was the final straw – the company was in play and open to purchase. Desmond himself graphically describes what happened next:

> ... [A] well-known publisher of central European origin[127] bought all the Cassell shares he could obtain on the market and offered them to the New York firm of Crowell, Collier, Macmillan, saying he thought that Cassell was ripe for a take-over bid. The Americans bought the shares, and if one of their directors was right about the price they paid him, he did very nicely. In due course they made their offer; it was a good one, but none of us were interested ... [but] Bill Angell [Newman Flower's trustee who controlled a large block of shares] pointed out ... [that if he did not accept it he] was guilty in law of betraying [the] trust. I was staggered: we were trapped and there was no way out. So the firm was sold against our will and we became part of a group of publishers ... (Flower, 1991, p.372)

So Cassell passed out of family control and into the unsympathetic hands of an American combine that would eventually become part of Maxwell's

127 This was, of course, Maxwell.

empire. The general book division was eventually closed after making massive losses in 1981. Flower and his colleagues were long retired by this time, and one wonders if they ever regretted their decision to invest in bricks and mortar rather than books.

Change also overtook the literary houses founded in the 1920s and 1930s as their once bright young leaders died or retired and gave way in their turn to new generations with new ideas and new objectives. At Cape, the founder was approaching his seventieth birthday in 1950 and. although he was still fit and energetic, he spent less time on the day-to-day running of the firm. Wren Howard's son, Michael, came into the business and eventually took over his father's role in production and general editorial management (Howard, 1971, part two). The early years of the decade were not good or profitable for Cape, whose aging directors rested too much on past glories. Sales declined and costs increased, deflating profits, while Jonathan relied too much on the advice of readers who were out-of-touch and cautious. As a result, he turned down many titles which might have revived his fortunes, including William Golding's *Lord of the Flies*, which eventually went to Faber. His luck changed in 1952 when the younger brother of an old schoolmate and literary editor of *The Spectator*, Peter Fleming, arrived with the manuscript of his first novel. His name was Ian Fleming and the book was *Casino Royale*, the first of the James Bond spy fantasies.

Jonathan initially dithered since he thought thrillers were beneath his imprint, and Wren Howard thought the cynical, louche Fleming a 'bounder' and his womanizing, hard-bitten and callous hero distasteful. Eventually Cape published the book in 1953, but initially it did not sell particularly well.[128] However, it and its sequels, especially after they were filmed in the 1960s, were in due course to be one of the mainsprings of Cape's revival. Hardback sales achieved hundreds of thousands of copies, and paperback licences and translations amounted to millions. Significantly, Jonathan asserted that he had never read any of the Bond novels and he only corresponded with Fleming when he absolutely had to (Howard, 1971, p.256).

It was not until 1955 that Jonathan was persuaded to appoint a

128 The first print run was 8000, with 4000 for Macmillan in the USA. This was not actually bad for a first novel from an unknown writer, but first editions now sell for thousands of pounds. Other contemporary publishers would probably have printed about half that quantity, and today a new thriller from an unknown author might have a print run of 2000-3000.

sales manager for his firm, and in an inexplicable move he then employed the American Robert Knittel, whose taste was very far from that of the British reading public, as senior editor. Jonathan then suffered the death of his third wife and a stroke in quick succession, and he passed more and more of the decision-making he would never previously have delegated to Knittel. A proposal to merge with the smaller literary house of Sidgwick and Jackson was put on hold.[129] Michael Howard, although a board member and a major shareholder, was not consulted about Knittel's appointment, and he recalls his frustration and anger at Jonathan's high-handed and wayward action:

> [Knittel] was to be paid rather more than double what … I received. I spent the week-end in a turmoil of indignation.
>
> I had nothing against Robert Knittel. Indeed, I knew nothing about him, and it was this that made me angry. The neglect to tell me … showed complete disregard for any feelings I might have … and even though he was my senior and had been in publishing for much longer than I, the terms of the proposal made to him devalued my own role. I was accustomed to the general reticence and lack of information about future plans, but this treatment seemed so cavalier that I felt I should be a great deal better off with some other publisher. I wondered, if Cape rated me so low, what I was really worth: and drove over to Henley to see Rupert Hart-Davis and unburden myself of my bewildered rage. He gave me sympathy, some account of his own tussle with the two recalcitrant old men [i.e. Cape and Michael's own father] and the encouragement to tackle them head on.
>
> Early the following week I stormed at them for an hour or more in Jonathan's flat. (Howard, 1971, p.271)

Michael Howard was eventually persuaded to calm down and stay, but the episode negatively coloured his view of Jonathan and his father's judgement, and their poor understanding of what the post-war market wanted. Knittel was not a good appointment. He knew American fiction and had a taste for translations of European writers, but few of his publications made any money. Winners of the French *Prix Goncourt* might be prestigious, but they did not appeal to the British reading public. Howard notes sourly that one new season's list in the late 1950s included four German translations, three from French, and others from Danish,

129 Sidgwick and Jackson remained independent until they were taken over by Macmillan in 1986.

Spanish and Italian 'and by no means all of them transplanted satisfactorily' (Howard, 1971, p.272). In 1959 more than half the thirty-nine titles announced as new books from Cape were imports from the USA or translations. The character of the list had shifted, and not in a positive direction.

As Jonathan entered his ninth decade in 1959, Howard was inconsolably gloomy in a memo to the chairman:

> One of the most disheartening experiences I've had recently was reading *The Bookseller*'s reports of Christmas in the book shops ... Not a single Cape title was mentioned ... Nor were our books noticeable in any of the book-sellers Christmas catalogues I've seen. And when I have asked them, I've been told why.
>
> ... This year we have had a lot of very saleable books [*not* what he was saying in private] and we ought to have sold a lot more of them than we did. It's no good having Robert [Knittel] to find merchandise if we can't shift it, particularly because so many of the books he finds demand powerful salesmanship; the potential is there, but they've got to be marketed in the right way: and ours isn't it. (Howard, 1971, pp.273-4)

Whether Howard's coded messages were causing Jonathan to have second thoughts is not clear, but he abruptly turned against Knittel, refusing to sell him shares in the firm (which he had apparently promised) although he procrastinated in the actual messy business of sacking him. Within a few weeks, in February 1960, Jonathan Cape was dead, apparently after suffering another stroke.

Michael Joseph, as we have seen, suspected rather earlier than most that his style of publishing was out of joint in the new conditions of the post-war world. Nevertheless, he and his energetic editorial director Robert Lusty were still open to new ideas, and one of the best was the creation of the *Mermaid Paperbacks* in 1952. At that period literary houses such as Joseph published their books in hardback only, licensing the rights after a decent period to paperback houses, predominantly Penguin, but during the 1950s also to a whole range of new 'paperbackers' such as Pan, Corgi and Fontana.[130] Apart from the latter (which was an imprint of Collins),

130 The rise of the mass market paperback houses, led by Pan, is considered later in this chapter. The rationale for the strict segregation between hardback houses publishing original books and paperback houses who largely published only reprints (although Penguin originated many of its own books by direct commissioning from almost its beginning) was that their markets were fundamentally different, and were implicitly

it was unheard-of for 'serious' publishers to issue their own paperbacks. As we shall see, it was an exact reversal of this structure and the creation of the 'vertical publisher' that was to transform and rescue literary publishing two decades later.

In principle the 'Mermaids' were innovative and an attractive idea commercially. They were reprints of successful novels, such as the *Hornblower* stories of C.S. Forester, published a few months after hardback release in paperback size but on better paper than the 'mechanical' wood-pulp material used for most paperbacks and bound in limp-cases with rounded spines. Their bindings were sewn and glued into endpapers rather than the cheap but prone-to-breaking 'perfect' binding used on standard paperbacks.[131] These were thus handsome and affordable alternatives to paperbacks, with their laminated cases, blue, black and yellow cover designs and stylish mermaid colophon giving them a distinguished look. They sold for four shillings and sixpence or five shillings

—

class-divided. Hardbacks were bought by the better-off middle classes (and libraries, both public and circulating), while paperbacks were bought by the poorer classes, including the 'temporarily poor' groups of students, artists and bohemians. There was somehow an unspoken but real sense that between the two groups there was a significant difference in taste and appreciation of quality. This crude and snobbish segmentation was never even partially true; it was anathema to Lane, who had triumphantly demonstrated that good literature for the masses at sixpence was better business than fashionable novelettes for the carriage trade at six shillings. Nevertheless, the myth that hardback publishing was somehow 'better' than paperbacking, and that the two approaches were so different in editorial decision-making and marketing that they should be rigorously separated, persisted long after all the evidence showed it to be nonsense. One even finds echoes of this pernicious attitude among some more *soigné* book people today, seventy-five years after Lane conclusively demonstrated its fallacy.

131 'Perfect' binding is not named for its quality but for its (American) inventor, a Mr Perfect. Adapted for long print runs, it involves the ends of the book sections being sliced off, and the resulting loose pages then being glued into a card case. The glue dries out over time, whereupon loose pages fall out and the spines tend to crack as the book is read. It was an early example of planned obsolescence. Since most paperbacks are also printed on high-acid wood pulp paper, which yellows and becomes brittle on exposure to the atmosphere, they tend to have a considerably shorter life than hardbacks printed on alkaline papers. In recent years, technical improvements such as better quality glues and 'slot' binding have made paperback quality better, and in general better paper is now used, in part to meet environmental requirements. Some have observed that production standards of hardbacks have in their turn declined, with unsewn bindings and poorer quality paper than hitherto.

each, a considerable saving on the standard six shillings or seven and sixpence 'cheap edition' hardbacks.

The 'Mermaids' deserved to fare better than they did. They were constrained by being confined to re-issues from Joseph's own list, but they were driven off the market by Collins's launch of the 'Fontana' series of paperbacks in 1954, which undercut the 'Mermaids' in price by up to half. Since Collins owned their own print-works, they could produce books that looked, superficially at least, as good as 'Mermaids', and much more cheaply.[132] Joseph suspended the series in 1955.

By this time, Joseph had decided that the time had come to cash in on his business. His wife had died and he had married his secretary, Anthea Hodson, later to become a notable editor in his imprint of popular authors such as Dick Francis and James Herriott. Joseph had no children, but he had an abiding love of cats, so he decided the best thing to do was to sell up and enjoy the fruits of his labours. As he noted at the time, he felt unsure that his particular type of publishing flair and sensibility had any longer a place compared to other publishers:

> The size of the list is an important consideration. We try to make our profit out of a relatively small number of titles. Fifty new books a year is about as many as we care to publish. One advantage of publishing for comparatively few authors is that we can, and I think we do, successfully establish the friendliest personal relations with our authors …
>
> We do NOT go in for big speculative books such a political memoirs, which require huge advances. To my mind such books are a gamble and do not add to a firm's literary reputation.
>
> We do not believe in publishing by committee. Decisions are often made within a couple of days and all the leading literary agents know that they can count on an immediate reading of anything important. Although I am always willing to, and often do read MSS at short notice, we have a pretty good panel of experienced readers …
>
> To sum up, our policy is to publish books of general interest and of literary quality, to keep the size of our list within manageable limits: and to publish as economically as possible. We keep down for instance, the cost of our press advertising: …

132 Fontana paperbacks had laminated card covers and were printed on rather better paper than, say, Pan Books, but they were still perfect-bound and liable to fall apart after one reading.

> I do not claim that there is no room for improvement. The editorial side of the business will undoubtedly need reinforcement to provide for the years ahead. I have some tentative plans in mind and shall be glad to outline them, at a convenient time (letter to Graham Smith, undated but 1954, quoted in *At the Sign of the Mermaid*, 1986, pp.29-30)

Unfortunately Joseph did not share what was in his mind with Lusty and he announced without consultation, a few weeks after writing the above, that he had agreed to sell his company to Sir John Ellerman of Illustrated Newspapers, although he would remain in day-to-day charge. Lusty had felt for some time that Joseph had become 'distant', but he had been convinced that, with his able deputy Charles Pick (who would later run Heinemann), he was operating the business successfully within Joseph's precepts. His abrupt abandonment came as a nasty shock, and he felt abused and betrayed. The last straw came when he was informed by rumour rather than direct communication that a literary gadfly named Derek Verschoyle was to join the company to add editorial spice.

Verschoyle was a snob and a fantasist who had disastrously run an eponymous publishing company that had collapsed. He wrote light books about social history (Lusty acidly remarks that his best-known work was entitled *Famous Balls*). Lusty was a gifted if irascible editor[133] who knew his own worth, and he found being subordinate to a *poseur* such as Verschoyle intolerable. He and Joseph rowed furiously, and Lusty even produced his original letter of appointment of 1935 to prove that he was in charge of editorial matters. In the event Verschoyle suddenly departed and was summed up later by Lusty as 'a sad man ... [whom] success eluded ... all along the line and continued to do so until he died.' (Lusty, 1975, p.165)[134]

Lusty and Joseph uneasily patched things up, but although the sale had made both wealthy, Lusty found his trust in his mentor had evaporated. Joseph was spending much more time with his cats and the racehorses

133 In his later years, his splenetic if witty broadsides on the malfunctions of the book trade, aimed from his retirement fastness of the Old Mill at Blockley in the Cotswolds, would enliven the correspondence columns of *The Bookseller*.

134 Lewis (2008) gives a contemporary assessment of Verschoyle which pulls no punches (pp.16-26). He was clearly a pathological inadequate with a deep and thoroughly erroneous over-estimate of his own ability. Verschoyle continued in a series of vaguely literary jobs, including editing a magazine for vegetable enthusiasts and running a bookshop in East Anglia until his early death in 1973 at the age of 62.

that he could now afford, advised by his author and champion jockey Dick Francis. His appearances in the office were confined to monitoring the petty rules and procedures that he insisted the new owners wanted. The man who did not publish by committee now delighted in demanding chits for expenses and other 'childish measures' unknown in the days of independence (Lusty, 1975, p.165). To add insult to injury, Lusty received a request from Hutchinson, where he had begun his career, to provide a reference for one Derek Verschoyle who had applied for the job there as the new Chief Executive; he provided a frank and unflattering assessment. Lusty was then asked if he himself would take the job. Normally he would have consulted Joseph, but felt he could not after what had passed between them. He resigned and joined Hutchinson, although he would later rebuild a friendship with Joseph. So a great publishing creative partnership ended in disharmony, as often happens in publishing when two volatile creative egos which originally combined to great effect gradually (or indeed suddenly) generate more heat than light. Joseph was to have a tragically short time to enjoy his new found wealth and leisure. He died in March 1958 at the age of sixty.

Gollancz was still a vigorous and innovative house in the 1950s, with Victor's energy and vision apparently undimmed by age or lack of understanding of the new era. The great Left-Wing radical continued his crusade to change the world, and he turned his attention to the dismantling of empire and the promotion of anti-racist politics. He regularly made trips to the United States to acquire titles, and he made his firm the leader in the new and *avant-garde* genre of science fiction with then unknown but now classic authors, thoroughly appropriate for the age of the Sputnik, such as Kurt Vonnegut, Poul Anderson, Ursula K. Le Guin and Robert A. Heinlein. But there were signs, too, that even he was not always sure in his editorial judgment and that he was not consistent in keeping up with the winds of change.

Although never a Stalinist he was nonetheless uncritical of the Soviet Union, and some of his publishing reflected this up to and beyond the Hungarian uprising of 1956. He became more fixated by control, and although he had brought his daughter Livia and nephew Hilary Rubinstein into the firm as directors – and potentially as his successors – in 1953 and 1952 respectively, he restricted their authority and never delegated enough responsibility to them. Livia stayed and did eventually succeed her father, but Victor treated Rubinstein meanly, despite his commissioning Kingsley Amis and Nadine Gordimer to the imprint.

He eventually left to become a literary agent of distinction.

Victor's reputation as a difficult taskmaster grew worse. Throughout the 1950s there was literally a swinging door in Henrietta Street as a succession of gifted and creative editors came and went with depressing regularity; few lasted more than a year. Victor also fell out with authors, although he kept his inexplicably cordial relationships with those arch-conservatives Ivy Compton-Burnett and Dorothy L. Sayers. More than any other of the pre-war houses Gollancz kept its character in the postwar years, perhaps because it had been ahead of its time when it was set up and also because Victor never lost his fire. He continued to find time for his social causes, and perhaps his greatest legacy is the abolition of the death penalty in Britain, a campaign he set up with Arthur Koestler (with whom he characteristically later quarrelled) which resulted in success in 1965. He was also active in the cause of Arab Palestine (which led him to be criticized in his own Jewish community) and the Campaign for Nuclear Disarmament. For Victor, as he entered his sixties in 1953, his books were never far from a good fight. Such a conviction would continue well into his seventies, until his death from a stroke in 1967.

A number of other houses briefly flourished in the 1950s, mainly set up by refugees from larger publishers. These included Frederick Muller, who had been at Hutchinson, and had built a successful general list before being absorbed by the Australian Consolidated Press. Herbert Jenkins, founded by a novelist in 1912 and once owned by the Royal Society for the Prevention of Cruelty to Animals, had for many years relied almost entirely on its one golden property – the comic novels of P.G. Wodehouse. The author survived accusations of wartime treason (he had broadcast for the Nazis) to become enormously popular in the 1950s. W.H. Allen, a sleepy traditional firm of eighteenth-century origin, was revived in 1940 by an American, Mark Goulden, and it developed a distinctive list of titles on entertainment, building an early interest in what would be termed today 'celebrity memoirs'. Goulden sold out to the American house Doubleday in 1961, only to buy his imprint back a few years later.

MacDonald and Company had been set up just before the war in imitation of Penguin to sell cheap books to Woolworths; they were taken over by Purnells, a printer based near Bristol who wanted a publishing vehicle to sustain their large-scale printing facilities (Goodman, 2004). They identified romantic and historical fiction for the female market as the way to do this and published Kathleen Winsor's *Forever Amber*, the prototypical 'bodice-ripper', in 1945. This led to their acquisition of their most remarkable author, Catherine Cookson, in 1950. Her long series of sagas featuring indomitable heroines overcoming poverty, abandonment, seduction, rape and crime to emerge as wealthy and influential matriarchs remain enormously popular, and are still consistently the most-borrowed titles from public libraries. She ultimately would sell almost 100 million copies of her novels for adults and children.

The company would eventually fall under the sway of Robert Maxwell, but it enjoyed a brilliant decade between 1950 and 1960. Buoyed on Cookson's sales, it acquired a number of famous and serious imprints, including John Lehmann, Max Parrish, Queen Anne Press and the ancient and eminent Sampson, Low, whose list included the lucrative and distinguished reference publisher Jane's Fighting Ships. It also pioneered part-works that would build in to encyclopedias, including the very successful weekly *Knowledge.*

Penguin, of course, entered the 1950s in fine form – transformed from a mere publisher to a fully-fledged cultural institution. As we have seen, Lane astutely combined his artful manipulation of paper rationing, his instinctive feel for branding and market segmentation and the recruitment of the most talented editors, designers, consultants, salesmen and agents to create the best-known publishing house in the world, and possibly of all time. His imprints had proliferated and Penguin had given birth to non-fiction Pelicans, artistic King Penguins, Puffins, created by the brilliant Kaye Webb, for children and the Penguin Classics, the greatest works of world literature available for the price of a packet of cigarettes. Lane employed the most gifted graphic artists and designers, led by the charismatic Jan Tschichold.

Trained in the clean and modern style of the Bauhaus, Tschichold had fled Germany to escape the Nazis and was given the task of creating a unified look for Penguins and their siblings by Lane. Described by Lewis (2005, p.244) as a 'ruthless perfectionist', Tschichold only worked for Penguin for twenty-nine months, in which time he designed over 500 books, driving typesetters and less punctilious graphic artists to distraction in the process with his uncompromising demands. When he left, he had created an unmistakeable image of what a Penguin should look like, inside and out, that was continued by his no less rigorous successor Hans Schmoller and which remains discernible in the look of Penguins today.

And it was another German who was to create the most original and distinctive strand of Penguin Books during the 1950s. In the canteen at Penguin corporate headquarters (now in the former Shell building in the

Strand) there hangs a large collective portrait by the fashionable artist of the 1950s, Rodrigo Moynihan RA (reproduced as the endpapers of this book). It was painted in 1955 and is entitled *After the Conference.* As it happens the group depicted here never actually were all assembled together at one time in one place – Moynihan took individual sittings and patched them all together later. The painting features the key figures in the management, editorial, sales and production hierarchy of Penguin at the height of its power in the 1950s, as well as its distinguished academic advisers. Those portrayed include Allen and Dick Lane, Eunice Frost, E.V. Rieu, Jack Morpurgo (whose son Michael became a noted children's author), Noel Carrington, C.A. Mace, Michael Abercrombie, Gordon Jacob, Alfred Ayer, Max Mallowan (husband of Agatha Christie) and John Lehmann, among several others.[135] Tucked in a corner is a slight, balding bespectacled figure. This is Sir Nikolaus Pevsner, editor and main writer of one of the most remarkable publishing endeavours ever conceived – Penguin's *Buildings of England.* This exhaustive census and description of every public building, church, private house and other construction of architectural merit in the country was organized on a county basis; it eventually ran to almost one hundred volumes, covering Scotland, Wales and Ireland as well.

Pevsner reputedly suggested the idea to Penguin over a cup of tea in Lane's garden towards the close of the Second World War. Without hesitation or consulting his colleagues Lane gave the go-ahead, and for the next fifteen years Pevsner, probably the most distinguished art historian of his generation and a world expert on English art as well as architecture,[136] indefatigably cycled, trained and motored across the country, gaining access to grand manor and tiny cottage. All were recorded with accuracy, affection and occasionally coruscating wit. It was a task of enormous complexity and unbelievable industry, triumphantly delivered. For several generations, no visit to any British city, town or village could be contemplated without a copy of the appropriate Pevsner to hand. It was a publishing feat that only Penguin could have conceived or carried out.[137]

135 Lehmann was a real publishing journeyman. After surviving the Hogarth Press and his own imprint, he edited *New Writing* for Penguin and founded *The London Magazine.* He died in 1987, aged 80, after a long career of literary entrepreneurship.

136 He was also a master of the laconic and quirky book dedication. One of the volumes of the series is dedicated to the manufacturers of ice lollies.

137 Sadly Penguin decided in the early twenty-first century that Pevsner was no longer a

When Penguin 'came of age' in 1956 it marked its twenty-first anniversary with the publication of a commemorative volume. *The Penguin Story* was written by Allen Lane's trusted editorial factotum William ('Bill') Emrys Williams, who had joined the company in its infancy and later became secretary-general of the Arts Council in 1951 and the leading cultural panjandrum of the age following a formative role in the creation of UNESCO, the idealistic cultural agency of the United Nations. This modest-looking paperback of 124 pages, designed by Hans Schmoller, celebrates the remarkable achievement of Penguin. Its cover shows browsers in W.H. Smith's bookshop in Richmond on Thames selecting from an apparently infinite 'face-out' display of Penguins, Pelicans, Puffins and Specials in the characteristic soft focus colour photography of the age. Its contents are a celebration of elegant typography and high quality printing, including plates in the expensive process of collogravure by the Queen's Printer Harrison and Sons.[138]

However, the most remarkable feature of the book is the complete catalogue of Penguin publications which occupies over half of the pagination. This records many thousands of titles spread over thirty-three imprints including classics, music scores, handbooks, selections from Hansard, as well as children's books and titles published in French and Italian. The sweep of coverage in fiction and non-fiction is breathtaking with hardly a subject, an audience or an interest neglected. Williams (1956, p.57) modestly ascribes this to 'a steady and logical process of evolution'. Penguin by 1956 was firmly established as a cultural institution and a national icon, its stature and presence very similar to that of the Reithian BBC which was just about to be challenged by the advent of commercial broadcasting.

Not that Penguin, even at its apogee was without challengers or competitors. The chief of these was Pan Books. Pan grew from a consortium of publishers Collins, Heinemann, Macmillan and Hodder and Stoughton who had set up the Reprint Society in 1939 to issue cheap reprints of their titles in hardback on the book club system. As Penguin's

flagship venture and the series was sold to Yale University Press, where it continues to flourish.

138 Collogravure is a photographically-based process that uses gelatine rather than metal plates (which break up easily and quickly). It produces a wide tonal range in the printed image, reproducing photographic originals more exactly than the more usual 'screened' reproduction. It was more often used for very high quality reproductions of paintings. Harrisons also printed British postage stamps.

success with paperbacks became apparent, this organization metamorphosed into Pan Books in 1944, concentrating solely on paperbacks for the mass market. Pan's editorial and marketing strategy was radically different from Penguin, although it sought – initially at least – a similar market. It concentrated on relatively few titles as opposed to Penguin's diversity and priced its books even more cheaply. It did this by printing in Paris on very low quality wood pulp paper and by cutting as many production corners as it could,[139] even maintaining its own barge on the Seine, the *Laloun*, to transport its books cheaply to port. Pan initially favoured brightly coloured cover artwork in the American pulp thriller style featuring tough guys, curvaceous blondes and fist action, regardless of whether the plot called for such illustration or not. Towards the end of the decade, however, its covers had become powerfully dramatic, imaginative and original with strong and iconic graphic impact, very unlike the refined and occasionally twee design that characterized most book art of the period (Bradley, 2008, pp.142-3).

By the end of the 1950s Pan had definitively positioned itself at the base of the market, and although this strategy was very successful it hardly nibbled at Penguin's sales. Peter Mayer, who would later lead Penguin, recalls that Pan had seized the popular but rather shallow and gung-ho market for action-packed memoirs of the Second World War such as *The Dam Busters*, which Penguin disdained (Bradley, 2008, p.143). Nevertheless, or perhaps consequently, Pan achieved sales of over 8 million books in 1955 from a list of only 150 titles, including the James Bond titles licensed from Cape. Unlike Penguin, it only published titles licensed from other publishers rather than creating 'originals' and its management ethos was sales- rather than editorial-driven, although its energetic publishing policy directed by Ralph Vernon-Hunt was sure in its judgement of public taste. Pan's sales outlets comprised not only bookshops (although it had a minimal presence in up-market retailers such as the royal bookseller Hatchards[140]), but Pan Books were widely stocked and enthusiastically

139 Most Pan books from the 1940s and 1950s are now brown, crumbling and broken. Very few will survive this century. An unfortunate cost-saving decision not to laminate the covers means that the lively and colourful art on them has faded and looks dull, unlike the still bright covers of contemporary American 'pulp' books which were protected by an application of clear plastic film or varnish.

140 Hatchard's renowned managing director Tommy Joy, who would personally select a reading list of suitable books for members of the Royal Family each summer, reputedly tried to keep Pan books out of his famous shop in Piccadilly.

sold by the now virtually vanished retail sector known as CTNs (confectioners, tobacconists, newsagents) – independent stores then thousands strong. Only the female-oriented romances published by Mills and Boon achieved similar penetration in distribution. As the 1950s advanced, Pan was quickly emulated by imitators such as Corgi, Panther and Fontana, but none of these mass-market paperbackers really caused Penguin much concern. By 1960 Penguin bestrode the publishing world like a colossus, providing literature, entertainment, instruction, enlightenment and pleasure to readers of all ages, classes and tastes, throughout the world at very low prices. Lane's dream was realized, and it had made him rich. He was now ready for the finest moment in his career.

7 'From the end of the Chatterley ban to the Beatles' last LP'

British publishing in the 1960s

My deliberate misquotation of Philip Larkin's *Annus Mirabilis* evokes a decade during which British society in cultural, economic, political and ideological terms transformed completely. It is thoroughly appropriate that Larkin used a publishing event to symbolize this since publishing was both a fundamental vehicle and reflector of the changes that characterized 1960s Britain. The processes and factors which brought this about included the end of deference, the altering roles of women, the emergence of teenage culture, Americanization, decolonization and the end of empire and a confident consumerism based on full employment, hedonism and wider availability of leisure and travel. All had, of course, begun during the previous decade, but they all came together right at the beginning of the 1960s. It may be ironic that the catalyst was a rather old-fashioned book inspired by the First World War and written by an author almost thirty years dead, whose life and experience had been shaped by class-based social rigidities that were nearly extinct. Nevertheless the publication of an unexpurgated edition of *Lady Chatterley's Lover* by D.H. Lawrence was to become the emblem and trigger for deep changes with an irrevocable impact.

As Alan Travis remarks, no twentieth-century writer was more pursued and harried by the official guardians of British moral rectitude than Lawrence – with the possible exception of James Joyce, whose toxic triple offences of Irishness, explicitness and flouting of literary and social convention had singled him out as a special target of disapproval (Travis 2000). As we have seen in Chapter 2 with *The Rainbow*, Lawrence had suffered an early brush with censorship, but he had found Methuen as his publisher less than supportive. He was a driven, complex author and artist for whom sex was a purifying and quasi-religious force. He was certainly no pornographer and, as he made clear in his essay *Pornography and Obscenity*, he was in fact rather prudish about crude descriptions of sexual activity, noting 'the insult it offers, invariably, to sex and the human spirit' (quoted in Montgomery Hyde, 1964, p.2 and p.10).

Nevertheless by the time of his death in 1930 Lawrence had become notorious as a writer and painter whose works were outrageous to public decency and which were in their full explicit forms denied a British audience. They might be published without cuts in France or Italy, but if they were imported into Britain they were seized and provided fuel for the 'King's Chimney' – the furnace operated by Customs and Excise to destroy banned publications. No book of his was more earnestly pursued than his final novel *Lady Chatterley's Lover*, written in 1928 and first published in Florence. It concerns the unfulfilled life of Constance Chatterley, married to a crippled and impotent aristocrat, and her exploration of her desires and longings with her husband's gamekeeper. The book is as much about class and the dehumanizing effects of war and industrialism as it is about sex, but inevitably it is its sexual passages, and particularly its use of taboo words, that excited both disapproval and interest. It had long been available in an expurgated edition from Heinemann in a collected edition, but 'complete' editions were officially banned and subject to destruction.

Many modern critics would contend that it is far from being Lawrence's best work, lacking the lyricism and poetry of *The Rainbow* or the vivid characterization of *Women in Love*, but it retains even now the power to shock and move.[141] F.R. Leavis was a Lawrence enthusiast and taught the novel to his Cambridge students with gusto in the 1940s and 1950s, although he would later claim that Lane had done Lawrence a disservice by exciting a prurient interest in the book; he petulantly refused to dedicate a copy of the Penguin edition of his book *The Common Pursuit* for Lane's collection (Lewis, 2005, p.332). Leavis's students in their turn moved on to teaching posts in new universities and colleges and to write for literary journals. After a quarter century of relative neglect since his death, Lawrence was beginning to enjoy a new vogue and popularity.

Penguin had previously published several Lawrence novels and collections and with the thirtieth anniversary of the novelist's death approaching, it seemed a good opportunity for the reissue of the

141 Interestingly in a class discussion in 2008 of the Chatterley case with a group of publishing MA students (only two of whom had previously read the book), the majority found the text 'shocking'.

complete canon. Another factor was the passing of a new Obscene Publications Act in 1959 from a Bill introduced by the young Labour MP Roy Jenkins, later to become a notable Home Secretary and for some the architect of the 'permissive society'. Jenkins was in fact the conduit of the recommendations of a committee on obscenity set up by the Society of Authors; chaired by A.P. Herbert; its only publisher members were Billy Collins and Rupert Hart-Davis. The Publishers' Association had otherwise declined to become involved with the issue (Bonham Carter, 1984, p.112).

The Act clarified the law on obscenity, which had previously been a common-law offence and muddled in its definition, and the powers it gave law enforcers, many of whom – police, watch committees and magistrates – allowed their personal views and predelictions to decide what was obscene and could be banned without reference to due process. Many clearly exceeded and abused their powers, and many thousands of allegedly obscene publications were seized and destroyed without compensation for authors and publishers throughout the 1950s. One of the victims of the old regime had been the postcard artist Donald McGill, whose cheerfully vulgar but hardly obscene drawings were regularly suppressed and prosecuted.[142] The test of an obscene article was now simply one that would 'deprave and corrupt', but a new defence of 'public good' was admitted if the publication could be shown to have artistic, scientific or literary merit.

The received version of the legend of the Chatterley affair suggests that Allen Lane wanted to test the new law, and by so doing strike a shattering blow for literary freedom and the right to publish without State interference. Lewis casts a little cold water on this heroic interpretation (Lewis, 2005, pp.313-16). When the Penguin directors discussed the proposal to issue a complete edition of the book during 1959, the only objection to it was raised by C.M. Woodhouse, the rather blimpish Conservative MP

142 Born in 1875 and dying in 1962, McGill had been drawing 'vulgar' or 'saucy' postcards since 1904, mainly for sale at seaside resorts. Although they were often banned by local watch committees at places such as Blackpool or Worthing during the 1930s, his cheerful cartoons were tremendously popular. But the reactionary attitudes of successive Conservative Home Secretaries saw McGill subjected to more and more official persecution. This culminated in his trial for obscenity at Lincoln in 1954 which found him guilty and imposed a fine. He was later invited to give evidence to the parliamentary Select Committee examining the need for a new obscenity law, and his conviction is widely seen as one of the main stimuli for reform (see Buckland, 1984).

whom Lane had employed part-time as editorial and sales adviser, despite his total lack of publishing knowledge. Since Woodhouse's stock was rapidly in decline with Lane, who was keenly regretting his decision to hire him, there is a suggestion that Lane only agreed to publish Lawrence's novel to spite him. Certainly at a later editorial meeting when the editor John Curtis wondered which version of the book they would publish Lane seemed bemused that there was more than one, and did not seem to know that the main issue with the text was the use of taboo words (Lewis, 2005, p.315). Later he candidly admitted that he did not see himself 'in the role of a crusader', but merely wished 'to chuck a jemmy in the works'.

Crusader or not, and by no means the only contrarian publisher to seek to test the mettle of the censors,[143] once Lane realized what the consequences of publishing might be he committed himself heart and soul to the objective. He was not unaware that success would bring enormous commercial gains, but although hindsight makes a victory look inevitable it was by no means certain when Lane decided to proceed. Effectively he bet his house on the changing taste of the time. It was both brave and foolhardy, but the old mischievous spirit of *The Whispering Gallery* was afoot and Lane did love a cause – although he would have certainly preferred not to have to go to prison for it.

In January 1960, the Penguin directors authorized a contract for the book, after having ascertained from Alewyn Birch[144] (the baby-faced and equally mischievous sales director of Heinemann, who held the rights) that they did not plan to issue an unexpurgated hardback edition themselves, and they paid the Lawrence estate an advance of £1000. Penguin envisaged a print-run of 200,000 basing their estimate on their previous sales of Lawrence's novels. Plans were made to publish in August 1960 at a price of three shillings and sixpence. One of the few printers who had the capacity to print such a quantity, Hazell, Watson and Viney of Aylesbury, were awarded the manufacturing contract. However, one of their compositors complained that he had been forced to set obscene

143 Two years previously, George Weidenfeld had braved the wrath of the Director of Public Prosecutions by publishing Nabokov's *Lolita*, and Fred Warburg had faced a jury trial over Stanley Kauffmann's *The Philanderer* in 1954.

144 Birch, for whom the term 'ebullient' seemed to have been coined claimed to be 'half Irish, half Dutch and half Italian'(!) (St John, 1990, p.315) and was one of the great characters of mid-century publishing. When I knew him, later in his life, he had jumped the divide to become a bookseller and was an inexhaustible fund of entertaining and scurrilous anecdote, some of which I have shamelessly borrowed in this book.

words for the book and Hazells – mindful that the law held the author, publisher and printer jointly responsible if obscenity was proved – refused to proceed. Rescue came from an unlikely quarter as the venerable and seemingly staid publisher of shorthand manuals and ready-reckoners, Sir Isaac Pitman and Company, on the equally unlikely recommendation of the Conservative Home Secretary, R.A. Butler, offered to print the book through their subsidiary Western Printing Services. In contrast to Hazell, their manager Anthony Rowe was prepared to face possible prosecution and imprisonment in producing the book.[145]

Lane's buccaneering instincts now took over. He ensured the forthcoming book was widely advertised and through his contacts in politics, newspapers and broadcasting worked both the public and the would-be guardians of public morals into an anticipatory lather. The Conservative Attorney-General, Sir Reginald Manningham-Buller, known unkindly but accurately as 'Bullying Manner', warned that the book was likely to be prosecuted.[146] As an unexpurgated edition[147] had already been published in the United States a few months earlier, a few clandestine copies had begun to circulate in Britain, although most were seized and destroyed by Customs. An advance copy of the Penguin edition mysteriously appeared in a branch of W.H. Smith in Peterborough (even though the prim chain bookseller had refused to subscribe the title generally) and was bought by a conveniently browsing police officer who passed it to his Chief Constable, who in turn sent it to the Director of Public Prosecutions, requesting that action be taken against the book. Legend has it that Lane himself had helpfully arranged the planting of the book on Smith's shelves and alerted the Peterborough police to look for it there.

The book was scheduled to be published on 25 August and almost all of the 200,000 copies had been subscribed to the book trade, W.H. Smith's prudery notwithstanding. On 16 August, two detectives visited Penguin's High Holborn office by appointment and were met by Sir William ('Bill')

145 Rowe, an elegant and self-effacing figure, later founded his own printing firm in 1983. He was a notable innovator in book manufacture, pioneering the use of paper printing plates for short-run works and digital systems for print-on-demand.
146 His daughter, Eliza, would later become chief of MI5.
147 Or more correctly several editions, since the copyright status of the book was unclear in the United States and following a court case brought by the United States Postal Service, which declared the book an article that could be legitimately sent by mail, editions were rushed out by the American paperback houses, Pocket Books, Dell, Pyramid and New American Library at the end of 1959 (see Lewis, 2005, pp.319-20).

Emrys Williams, the senior director available and also at the time Secretary-General of the Arts Council, on behalf of the Penguin board. With superb nonchalance, Lane was not there but on holiday in Spain (Hare, 1995, pp.240-1). Williams handed over twelve copies of the as-yet unpublished edition to Detective Inspector Monahan, who remarked that he would be in touch.[148]

Events now moved quickly. Publication of the book was suspended and the already distributed stock was recalled. Lane was brought back from his holiday by telegram on 16 October. The following day a summons was served naming Lane and fellow director Hans Schmoller as defendants representing the board of Penguin. The charge was that in contravention of Section 2 of the Obscene Publications Act 1959 Penguin Books had knowingly published an obscene article; if found guilty Lane, Schmoller and other Penguin directors, as well as the printers, would be liable for substantial fines and terms of imprisonment. Section 2 allowed for the defendants to elect for trial by jury, which they did, in retrospect an extremely wise decision. The action *Regina v. Penguin Books Ltd* was set down for trial at Court 1 of the Central Criminal Court of the Old Bailey in London on 20 October 1960. The stage was set for one of the most dramatic and significant criminal trials in publishing history (Rolph, 1961, 2005).

The legend, not least as retailed by Lane and the chronicler of the trial 'C.H.Rolph',[149] is that Penguin, representing the revolutionary forces of change and the progressive values of a new generation, were bound to win, especially since the prosecution was inept and hidebound into the dead values of Victorian morality and class bias. As Hare observes, however, 'right up to the moment the jury returned their verdict, [there was] a very real possibility that Penguin would lose the case' (Hare, 2005, pp.241-2). Penguin's solicitor Michael Rubinstein was not over-optimistic, and he quickly attempted to assemble a cast of expert witnesses to testify on Penguin's behalf, using Bill Williams' connections in the arts world. Among those who were willing to speak included the great and good of Literature, such as E.M. Forster and J.B. Priestley,

148 Williams later got cold feet about his role and worried about his legal position as the person who had 'published' the potential offending obscene article, especially with his considerable official role as an arts mandarin. He telephoned Monahan and asked if the official record could show that another Penguin director, Hans Schmoller, had handed the books over, which was duly agreed (Hare, 1995, p.241).

149 The pseudonym of literary journalist C.R. Hewitt.

although others like Laurence Durrell, Robert Graves and Graham Greene were reluctant and Evelyn Waugh, predictably, was downright hostile. Some bizarre potential witnesses were canvassed such as Godfrey Winn, a columnist renowned for his optimistic effusions in women's magazines, and the children's writer Enid Blyton who wrote a cheery but rather bemused reply to the invitation:

> I cannot IMAGINE why Penguin Books Ltd have put my name on their *Lady Chatterley's Lover* list … Don't you think there is something slightly comic about E.B. solemnly declaring that *L.C. Lover* is a fit and proper book for everyone's reading?
>
> I'd love to help Penguins Ltd – they are doing a fine job with their publications – but I don't see how I can. For one thing I haven't read the book – and for another thing my husband said NO at once. The thought of me standing up in Court solemnly advocating a book 'like that' (his words, not mine – I feel he must have read the book!) made his hair stand on end. I'm awfully sorry – but I don't see that I can go against him. I feel impelled to read the book now of course (what MARVELLOUS publicity it is having, and how pleased Penguins must be!) though a woman author (for adults) once told me it was dull and badly written. (Quoted in Hare, 2005, pp.243-4.)

Publishers eventually rallied in support, although Victor Gollancz was ambivalent about testing the law with 'a pretty bad novel, and a pretty badly written one too', despite admitting that he had enjoyed the sex scenes. Geoffrey Faber, T.S. Eliot, Rupert Hart-Davis, Desmond Flower, John Lehmann and even Stanley Unwin, who had, after all, experience of being pursued for obscenity, all offered to appear in Penguin's support. However, the star performer, as we shall see, was to be Richard Hoggart, then an obscure English lecturer at Leicester University.

The trial opened under Mr Justice Byrne, a Roman Catholic of strong moral principle[150] and felt to be no friend of modern sensibility, with a jury of nine men and three women. The defence was conducted by barrister Gerald Gardiner, assisted by Jeremy Hutchinson and Richard du Cann. The prosecution was led by Mervyn Griffith-Jones, an experienced advocate with a fearsome reputation who had successfully pursued obscene books in the past. Although he is often portrayed as a dry,

150 Bizarrely Byrne's wife sat alongside him on the bench, radiating disapproval as each offending passage was read out.

unemotional and out-of-touch relic of a former age, he evidently possessed a mordant wit. Asked why he wished to take the case, he replied, 'I put my feet up on the desk and start reading. If I get an erection, we prosecute' (quoted in Lewis, 2005, p.327). Lane and Schmoller were allowed to sit in the well of the court rather than the dock.

The opening exchanges were bland and courteous. Griffith-Jones carefully explained the provisions of the new Act and advised the jury that if they found the book capable of depraving and corrupting – which he defined as 'induc[ing] lustful thoughts' – but of redeeming artistic merit, they must acquit. He summarized the plot, enumerating the number of times forbidden words were used, and made his famous remark 'Is this a book you would have lying around your house? Is this a book you would even like your wife or servants to read?' (Rolph, 2005, p.4). Despite its later notoriety, this observation passed almost unnoticed by observers in the court, except by the sharp-eared Gardiner. In the court reporting much more emphasis was placed on Griffith-Jones's shocked assertion that Penguin would be making the book available to a class of persons who only had three shillings and sixpence to spend. Gardiner countered by first agreeing with Griffith-Jones's description of the book, but by eulogizing Penguin and 'a man called Lane' who wanted cheap books for 'ordinary people'. He cleverly implied that it was wealth alone that determined who could read the book with impunity while those 'ordinary people' (looking directly at the jury as he spoke) were denied because they could not afford to buy it. Penguin were on their side in their mission to democratize literature.

The jury were then sent away for three days to read the book in the chilly and uncomfortable setting of an Old Bailey jury room while Byrne heard another case.[151] Griffith-Jones called only one witness, Inspector Monahan, who simply confirmed that he had received the dozen copies the jury had read from Penguin and nothing more. The prosecutor was content that the good sense of the jury would deliver his desired verdict. Gardiner proceeded to call over thirty expert witnesses, although some such as Rebecca West proved tongue-tied and discomfited by the sarcastic questioning of Griffith-Jones and the sometimes heavy-handed interruptions of Judge Byrne. Others were incoherent or inaudible, and Kingsley Amis was called but failed to appear. Rubinstein, without a trace

151 An otherwise rather good BBC dramatisation of the trial in 2000 imagined that a woman and man on the jury, inflamed by the writing, conducted a tempestuous affair during this interlude. This seems unlikely given the Spartan conditions.

of obvious irony, later wrote to him that his failure to testify had probably helped their case.[152] The case was not going well for Penguin and when the Bishop of Woolwich answered a rather leading question from Gardiner with the assertion that this was a book that all Christians should read, it looked lost. Lane showed no emotion, but was perhaps recalling the way the mood of the court had swung over *The Whispering Gallery*.

In the event it was Richard Hoggart's testimony that saved the day. The defence had been uncertain about calling a young unknown provincial academic to speak for the book, but his earnest and down to earth style swung the jurors decisively in favour of the book. He was helped by Griffith-Jones's disastrous attempts to patronize him and ridicule his background. Hoggart responded to this and to some rather hostile comments from the judge with impressive dignity and clarity, showing himself in Rolph's words to be a 'self-composed, determined and unshakeable witness' (Rolph, 2005, p.22). The jury clearly agreed with Hoggart's judgement that the book was moral, even 'puritanical', despite the clear lead from the prosecution (and the judge) that this was nonsense. Lane for his own part seemed less convinced and he gave an unimpressive performance in the witness box, as did the other publishers like Stanley Unwin. The latter had prepared a detailed testimony, but was ignominiously dismissed by Griffith-Jones with a peremptory 'no questions'.

In his closing address, Gardiner chose to be concise and to the point, arguing Penguin's social mission against literary elitism was exemplified by this act of publication: 'the whole attitude is one that Penguin Books was formed to fight against, which they have always fought against, and which they will go on fighting against.' He mischievously hoped that he would not offend if he remarked that 'a certain number of people nowadays ... don't *have* servants.' He invited the jury with confidence to judge the case on the basis of Penguin's reputation.

Griffith-Jones, by contrast, chose to be florid, orotund and verbose: his closing speech was almost twice as long as Gardiner's. He harped on standards and ridiculed the quality of the experts, but did not return to his initial theme of cheap editions nor mention wives or servants. Too late, he appealed to the jury as ordinary men and women to whom the book must 'lower the general standards of thought, conduct and decency'.

152 He quickly added, 'the jury may very well have tended to be bored by the prolongation of the evidence' (Hare, 2005, p.249).

The judge summed up fairly, but indicated clearly that he thought the jury should convict. But they did not. After a short retiral, they returned a verdict of 'Not Guilty'. Gardiner requested an order of £13,000 costs for Penguin, but Mr Justice Byrne, with a trace of a smile and using the only weapon at his disposal, refused. That evening, Lane hosted a victory party and basked in the glory and congratulations of his colleagues, authors and the apostles of social change. Penguin was the harbinger of a new age of permissiveness, freedom and, for some, licence and decline.

Actually, it is easy to claim too much for the Chatterley trial. There was already unease with the 1959 Act and it was swiftly replaced by a new law in 1964, which created a new offence of 'having an obscene article for publication for gain'. Widely seen as a backlash to the Penguin judgement, this made booksellers liable as well as publishers (Bonham Carter, 1984, p.114). Under this regime, Penguin would conceivably have been found guilty, and it was the acquittal of *Last Exit to Brooklyn* in 1967, published by John Calder and Marion Boyars that definitively broke the stranglehold of official censorship, at least as far as sexual content was concerned.[153] It was this case that also led to the end of theatrical censorship by the archaic system of 'Aunt Edna' with play scripts being vetted by the Lord Chamberlain. The State lost all taste for official pursuit of obscenity although the occasional private prosecution continued, such as Mrs Mary Whitehouse's action against gay poet James Kirkup in 1997.[154]

Nevertheless, even if the trial did not immediately transform Britain, it certainly changed Penguin. Despite the outrage of the Beaverbrook Press, particularly the *Daily Express*, the ordinary public, some rather shamefacedly, flocked to buy the newly liberated book guided by posters simply saying 'Now YOU can read it.' The 200,000 copy print-run disappeared almost overnight and a further printing of 300,000, some ironically printed by Hazells, was absorbed by Christmas. Eventually over 3 million copies were sold and Lane commissioned an introduction for a new

153 Interestingly, John Calder, a notable defender of publishers' rights and an iconoclastic publishing independent, had little faith in the wisdom of ordinary jurors. He complained that those who tried him had little knowledge or qualifications to judge the value of his publications.

154 Technically, the charge was 'blasphemous libel', since the offending poem imagined a gay relationship between Christ and a Roman centurion. Although the publisher, *Gay News*, was found guilty, it is widely considered that this case positively discredited the laws of obscenity and blasphemy and it is widely-held legal opinion that no future cases under these laws could be successfully brought (see Jones and Benson, 2002).

edition from Hoggart in 1961. This edition (which remains in print) contains the following extraordinary dedication written by Lane himself, leaving no doubt about his personal view of the verdict:

> PUBLISHER'S DEDICATION
>
> For having published this book, Penguin Books were prosecuted under the Obscene Publications Act, 1959, at the Old Bailey in London from 20 October to 2 November 1960. This edition is therefore dedicated to the twelve jurors, three women and nine men, who returned a verdict of 'Not Guilty' and thus made D.H. Lawrence's last novel available for the first time to the public in the United Kingdom. (Lawrence, 1961, p.xvii)

Rolph's account of the trial was rushed out and became a bestseller in its own right. Prior to its general publication, Lane had a special hardbound edition made of it as his personal Christmas book which he signed and numbered himself to send to 2000 friends and associates, not all of whom appreciated the gift.[155] Triumphalism aside, the successful outcome enormously increased Penguin's turnover and profits and indelibly linked them in the public mind with progressive causes. Lane used some of the income to refurbish his Spanish villa which he renamed 'El Fénix' in Lawrence's honour.[156] Penguin's pre-tax profits had tripled and were just a point short of 20 per cent of turnover, a unheard-of return from book publishing. As so often, it was at this peak moment of triumph that events began to unravel and Lane embarked on a course of action that would eventually lead to personal strife and corporate mayhem.

The Penguin directors had previously discussed turning the company public and Lane chose the post-coital afterglow of the Chatterley verdict as the right moment to do so. The City brokers were enthusiastic, referring to the newly available shares as 'Chatterleys', and it looked as if the issue would be many times over-subscribed. Because many of his old colleagues who had been with the company from the start were due to retire, Lane could easily convince them about going public as the shares would usefully enhance their pensions. However, he found his brother Dick less tractable. Allen wanted to retain overall control in the firm, but

155 Stanley Unwin complained that the poor quality of the paper made the drawing of him by Paul Hogarth 'unrecognizable' (Lewis, 2005, p.332).

156 The Phoenix device was Lawrence's chosen emblem and was used on the cover of the 1960 edition.

knew that the share issue would make him a millionaire if he sold a minority holding into the prevailing bull market. To achieve both he needed to buy Dick's shares to add to his own, but he rather meanly and inexplicably only made him a derisory offer for his holding. To add insult to injury, he also asked Dick to resign his board seat and relinquish his management of Penguin Australia. Dick, hurt and rather resentful, reminded his brother that it was he who had provided the initial capital in 1935 and thus deserved better. Exchanges between the siblings became increasingly acrimonious and bitter, especially after Allen eventually and reluctantly offered Dick only between eight and nine shillings per share – about one-third less than independent brokers were anticipating in press reports.

Allen eventually acquired Dick's shareholding, but relations between the brothers were irretrievably soured and the two afterwards remained distant if not estranged. The public share issue was made in April 1961, with the price set at twelve shillings, which valued the company at £1,350,000. The issue was oversubscribed 150 times and those outside investors who received an allocation were limited to 200 shares each. Lane and family interests retained 70 per cent of the company, and by the close of business of the first day's trading the shares were 44 per cent up on the issue price. Allen, with a personal holding of 51 per cent, was at last a millionaire (de Bellaigue, 2004, p.31).

If Allen does not emerge with much credit from this episode, he behaved even worse in his relations with staff and associates and his vision for the future of the company. He had always been autocratic and with a perverse streak, but it is almost as if the Chatterley victory had convinced him of his own infallibility and his unchallengeable right to do as he pleased. He indicated his intentions early by sacking Rubinstein, the hard-working and dedicated solicitor who had made no small contribution to the Chatterley success and whose firm had represented Penguin since 1935, replacing him with a commercial lawyer from a City firm. Eunice Frost, Lane's loyal secretary and lieutenant, was frozen out, although Lewis suggests that her diminishing role may have been because of his concern for her health. Others, such as Alan Glover, were treated with less consideration (Lewis 2005, p.305). Like his Uncle John before him, Lane had become obsessed by his legacy; even before the Chatterley case he had began searching for a suitable heir to inherit his increasingly grandiose vision.

His first choice was Tom Maschler, a pushy and ambitious young editor who had moved swiftly and without much trace through jobs with André Deutsch and MacGibbon and Kee to join Penguin in 1958. In his rather disingenuous and self-regarding memoir Maschler recalls visits to Lane's country home and implies that he was being groomed for the succession (Maschler, 2005, pp.48-9). But he was impatient and resigned in May 1960 to join Cape because 'I did not find working at Penguin satisfying'. Others at Penguin, such as Paul Scherer, later to run the mass-market paperback house Transworld with distinction, found Maschler difficult. When Lane toyed with the idea of investing his new wealth in acquiring Cape, it was the presence there of his fled prôtegé that scuppered the deal (see Lewis, 2005, pp.338-9). Before he left, Maschler performed one fateful and ultimately very destructive service. He introduced Lane to his friend Tony Godwin as his potential successor.

Godwin was a perplexing, energetic, emotional, exasperating, uninhibited and brilliant character who loved books and authors. He could also be scheming, ill-disciplined, naïve, impetuous, indiscreet, overbearing and wrong-headed, but never dull or predictable. He entered the book trade in 1946 when he took over the rundown shop Better Books in Charing Cross Road, and following his personal predelictions and the mood of the times turned it into London's leading *avant-garde* and fashionable bookseller and a venue for progressive arts events. He also, less glamorously, ran the wholesaler Bumpus. He contributed a chapter on London bookselling (as 'Anthony Godwin', nomenclature to which anyone who knew him never recalls his answering) to Hampden's *The Book World Today* in 1957; it shows an impressive grasp of the business minutiae of bookselling. He was quite critical of publishers' attitudes to bookselling, not least over the perennial issue of discount terms, and, tongue doubtless firmly in cheek, declared that bookselling is the vocation 'for one of my ruminative nature' (Hampden, 1957, p.140). Just over three years later, after a brief meeting with Lane, he replaced Maschler as editor at Penguin, just in time to witness the Chatterley trial from inside the company.[157]

Godwin sensed that following the verdict and the flotation change was in the air and he was to be Lane's chosen agent. His rise was meteoric. Before the end of 1961 he had moved from being fiction editor to editor-in-chief and a seat on the board. He was given *carte*

157 Although he continued to own and manage the shop during all the time he was at Penguin.

blanche over book acquisitions and set about shaking things up fundamentally.

One area that seized his attention was cover design which at Penguin had always been restrained and dignified; using austere typography and bands of solid colour gave Penguin books distinctiveness and unity, while garish illustrations and immodest cover blurbs were left to vulgar paperbackers such as Pan or Corgi. Much to the horror of older retainers like E.V. Rieu, Godwin abandoned the sober legacy of Tschichold and hired the modish Italian graphic artist Germano Facetti as art director. Penguin covers became dramatic, colourful and in the term of the time 'cool'. Artwork was provided by trend-setting new artists such as Quentin Blake or David Gentleman, who was also shaking up the staid Post Office with flamboyant and revolutionary stamp designs encouraged by a radical Postmaster-General called Tony Benn[158] (Gentleman, 2002, pp.110-14). Modernization was long overdue, and Godwin placed Penguin in the *avant-garde* of 'swinging London' in which design was a new and rather unsettling currency. He was, of course, right, but the transition was sudden, un-nerving and expensive.[159]

Godwin's restless and intuitive intelligence soon strayed outside his initial fiction remit. He refashioned Penguin Specials and Pelicans into a visually interesting and cutting-edge non-fiction series that included trend-setting academic authors such as Max Nicholson and R.D. Laing. The timing was just right to capture the hordes of new university students who were crowding the campuses at Sussex, Lancaster, Essex, Norwich and Stirling, set up in the wake of the vertiginous expansion of higher education following the Robbins report of 1963. His most radical idea was to create a hardback imprint within Penguin (eventually to become Allen Lane the Penguin Press) which seemed to cut against all the founding principles of the company. His thinking in many ways anticipated the creation of 'vertical' publishers twenty years later, but at the time hard-

158 Those who knew them both say that there was a remarkable similarity between Benn and Godwin in their ability to incense, inspire, exasperate and irritate. Gentleman provided thirty-two cover designs for the 'New Penguin Shakespeare', using the block colour and wood engraving technique that he had developed on his controversial designs for the Shakespeare Festival stamps of 1964 – the first British issue to portray any person other than a member of the royal family.
159 Some older authors hated their new covers. Graham Greene was so upset that he asked Heinemann to take his rights away from Penguin, forcing Lane to fly out to Antibes to pacify the great man (Lewis, 2005, p.351).

back publishers and paperback publishers were rigorously segregated species, dependent on each other but never to cohabit. Set up in 1965, perhaps symbolically in the old offices of John Lane in Vigo Street, the list included authors such as Hunter S. Thompson, Al Alvarez and Studs Terkel. It was both spiritually and physically a long way from Penguin's workaday office and warehouse at Harmondsworth on the edge of Heathrow Airport, but uncannily in tune with the taste of Carnaby Street and the Summer of Love. Sadly the denizens of 'swinging London' bought few books and the venture was not a financial success, although it was enormously culturally influential.

Godwin as a bookseller knew the value of marketing and merchandizing, and he appointed Penguin's first sales and marketing director, Richard Holme, from Unilever; he was later to be a prominent Liberal politician. Lane found Holme's methods unsettling and his demands for large promotional budgets uncomfortable. Holme fell out with Lane and quickly departed. Lane, who had watched Godwin's energetic transformation of his company, initially with pride then bemused but benign tolerance, now began to feel more and more disenchanted and his feelings moved from irritation to rage and then finally hatred. The look of the books had changed, but so too had the authorship as the imprint moved downmarket to compete directly with Pan by producing thrillers and pot-boilers. Godwin even publicly criticized Lane's founding principle of good literature at cheap prices.

The incident that brought the rift between the two to a head came in 1966 when a young editor appointed by Godwin, Jill Norman (who later created a distinguished cookery list) proposed to publish a collection of cartoons by the French artist Siné, well known for his anti-clerical and lavatorial humour. The selection entitled *Massacre* was actually quite restrained and mainly poked mild fun at monks, nuns and priests. At the editorial meeting at which the book was approved Godwin rather unwisely pointed out that this type of publication would appeal to younger people; those of an older generation, of course, would not understand the jokes. Lane bridled and made his disapproval clear. The decision was put to a vote with Lane and his older colleagues against, Godwin and his younger acolytes for, and the book went ahead to be a lead title for Christmas.

When *Massacre* appeared, Penguin was inundated with outraged complaints from readers and booksellers. Lane confessed himself to respected retailers like Una Dillon and John Heffer to share these views and blamed the book on 'a young and energetic editorial staff ... [to whom] I ... give ... as free a hand as possible' (Lewis, 2005, p.362). Godwin issued an ill-advised press release making clear the book had been the subject of internal disagreement, but was an essential part of Penguin meeting the new sensibilities of the age. The new satirical weekly *Private Eye* – itself a product of 1960s *lèse-majesté* – gleefully mocked a venerable institution vainly trying to be 'with it'. Privately Lane seethed, both at the insubordination and the public humiliation. The hero of the Chatterley trial plotted a bizarre and unworthy revenge on his erstwhile heir.

At midnight on a cold December night a hired van containing Lane and a few trusted associates drew up outside the Harmondsworth warehouse. Stealthily, they opened the door, removed the entire stock of the offending Siné[160] and decamped to Lane's nearby farmhouse where the books were reputedly dumped in a silage pit. Godwin never confronted Lane directly about the incident, but confided to friends that it was the end of their productive relationship and any personal affection. His descent was a rapid as his promotion. He was relieved of his fiction editing overnight and his responsibility for art direction was taken away. His health suffered and he began to spend whole days in bed nursing his grievances. Some of his illness may have been psychosomatic, but in February 1967 he nearly died from an asthma attack which hospitalized him. Lane barely hid his contempt and referred to him as 'that shit Godwin'. In turn Godwin thought Lane 'an unspeakable buffoon'.

Events came to a conclusion in April 1967 when Lane took him out to dinner and peremptorily told him he had to leave. Godwin, still unwell, was shaken and upset, but Lane was adamant. Whether by Godwin himself or his sympathetic colleagues the sacking became public, and the Press portrayed it as a reactionary victory over an exciting new talent. An emollient press release did not calm speculation and a group of Godwin-appointed editorial talent, including Charles Clark, who would later run Hutchinson, Jill Norman, Giles Gordon, who became a leading literary agent, and the legendary editor of the children's imprint Puffin, Kaye Webb, wrote an extraordinary letter to *The Times* praising the way 'he [Godwin] extended the range of the list with vision, and we who were his

160 Apart from a few copies left on the picking bench for morning despatch which were overlooked and later mysteriously vanished as well. Returns were destroyed and the book was declared out of print. It is consequently one of the rarest and most sought-after Penguins among collectors and commands a very high price.

editorial colleagues felt at every point his intense concern for quality and purpose'. Perhaps prudently, they added 'we know that these feelings are shared by Sir Allen Lane and his fellow directors'. Godwin himself characteristically spent 17 May as his last day in the office writing friendly letters to authors and saying his farewells. He later that year became Managing Director of Weidenfeld and Nicolson and later moved to the United States, but on the testimony of his ex-wife Fay, the noted photographer, his health never recovered from the shock of leaving Penguin. He died in 1976 at the age of fifty-six.[161]

An assessment of Godwin's contribution to Penguin is problematical. A modern critic such as Rylance (2005) sees him as an essential cultural catalyst, essential to adjust Penguin's mission and output to a reading public with whom its founders had lost touch. Whether he actually saw himself that way, or was simply a quixotic and mercurial careerist seeking to supplant his benefactor (there is plenty of anecdotal evidence that he was not averse to political plotting), as some detractors claim, or simply an idealistic and gifted editor with an instinctive understanding of *Zeitgeist* and a commercial nose for what would work in a new publishing world, as his admirers would contend, must await a full biography to elucidate. My feeling is that he was probably all three. Under his guidance, Penguin's turnover more than doubled to £4.4 million and profits remained in high double-digit percentages, although they had begun to fall towards the end of his tenure as some of his more expensive projects came home to roost (see Table 5 in de Bellaigue, 2004, p.35). His lasting legacy was to convince Lane that Penguin could not continue as before but that a young, uncontrollable, heir-apparent was not the solution to securing the firm's future. During Lane's last years up to his death in 1970 he retrenched, appointing the fearsome publishing accountant Christopher Dolley as Managing Director, regarded by Godwin's appointees as a soulless philistine.[162]

There were still some notable developments such as the success of the textbook list Penguin Education under Charles Clark, but overall there

161 A memorial trust was established in his memory to award grants to young publishers, but it appears to have been inactive since 2005.

162 Dolley, who reputedly only spoke in terms of cash flow and returns, did much to keep Penguin afloat, however, and prevented the worst excesses of editorial enthusiasm. He wanted to close down Allen Lane the Penguin Press, but never succeeded. Interestingly, when Penguin merged with Longmans, he did not survive long, leaving suddenly in 1973 for (in the ominous but oft-used phrase) 'a wider field of business activity'.

was the distinct impression in the later 1960s that Penguin had lost its way and Lane had lost interest. Margins eroded and financial controls were lax. Lane became ill (eventually diagnosed as cancer) and he seemed most interested in disposing of the company rather than ensuring its independence after his death. He considered a sale to the British subsidiary of American publisher McGraw-Hill, and reputedly the ever-predatory Robert Maxwell was preparing a bid. In 1968 the venerable house of Longmans had been sold to the industrial conglomerate S. Pearson and Sons, but the publisher's last remaining family director, Mark Longman, stayed in charge. Just before his death Lane reached an accommodation with Mark for Pearson-Longman to take Penguin over in a deal which valued the company at £8.44 million with much talk of joint ventures and international collaboration, particularly within educational publishing. The new company, Longman-Penguin, with the prospect of great potential growth from Pearson's access to enormous capital assets, did not survive long as Mark himself unexpectedly died in 1972 at the age of fifty-six and Pearson decided to separate the two companies under a holding group. Thereafter, as we will see in the next chapter, their fortunes diverged markedly, and although there was some collaboration and synergy it was nothing of the scale or substance that Lane and Mark Longman had envisaged or hoped for.[163]

I have dwelt on Penguin's vicissitudes during the 1960s at length because they exemplify the kinds of problems with which many publishing houses in the period had to contend. Publishing models created in the 1930s, or even before, were becoming outdated, and structures created by charismatic and skilled but aging entrepreneurs were looking tired in the face of rapid and bewildering social change. This was certainly the case at Collins which had entered the decade as the largest, and arguably most successful, family-owned publisher in Britain. During the 1950s and early 1960s 'Billy', the fifth William Collins to bear that name and head the company, had shown great energy and vision in building up a diverse and extremely profitable publishing list. In fiction, middlebrow writers such as Agatha Christie and Alistair MacLean regularly topped the best-seller lists for Collins, and the late but enormously successful creation of a mass-market paperback list, Fontana, quickly became a major challenger

163 Although there were occasionally surprising links: when in 1979 I argued to an unwilling Longmans personnel manager that an unforthcoming salary benefit was 'what they got at Penguin', my request was granted on the grounds of equity with the sister firm.

to Pan and other mass-market paperback houses, although it had little competitive impact on Penguin.

However, it was in the less glamorous but highly profitable sectors of education, reference, bibles and religious publishing (the latter directed with aplomb by Billy's wife, Priscilla, always known as Pierre) where Collins really made its money, particularly from overseas markets. Billy was knighted in recognition of his contribution to export rather than literary achievement. These sectors were located at the firm's historic base in Glasgow, while literary and trade publishing was concentrated in London. During the 1960s, Collins built a major, state-of-the-art printing facility and offices in the run down east-end slum district of Cathedral Street in Glasgow – a project intended to reinforce the centre of gravity of the company's business as emphatically Scottish.[164] However, this was an uncharacteristically false move from Billy. He misread the changes that were overtaking printing and the costs of modernizing plant. Owning one's own manufacturing equipment, once a great strength allowing flexibility and speed, became a liability.

This structural feature was a contributor to the decline of Scottish publishing generally. Publishers who were also printers were a particular feature of the Scottish book business. Apart from Collins, firms which owned their own print works included Blackie, Nelson, Bartholomew, Pillans and Wilson and several other publishers. Even the tiny Oliver and Boyd owned its own bindery. In England, only Dent (the Aldine Press) and the university presses had their own printing facilities, although some printers, like Wills and Hepworth of Loughborough (who produced the Ladybird series) launched into publishing to make use of idle time on their presses (see McLeery and Finklestein, 2007).

Tensions grew between the metropolitan aesthetes in Collins London office, who saw themselves as intellectually superior, and the printers and preachers of Glasgow (Stevenson, 2007c, pp.323-5). Jeremy Lewis provides an entertaining account of the London office of Collins and the foibles of its staff during the 1960s, which then included the later-to-be prominent journalist and bodice-ripping novelist Jilly Cooper (Lewis, 1995). They clearly saw themselves as having little in common with their Scottish colleagues and felt (erroneously in fact) that they were contributing more

164 The building still stands as part of the University of Strathclyde, appropriately housing a library and bookshop. The district has been gentrified out of all recognition and most of the grimy tenements which surrounded the futuristic (for its time) Collins building have disappeared.

than their fair share to the company's prosperity. The appointment in 1967 of two non-family directors, Ian Chapman and David Nickson, was an attempt to strengthen the company and secure its future. Collins had always been good at succession planning, and this move did succeed in keeping the company together and smoothing over immediate problems (de Bellaigue, 2004, p.139). However, it also led to the final unravelling of the company's independence in the following decade (see Chapters 8 and 9).

Collins's compatriot, Thomas Nelson and Sons, had a very similar profile in both strengths and problems but succumbed earlier. During the first half of the twentieth century, Nelson had been successful in religious, educational, children's and illustrated books, and operated a large and lucrative international business from their Edinburgh base at Parkside Works. They were the first British publisher to establish an American office (in 1854) and by 1960 they also had large and successful operations in Canada, South Africa, Australia, New Zealand and India, as well as, uniquely for a British publisher, a thriving French company. Like Collins there was a distinct sense of the printing tail wagging the publishing dog with Nelson, and when they were bought by the Canadian media conglomerate Thomson in 1960, their publishing model was already looking very outmoded. They survived in Edinburgh until 1968, when Thomson decided to close the print works and remove their publishing from Scotland. Their imprint survives in the United States on popular religious books and in the United Kingdom as Nelson-Thornes.[165]

For some trade publishers, the 1960s were a time of regeneration and renewed energy. This was best exemplified by Cape. When Jonathan died in February 1960, he had still not grappled with the problem of Robert Knittel's idiosyncratic publishing, and despite flirting with selling the company he intended that his shareholding should pass to his son Tim. Tim, however, did not want to take the business over and eventually the chairmanship went to Wren Howard and the direction of the firm came to Wren's son Michael. Michael recognized that speedy and dramatic action was needed to stop the Knittel rot: he probably also harboured some lingering resentment over Knittel's appointment.

165 Stanley Thornes had been an educational representative for Longmans. Recognizing that most books for schools in the 1960s were becoming more and more unsuitable for rapidly changing teaching methods and curricula, he left to set up his own company. It became very successful and Thomson bought it, merging it with Nelson, which by that time was confined to educational publishing. It is now owned by Dutch publisher Wolters Kluwer.

In fact, just before Jonathan's death, Howard had suggested to him that Tom Maschler from Penguin should come to Cape to replace Knittel, but the old man did not live to actually meet Maschler. Howard had no doubts though about Tom's suitability, and as soon as the funeral dust settled he appointed him as literary director with some glee, only later telling Knittel, who promptly resigned. It is quite instructive to compare Howard's and Maschler's differing memoirs of these events, casting as they do unconscious light on both men's motivations and expectations, but there is no doubt that Tom, never short of *amour-propre*, was seen by both as the means to transform the house's fortunes profoundly (Maschler, 2005, Howard, 1971). A new and energetic team was swiftly put in place. A new publicity manager, Tony Colwell from Collins, arrived a few days after Tom, who then promptly departed for New York to acquire new titles (he had little to sell from the Knittel-era list). One of them would be Joseph Heller's *Catch-22*.[166]

When Tom was in New York, events in London very nearly strangled his career with Cape at birth. Ever since Michael Joseph had sold out there had been spasmodic discussions between Wren Howard and the so-called 'Trinity' of remaining Joseph directors, Peter Hebden, Roland Gant and Charles Pick, to join their firm, Cape. There is some evidence that Wren thought they might counterbalance what Michael Howard called Tom's 'confidence and brash directness' (Howard, 1971, p.291). The proposal brokered by Allen Lane – who may have wanted to make mischief since he had been unhappy with Maschler's abrupt departure from Penguin – was to restructure Cape as a co-operative in which the Trinity and the Howards all held shares but none would hold a decisive majority, although in a split vote Michael Howard's decision would prevail. Lane even offered to finance the Trinity's purchase of Cape shares. Norman Collins, the head of Associated Television (ATV), was also to provide finance.[167] There was no discussion of any participation by Maschler in the equity.

When Michael perhaps rather casually revealed these plans to Tom by letter to New York, the latter felt threatened and upset; he promptly telephoned Michael to seek reassurance and to complain. Michael seemed

166 Actually entitled *Catch-18* at the time (Maschler, 2005, p.57).

167 The independent television companies, famously described by Roy Thomson, owner of Scottish Television, as 'a licence to print money' were created in 1955. By the early 1960s they were keen to invest in book publishing on the burgeoning growth of advertising revenue to create what later observers would call 'cross-media alliances'.

surprised that his new employee should be worried, even when Tom suggested that Michael's own position might not be secure under the new arrangement. With some *sang-froid* and perhaps typical arrogance Tom did not return to London immediately but stayed in New York since '[he was] determined to complete the work that [he] had planned ... [being) on to some important books' (Maschler, 2005, p.55).

When he did eventually come back he discovered that details of the plan had been leaked to the Press and demanded that he be included in all future discussions on the firm's future – a remarkably assertive position from a twenty-seven-year-old barely a month in post who owned no shares. The Howards, perhaps regretting their actions, acquiesced, and Maschler did not neglect to tell them that unless they were careful, 'in the event of [him] being pushed out it would not be long before ... [they] were also out' (Maschler, 2005, p.56). Howard and Maschler's accounts of the events differ subtly, but it became clear that the Trinity could not agree to Tom being in editorial control and he would have to leave if the plan was to go ahead.

At an extraordinary final meeting, with Tom present, Peter Hebden announced bluntly 'I am sorry to say this in front of you, Tom, but you must go'. Wren Howard then briskly announced 'that's that', and made it clear he was backing Tom. Faced with energetic youth or proven experience, he had chosen youth. The Trinity departed crestfallen, Hebden back to Michael Joseph, where he became Managing Director until his early death at the age of fifty-three in 1970, Pick to run Heinemann and Gant to Secker and Warburg. The Howards and the Trinity were deeply embarrassed by the affair, and especially by its public conduct, but it secured Tom's position and gave him the power base to take the company forward in the way he wanted. A large proportion of the shares (41.7 per cent) were eventually bought by the television mogul Sidney Bernstein of Granada, Norman Collins's great rival. He became a close ally of Maschler and eventually sold him 'approximately' 10 per cent of the company.[168]

With Tom firmly in charge of editorial matters, although the Howards retained overall management responsibility, Cape's publishing expanded dynamically. Probably more than any other hardback house, it reflected in its content and direction the new concerns and cultural values of the decade. New, taboo-breaking authors such as Edna O'Brien with her witty

168 De Bellaigue says his share was 7 per cent. Given Tom's tendency to occasionally self-aggrandize, I would prefer this figure.

and sexually frank tales, Len Deighton with his complex and demanding spy stories, and John Fowles with his dark and psychologically powerful novels like *The Collector* (1964) and *The French Lieutenant's Woman* (1969) brought both critical and sales successes which pushed the boundaries of popular taste. Perhaps the most iconic book came in 1964 when Tom published *John Lennon in his Own Write*, recognizing that the mercurial lyrical genius of the Beatles was not a mere pop singer created by the commercial music industry, but a serious creative writer. It also sold enormous quantities to fans.

Tom was always both an instinctive editor with good taste and an eye for quality as well as a grounded commercial publisher. He also surrounded himself with young colleagues who shared his energy, enthusiasm and outlook, none more so that Graham C. Greene, who joined from Secker and Warburg in September 1962 to take up the newly created post of Sales Director at the age of twenty-six. Bespectacled, besuited and a scion of the Suffolk brewing family, Greene was temperamentally and by background very different from the casual and often chaotic Maschler, but he was a salesman of genius. His father was Hugh Carlton Greene, the Director General of the BBC who famously liberalized the broadcaster during the 1960s with programmes such as *That Was The Week That Was* and set much of the context for the great change in the morals and manners of the period. Greene was also the nephew of the novelist Graham Greene and, as we shall see in the next chapter, played a decisive and not always blamelessly straightforward role in Cape's final disposition and the unravelling of his uncle's own publisher, the Bodley Head.

Together Greene and Maschler made Cape the highest profile publisher of the decade. Tom found new writers but also repackaged the glorious backlist, including Ernest Hemingway, Ian Fleming and T.E. Lawrence (the latter two authors' works benefiting from major successful films in the decade). Sometimes their restless energy took them in surprising directions, as with the creation of *Jackdaws* in 1963. These, collections of facsimiles of historical documents contained in flapped foolscap wallets, were a revolutionary venture for a literary publisher. They were difficult to produce and the book trade treated them with suspicion, partly because the contents were only loosely inserted and could be easily stolen.[169] Greene energetically promoted them, and they began to sell

169 This problem was later solved by sealing them in cellophane wrappers, probably the first publications to be so treated. Today, expensive or delicate books are shrink-wrapped in clear PVC, as cellophane tends to tear.

widely to schools as teaching material and at heritage sites. They became so successful that by 1966 Cape formed a separate company to publish them under Greene's chairmanship. At the launch party for the new company a speech in their honour was made by Tony Crosland, Secretary of State for Education and architect of revolutionary changes in teaching at schools and universities.

Cape began to range much more widely from its literary heartland. Non-fiction titles, echoing its founding title *Arabia Deserta* of 1921, appeared but had variable success, although Desmond Morris' *The Naked Ape*, (1967) was a great bestseller, helped by the public's recognition of the author as a famous television presenter[170] and spawning a new genre of popular anthropology. An alliance with a small private press, Goliard, resulted in a joint-venture company in 1967 that brought prestigious authors such as Lévi-Strauss, Barthes, Neruda and Havel in short serious monographs. They probably did more for the house's reputation than its bottom line.

Nevertheless Maschler and Greene's partnership more than doubled the firm's turnover to over £600,000 by 1965. They were rewarded with board seats and the joint Managing Directorship in 1966, with Michael Howard as Chairman. Howard, who had suffered a serious illness in early 1965, progressively withdrew from day-to-day operations, eventually retiring in 1970 with Tom succeeding him as Chairman. Before his departure Howard looked to direct the firm's greatly enhanced revenue stream towards making a major company acquisition – partly to ensure that Tom, whose reputation as an editorial magician was now very high, would not be poached by other houses.

He first looked at buying Secker and Warburg out of Heinemann in 1968. Its managing director, Maurice Temple Smith, had left to found his own eponymous publishing house and chairman Fredric Warburg was set to retire. As the publisher of George Orwell, Angus Wilson and Thomas Mann, the company would have fitted Cape well and Howard thought them 'friendly and familiar' (Howard, 1971, p.327). Although Heinemann was initially receptive, the company eventually withdrew. Howard then turned his attention to the old-established firm of Chatto and Windus whose director, Ian Parsons, had been in spasmodic dis-cussions for an alliance with Cape since 1967. In April 1969, an agreement was reached

170 Morris is arguably the first 'celebrity author' created by television, and his book one of the earliest examples of a 'TV tie-in'.

that the two firms should merge. Chatto was the smaller company with sales of just over £580,000 to Cape's almost £800,000, but it was more diverse and included an educational and children's division as well as the Hogarth Press. The eventual arrangement, brokered largely by Greene, gave Cape and Chatto shareholders equal control with Howard and Parsons as joint chairmen. When they retired shortly afterwards their positions were taken by Greene and Norah Smallwood of Chatto – the first woman formally to head a major publishing house, Margaret Boon's brief regency at Mills and Boon notwithstanding. The agreement guaranteed the imprints' editorial independence, but allowed them to pool services and functions, a model that would become important in the succeeding quarter century as publishers continued to consolidate.

The other trade publisher that rose to prominence in the decade by surfing the changing *Zeitgeist* was Weidenfeld and Nicolson. Founded in 1949 by yet another east European *emigré*, George Weidenfeld, who had worked as a journalist for the BBC, and his partner, Nigel Nicolson, son of Harold Nicolson and the aristocratic gardener and writer Vita Sackville-West, the imprint had grown out of a venture in current affairs publishing, Contact Books.[171] Its earliest publications were packaged books under their own imprints for chain stores, but after Nicolson sold him his shares in 1956 (although he retained a directorship), George Weidenfeld guided the company forcefully in a distinctive direction. He concentrated on history and serious biography, and with both he surprised the sceptical book trade with its success.[172] He launched a paperback textbook series for higher education under the title 'World University Library', distinctive for its non-English authorship, its lavish use of colour and its tendency for its volumes to fall apart.[173] It eventually ran to 80 titles and was sold in 1969 to Granada, who were diversifying their profits from independent television in educational and professional publishing.

171 The initial plan had been to establish a current affairs magazine, but the partners found it impossible to obtain sufficient paper quotas, so sold their first issues in hard covers as 'books' which ensured a larger paper ration.
172 Although not Stanley Unwin, who was attracted by the energetic and cultured young German and freely proffered him advice, including 'Books about Mary Queen of Scots sell, but not books about South America'. As the eventual publisher of Antonia Fraser's highly successful biography of the Scottish Queen and the Nobel prize-winning writings of Gabriel Garcia Marquez, Weidenfield proved he could successfully sell both.
173 They were printed in Eastern Europe and, although the print quality was excellent, the binding was poor and broke easily.

Weidenfeld was renowned for his networking ability and his political connections in Britain, Europe, North America and Israel. He had published the little-known academic economist and politician, Harold Wilson, in 1949, and when the latter became Prime Minister in 1964, Weidenfeld became part of the inner circle of the Labour government. Wilson gave him a knighthood and eventually a peerage (in 1976),[174] the first publisher to be so honoured. More importantly, he gained access to the leading political personalities of the day and made a speciality of publishing their memoirs. By 1968, he was publishing 250 new books a year, many of real distinction – such as Antonia Fraser's *Mary, Queen of Scots* (1969) – which became deservedly best-sellers, supplemented by pot-boilers and political titles aimed to gain him influence and repay favours. A solid stream of revenue came from the much less exciting but reliable publications of his Arthur Barker imprint, which specialized in sports and pastimes. As we have seen, he briefly employed Tony Godwin to give new energy to his list, but the association was short-lived as he found Godwin's tendency to pay large advances unpalatable.

Some observers have detected a whiff of Maxwell about some of Weidenfeld's activities, but while there have always been those critical of his methods (some of which stems undoubtedly from jealousy of his success), there was definitely no dishonesty or sharp practice in his dealings. Norrie (1982, p.128) has compared him to the young William Heinemann, and he certainly shared some of that creative, restless energy and entrepreneurial flair as well as an international outlook. He could work the establishment and yet be rebellious – a very 1960s combination. His relocation of his publishing house to unfashionable Clapham in southwest London recalls Heinemann's pioneering use of Covent Garden, although few followed Weidenfeld to south of the River Thames. He would remain active for a further three decades, but it was during the 1960s that his publishing style, responsive to the flavour of the times and alive to emerging trends, was forged and his influence was probably then at its height.

While Britain underwent great and exciting social change at home, the decade of the 1960s also saw profound transformation in its global role. The independence of India and Pakistan in 1947 had started the dismantling of the British Empire, which gathered pace with independence for Ghana (1957), Nigeria (1960), Kenya (1964) and a whole swathe of

174 This was in Wilson's resignation honours list, the infamous 'lavender list'.

26 Michael Joseph, 1938.

27 The former Michael Joseph office at 26 Bloomsbury Street.

28 Portrait of George Rainbird by J.F. Doeve, 1951.

29 Entrance step to the former Thames and Hudson office in Bloomsbury Street with the 'dolphins' colophon worked in ceramic tiles and the signs of the zodiac.

30 Sir Stanley Unwin by John Gay, 1947.

31 Robert Maxwell by Ida Kar, circa 1958.

32 Sir Victor Gollancz in the late 1940s.

33 Sir Allen Lane at Harmondsworth, 1947.

34 Sir William Roy 'Billy' Collins, circa 1950.

35 Desmond Flower, examining a Chinese porcelain bowl, in the Cassell offices, near St Paul's Cathedral, 1947.

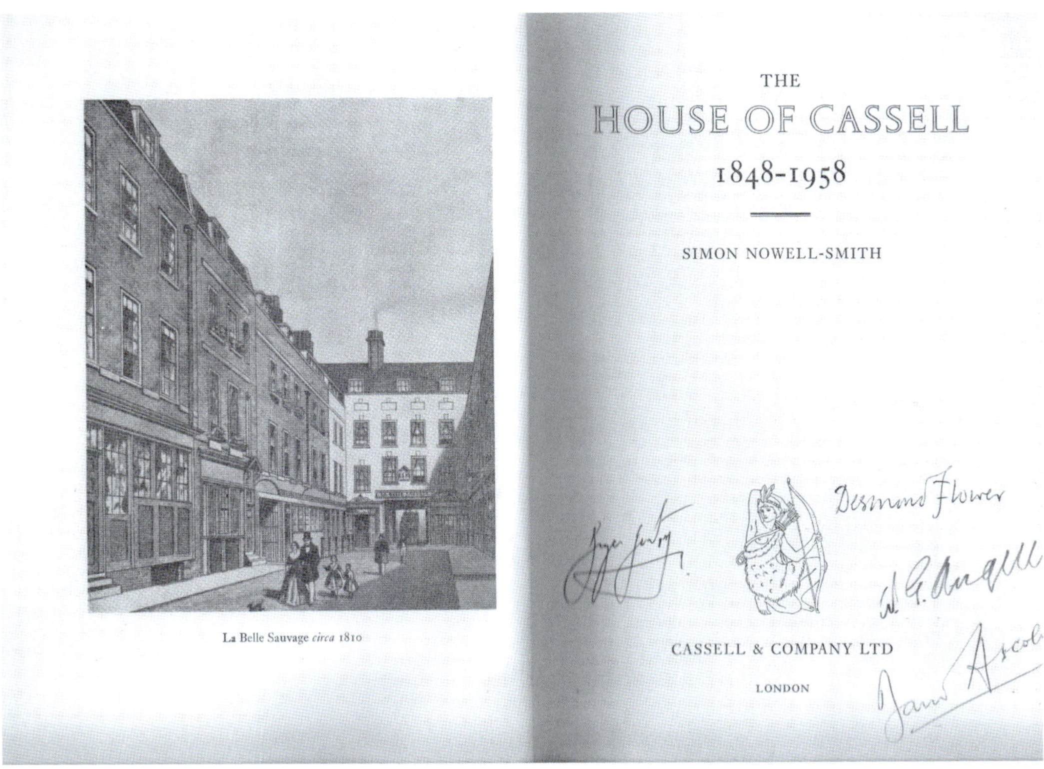

36 Title page opening of *The House of Cassell* by Simon Nowell-Smith (1958) signed by all the Cassell directors.

37 The cover of *The Penguin Story* (1956) with Allen Lane's compliments slip.

38 Longman House built to a design by Sir Frederick Gibberd at Harlow New Town in 1972. Described as 'the most modern publishing house in the world', it was meant to resemble stacked bookshelves. It was demolished in 1997.

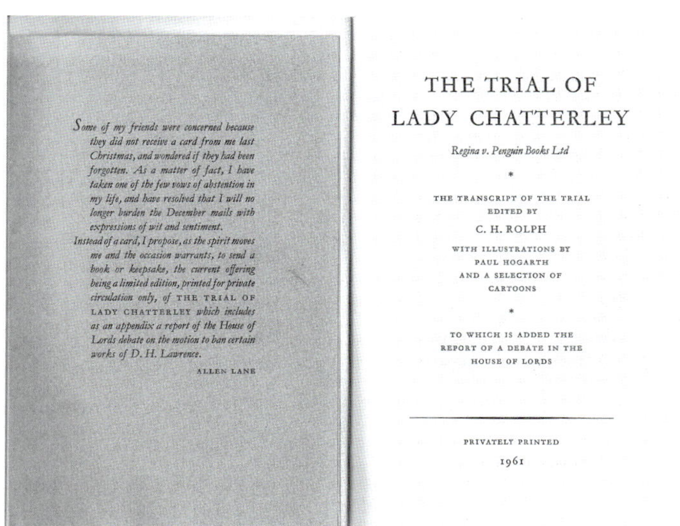

Some of my friends were concerned because they did not receive a card from me last Christmas, and wondered if they had been forgotten. As a matter of fact, I have taken one of the few vows of abstention in my life, and have resolved that I will no longer burden the December mails with expressions of wit and sentiment.

Instead of a card, I propose, as the spirit moves me and the occasion warrants, to send a book or keepsake, the current offering being a limited edition, printed for private circulation only, of THE TRIAL OF LADY CHATTERLEY *which includes as an appendix a report of the House of Lords debate on the motion to ban certain works of D. H. Lawrence.*

ALLEN LANE

THE TRIAL OF
LADY CHATTERLEY

Regina v. Penguin Books Ltd

*

THE TRANSCRIPT OF THE TRIAL
EDITED BY
C. H. ROLPH
WITH ILLUSTRATIONS BY
PAUL HOGARTH
AND A SELECTION OF
CARTOONS

*

TO WHICH IS ADDED THE
REPORT OF A DEBATE IN THE
HOUSE OF LORDS

PRIVATELY PRINTED
1961

39 Title page opening of the privately-printed edition of *The Trial of Lady Chatterley* by C.H. Rolph which Allen Lane, as his loose inserted slip explains, used as a Christmas card for friends in 1960.

40 Frederic Warburg in the late 1950s.

41 Tony Godwin photographed in the mid 1960s by his wife Fay.

42 Paul Hamlyn, by Lewis Morley, circa 1966.

43 Alan Hill in the mid 1970s.

44 Norah Smallwood in her office at Chatto and Windus in the late 1970s.

45 Max Reinhardt in the early 1980s.

46 Sir Geoffrey Cass by Gareth Hawker, 1997.

47 Tim Hely Hutchinson, 2000.

smaller colonial territories in Africa, the Caribbean and elsewhere. By 1970 most of the former British Empire had gained political independence and stood in a new relationship to their formal imperial power. Business structures altered in response, and publishing was by no means immune. The British Empire had been a vast and lucrative market for traditional British publishers such as Macmillan, Longmans and Nelson, and while these relationships survived independence, they were transformed by the new political structures. Harold Macmillan, who had predicted the 'Wind of Change' to the unappreciative members of the South African parliament in 1960, saw his family firm create what was effectively privately-owned state publishing in some newly emergent African nations, for example Macmillan Boleswa in Swaziland, Lesotho and Botswana and a more-or-less exclusive market for textbooks in Ghana. Longmans for its part dramatically expanded its participation in educational publishing in former colonial territories during the decade. It had to if it was to compete effectively. In 1962, it owned only three overseas companies, in Hong Kong, Malaya, and Nigeria, mainly acting as distributors, and only had minority shareholdings in companies that bore its name in India, Canada and South Africa (Briggs, 2008, p.437).

Under the determined direction of John Chapple, who had replaced C.S.S. Higham in 1957 as director of overseas education, Longmans focused its energies on developing strong textbook publishing in Africa. After an abortive attempt to challenge Macmillan's stranglehold in Ghana, it concentrated on Nigeria where it established an 'indigenous company' in 1965, publishing locally as well as importing. Despite the debilitating civil war of the late 1960s, Nigeria's growing oil wealth made it the mainspring of Longmans' growth and profitability until the abrupt economic collapse in 1982. Longmans' strategy was to promote local managerial and editorial talent, and shortly following independence it took on the bright and well-connected civil servant Felix Iwerebon. He quickly rose to direct Longman Nigeria.

Similar models were put in place in Kenya in 1965 as well as subsequently in Malawi, Tanzania and Zambia. The local companies worked closely with Ministries of Education, producing innovative and highly lucrative publishing closely attuned to market needs, such as the *Black Orpheus* magazine showcasing African writing talent. Even in Rhodesia where the white minority was about to rebel and reject majority rule in 1965, Longmans courageously africanized its local company.

Longmans energetically expanded its international operation elsewhere in the former Empire, and indeed in wider realms. Companies were expanded or acquired in Canada, Australia and New Zealand, the latter two directed with verve by Bill Kerr.[175] He had cut his teeth on the African expansion and led its early concentration on publications for teaching English to non-native speakers (referred to as ELT) which later enabled it to gain important markets in the Middle and Far East, and in Europe. It pioneered partnerships with local publishers and distributors such as *Librairie du Liban* in Beirut which went on to give Longmans a dominant position in language teaching in Arab countries. It also brought success to authors like L.G. Alexander, whose innovative courses such as *Profile* and *New Ways to English*, using audio-visual as well as printed material, became famous titles among learners of English.[176] Even before Mark Longman's death in 1972, Longmans had definitively abandoned general publishing and pinned its future to educational, professional and academic publishing.

The impetus for this came from Chapple and his counterpart in the home market, John Newsom, who had joined the company in 1957 and was appointed as joint Managing Director with Chapple[177] in 1962. Newsom, as well as energetically building up Longmans as the leading educational publisher, was extremely well-connected and influential with the social engineers of the Labour administration which came to power under Harold Wilson in 1964. Despite his responsibilities at Longmans, he continued to have a glittering career in educational administration and public service. His report *Half Our Future* in 1963 (for which he was knighted the following year) was highly critical of the grammar-secondary modern divide in schools, and prepared the way for the introduction of the comprehensive school system.[178] It was Newsom who

175 When I visited the New Zealand company Longman Paul in 1983, I was offered refreshment from the 'Bill Kerr Memorial Drinks Cabinet' which the staff had decided was a fitting tribute to his leadership following his death.

176 A later fruit of the Longmans-*Librarie du Liban* collaboration was the *York Notes* series of student guides to literary texts, launched in 1984, primarily for ELT students but which have since become the best-selling books in their field among students of literature in general.

177 This odd form of consular governance was to become a feature of Longmans over the next two decades and reflects the balance between the domestic and overseas business.

178 Despite being commissioned during the dying months of Macmillan's outgoing Conservative government, it was the enthusiastic new ministers of Wilson's 'white heat of technology' revolution to whom Newsom spoke loudest. They took up his

masterminded the company's removal from Mayfair in London to a purpose-built, ultra-modern building (since demolished) in Harlow New Town, twenty miles north of London.[179] He also oversaw the change of name from the historic and euphonic 'Longmans, Green and Co.' to the practical and accurate 'Longman Group' in 1969. He died unexpectedly two years later at the age of sixty-one, leaving Chapple in overall charge.

Even smaller publishers sought to emulate Longmans' success in the rapidly growing education markets in former colonies. One was Edward Arnold, founded in 1890 by a grandson of the famous Victorian headmaster Thomas Arnold and nephew of the poet Matthew Arnold (Bennett and Hamilton, 1990). For most of its history, it had combined a solid but rather unexciting general list (its most distinguished author was E.M. Forster) with school textbooks, scientific reference books and sheet music.[180] During the 1950s it had begun to make tentative forays into overseas markets, but the enthusiasm of its chairman, Brian Fagan, who had observed how companies such as Longmans and Evans Brothers had successfully expanded in post-independence Nigeria, encouraged them to set up 'an overseas department' including an ELT list. The company never had the resources to establish local publishing, but for a time its textbooks, particularly in medicine, carved out an important market in newly created or expanding universities in post-independence countries.[181]

—

recommendations with fervour, particularly Tony Crosland, who became Secretary of State for Education and Science in 1965.

179 It has been said that Newsom favoured Harlow as a base because it was a less than fifteen minute drive from County Hall in Hertford where he maintained an office in the Hertfordshire education department, and he was also a member of the Harlow Development Corporation. 'Longman House' (RIP 1997) was designed by the visionary architect Sir Frederick Gibberd who was responsible for the overall design of the new town, including its famous 'Green Lungs'. Surrounded by parkland and adjacent to the railway station, it was bright, airy and convenient, and included among its facilities a modern canteen and a staff bar. Longmans' distribution facilities were also established in Harlow, although there was not much interaction between the sites despite their being less than half a mile apart. Gibberd's design was thought to be inspired by either stacks of bookshelves or a galleon in full sail, both of which would have been highly appropriate to the company's heritage.

180 Sheet music always caused book publishers problems since their outlets were different from books, and it was supplied under a complicated discount structure. Arnold sold their sheet music business to the specialist company Novello in 1959.

181 Arnold, like many other tertiary-level publishers, benefited from an innovative subsidy scheme operated by the British Council under the name 'English Language

However, this activity may have over-stretched its resources, and by the end of the 1960s Edward Arnold had run down its overseas list to concentrate on domestic markets.

At the same time Oxford University Press, and to a lesser extent Cambridge, were also expanding into former colonial territories. Oxford was particularly active in eastern and central Africa, with a key focus in South Africa. Here it rather uneasily served the educational needs of the apartheid regime whose policy of separatist 'Bantu education' became more hardline after the Sharpeville massacre of 1960 and the imprisonment of Nelson Mandela and his fellow political activists. There was at the time and since much criticism of OUP for maintaining its South African publishing branch during this period (although other British publishers also did so, but perhaps with a lower profile) as being collaborative with a distasteful regime inappropriate for a university press. Less controversially, OUP also established a branch in Ethiopia following the successful acquisition of an exclusive contract from the Ministry of Education, but this proved ephemeral and did not survive the fall of the Haile Selassie regime in 1974.

Despite the impressive and important developments by Macmillan and Longmans to support and expand educational publishing in the Commonwealth and elsewhere in the world, the most significant and culturally resonant British publisher who helped shape the post-Imperial world of publishing overseas was Heinemann Educational Books (HEB). Since the end of the Second World War, Heinemann had had a chequered history, with its publishing drifting somewhat under the benign but rather lacklustre leadership of A.S. Frere. Like other houses of similar vintage and orientation, including Cassell and Hodder and Stoughton, it clung to out-moded markets and pre-war models. It had survived an action for obscenity in 1954 for Walter Baxter's *The Image and the Search*, outraging the fearsome and legendary Editor of the *Sunday Express* John Gordon, who campaigned for its withdrawal. The prosecutor was Mervyn Griffith-Jones, but this was no heroic struggle between the establishment and a modernizing publisher. At both the first trial and the retrial, the

—

Book Society' (ELBS) which made special editions of key textbooks largely in law, the sciences and medicine available at one-third of the list price in designated 'developing countries'. Launched in the 1960s, it was a boon both to publishers, since it both countered piracy and extended sales, and to students, but it was a victim of budget cuts and a changing attitude towards books within the Council and was wound up in 1984.

jury failed to reach a verdict, and although Heinemann was acquitted at a third trial, this was only because the prosecution offered no evidence. St John (1991, p.410) describes Frere as 'a hero', but actually he looked rather foolish and indecisive, traits which characterized his stewardship of the company.

Between 1950 and 1960, Heinemann's turnover had barely increased to just under £600,000, but overheads doubled and profits plunged to barely £20,000 (Hill, 1988, p.154). It had the added problem of maintaining a large and costly printing works at Kingswood in Surrey, and unlike Collins, was dithering over publishing paperbacks which would have made good use of the facility. It made ill-advised acquisitions, such as Peter Davies and Hart-Davis, which were loss-making and by 1957 it was rapidly running out of money and options. It was temporarily rescued by a substantial minority buy-in from the conglomerate Thomas Tilling who had large transport interests and were known disparagingly to some, at least at Heinemann, as 'the bus people'.

When Tilling got to grips with Heinemann's desperate finances they were horrified, and by 1960 were loudly complaining of profligate mismanagement. One of their directors pointedly asked: 'How much longer ... are we going to throw money out of the window just to satisfy this whim of being civilized – which we are not?' (St John, 1991, p.422). Frere, perhaps recalling the white knight of Doubleday who had saved the firm forty years before, decided the only way out was to sell the whole operation to an American company, eventually settling on the highly corporate and highly incompatible New York firm of McGraw-Hill. Whether they would have saved Heinemann or simply asset-stripped it is an highly debatable point, but they never got the chance. Members of Frere's own board resisted the proposal and the deal foundered in a welter of recrimination and bad faith, not helped by extremely unfavourable press comment. Frere continued in the purely honorary role of President for a few months, but eventually left the company completely at the end of 1962 in an very bitter atmosphere.

The one bright spot in a miserable performance was Heinemann's educational business. This had increased four-fold between 1953 and 1959, and by 1960 was contributing almost one-third of the company's turnover and almost all its profit. This had been achieved largely by the brilliant leadership of one of the century's greatest and most creative publishing entrepreneurs, Alan Hill. The son of a village schoolmaster, he joined Heinemann in 1936 after taking a history degree at Cambridge. His university contemporaries and friends had included Jacob Bronowski, Alistair Cooke and Robert Gittings (all of whom he would later publish), and he combined his radical non-conformist faith in the power of education to transform lives with an appreciation of the value of critical scholarship.

Hill had originally only intended to work at Heinemann temporarily to fund his plan to study as a barrister, but he found publishing much more to his taste. Initially employed as an assistant editor for schoolbooks, he learned his craft the hard way by selling texts directly to teachers. He quickly made a positive impression on Heinemann's chairman, C.S. Evans, and was given responsibility for commissioning textbooks under the direction of R. Welldon Finn. Finn had built up in the space of a few years a school list that was beginning to rival that of Longmans and Macmillan (Hill, 1988, pp.42-6).

Following war service in the RAF, Hill took over Finn's position in 1946 with a brief to make Heinemann the leading educational publisher. He interpreted this to mean 'not simply schoolbooks ... I proposed to publish across the whole range of writing intended for enlightenment, as opposed for entertainment' (Hill 1988, p.67). This vision he energetically pursued by signing up a new generation of young non-fiction writers with a particularly strong suit in the sciences. His Cambridge connections brought him Bronowski and the iconoclastic astronomer Fred Hoyle. Important lists were built in English, politics and history, with Alan's personal political radicalism and enthusiasm for social engagement resulting in books that were well ahead of their time and often controversial. In 1955 the success of his plans saw him appointed to the Heinemann board, and from then on he was able to make his particular vision of education in the broad sense the core of Heinemann's growth, with particular emphasis on overseas markets.

He established subsidiary companies in Australia, New Zealand, Hong Kong, Canada, Malaya, the Caribbean and most significantly in several African countries. While the rest of the company put in an indifferent performance, he was left alone to build a highly distinctive and highly profitable publishing structure. As he explained:

> I departed radically from the firm's management style in building up the educational organisation – where the close integration of the publishing and sales sides was fundamental to future growth. On the other hand I must admit that Frere's editorial policy suited me well.

> I benefited greatly from the publishing freedom I enjoyed, reporting only to my own educational team (a self-imposed responsibility) and not to any higher authority. But the same could not be said for our lack of financial control. As there was nobody to consult before committing the company's funds, we had no idea of the impact of our ever-increasing projects on the firm's financial position. In retrospect, it must have been considerable. (Hill, 1988, p.158)

Heinemann for their part were extremely lucky to have such a visionary and committed entrepreneur in at least one part of their business. Hill and his small team which included Tony Beal, a gifted sales manger who eventually succeeded Hill, were energetic, forward-looking and open to new ideas. They were also highly market-oriented and aware of the great political and cultural changes overtaking the former British *Imperium*. Perhaps their most important and lasting achievement was the creation of the 'African Writers' Series, giving a rising generation of creative writers from newly emergent countries an outlet for books born out of the independence struggle that would not have been published elsewhere. The series began in 1958 with the Nigerian Chinua Achebe's *Things Fall Apart*. By the end of the 1960s, the series comprised eighty titles – mainly novels from virtually every country in sub-Saharan Africa, but also plays, poetry and political studies. They included translations from writers in French, Arabic and Portuguese, as well as works from South Africa that were banned in their writers' homeland. Although others later copied the format, Hill's enterprising faith in the value of local writing and heterodox view of education created a whole new genre in world literature which has included several Nobel laureates.

After a brief and unhappy time as Managing Director of William Heinemann during the McGraw-Hill débâcle, Hill was eventually rewarded with the creation of his own company: HEB was incorporated separately in July 1961. He spelt out his ambitions in its prospectus:

> … [W]e are now well-poised for even more rapid expansion during the next ten years. Our staff have a self-confidence and dynamism, which has been quite unshaken by the vicissitudes of the Heinemann Group during the last year … I do not disguise the fact, that during the next decade, we hope increasingly to rival Longmans. Above all it is our ambition to build up a long-life business, one which will be a household name when other firms have become merely memories. (Hill, 1988, p.176)

He was as good as his word. From sales of £350,000 in 1960, HEB steadily expanded and achieved turnover of £1 million by 1967, becoming the largest company in the Heinemann Group. The overseas companies flourished with local publishing and increasingly local management. While never outstripping Longmans in key areas such as Nigeria, they produced strong results, generating £700,000 turnover overseas by 1970, almost a third of HEB's revenue. Over the decade, HEB produced over 1500 new books and profitably pioneered areas that other educational publishers had ignored, such as archaeology and music and theatre studies. The latter included John Gielgud among its authors, with his *Stage Direction* (1963) becoming a bestseller among students and practitioners. Other new fields which Hill pursued included criminology and management studies based on the works of the versatile and prolific Peter Drucker.

Hill ascribes his success to his 'Protestant work ethic', but while he certainly had a driven, occasionally messianic zeal he possessed in stronger measure the ability to spot new trends, take calculated risks and above all to delegate and trust others to do likewise. He was an immensely likeable and friendly man who valued harmonious personal relationships among his staff and authors above all else. He was as far from the autocratic Cape, the neurotic Joseph or the self-important and ineffectual Hart-Davis as it is possible to imagine.[182] Almost uniquely among the publishing personalities written about here, he is recalled universally with genuine warmth both by colleagues and rivals. In many ways, Hill was the model for a new breed of publisher, quite unlike the individualistic Cape, Lane, Gollancz or Warburg – or even his much admired founder Heinemann – who had relied primarily on flair and instinct to create their businesses. Hill was collegiate, business-oriented and informed by market research. He could read and judge balance sheets as well as great literature, and was probably the first publisher to describe himself as an 'executive'.[183]

182 A revealing anecdote is that when on his way to a company function, he suddenly found he could not recall the first name of a colleague's wife who was going to be there. He promptly stopped his taxi and rang his secretary from a nearby phone-box to ascertain the lady's name. When he greeted her later, he called her by first name, adding 'how lovely to see you again'. They had only met once before, but the lady in question felt suitably gratified.

183 Alan's younger son, David, also forged a notable publishing career. He began as a junior editor at HEB, then moved on to run the British end of the American academic house Sage, finally becoming editorial manager of the educational publisher David

As the expansive and optimistic 1960s drew to a close, to be replaced by a much more turbulent and difficult decade, publishing would need the kinds of careful planning and management skills that Hill exemplified to meet the challenges that lay ahead. The book business underwent enormous change in the decade, and some of the trends and features that would emerge more clearly during the remainder of the century, and indeed up to the present day, were laid then. These included the first stirrings of corporatism and an awareness of wider business concerns, with the gradual erosion of the influential individual relying on his taste and judgment alone to determine what was published. Marketing and subsidiary rights emerged from the shadows to become important parts of the business mix. The role of women, for long the vital and unsung underpinning of the industry in all sorts of administrative, editorial and sales functions, changed, and they became more prominent in executive positions, albeit still under-represented at the highest levels. Anne Walmsley at Faber and Faber could recall that as late as the 1960s the 'Faber young ladies' were still rather 'jerseys and pearls' [who] ... went to the country for the weekend' and were in awe of the tall, bowler-hatted figure of T.S. Eliot as he stalked the Russell Square offices (Bradley, 2008, p.23).[184] Elsewhere, the cliché of the long-suffering, secretarial helpmeet of the gentleman publisher gave way to an influx of lively, career-minded and ambitious young women with degrees from one of the new 1960s universities such as Sussex or Warwick, and from a much more diverse class background. No longer would they – nor could they afford to – subsidize meagre publishing salaries with private incomes. They wanted proper jobs and prospects, and slowly they transformed the way publishing was done. The first inroads were in sales, rights and marketing, but eventually they achieved prominence in editorial and general management.

It would be wrong to suggest that this transition was easy and that it was completed without resistance to a great degree during the 1960s. Women in executive roles were not everywhere welcomed, but publishers

---

Fulton. As well as his energy, David shares his father's radical outlook and strong social conscience.

184 It was remarked to me by one 'young lady' that Eliot hated to hear them swear, and when she casually remarked about the people in the Square outside her window doing 'bugger all' she suddenly became aware of the disapproving presence of Eliot behind her, whereupon she fled, red-faced.

such as Cape, Bodley Head and probably most of all Paul Hamlyn encouraged female talent and rewarded it. Nevertheless, it would take forty years for women to achieve anything like parity with men in senior roles. Some would argue that there remain yet lingering traces of pre-1960s attitudes in some publishing houses.[185]

Perhaps the most lasting legacy of the changes of the 1960s was a definitive transformation of the social position and composition of publishing output. The 'mass market' for books had, of course, existed since at least the middle of the nineteenth century, and was much boosted by Lane's Penguin revolution – but it was during the 1960s that the last vestige of the idea of books as the province of a social elite were dissipated. The last subscription 'circulating library' (Boots), a bastion of upper-middle class taste and attitudes as we have seen in Chapter 1, closed its doors in 1966. If they had not become truly democratic, books had become at least accessible to a wider range of readers, not least through Hamlyn and his unorthodox choice of titles and ways to market. Improved education, new universities, liberated social attitudes and the end of deference all created new wider markets to which publishers – some, it must be admitted, more slowly than others – responded with a wider range of titles and subjects. Children's publishing, for example, previously long dominated by class-bound tales featuring (and aimed at) the white, privately educated sons and daughters (the latter were often in subsidiary roles) of prosperous home counties parents – provided, for example, by Enid Blyton and Anthony Buckeridge – saw, during the 1960s, the emergence of books drawing on more diverse experiences and aimed at a wider junior readership. The work of Kaye Webb at Puffin and the Bodley Head's Judy Taylor (who founded the Children's Book Circle) was critical in inducing this change (Bradley, 2008, pp.96-106). Women editors were often the instigators of the new children's publishing, but there were also significant male revolutionaries such as Klaus Flugge at Andersen Press and (a little later) Sebastian Walker at Walker Books.

The decade also saw the beginnings of the social transformation of those who worked in publishing. As we shall see in the next chapter, the 'gentleman publisher' myth took quite a long time to die, and was never

185 The tendency of some trade publishers to 'employ' young women of high social status (and possessing trust funds) as 'interns' for little or no salary still persists today. These 'Samanthas' (as I have heard them called) think publishing 'glamorous', but often (with a few honourable exceptions) find their roles being confined mainly to photocopying and tea-making.

in any case as complete a description of those who ran publishing as has been imagined. Many substantial publishing figures – from Heinemann, Dent, Lane and Cape to Hill – had emerged from quite modest social backgrounds, as did most of those who worked in sales, production and administrative positions. Nevertheless it is not a baseless caricature to note how many of those who controlled publishing up until the end of the 1960s were still male, privately-educated, Oxbridge graduates with private incomes who frequented the Garrick Club. The social changes of the 1960s initiated challenges to their tastes and the structures of their businesses, and the companies that would prosper were those who recognized and reacted to those changes.

8 'No more Gentlemen'

British book publishing in the 1970s

When Fredric Warburg published the first volume of his autobiography in 1959 he entitled it *An Occupation for Gentlemen* (Warburg, 1959). Warburg, who had begun his publishing career with Routledge after the First World War and had with Roger Senhouse bought the business of Martin Secker to create Secker and Warburg in 1936, was nostalgic for the days when publishers were cultured dilettantes, interested in quality and literary merit but 'fool[s] in handling money and incompetent in dealing with sales' (Warburg, 1959, p.277). Whether or not Warburg's conduct was that of a gentleman – and his defenestration of Martin Secker from the firm he founded may suggest otherwise – his picture chimed with a general view that publishing was a business that was not quite business-like, the last resort of the effete amateur, mannerly, dreamy and impractical.

The previous chapters have shown that this myth was only ever fractionally true. Publishing had always possessed its fair share of rapacious, ruthless and restless entrepreneurs, as handy with a balance sheet as a manuscript, and while individuals such as Cape, Joseph, Warburg himself and many others may have cultivated the image of literary gentility, they had no shortage of business acumen. Nevertheless, up to the end of the 1960s the public continued to regard publishers as tweed-jacketed *literateurs*, privately educated and supported by private incomes. These fortunate ones spent their mornings reading in well-appointed Georgian drawing rooms in Bloomsbury and their afternoons, following long, claret-fuelled lunches with importunate authors, in the leather armchairs of the Garrick or Savile Clubs. And they were always men.[186]

186 Interestingly, the myth continues to be perpetuated by the publishing comic strip in the satirical fortnightly *Private Eye*, which recounts the fictional doings of Snipcock and

And then something happened. When Warburg finally completed his second autobiographical volume entitled *All Authors Are Equal* in 1973, two years after his retirement, the earlier optimistic tone that had summarized his publishing style as 'the pride of my craft and the secret of my happiness'[187] had darkened. His take on the publishing world he had just left was elegiac and bitter as he lamented the passing of the old order:

> … [W]e are nearing the point when a publishing house is no longer a mystique, an adventure or a quality system, but an organisation for the production of profitable commodities on an ever greater scale. Soon their sons, the teenagers and twenty-year-olds of today, already in revolt against their elders' ideas, are likely once more to change the face of publishing in ways which cannot now be foreseen. Already it is clear however that many of them, including some of the most brilliant executives, are leaving firms where they had previously been happy. Some because the growth in size of the firm and its exclusive concentration on profits has disgusted them. Some because they fear, rightly or wrongly, the American ownership or part-ownership of British firms. This has grown substantially in the last decade. They believe, as I do, that book publishing is a direct reflection of the British character and way of life, and should not therefore be in foreign hands. (Warburg, 1973, p.144)

This was more than just an old man's dyspeptic resentment of a rising generation. Publishing had indeed changed in both its organization and ownership, and its structure would continue to evolve more dramatically in the 1970s than in any preceding decade. Trends then set in place continue to the present. Why this happened was due both to shifts of emphasis and new business priorities within publishing and to the exigencies of a much less certain and settled economic climate.

Since the end of the Second World War until the late 1960s, the British economy had grown steadily with low inflation, full employment and rising prosperity. The social changes of the 1960s encouraged consumerism and expectations of constantly improving living standards and rising disposable income. But even before the end of the 1960s there were

---

Tweed who uniquely still inhabit a Bloomsbury house and sport bow ties and tweed jackets. While they comment on contemporary publishing issues, their context is anything but, such is the power of the icon of the gentleman publisher.

187 These are the concluding words of *An Occupation for Gentlemen* (p.280).

signs that the long postwar boom was beginning to falter. Traditional industries such as engineering, shipbuilding, textiles and motor manufacturing were starting to look uncompetitive compared to elsewhere, and unemployment figures began ominously to increase. The Labour government of Harold Wilson, which had devalued the pound in 1967, was looking tired and out of touch, but its defeat at the hands of the Conservative Edward Heath in June 1970 came as a surprise. Heath was initially popular, but he found the economic forces he had to contend with intractable. Unemployment inexorably rose to over one million, a wages and prices freeze was introduced to tackle inflation, and industrial unrest became commonplace. A definitive new direction that would profoundly change British business came with membership of the European Economic Community in 1973, although at the time it was hotly contested. The outbreak of a prolonged miners' strike at the end of that year brought economic chaos resulting in widespread energy shortages and the 'three day week' which inflicted lasting economic damage on already debilitated industries.

Heath called an election on the slogan of 'Who Governs Britain?' in 1974 which he narrowly lost, returning Wilson to power. However, he only stayed in office for two years, abruptly resigning in 1976 and allowing James Callaghan to succeed as Prime Minister. Economic problems were paralleled by social disaffection and unrest, not least in Northern Ireland where traditional rivalries between the unionist and republican communities had simmered for decades. Although there had been attacks on the mainland before, a renewed and sustained campaign of random bombings and political assassinations by nationalists of the Irish Republican Army in the 1970s brought a new sense of fear to the British public. Two bombs in Birmingham in November 1974 killed twenty-one people and initiated a series of murderous attacks that fostered general insecurity. Overseas, the war between the Arabs and the Israelis in 1973 led to the rapid increase in the price of oil that permanently destabilized the global economy. By the mid 1970s the old certainties had gone and the world appeared a bleaker, less confident and more challenging place.

Publishing was not immune to the new economic environment. For only the second time since records had begun to be kept in 1947, fewer new books were published in 1975 than in the previous year (Stevenson, 2008, p.279).[188] Rising costs, tighter credit and reduced spending power

188 The only year in which this had happened previously was 1959.

among book buyers obliged publishers to look critically at their cash flow and their decision-making. Inefficient and picturesque business practices, such as the publishers' trade counters and generous credit periods, came under scrutiny and were abandoned or curtailed as it became obvious that the overheads they generated were increasing unsustainably. Collins closed their London trade counter in King's Cross in 1975 and centralized all their distribution from their Glasgow warehouse. By 1970 Allen and Unwin had moved their warehouse and trade department to the new town of Hemel Hempstead, twenty miles north of London (Unwin, 1972, pp.166-7). Heinemann maintained their central London trade counter a little longer, but were increasingly servicing smaller orders through a third-party distributor, the Book Centre (St John, 1991, p.488). Predictably the last publisher's trade counter in central London was operated by John Murray from their cramped and Dickensian warehouse in Clerkenwell, but it too eventually closed.

But most significantly, as Warburg observed, the ownership and management of publishing houses began to change. The need to find economies of scale obliged mergers like that of Cape and Chatto to reduce distribution overheads. Although Warburg saw American ownership as a major threat, this was in reality neither a new feature nor particularly significantly disruptive. After all, as we saw in Chapter 3, Doubleday had been the saviour of Heinemann in the 1920s and his rule had been notably benign. McGraw-Hill had operated its own subsidiary in Britain since 1909, and although it had attempted to widen its presence with moves to take over British publishers – including Heinemann and Penguin – it met with little success. Its energetic Managing Director Gordon Graham had developed a strong British company, but he left in 1974 to run Butterworths, significantly concluding that '[t]he Atlantic (had) bec(o)me too narrow' (Norrie 1982, p.135). When John Wiley, the old-established New York scientific and educational publisher, established their own UK company after many years being represented by Chapman & Hall, they perhaps symbolically chose to locate in Chichester. It was certainly a pleasant town, but also remote from the London publishing scene.[189]

189 The choice of this location, which remains Wiley's headquarters for Europe, Africa and the Middle East, was reputedly influenced by their original director's proclivity for sailing and the proximity of Chichester Harbour and the Solent. Nevertheless Wiley have prospered in West Sussex; they are now the largest private-sector employer in the town and a major presence in nearby Bognor Regis, where their distribution facility is located. It is interesting, and perhaps significant, that the British subsidiaries of many American

Warburg's disaffection with what he saw as the growing corporatism and conglomeration of British publishing had come from his own experience within the Heinemann group. This association began in 1951 when, following a cashflow crisis, Warburg agreed that Heinemann should take over his firm's distribution and guarantee its overdraft (Thomson, 1986, p.44). Shortly afterwards Heinemann acquired most of Secker and Warburg's capital. Apart from occasional, rather futile attempts to impose financial control under Frere's benevolent if ineffectual guidance and during the early years of the Tilling Group ownership, Warburg was left to do as he liked. This, it emerged, was to publish literature that attracted high regard and brilliant reviews but by and large made little or no profit. Despite discovering authors as commercial as Angus Wilson and Malcolm Bradbury, Warburg stubbornly clung to his high-toned literary values, and although he published some titles that well reflected the *Zeitgeist*, such as Margaret Forster's *Georgy Girl* (1965), he was much more interested in prizes and prestige than profits.[190]

After Roger Senhouse resigned in 1962 for reasons that still remain obscure, Warburg increasingly shrugged off the irksome constraints of his owner's attempts at financial controls. However, he was certainly innovative in his editorial management, exemplified by his engagement of the creative editor Barley Alison from Weidenfeld in 1967 to find and nurture new authors. She was not paid a salary but published under her own imprint (The Alison Press), with Warburg paying production and overheads and any profits being eventually shared.[191] The company also set up a like type of co-operation with the publisher of military history Leo Cooper after Warburg had left the firm. This kind of arrangement – dependent as it was on the protagonist having private means

—

publishers chose to locate in extra-London sites, including McGraw-Hill in Maidenhead and Holt-Saunders in Eastbourne.

190 There is no denying the cultural importance of Warburg's publishing. His authors included Günther Grass, Federico García Lorca, Alberto Moravia, Yukio Mishima, and Nobel laureates Heinrich Böll and Yusunari Kawabata in translation, as well as playwright Arthur Miller and poet D.J. Enright.

191 Warburg rather laconically remarked in his memoirs that '[o]bviously a plan of this type will only be acceptable to a person of sufficient means to wait for the profits which, after all, may never come. Such means were available to Miss Alison.' He quotes, apparently without irony, as an example of Alison's commissioning John Hopkin's travel memoir *The Attempt* (1968) '[which] has made £43 after only two years, even allowing for the cost of overheads' (Warburg, 1973, p.293).

to support themselves – was rather out of joint with the changing nature of the people coming into publishing, so was not widely emulated later, although, as we shall see, Max Reinhardt would develop a similar symbiosis with Penguin.

Warburg's stature and influence within Heinemann was enormous. It was he, together with Hart-Davis, who had been the main objectors to the abortive McGraw-Hill takeover, but as his imprint's losses mounted the Heinemann board and Tilling owners grew restive. In 1966, he appointed Maurice Temple Smith as editorial director and, it was widely thought, his eventual successor. Although Warburg described his relationship with Smith as 'happy enough', other observers saw friction between the two that recalled Lane and Godwin's tussles at Penguin.

Charles Pick had been taken on at Warburg's suggestion as group Managing Director in 1962. He came from Michael Joseph after the Cape fiasco to guide the post-Frere Heinemann and had initially, perhaps out of respect for his benefactor, kept out of direct involvement with the running of Secker and Warburg. By the mid 1960s, however, he insisted on attending all decision-taking meetings.[192] He found that overheads were running close to 40 per cent of revenue (compared to below 30 per cent elsewhere in a tightly-run company) and there were wasteful duplications such as separate sales and production departments for the imprint. Pick tried to micro-manage the irascible Warburg, insisting that no new books could be signed without his approval. Warburg, unsurprisingly, chafed under these constraints and relations between him and Pick became strained.[193] Warburg was by nature prickly and abrupt, and as he grew older he became more cantankerous. Robert Lusty, who had published Warburg's memoirs at Hutchinson, acerbically remarked that '[t]o have published Fred Warburg ... and to have retained [his] friendship is, even when said in the greatest possible humility, something of an achievement' (Lusty, 1975, p.188).

When Temple Smith and a colleague, without consulting Warburg, attempted to buy the firm from Heinemann, they represented that they wished to save the imprint's essential character. The proposal was

192 Secker & Warburg remained a separate company within the Heinemann group until its eventual sale to Octopus in 1985. Pick became its Chairman in 1973, until on his retirement he was replaced by Nicholas Thompson from Pitman in 1985.
193 Warburg does not mention Pick at all in his memoirs.

rejected, and Smith was required to resign; he eventually set up his own eponymous firm.[194]

Warburg ostensibly accepted the new stringent regime, but shortly after Temple Smith's departure he too put together a bid to buy his firm back in association with Graham C. Greene of Cape. The Heinemann board initially listened to this proposal favourably and got as far as exchanging financial statements, but when Pick learned what was afoot he violently objected. Warburg claimed that he was not the prime mover in the scheme, but merely 'a commodity being thrown about in the middle' (St John, 1991, p.571). Pick, exasperated, put Warburg under increasing pressure to retire and initiated a search for a successor who would show more financial discipline while maintaining high-quality editorial standards. Warburg reluctantly accepted the largely honorary role as President (without executive powers) and eventually retired completely in April 1971, following a year when ironically his company, responding to Pick's medicine, showed a profit for the first time in many years.

The right candidate to replace Warburg was found by chance. Alan Hill, who at the end of 1970 was looking around for companies to acquire, invited Tom Rosenthal, the managing director of the fine-art publisher Thames and Hudson, to lunch to explore whether his company might be bought. Rosenthal thought he was being sounded out as Warburg's replacement and enthusiastically told Hill he would do the job. Hill was initially nonplussed, but by the time he returned to the office he was convinced that Rosenthal was the man for the job, and he told Pick (now Heinemann chairman) and the group Managing Director Dwye Evans so[195] (Hill, 1988, pp.253-4). They agreed, and in September 1970, after some convoluted negotiation about share ownership and job title, Rosenthal was confirmed as the new Managing Director of Secker and Warburg.

Warburg rather coolly dismissed the new man's arrival with a curt sentence: '[h]e was almost exactly half my age' (Warburg, 1973, p.302). Fred clearly regarded himself as the last of the gentlemen. The upstart Rosenthal was assertive, occasionally bombastic and gauche, but he

194 Interestingly, his own company specialized in academic publishing, building notable and lucrative lists in history, social science, psychology and some of the earliest titles on environmental activism. It remained independent until 1981 when it was sold to East West Publications and was later absorbed by the Gower Press of Aldershot, now part of Ashgate Publishing.

195 Hill was to succeed Evans as group managing director in 1973.

combined both a shrewd financial brain and a cultured sensibility.[196] He attacked the task of rebuilding the list with characteristic verve. The imprint maintained its distinguished literary cast, but added books by more commercial writers such as the humorous satires of Tom Sharpe, the racy feminist tales of Erica Jong and the campus novels of David Lodge. The range of the list broadened enormously and for the first time crime stories, science fiction and current affairs reportage, including Bernstein and Woodward's *All the President's Men* which exposed the Watergate scandal in 1974, were included. Cover design, which under Warburg had been restrained and quietly elegant, became brash and noisy, with much use of metallic foil and dramatic typography. More prosaically, Rosenthal was a vigilant cost-cutter who scrutinized expenses and rigorously excised all spending he regarded as unnecessary. He was a tough negotiator with authors and agents, introducing a number of now commonplace innovations to author-publisher dealings such as the three-book contract. He nevertheless also recognized the value of continuity, and his supportive treatment of Warburg's long-serving editorial director, David Farrer, and Barley Alison – who were rewarded with board seats – was returned with great loyalty and renewed creativity.

What Warburg thought of these changes is not recorded, but Rosenthal's approach certainly brought speedy and positive results. By 1980 the firm's turnover had increased eleven-fold in a decade to over £2,750,000. Far from being a drain on Heinemann's resources, it was now second only to HEB as a net contributor to the group, with annual profits exceeding £300,000. Such an achievement would have been remarkable at any time, but in a period of economic hardship and uncertainty it was a truly remarkable turnaround.[197] Rosenthal's restless energy, drive and occasionally overblown and grandiose manner may have disconcerted some, but his ability to think laterally, seize opportunities and make shrewd business choices gave him the competitive edge. He – unlike others – could operate effectively in the new world of corporate consolidation that was beginning to overtake publishing.

Typical of the new massive conglomerates that increasingly came to dominate book publishing was the International Publishing Corporation (IPC). This had begun as a newspaper and magazine publishing company

196 Rosenthal is widely regarded as the model for *Private Eye's* Snipcock, whose rotund, bow-tied persona regularly deflates with sharp-tongued realism the editorial flights of fancy of his refined editorial partner, Tweed.
197 Although this figure should be put in the context of the period's high inflation.

directed by Cecil Harmsworth King, the nephew of Lord Northcliffe (Bourne, 1990). The core of his business was the Labour-supporting tabloid newspaper *Daily Mirror*, and although throughout his career King concentrated on newspapers – not least for the political power they gave him – he created almost willy-nilly a vast cross-media publishing empire in which books played an increasingly important part. He had acquired the Northcliffe-founded Amalgamated Press in the 1950s mainly for its magazines, but this brought him the sizeable technical book list of Iliffe. The later acquisitions of Odhams and Newnes, both long-established publishers of practical and reference works for the masses, also introduced considerable non-fiction book publishing.

Odhams, originally a printer founded in the nineteenth century, became a publisher in 1906 and founded the political weekly *John Bull*, edited by the notorious crank and conman Horatio Bottomley. Despite (or perhaps because of) this, they prospered and especially after parting company with Bottomley in a famous and acrimonious dispute became more and more identified with Labour party and trades union politics. Their list was wide and concentrated on education for the masses, often sold through mail order and via their mass circulation newspapers such as the Sunday *People*. They had in the 1930s a monopoly of colour photogravure printing, giving their reference books a glamour and attraction that other publishers could not match. Later books were used as premiums to encourage subscriptions to their newspapers in aggressive, mail-based campaigns. Their list was always serious, high minded and improving, including, for example, the first books of the young historian Asa Briggs, but it could be eclectic. For many years they published *Debrett's Peerage*, hardly an essential work for trades unionists (for further details, see Odhams, 1935).

George Newnes, founded in Manchester in 1881, had a very similar profile in markets, but concentrated more on magazines than books; through its *Strand Magazine* it was the original publisher of Sherlock Holmes, although those rights in volume form eventually passed to John Murray. Among its many periodicals was the *New Musical Express*, which became in the 1960s and later the main organ of the pop music industry. Newnes established a book publishing subsidiary, the Educational Publishing Company, which specialized in reprinting classic adult fiction and storybooks for children (often sold to its periodical subscribers by mail order). It also published an extensive original list of ready reckoners, household maintenance guides, cookery books and treatises on pastimes, from fishing to photography, noted for their accuracy and earnestness.

There was a natural fit when IPC brought these two companies together in 1968, particularly when it added the British lists of the American-based school book publisher Ginn, since they shared many markets. Or at least that was what claimed. Despite the group's Left-Wing credentials and trades union heritage, IPC's real reason for the merger (which included the Fleetway Press, which largely published juvenile comic magazines) was, in a term that would become ominously familiar in subsequent years, 'rationalization' – effectively to eradicate inter-group competition by down-sizing. Many jobs were lost and their book publishing in particular lost impetus.

King had developed an admiring friendship with Paul Hamlyn, and in 1964 IPC paid £2.25 million for Hamlyn's book publishing company and gave him a seat on the IPC board. The following year all IPC's book publishing interests were consolidated, significantly under Hamlyn's name.[198] King had reputedly promised Hamlyn that he would become the head of the world's largest book publisher in the world (Rix, 2004).

King then turned his attention to buying Butterworths, in which he had previously acquired a small shareholding. The Butterworths chairman Richard Millett, appointed in 1965, was an aggressive and impatient solicitor who had been one of the trustees of the Bond estate, but he did not favour the installation of either of Bond's sons as Butterworths directors[199] (Graham, 2006, pp.74-83). He had become famous among City observers and reporters for his acerbic Chairman's statements – which lambasted government policy towards business – and while his rudeness and barely-concealed contempt for his staff recalled Stanley Bond at his worst, he had begun to improve Butterworths' lacklustre financial performance, particularly in the languid scientific and medical department. He became convinced that the company had to merge or be taken over to secure its future.

He had discussed the possibility of an arrangement with Longmans, but it came to nothing. Less welcome was an unsolicited bid in 1967 from Robert Maxwell's Pergamon Press to acquire the company, which Millett characteristically and forcefully rejected.[200] He was, however, more

198 First as Paul Hamlyn (Holdings) Ltd in 1965 and as the Hamlyn Publishing Group in 1967.

199 Ian Bond, the elder son, worked for a short time for McGraw-Hill, but left publishing in 1967. Brian Bond, the younger son, became an insurance broker.

200 Millett was perspicacious in that he publicly stated his doubts on Pergamon Press's

receptive to King's overtures, although he regarded the initial offer as insufficient. The Pergamon bid had put Butterworths in play, and the shareholders demanded a speedy resolution. A counter-offer by the American house Crowell Collier Macmillan, who were seeking to enter the British market, was financially adequate, but evoked reservations about the leading British law publisher becoming American-owned.

King and IPC increased their offer, albeit in paper rather than cash, which valued Butterworths at almost £7 million. It was an unheard-of valuation of a publishing company that, although improving, had until lately been making sustained losses for over a decade and turned over just over £3 million.[201] Butterworths passed into IPC ownership in December 1967, with King as chairman. Paul Hamlyn heralded the new regime, arriving at the Butterworths offices to greet their sober-suited staff 'dressed in a (then) dazzling concoction of greens, liberally sprinkled with purple polka dots' (Kay Jones, 1980, p.233), as head of the IPC Books Division.

Events then unravelled quickly. Barely five months later, King, who had become increasingly paranoid about the domestic political situation, used the front page of the *Daily Mirror* to demand Harold Wilson's resignation in a signed article.[202] Despite his apparently unassailable position as the creator of IPC, King had overstepped the mark and miscalculated disastrously. His fellow-directors summarily dismissed him. He had always intended to step down as chairman of Butterworths, and indeed his chosen successor, Norman Fisher, who had been a director of MacDonald & Co (ironically later to be owned by Robert Maxwell), took up the post in July 1968. Hamlyn, who remained as titular head of the Book Division, found Fisher an uncongenial colleague and thereafter had little to do with Butterworths. In fact Hamlyn, certainly after the loss of his protector King, chafed increasingly at the demands of corporate management which he never really enjoyed or had much aptitude for. He left more and more of the day-to-day business to his Managing Director, Philip Jarvis, and

—

financial stability at a time when Maxwell was held in high regard by the City and the government (Kay Jones, 1980, p.228).

201 The 'multiple' method, one of the techniques used to value publishing companies, applies a factor to annual turnover to arrive at a bid price. The factor ranges generally from 0.5 for less-profitable trade publishers to 3.0 for highly profitable, subscription-based companies. (See Gasson, 2001, for a more detailed discussion.)

202 He had apparently also discussed the possibility of a *coup d'état* with other business leaders, and asked Lord Louis Mountbatten, cousin of the Queen, to accept the role of figurehead leader following his revolution. Mountbatten refused.

busied himself with his recorded music business Music for Pleasure, founded in 1965.

In March 1970, the paper manufacturer Reed, in which IPC had a substantial shareholding, took over IPC, and the already discomfited Hamlyn resigned in protest. The new company was renamed Reed International and, under the direction of Labour insider Sydney 'Don' Ryder, it became one of the largest business enterprises in the United Kingdom and the biggest integrated paper, printing and publishing conglomerate in Europe, with over 80,000 employees. Ryder was one of the most controversial business figures of the 1970s. Originally a financial journalist and editor, he had run Iliffe publications so knew IPC well from having served on its board, albeit before King's great expansion. He left IPC to become Chairman and Chief Executive of Reed Paper and – through an aggressive policy of expansion – had gained a dominant position in newsprint supply.

When King was removed Ryder saw his chance to further aggrandize his empire by merging his smaller company with IPC, and he less than scrupulously used his political connections to avoid the takeover being scrutinized by the Monopolies Commission. This effectively scuppered a rival bid from the competing industrial conglomerate Courtaulds. When Ryder left Reed in 1974 to chair the National Enterprise Board, the state instrument of industrial policy, many of his ill-advised expansions and acquisitions overseas were quickly divested to save the company from insolvency. As what would be called today the Government's industrial 'czar', Ryder presided at the NEB over the disastrous attempts to reorganize the ailing motor manufacturer British Leyland. His infamous 'Ryder Plan' collapsed, amid accusations of corruption (which was never proved and for which claim he received damages from the *Daily Mail*), and he retired from public and business life in 1976 having received a peerage for his efforts.

Ryder appointed the logistics and systems expert Ken Stephenson, initially to sort out the poor profitability of the Hamlyn imprints but eventually to head Butterworths as well. Stephenson was, in true Butterworths tradition, forceful, abrasive and energetic, and he was keen to impose Ryder's brand of industrial conglomeration on what he saw as a poorly-run and insufficiently profitable publishing operation. To his credit, he opposed some of Ryder's more bizarre ideas, which called for companies within Reed to be grouped geographically rather than by function and which brought enterprises in totally different markets and structures under the same management. He was nevertheless unable to prevent Butterworths' Australasian subsidiaries being decoupled from their parent and incorporated within an unsympathetic Australian manufacturing company (Reed Consolidated Industries).

One of Stephenson's other innovations was to become something of a trend among publishers of the period – the removal of key publishing functions such as warehousing, accounts, sales and even editorial from congested city centre sites to rural 'green field' locations. Some publishers, such as Heinemann and Dent, had established out-of-town factories much earlier, of course, but they were essentially printers and binders and their editorial bases remained in London.

The flight to the countryside of the decade of 1965-75 was something new and different. It was very much in tune with the *dirigiste* planning ideas of the prevailing political ethos which was encouraging the decentralization of the economy. Macmillan had led the way in the early 1960s by relocating its warehouse and some sales and editorial functions to Basingstoke.[203] Longmans, as we have seen, moved virtually all their operations to Harlow in 1968, while Allen and Unwin created a large distribution and office complex in Hemel Hempstead between 1964 and 1970, leaving only a few 'whose presence in London were essential' in their Museum Street premises (Unwin, 1972, p.167).[204] Stephenson had originally planned to move Butterworths' entire operation, including editorial, to Bath in 1971, but changed his mind, eventually settling on, appropriately, a disused paper-mill at Borough Green in Kent. A new warehouse and office block were developed in 1973 and for at least a decade 'Borough Green' was 'place of publication' on Butterworths' imprint.[205]

Other publishers sought similar rural settings. Routledge and Kegan Paul constructed a warehouse and office block at Henley-on-Thames in

203 This was reputedly in response to a 'tricky' by-election in Hampshire that Harold Macmillan hoped to influence.

204 Both Harlow and Hemel were 'designated' New Towns and offered companies which relocated there significant financial advantages, including reduced business rates and subsidised housing for staff. Longmans' building was actually designed by the idealistic architect and creator of the Harlow master plan, Sir Frederick Gibberd and featured for many years in the Harlow Development Corporation publicity materials.

205 Other 'ruralized' publishers still tended to use 'London' as their 'place of publication' on the grounds that their registered offices were still in the capital. Longmans, for instance, apart from a very brief period in the late 1960s, never indicated Harlow as their publishing base.

the late 1960s. Hodder and Stoughton constructed a new warehouse and office complex at Dunton Green in 1974, only five miles west of Borough Green. The main factors in determining these locations was the proximity of the new M26 motorway, which gave swift access to the Tilbury container port for exports and imports and the new distribution centre created by W.H. Smith at Swindon, as well as a swift passenger train service to London.

Hamlyn, as we have seen, had been unhappy during his last years at IPC and had devoted much of his restless energy to planning his escape. In the event, the Reed merger provided a convenient cover for his resignation, and when he re-emerged a few months later, his new guise astounded even those expecting him to do the unexpected. The surprise when it was announced he had been appointed joint Managing Director with Rupert Murdoch of the Australian newspaper company News International (NI) was palpable.[206] This was prior to Murdoch's enormous expansion into British newspapers and other media, and although Hamlyn's executive position with Murdoch was short-lived, the rather unlikely colleagues did continue to work together harmoniously and productively; Hamlyn remained a director of NI until 1986 (de Bellaigue, 2004, p.91). Their political and cultural differences were enormous, but were subsumed by a great and genuine mutual regard for the other's entrepreneurial skill and drive.

However, Hamlyn had never intended to stay in an executive role with Murdoch for long.[207] He used the considerable financial and other clout of NI to launch his last great publishing enterprise, Octopus, a plan which had apparently been forming in his mind for some time. His intention was to unite his instinctive feel for marketing and ability to think globally with his belief that good books at the right price would always sell better than book trade traditionalists imagined. To realize his vision, he shamelessly cherry-picked his staff from IPC, bringing Sue Thomson, a versatile and experienced production executive, as Managing Director. This was a characteristically bold and shrewd move in an industry where

206 News International was Murdoch's family company. It was founded by his father Sir Keith Murdoch, knighted for his distinguished war career and subsequent promotion of American Australian cultural relations. Sir Keith Murdoch fellowships are regarded as the most prestigious academic awards available to Australians studying in the United States.

207 De Bellaigue reports that he himself characterized the joint role as 'daft' (de Bellaigue, 2004, p.91).

production managers were almost unheard-of as Chief Executives, let alone women. Thomson was shortly joined by Ronald Setter as publishing director and Peggy Singleton as marketing director and general manager, both of whom had impressed at IPC, as well as a number of more junior managers from the Hamlyn imprint. Significantly, no-one from Butterworths was recruited.

The key element of Hamlyn's success had always been value for money and he realised that good-quality cheap colour printing – which could not be obtained in Britain – was the key to this. In his previous 'Books for Pleasure' incarnation he had sourced this in eastern Europe, particularly Czechoslovakia, but now Hamlyn turned to the Far East for book manufacture. Despite the formidable logistical obstacles, one of his first acts was to establish Mandarin Publishers in Hong Kong under the direction of Geoffrey Cloke, another IPC veteran. Mandarin was in fact a print broker rather than a printer, obtaining flexible printing of very high quality at rock-bottom prices from a range of suppliers in the then British colony. Now commonplace, the model offered by Mandarin of a global supply chain which completely integrated editorial management, production, sales and distribution was a revolutionary concept that gave Octopus unique advantages in the market.

Once he had established his team and his publishing base Hamlyn bought his new company out of NI (with Murdoch's blessing) in 1972. In its first year of independent trading, it was already turning over almost £2 million, with an operating margin approaching 15 per cent. This is significant as even in good times most book publishers – apart from those in secure, demand-inelastic markets such as law or education – struggle to achieve double-digit margins. In the succeeding decade Octopus would grow to an annual turnover of almost £25 million. While it is true that its margin slipped to just below 7 per cent in the economically gloomy years of 1979-80 (still considerably above the industry average), growth was sustained for most of the period and Octopus generally bucked the stagnant trends in the British book market as the economic woes of the decade mounted.

Hamlyn's secret was to manage his risk and exposure to returns extremely cautiously, especially in the early years. The strategy involved the re-use of his content in appropriately edited forms in secure markets, both at home and overseas. One of his earliest deals was to produce an 'own-brand' exclusive book series for the chain bookseller W.H. Smith; they guaranteed to buy the titles 'firm', but at a discount of 60 per cent.

This seemed appallingly high to other publishers, who offered a maximum discount of 35 per cent but accepted the risk of returns. Again, such arrangements are not unusual today, but it was Hamlyn and Octopus who pioneered them. He later repeated the arrangement for other high street stores such as Marks and Spencer. Despite their evident quality and good value, these publications attracted the sneering dismissal of some publishers as 'council estate coffee-table books' (de Bellaigue, 2004, p.94).

Not that Hamlyn cared. He was too busy making money and demonstrating that by his relentlessly commercial approach he could overturn many cherished nostrums of traditional book publishing. Many of the Marks and Spencer titles (at their peak, he was producing over fifty new books per year for the retailer with some, such as *The Microwave Cookery Book*, selling almost one million copies) were easy to repackage since he had retained ownership of the illustrations and text; they did extremely well through a well-developed network of overseas agents. By 1980, 40 per cent of Octopus sales were made overseas, a figure only usually matched by the major educational publishers like Longmans or Macmillan, and certainly undreamt-of by trade publishers. It is also significant that a large proportion (60 per cent) of Octopus's revenue came from backlist, again a feature much more typical of educational than trade publishers. Hamlyn also ran an extremely tight ship in staff terms. Although a Labour supporter, and actually a generous and well-liked employer, he had been appalled by the heavy unionization and over-manning that he had encountered at IPC and proved to be ahead of his time in his frugal approach to staff. In 1982 Octopus employed only 250 people, each generating over £120,000 of turnover.

Unlike his earlier ventures, Hamlyn was no longer content to confine himself to non-fiction 'lifestyle' titles that he himself generated. He sought to widen his range by acquiring rights from other publishers and repackaging them in his distinctive format – and at startling low prices. An early example was an agreement with the British Printing Corporation (BPC) who as Purnell had, under the direction of Norman Marshall and Patrick Cavendish, introduced the concept of the 'partwork' to British publishing. They produced the highly successful *Knowledge* in 1961, a weekly encyclopedia aimed at children, as well as a number of other, more adult-oriented periodical reference works (Goodman, 2004). When Marshall and Cavendish left in 1967 to found their own company, which quickly came to dominate this highly specialist market, BPC – weakened by an unfortunate dalliance with Robert Maxwell – rather lost their publishing way. They were relieved to license their material in 1975 to Octopus, who used it to create a series of highly successful and very good value reference books on subjects such as warfare, history and even witchcraft.

Perhaps Octopus's most innovative rights licensing initiative came in the following year: an arrangement to republish titles from the Heinemann and Secker and Warburg backlists. Rosenthal and Pick had come up with the idea of creating 'omnibus' collected volumes of their leading classic authors, such as Hemingway and Orwell, in thousand-page hardbacks, each containing four or five novels. However, they had been frustrated by the discovery that within their editorial and production systems and traditional marketing, these volumes could not be published at anything less than a prohibitive price.

Despite some of his colleagues regarding Hamlyn as a vulgarian *arriviste*, Pick thought he might have the solution, and went to consult him in December 1976. Without hesitation, Hamlyn saw the potential, and said that he could produce the books to retail at £3.95 (the best Heinemann could do was £12.50) in minimum print runs of 50,000. The books were to be sold exclusively in Britain through W.H. Smith, and then worldwide through Octopus agents. The two agreed to a joint-venture sharing profits under the Heinemann-Octopus imprint, and the first ten titles were launched only a few weeks later in spring 1977. Bound in full cloth and elegantly printed on high-quality paper they looked good and were unbelievable value. The Bedford Square nay-sayers[208] were nonplussed and silenced. The initial list of titles had cunningly mixed highly commercial authors like Nevil Shute and Erle Stanley Gardner with 'serious' authors such as Somerset Maugham, Franz Kafka, John Steinbeck and D.H. Lawrence. The reaction of the market was ecstatic right across the list. Most of the initial printings sold out in a week, and reprints amounting to a total of a million copies were ordered and quickly absorbed. Other publishers clamoured to join the scheme.

Hamlyn was characteristically canny. He waited almost a year before adding four new titles, with the choice of authors again ranging from mid- to high-brow. They comprised collections of H.G. Wells, Ernest Hemingway, Graham Greene and C.S. Forester. The success of the

208 Bedford Square in Bloomsbury was then the centre of British trade publishing. Until the 1980s, most leading houses maintained offices in the Square, as did the Publishers' Association. Today the British office of Yale University Press is the only publisher who remains there.

omnibus republication model was assured, and by 1983 the joint-imprint had produced sixty-five editions known incongruously as 'Pickles'.[209] They had sold almost four million copies with a cumulative turnover of almost £8 million, and profits exceeded £2 million (St John 1992, pp.449-50). Authors ranged widely from Evelyn Waugh, Scott FitzGerald and Morris West to Georgette Heyer, Dennis Wheatley and Raymond Chandler. There is more than a touch of similarity between Lane's social purpose with Penguin and Hamlyn's bringing of good literature to an entirely new audience with the Pickles. Like Lane, he always put the business and its balance sheet first (and enjoyed the fruits of his enterprise with lavish living), but he got a lot of personal satisfaction from making money out of creating new readers.

Other profitable new ideas that arose from his lateral thinking and inspirational entrepreneurship included the creation of a stationery brand, Tigerprint, exploiting his powerful sourcing of raw materials and access to design flair.[210] He also showed his shrewd and original sense of market potential by creating branded products for emerging design-oriented companies, such as the clothes and furnishing retailer Laura Ashley. Hamlyn was an early exponent of the value of branding in book titles, and he was notably subtle in getting the best out of customized titles and convincing difficult but prestigious partners to endorse his books. He gained a reputation for being punctilious in involving partners closely at all stages and making sure they approved content. An alliance with the fashion magazine *Vogue* – whose owners, Condé Nast, were extremely protective of their titles – produced over a million sales for *Vogue Complete Beauty* in a market where exclusivity rather than mass appeal was the watchword. Octopus's unique skill was to deliver the appearance of the former with the results of the latter.

Hamlyn was also very good at sensing the way markets were changing and seizing opportunities even out of apparently unfavourable prospects. As the economic conditions at the end of the decade worsened and recession loomed, he created the imprint Bounty Books. This sought

209 This was because Hamlyn, who was much given to cloak-and-dagger scheming (and very bad puns), had kept the plan hidden under the code name 'Operation Pickles' until he was ready to go public. There is a suggestion that he playfully used his co-conspirator's surname to suggest the name.

210 Tigerprint was a successful and profitable addition to the business, turning over almost £7 million by 1984 – although many at the time were sceptical that a publisher could make a success of an essentially consumer product range.

to republish a 'budget range' of books at very low prices, often used as promotional items by non-book retailers. He used the distributor Websters (whom he would eventually buy) to sell these titles to a whole range of non-traditional outlets. While other publishers were floundering and barely making ends meet, Octopus enjoyed almost unrelieved success during the 1970s. By 1979 the company was reorganized as the Octopus Publishing Group. It was poised to become public and then embark on even more spectacular growth and diversification in the following decade, as we shall see in the next chapter.

De Bellaigue (2004, p.110) remarks that when Octopus was set up, observers might have concluded it was simply a recreational activity for its founder without many prospects. Others have contended that Hamlyn was simply lucky. His timing was always good and his decision-making clear-sighted and informed, if at times instinctive. He employed good people whom he trusted and who returned his trust with loyalty. Hamlyn saw opportunities others did not and backed them with serious investment. Brave without being foolhardy, he was good at both detail *and* strategy – but, most of all, he knew his limits. As he remarked famously in an interview with the *Sunday Telegraph*, 'I only understand one kind of publishing and that is books of wide appeal that improve the quality of life from the stomach to the mind' (quoted in de Bellaigue, 2004, p.92). He never lost sight of that simple formula, building from it more than one publishing house that brought him great wealth and great enjoyment – as well as changing the lives of millions who had never been touched by books before.

In contrast to Hamlyn's sure and brilliant management the consolidating tendencies of the decade elsewhere brought other, less positive results. Robert Maxwell had been building up the Pergamon business steadily, and when he floated it on the Stock Exchange in 1964 (diluting his personal shareholding to less than 30 per cent), it was publishing 600 new books per year and 70 journals in a wide range of scientific and academic fields. We have already seen that his methods both as an entrepreneur and a publisher had been questionable from the outset of his career, but it is during the 1970s that a series of scandals emerged into public view that began to call his integrity and reputation more generally into question (and would hold ominous echoes for future events).

There is no doubting Maxwell's vision, even if his means of executing it was not always 'whiter than white'. He was among the first to recognize the importance of computing in education and research, and he foresaw the role of networked personal computers in delivering information. He had invested in a computer company manufacturing the Modular One range, and in June 1969 he entered into discussions with an American data processing company, Leasco – managed by an entrepreneur at least his equal in guile and ruthlessness, Saul Steinberg – to merge their two companies. Maxwell would become 'second shareholder' and director of Leasco's international operations. The concept was simple and brilliant: Pergamon had the content and Leasco had the means (at least in theory)[211] of delivering it electronically to libraries and professionals (Cox, 2002, p.277). It was an idea at least two decades ahead of its time.

Leasco made an offer of £25 million for Pergamon, but it quickly emerged that Maxwell had inflated his company's value. He had done so by using a series of secretive trusts and private companies based in Liechtenstein and elsewhere to buy book overstocks and inflate journal sales. These companies had also covertly bought Pergamon shares to inflate their price. As Cox observes, Maxwell had, despite the flotation, continued to treat Pergamon very much as his personal fiefdom. However, he had miscalculated Steinberg's cunning and the growing disaffection of his institutional shareholders.

At a shareholders' meeting in October 1969, Steinberg ousted Maxwell from his own company. For almost five years he ran it as a cash cow, but without any electronic publishing – or indeed other new publishing ventures – being initiated. Cox recalls it as a 'sterile period' and acidly remarks that 'Leasco failed to introduce a publisher on the board of directors' (Cox, 2002, p.277).

Attention having been drawn to the dubious methods whereby Maxwell had ran Pergamon's business, he was investigated by Department of Trade inspectors. They concluded in a famous judgment in 1971 that 'he was not … a person who can be relied on to exercise proper stewardship of a publicly quoted company' (Bower, 1988, p.222). Subsequent investigations into the corporate governance of his private companies, and irregularities in the encyclopedia business (which had been mainly responsible for gaining Pergamon the Queen's Award for

211 It is very debatable whether Leasco actually had the technology to deliver 'electronic publishing' with the speed and flexibility that we know today. Its data processing capabilities were slow and laborious by modern standards, and the concept of the Internet as envisioned by Sir Tim Berners-Lee was at least 25 years away. Nevertheless the idea that underlay Maxwell and Steinberg's proposals was essentially the principle of contemporary digital publishing.

Export Achievement in 1966), published in 1972 and 1973, found highly questionable and indeed illegal activities. It was remarkable that, despite these findings, there was no decision to prosecute him. Some have concluded that Maxwell's political influence (he had been a Labour MP between 1964 and 1970, and stood unsuccessfully in the elections of 1970 and 1974) may have protected him.

Even more remarkable was the way in which an influential group of authors and journals editors put Leasco under pressure to sell their share of Pergamon back to Maxwell. He (or his ghostwriter) predictably cast Steinberg as the villain in the whole Leasco affair, but there was no disguising the triumphal reversal of his fortune (Maxwell, 1988, p.12). Led by Sameul Eilon, the management academic from Imperial College, London and the physicist Brian Spalding, the Pergamon editors issued an uncompromising ultimatum at the beginning of 1973:

> We consider the involvement of Robert Maxwell – whose life work Pergamon represents – essential to the restoration of confidence in the management of the company. His past record indicates that he will bring the required leadership to the publishing management so that the company can again implement urgent innovations demanded by changing needs. It is our obligation to our colleagues, who entrust us with their manuscripts, to make responsible arrangements for efficient, economic and rapid publications and worldwide dissemination. With Robert Maxwell in charge of publishing activities, we are certain that Pergamon will meet its obligations. Without him, we shall be forced to reassess our relations with the Company and make alternative publishing arrangements. (Eilon in Maxwell, 1988, p.635)

Maxwell and his family still owned 28 per cent of Pergamon's shares, but if Leasco (with 36 per cent) could keep the institutional shareholders (with 18 per cent) on board, Steinberg felt he could get rid of Maxwell for good and all. He rudely told the other board members that he was 'fed up' with the situation and dismissed the academics as unimportant trouble-makers.[212] This was a fundamental miscalculation. In October 1973, Spalding went public with a statement to the Press, bluntly stating that '[I]t appears only to be Mr Steinberg who stands in the way ... [H]e must

212 At a later board meeting he 'contemptuously' dismissed the editors' concerns, stating that they were 'ten-a-penny' and he could line up dozens ... to take the places of those who chose to resign or who would be sacked' (Eilon in Maxwell, 1988, p.640).

see that, if the journal editors withdraw their support, the Pergamon operation will collapse. And he should be in no doubt that the editors want Mr Maxwell back' (Eilon in Maxwell, 1988, p.639).

In the event Steinberg's pugnacious attitude scared rather than reassured the institutional shareholders and they caved in to the editorial threats. Leasco dragged their heels, but they eventually withdrew with a bad grace and Maxwell was able to buy the company back for just over £1.5 million, a small fraction of what he had sold his shares for in 1964. The astonishing display of author power,[213] combined with craven behaviour by institutional and other investors and the American misunderstanding of British business protocol evinced by Steinberg, enabled Maxwell to return Pergamon to his private ownership. He was reinstalled as chairman in April 1974. No matter what the government inspectors had said, he was now unassailable and knew that his authors and editors would follow him anywhere. Unwittingly it was they, leavened a little by Steinberg's stupidity, who would enable Maxwell to pursue with tragic inevitability the great frauds that concluded his career and precipitated his presumed suicide in 1991, since never again would he subject any of his companies to the scrutiny of public shareholding.

The death of Billy Collins in 1976 brought to the fore problems that would eventually lead to the loss of Collins' independence. Billy had planned and expected that his eldest son Jan would succeed to the chairmanship on his death, but he had also brought in experienced non-family directors such as Ian Chapman and David Nickson to strengthen the board. Shortly before his death, he also recruited the tough-minded accountant George Craig from the soap manufacturer Procter and Gamble to manage an increasingly complicated and intractable financial structure. While Billy lived, criticism of Jan and his decision-making was muted; and although Nickson and Chapman had told Jan privately they did not have sufficient confidence in him as a future chairman as early as 1974, they did not share these reservations with Billy (de Bellaigue, 2004, p.160).

Superficially Billy left what looked like an extremely healthy company. With sales of just under £50 million it was the largest British independent publisher, and the largest non-corporate British enterprise in what were just beginning to be called the 'media industries'. Its pre-tax margin was a

213 Eilon compared the events to the popular 1960s television serial 'The Power Game', which starred Patrick Wymark as a ruthless industrialist who bore an uncanny physical resemblance to Robert Maxwell.

refulgent 10.6 per cent. Jan used his new position to attempt to dominate all areas of the company's activity. 'My own role', he wrote in the 1977 Chairman's report '(is to have) an interest in all areas of the company with a special interest in the American company, children's, bible, and reference divisions, and the manufacturing division and finance' (quoted in de Bellaigue, 2004, p.162). With support from his formidable mother Lady Priscilla Collins, who ran the religious books imprint, he gave notice that he was to be firmly in charge and the influence of his erstwhile board rivals was to be severely curtailed. Even for an energetic and highly competent executive like Tom Rosenthal, the management portion Jan had sliced out for himself would have been daunting. Unfortunately Jan was no executive magician, and Collins's financial performance began to decline almost immediately on his assumption of power. Although sales continued to increase initially, within three years its earnings had fallen from over £5 million to a loss exceeding a quarter of a million pounds.

To be fair, the reasons for some of this were down to structural problems within the firm that had gone uncorrected in Billy's heyday, as well as factors beyond a single company's control. Increasing inflation and the strengthening of the pound against other currencies, for example, severely hampered a major exporter like Collins. Others were, however, directly attributable to Jan's management style. In 1974 he had convinced Billy and Priscilla that Collins should buy the World Publishing Company from the American Times Mirror Group, arguing that its religious and children's publishing was a good fit and provided access to a market where Collins could expand. The expectation of World proved wildly over-optimistic, and it was eventually disposed of at a loss. Collins was also the first major publisher to accede to booksellers' demands for higher discounts. It increased standard terms from 30 to 35 per cent, thus initiating a margin-paring spiral in a financial relationship established for decades. Such a trend would continue to destabilize book trade economics up to the demise of the NBA, and to the present.

The combination of a difficult economic environment and internal organizational challenges (Collins had between 1972 and 1979 spent over £17 million on establishing a new manufacturing and distribution base at Bishopbriggs north of Glasgow)[214] required united and determined

214 De Bellaigue (2004, p.163) notes that the actual cost was closer to £5 million, allowing for the generous grants and tax relief that were available for industrial relocation in 'special' areas. The historic factory and office building in Cathedral Street, expensively refurbished only a few years before, was sold to the University of Strathclyde.

management to overcome. Unfortunately the Collins board was openly at war, with Jan and his mother in one camp and Chapman, Nickson and Craig in the other. Each selected compliant non-executive directors to add to their strength, but it was clear that the impasse had to be broken to resolve the issues that divided them. Jan made it clear that he wanted to remain as Executive Chairman with a new Chief Executive to do his bidding and the non-family interlopers introduced by his father dismissed. He did in theory control over 50 per cent of the shares, but he was not sure he could count on a board majority. For their part, Chapman and his supporters wanted Jan stripped of executive authority, although they would suffer his continuation as figurehead Chairman. Jan's younger brother Mark, who with his sisters Deborah and Sarah (who had died tragically at the age of 34 in 1967 and had pioneered the sale of foreign rights) had worked for the firm and was being groomed as a more acceptable and steady replacement for the increasingly erratic Jan. Lady Priscilla remained steadfast in her support of Jan, but not even she could prevent his demotion.

In August 1979, Jan reluctantly accepted the board resolution that he should become non-executive Chairman, with Chapman as Deputy Chairman and Nickson as group Chief Executive. This new arrangement crucially gave the non-family executives total responsibility for all Collins book publishing, thereby excluding Jan from the expensive editorial meddling in which he had previously indulged. The medicine administered by the new board was strong and emetic. World was disposed of peremptorily in three sales and the freehold of the London office was sold – it yielded only £3.6 million, but indicated that no part of the company's operations was sacrosanct.[215] More radically, there were more than 600 redundancies in the UK operation and Collins in Australia was severely pruned in staff and scope.

Jan and his mother were not completely bested, however. To his credit, Jan was aware that shareholder and board disharmony might make the company liable to unfriendly attentions; the one he most feared was the incursion of Robert Maxwell, who had made his intentions towards

—

Collins took over some of the site vacated by their Glasgow competitors, Blackie, who had given up printing in 1966.

215 The elegant town house at 12-15 St James' Place had been Billy's pride and joy; here he had delighted to entertain authors and booksellers, and hold literary salons.

Collins more than clear.[216] He was also aware that Chapman longed to replace him as chairman. It was at a dinner hosted by Paul Hamlyn in May 1981 that Arnold Goodman, a renowned political and business fixer,[217] mentioned to Rupert Murdoch that Jan and Lady Collins would be willing to sell out their shareholdings in the family business. Initially dismissive, declaring 'Why do I want to be in book publishing?' Murdoch, perhaps at Hamlyn's urging, quickly grew interested. He made a decisive move less than eight weeks later. Jan arrived at what was planned to be an uneventful board meeting to prepare for the Collins's annual general meeting. He was hours late, whether by design or by genuine travel difficulties, and his first intervention in the meeting was to announce casually that he and his mother, as well as some family trusts, had agreed to sell their shares to Murdoch. A formal announcement of the intention of News International (NI) to acquire Collins would be made the following morning. There was uproar. The other directors summarily voted to remove Jan from the chairmanship and board, and Chapman was elected in his place. Mark Collins declared himself nonplussed and outraged.

The board was resolute in their determination to reject the bid, but in any case when the formal document was published it seemed that NI's offer was derisory. The entire company was valued at £22.75 million, less than one-third of its annual turnover, and seriously under-pricing its asset value. Chapman and his colleagues angrily rejected the offer and, despite a powerful media campaign orchestrated by Murdoch's papers, they slowly turned the tide against the bid among the remaining shareholders. A sticky moment came when Maxwell, who had quietly built up a holding of almost 10 per cent, promised Chapman that he would never sell to Murdoch – and then promptly did so.[218] Nevertheless, the Collins

216 The prospect of Maxwell holding the letters-patent to the King James Bible and control of Collins highly moral religious list is one of the more engaging counter-factuals of publishing history.

217 Goodman, a talented solicitor and arts magnate, was something of a publishing insider. For many years, he used the Macmillan boardroom in Little Essex Street as a convenient base for the Royal Courts of Justice and the nearby Inns of Court. I recall meeting him in the ground floor corridor there. His reputation has recently been called into question with allegations of financial misdemeanours, although nothing on a Maxwellian scale. It is significant that he made no bones about his hatred of Maxwell (and another great publishing buccaneer, Sir James Goldsmith).

218 De Bellaigue (2004, pp.170) notes that this 'curiously' coincided with the sudden resolution of some long-standing disputes and the extension of contracts between Maxwell-owned printers and Murdoch newspapers. Pure chance synchronicity, clearly.

board prevailed and in July NI withdrew the bid. However, Murdoch retained his shareholding of just over 40 per cent, giving him and a NI colleague Collins directorships. The wily Australian fox was content for the moment to bide his time and lick his wounds while keeping a close eye on Collins from the inside. What he did next we will see in the next chapter.

Other family publishers also felt the cold financial winds of the 1970s, and while they did not experience so dramatic a meltdown as Collins, they too were not immune to the pressures to abandon old dynastic practices and admit new blood. Even as venerable and gentlemanly a house as John Murray – which conducted its business from the famous Mayfair drawing room in Albemarle Street where Byron and Scott had met, and had for over two centuries been directed by a succession of Johns Murray in a rather unworldly fashion[219] (at least in the twentieth century) – felt the need to introduce a new breed of publishing entrepreneur to stiffen their sinews and enable them to take on a new commercial world (Carpenter, 2008). This they found in Nick Perren, who had joined the company from university in 1970 as an inspection copy clerk and enjoyed a meteoric rise, becoming a director in 1978 and ultimately managing director. Perren was (and remains) an energetic, lively and clear-sighted publisher with a good eye for business realities and opportunities. He concentrated on building up the company's unglamorous but lucrative educational business, the foundation of which had been laid by John Murray VI ('Jock'). Despite cultivating the persona of a literary *boulevardier*, Jock proved a shrewd judge of both commercial fiction and educational publishing.

Perren created an exciting and highly profitable textbook company which competed aggressively and successfully with the larger educational houses such as Longmans and Oxford University Press while retaining the high-quality general trade book publishing. He entrusted the latter to the gifted and level-headed Grant MacIntyre, who had cut his teeth in academic publishing. It was probably by the efforts of this pair, supported wholeheartedly, let it be said, by the current (and perhaps last) member of the publishing dynasty, John VII, that allowed the relatively small house to thrive and remain independent for another two decades.[220]

219 Although Byron may not have agreed, since he coined the famous epigram 'Now Barabbas was a publisher' about the John Murray who published him.
220 Murray was eventually sold to Hodder-Headline (now part of Hachette) in 2002. Perren retired and now operates a publishing consultancy.

Even Macmillan felt the need to restructure and streamline its business to meet the new, tougher circumstances of the age. Maxwell had famously predicted that Macmillan alone of all the traditional family companies would survive the 1970s without being taken over, merged or otherwise transformed into a conglomerate. While he was ultimately proved wrong, he was perspicacious enough to discern the underlying strengths in Macmillan's broadly-spread and diversified publishing, particularly its magazines and the scientific journal *Nature*, the financial jewel in their crown. Yet diversification had been achieved in a piecemeal fashion and the Macmillan management structure was rather ramshackle and outmoded. When Harold Macmillan retired from government in 1962 and returned to run his family publisher, there seemed little chance of the old showman agreeing to wholesale reorganization. However, as he gave way progressively in the following decade to allow the ground to be prepared for the succession by his son Maurice,[221] it became clear that a radical restructure was required. This was master-minded, in the spirit of the times, by a non-family member, Nicholas Byam Shaw.

Byam Shaw, the scion of a distinguished artistic and theatrical family, had been a long-serving Macmillan employee[222] and enjoyed the complete trust of the Macmillan family. He had begun his publishing career in sales with Collins, but he felt rather frustrated by Billy Collins's failure to promote him. He was recommended to Harold Macmillan by Alan Maclean, Macmillan's publishing director who had also been at Collins, and Byam Shaw quickly rose to become sales director (Maclean, 1997, p.164).

A saturnine, rather forbidding character, Byam Shaw possessed sharp business instincts and a clear sense of strategy. He devised a hierarchal structure of operational companies, each with their own directors, targets

221 Maurice Macmillan (1921-84) also had a political and ministerial career, but had retained a close association with the family firm throughout (he had been an early exponent of Pan books). He died unexpectedly before he could take up fully the place that had been prepared for him, with the crown passing rather sooner than was intended to his son, Alexander, now the 2nd Earl of Stockton.

222 It was a tradition that Macmillan staff either worked there for a short time, passing through en route for somewhere else (such as Tim Hely Hutchinson, Christopher Helm and indeed myself) or spent their entire careers there. Examples of the latter were literary editor Thomas Mark, who joined the company in 1914 and retired in 1962, and the legendary G.J. Heath, who joined as a boy at the age of thirteen in 1877 and 'never retired', dying in harness as general manager after sixty-two years service in 1939.

and budget, answerable to a holding company board. Each company was incorporated separately and reported results individually. Macmillan's British-based publishing was divided into four autonomous areas: Macmillan London for trade and general books; Macmillan Press for academic and reference publishing; Macmillan Education for school books and the increasingly important materials for teaching English as a foreign language; and Macmillan Magazines for *Nature* and a stable of other titles, including *Nursing Times* which had an enormous circulation and readership in the 1970s.[223] Service functions such as accounting and information systems were organized into their own companies like Macmillan Distribution Limited (MDL), providing warehousing and logistics, and cross-charged the publishing companies for services provided. There was even a film production company MFPL, but it is not clear whether it actually traded.

Macmillan's extensive overseas operations were incorporated in similar fashion, in Australia, South Africa and a string of emergent African countries. Some un-remunerative assets were disposed of, such as the Macmillan Company of Canada, founded in 1905 and sold in 1972. Harold's disastrous decision to withdraw from the United States in 1951, thereby losing the right to use the Macmillan name there for over forty years (until it was expensively re-acquired from International Thomson in 2000), had been to an extent recovered in the intervening two decades by a new American subsidiary, St Martin's Press.[224] Under its energetic and charismatic general manager and director Tom McCormick, St Martin's had become one of the United States' leading publishers, both in trade books and in academic, reference and college textbooks. As was inevitable with two powerful personalities, there was tension between Byam Shaw and McCormick, and St Martin's stayed outwith the operating structure, reporting directly to the Macmillan holding company.

Nevertheless, Byam Shaw, as Chairman of most of the operating companies, exercised effectively almost complete control. He carefully

223 *Nursing Times* had a circulation of over 100,000 and enormous revenues from pharmaceutical and recruitment advertising. Macmillan sold it in the late 1980s, arguing that it was non-core to their business. Some observers thought it was 'selling the family silver'.

224 Named for Macmillan's then street address in London, which in its turn was sold in 1965 when they moved most of their business to Basingstoke. The main editorial office was relocated to Little Essex Street at the western end of the Strand, near St Clement Danes.

excluded Macmillan family members from their boards, preferring to appoint trusted executives such as John Jackman, Sidney Josephs, Adrian Soar, Ray Barker and the uniquely creative academic editor Tim Farmiloe to deliver his vision of a highly profitable, diversified, international publishing organization with tight financial control and clear lines of accountability. The complete structure was in place by 1980, and there is little doubt that the rather corseted and perhaps over-elaborate edifice delivered good results and made Macmillan a difficult target for corporate takeover, thereby securing its independence. Some may have suspected that such a dense forest of companies in many jurisdictions gave opportunities to bury problems and hide excesses, but there is no doubt that it fostered a uniquely creative and innovative atmosphere. In no other company of similar size (Macmillan's UK-based turnover in the 1970s was about £30 million) could the investment have been found for major, slow-returning reference projects such as the new edition of the *Grove Dictionary of Music*, the *Macmillan Dictionary of Art* and the *New Palgrave Encyclopedia of Economics*.[225]

Macmillan continued both to win Booker Prizes for literary fiction (four between 1969 and 1981) and profits from mass-market paperbacks, textbooks, scientific journals and academic monographs, an almost unique combination in an integrated company. New formats were pioneered like the slightly taller so-called 'egg-head' paperbacks, covering more intellectual and serious non-fiction subjects, under the Picador imprint, as well as children's books featuring elaborate 'paper engineering'. Byam Shaw was a rather remote and retiring character whom it was difficult to get to know,[226] but he deserves great credit in shaping a lean and forward-looking Macmillan that remained financially strong

225 All but the Palgrave Encyclopedia (on which I worked) were sold to Oxford University Press in the first decade of the twenty-first century after Macmillan had finally lost its independence. They were among the first major reference works to be planned with a deliberate digital component, but were enormously consumptive of time, resources and investment. The *Dictionary of Art*, delivered with great aplomb and skill by its publishing director Ian Jacobs, took almost twenty years from conception to publication. Some have argued that it was the cost of these major projects that eventually made Macmillan a target for sale. If so, it was a heroic way to go.
226 He tended to shun publishing and book trade meetings and committees, and never served on the Publishers' Association council (where Macmillan Chairmen had been almost permanent fixtures since its foundation). However, he did chair the influential anti-censorship Freedom to Publish Committee, which may provide a key to his attitudes and wider interests.

through some very turbulent times. He might have appeared a gentleman, but that was a thin veneer on a very shrewd and business-like manager. He remained firmly in charge until he oversaw the sale of the company to the German media company Holtzbrinck in 1995.

Other traditionally organized publishing companies found the economic turmoil of the decade daunting and demanding. We have already seen that Cape and Chatto had formed an alliance to share overheads in sales and distribution, and in 1973 they were joined by the Bodley Head. The ailing shell of Lane's ancestral publishing house had been rejuvenated by the charismatic and elegant Max Reinhardt, who had bought it from Stanley Unwin in 1957 with the help of his theatrical friend Ralph Richardson and the merchant bank Henry Ansbacher (Adamson, 2009). Reinhardt was a tall, athletic and meticulously dressed man with matinée-idol looks who moved effortlessly in theatrical and clubland circles.[227] His background was exotic: he was born in Constantinople, studied in Paris and originally possessed Italian nationality, causing him to be briefly interned during the Second World War. He then worked in British military intelligence and entered publishing by acquiring a small firm, HFL, which specialized in the unlikely area of accountancy textbooks.[228] Rather like Cape, he cultivated the persona of a dilettante *boulevardier* of high literary sensibility, but as Rosenthal observes, he also disdained 'that beloved English affectation of semi-idiotic amateurism' that Warburg exalted among publishers: 'beneath his entirely genuine charm lay a steely professional publisher' (Rosenthal, 2004).

A botched merger attempt with Heinemann early in his career had made Reinhardt wary of business links with other publishers, but it had become clear by 1973 that the firm could no longer survive on its own (Lambert and Ratcliffe, 1987, pp.330-1). A holding company to own the three publishing houses was created with Reinhardt and

227 His first wife, Margaret Leighton, was a noted film actress and his second, Joan MacDonald, a casting director. In 1966 he moved his offices to Bow Street, adjacent to the Royal Opera House, Covent Garden.

228 HFL, named for H. Foulks Lynch who had established an accountancy correspondence college in 1884, was owned by the accountants Spicer and Pegler, who acted for Reinhardt. They sold him the publisher (together with its loss-making printer, Stellar Press) for £5000 in 1947, reputedly because they felt that he, with his society and government connections, could get around paper rationing restrictions more easily than they could. Although Reinhardt was not much interested in the subject matter of the books, their steady sale later underwrote his more risky literary publications (Adamson, 2009, pp.30-1).

Graham C. Greene (nephew of the novelist and Managing Director of Cape)[229] as joint-Chairmen, with Ian Parsons of Chatto as director. The arrangement allowed the imprints (later joined by the Virago imprint, specializing in feminist and women's writing) to keep their editorial independence and distinctive sales styles while sharing services and creating an effective modern distribution facility at Grantham in Lincolnshire. The role of the finance director, John Hews, who had been with Reinhardt since his early days as an accountancy publisher, was crucial in identifying the warehouse site and setting up computerized systems for stock control and royalty payments. The new facility cost the then-unprecedented sum of £420,000 – a figure that none of the component firms could have afforded alone in good times, let alone at the height of a recession. When it opened in 1975, it was the most modern in Europe, although in the fashion of the times highly unionized (de Bellaigue, 2004, p.140).[230] By 1980 CBC, as it had become known, was generally regarded as the most efficient book supply operation in the UK.

However, the new arrangement produced only short-lived harmony. Reinhardt's style in the management of both staff and authors was at odds with the brasher and less reflective style at Cape and Chatto. Long-serving and trusted editorial and sales staff such as Judy Taylor found the new environment uncongenial and left. The departure of Taylor was particularly a body blow, since Reinhardt had long thought of her as his successor. She was the first woman to be elected to the Council of the Publishers' Association and was the key figure in creating Bodley Head's children's list, generally regarded as the best of its era. She reached her decision only after much soul-searching, and there is no doubt that with her left a great deal of the creative energy of the house.

Judith Adamson (2009, Chapter 14) has described in detail the growing unease with which Reinhardt saw the fun and conviviality leach out of the business he loved, to be replaced (ironically given his earliest publishing) by a preoccupation with management accounts. Although he was too gentlemanly to say so, he found the methods and ideas of those now in the ascendancy in what became known as the Triad, particularly Tom Maschler and Carmen Callil of Virago, not to his taste (although he

229 Graham Greene (the novelist) was himself also a Bodley Head director.

230 It was opened by Michael Foot MP, who in the succeeding decade became leader of the Labour Party to whom the father of the chapel (Union chairman) of SOGAT (Society of Graphical and Allied Trades) confided that the new centre was overmanned, but 'there were plans'.

admired and remained on friendly terms with Callil). He even found his erstwhile friend Graham C. Greene unsupportive and duplicitous.[231]

The Bodley Head were obliged to move from his beloved office in Bow Street to unsuitable offices in Bedford Square next door to Cape.[232] His colleagues progressively shut him out of the key decisions in the business despite his controlling the largest block of shares and, although the three companies were supposed to be equal in influence, it was generally felt that preferment and preference were given to staff and projects from Cape (Adamson, 2009, pp.148-50). The corporate name Cape, Virago, Bodley Head, Chatto (abbreviated as CVBC) clearly showed the pecking order within the organization. The stress of the situation clearly contributed to Reinhardt's near-fatal heart attack in 1984, which occurred perhaps symbolically in the Cape boardroom. Although he recovered the unhappy situation persisted, and Greene in particular both publicly patronized and privately cold-shouldered him, much to Reinhardt's bemusement. He shared with Deutsch a trusting belief in the straightforwardness and honesty of English public school men, which proved to be sadly misplaced.

Eventually Reinhardt resigned, ironically just as Bodley Head marked its centenary.[233] He had sold off the professional publishing of HLF to Butterworths, but retained the name and company incorporation. This he used to set up a unique partnership with Penguin in which he could run his own publishing house, with Penguin providing production services and warehousing but giving Reinhardt complete editorial

231 In his memoir *Publisher*, Maschler is very dismissive of Reinhardt and does not even do him the courtesy of spelling his surname correctly (Adamson, 2009, p.157).
232 Judy Taylor recalls that Reinhardt was particularly fond of lunching at Rules in Maiden Lane where the traditional English cuisine – especially the steak and kidney pie washed down by at least three bottles of Beaujolais, often shared by herself, Graham Greene and Hugh Greene – was much to his taste. After the move to Bedford Square he was rarely able to visit this lunch haunt (Bradley, 2008, p.165).
233 There is a notably uninformative and bland account of Reinhardt's disengagement from Bodley Head in Lambert and Ratcliffe's centenary volume (1987) – hardly surprising given that it emerged from Bedford Square just as he resigned. (My copy belonged to A.L. Rowse who annotated the volume with his characteristic libellous scurrility.) Adamson's sympathetic biography of Reinhardt does much to redress the balance. It is the definitive account of his last unhappy decade with the imprint, making the point that despite the distractions of board room games he produced much important publishing (Adamson, 2009). His own privately published memoir (Reinhardt, 1998) is much too generous and kind to those who wronged him, but that is the measure of the man.

autonomy. Reinhardt Books set up in 1985 and successfully operated as a tenant within Penguin until 1996. It provided something of a minor bulwark of older publishing values against a rising tide of corporatism.

It might be thought that Penguin, as one of the first publishers to come into corporate ownership following Lane's death, would be better placed than many to cope with – and indeed benefit from – the choppy economic and business waters of the 1970s. In fact, the decade proved very difficult for Penguin, and it rather lost its way both editorially and financially. The merger with Longmans turned out only to be short-term. In August 1971, Pearson as parent of both bought the remaining minority shares in Penguin and established the two publishers as separate subsidiaries with little financial or operational overlap. Much of Longmans trade publishing, including the bestselling classical historical novels of Mary Renault and Stella Gibbons's *Cold Comfort Farm*, had already been transferred to Penguin, and the hopes expressed of joint ventures generally went unrealized. During the 1970s the two Pearson-owned publishers pursued distinct and more or less unrelated paths. Longmans enjoyed a brilliant revival by concentrating on home and overseas educational and professional publishing, especially in the rapidly advancing field of textbooks for teaching English as a foreign language and African, primarily Nigerian, school and college markets. This strategy, pursued by the new Chief Executive Tim Rix (appointed in 1976) brought large profits and steady growth, while Penguin put in an unsteady and quixotic performance (Briggs, 2008, Chapter 8).

As de Bellaigue (2004, p.37) observes, a frequent consequence of merger and restructuring is the departure of key personnel. Such moves certainly adversely affected Penguin, with the loss in short order of highly creative publishers such as Charles Clark, who left to run Hutchinson, and Dieter Pevsner and Oliver Caldecott (who set up their own company, Wildwood House, in 1972). All had weathered the storm of the Lane-Godwin years, but found Pearson ownership uncongenial. They were replaced by some imaginative and potentially very promising appointments. Peter Calvocoressi, a politics and international relations academic, became editorial director in 1972 and Peter Carson,[234] one of the brightest editors of his generation, joined in 1973 to run the hardback imprint Allen

234 Carson, who actually came over from Longmans, was one of the few staff exchanges between the companies, although Calvocoressi's admired textbook on international relations since 1945 was published by Longmans.

Lane. However, the structure they inherited was flabby, and the weaknesses of the end of the Lane era – which had been containable in times of economic well-being – were cruelly exposed when circumstances became less propitious.

Superficially it looks as if Penguin did well in the period, with sales increasing from just over £8 million in 1972 to £36 million in 1980. Most of this 'growth' is actually accounted for by inflation, and the underlying measures tell a sadder tale of erratic performance and decline. Initially there had been real growth, but as the economic crisis deepened Penguin found itself vulnerable and weak in a number of its key markets. An expensive and revolutionary scheme for teaching English in schools failed, and eventually the entire Penguin Education list was abruptly closed down in 1974. Between 1974 and 1979 volume of units sold fell from 44 million to 39 million and although a record pre-tax profit of £2.7 million (at a respectable margin of almost 15 per cent) was achieved in 1976, it rapidly went into freefall, barely reaching £240,000 in 1980 with a pre-tax margin of less than 1 per cent. Hardback sales were particularly poor and the Allen Lane imprint was starved of investment; although it limped on, its closure looked probable. The only bright interlude in the era was the acquisition of the New York literary and trade publisher Viking for $9 million in 1975, although this may only have occurred because Pearson needed to find a home for the United States surplus of its oil industry company (de Bellaigue, 2004, p.41).[235]

Calvocoressi, who had become chief executive, found Pearson executives interfering more and more in his company's management and increasingly constraining his freedom to operate. He formed the view that Pearson did not understand publishing, and particularly not Penguin's symbolic role as a cultural guardian not unlike that of the BBC, albeit without public funding. He expressed his exasperation and frustration more and more openly to colleagues and to the owners. This led to a crisis and he was dismissed abruptly in July 1976, ironically just as the company achieved its highest-ever profits. A rather chaotic interregnum under an

235 The ultimate Penguin holding company, S. Pearson and Sons, was a diverse industrial conglomerate in true 1970s style. Apart from publishing and newspapers (it owned the *Financial Times* and the Westminster Press), it also owned sanitary ceramic manufacturer Royal Doulton, various transport and property interests and, perhaps most bizarrely, the first growth vineyard in the Médoc, Château Latour. This last connection was much appreciated by executives like me who sometimes received cases of the fabled wine at Christmas.

out-of-depth salesman, Tony Mott, who later became a highly successful paperback publisher at Transworld, contributed significantly to the company's increasing woes, but two years later Pearson fortuitously recruited the man who turned out to be Penguin's saviour, the American publisher Peter Mayer. His story belongs mainly to the 1980s and is recounted in the next chapter.

The turbulence and economic displacements of the 1970s affected trade publishers most since their products were very susceptible to pressures on consumer spending. Most academic, educational and professional publishers actually continued to do rather well. Writing in 1974, Peter Allsop, Chairman of law publishers Sweet and Maxwell, remarked on how the market was expanding and he was more concerned with the possible impact of new technology than a decline in sales on his business (Allsop, 1974, pp.146-8). Schools and particularly universities were still growing, and their demand for books continued to increase strongly. Companies such as Longmans, Macmillan, Evans Brothers, Pergamon, Routledge, Methuen, Heinemann, Harrap, Pitman, Butterworths and a host of smaller specialist imprints prospered, particularly in export markets. The exceptions to these were the two major university presses. Both were unprepared for the financial problems of the time and had to take drastic action to survive.

Perhaps the most serious problems were experienced by Cambridge University Press (CUP). In 1970 it was still more or less unchanged in structure since Sydney Roberts' time and, although its operations had grown both at home and overseas, it still operated under a cumbersome administrative structure overseen by a group of academics, the Press Syndicate. There was tension between the head of the publishing arm of the Press, Richard David, and Brooke Crutchley, the University Printer, on the respective importance of the printing and publishing businesses, and there was little in the way of financial control. Effectively CUP had run out of money and was surviving on a bank overdraft amounting to £250,000. There was much donnish hand-wringing but as the financial situation and the general economic climate worsened it was clear that there needed to be a far-reaching and immediate change in the way that CUP was run. Uncharacteristically the university took brisk and decisive action. It reviewed the publishing activity (printing was regarded as sacrosanct), recommending the closure of the London office and the simplification and consolidation of activities in Cambridge. It also recognized the need for a forceful and visionary leader from the commercial sector. This they found in Geoffrey Cass, Managing Director of Allen and Unwin which he had joined after overseeing their move to Hemel Hempstead as a management consultant.

Cass joined CUP in December 1971 and he quickly turned its fortunes around, despite facing what initially looked like overwhelming problems. The overdraft had increased to £1.75 million in 1972 and Cass demanded, and received, more or less complete autonomy in financial matters from the University and the Press Syndicate. He won over the staff by pledging to avoid redundancies, although his briefings were recalled by some as 'bracing' or 'brutal'. Cass's cost-cutting and restructuring measures brought swift returns, and by the beginning of 1973 CUP had cut its borrowings to zero and had money in the bank. New appointments were made in arcane disciplines such as marketing, which greatly improved the sales operation. The backlist was critically scrutinized, re-priced or remaindered.[236] By the time the recession was in full swing in 1976, with unprecedented rates of inflation, CUP felt strong enough to increase its publishing output and invest in some major new projects. Cass then achieved arguably his greatest coup. He successfully put the case that CUP's activities justified charitable status; this was granted in 1976, thereby absolving it from Corporation Tax and giving its balance sheet a powerful fillip. Although problems remained there is little doubt that Cass – against all the odds – saved CUP from collapse at probably the most dangerous period in its history (Black, 1984).

Oxford University Press (OUP) had enjoyed, in the words of Sutcliffe (1978, pp.269-70), a more or less 'benign era' from the end of the war until 1970. It had grown internationally with 'branches' throughout the English language world, and indeed elsewhere, and had used its long-established London publishing house, first at Amen Corner near St Paul's Cathedral and later at Dover Street in Mayfair, to develop a reasonably lucrative trade list, even experimenting with paperbacks.[237] While CUP had always kept a more academic profile in its publishing, OUP's list had become

236 Cambridge had a reputation, as did Oxford, for never writing off backlist titles, and it was reputed that as late as 1975 both Presses' warehouses contained titles printed in the eighteenth century. There was certainly no systematic regular programme of price increases, an innovation Cass introduced.

237 Until the retirement of Geoffrey Cumberledge who had been OUP 'London Publisher' between 1945 and 1956, a peculiarity of Oxford practice had been that London books were published under the personal imprint of the publisher himself, rather than that of OUP.

much more diversified.[238] It published poetry, music, children's books and a wide range of educational material. Its reference books, atlases and its incomparable English dictionary, first published in 1928 and still being revised, were established as standard works. The core of the Press publishing was, nevertheless, the academic monographs and treatises published under the imprint 'Clarendon Press'. Their acquisition was decided by a committee of Oxford University academics known as the Delegates, with decisions made mainly on academic rather than commercial grounds. The Chief Executive of OUP's publishing arm's official title was 'Secretary to the Delegates'.

As a department of the University, the Press drew largely but not of course exclusively on its host institution for authors, staff and management. Its reputation was high for academic quality, rather less so for financial expertise, and it was saddled with an expensive manufacturing operation, even owning its own paper mill at Wolvercote on Oxford's north-western fringes. By 1970, the British operations of OUP were selling £10 million worth of books, but its structure was sprawling, with no clear strategy or central planinng mechanism. A rather half-hearted investigation of OUP's business (the Waldock Report) concluded in 1970 that re-organization and focus were necessary, but was dismissed by OUP publisher Dan Davin with typical robustness as merely an example of the 'penitential navel-gazing, hair-shirt, apologetic, prostrate defeatism that was rife in Oxford' (Sutcliffe, 1978, p.282).[239]

Nevertheless its recommendations were acted upon, if not quite as forcefully as at Cambridge. The decision-making role of the Delegates was circumscribed, the management and divisional structure was streamlined and proper financial planning and reporting introduced. More controversially, it was decided to close the London branch and concentrate all United Kingdom publishing in Oxford. Economies and new reporting structures were introduced by a new head, George Richardson, appointed in 1974 and now called 'Secretary and Chief Executive' for the first time. (The 'Printer' still oversaw manufacturing and kept his separate status

238 It was CUP's academic 'purity', compared to OUP's 'trade orientation' that Cass had used in his argument with the authorities to obtain charitable status (Black, 1984, chapter 15).

239 Davin, a rumbustious New Zealander who was Deputy Secretary to the Delegates, had a lively turn of phrase and a sharp eye for cant and Oxford 'lost causes'. He was much loved by his staff and OUP authors, and is still remembered with affection for his frequently outrageous comments.

and precedence.) Nevertheless Richardson was still an Oxford insider, since he had been a Fellow of St John's College and a Delegate. He was also, however, a shrewd academic economist who had observed the success that Cass had achieved at CUP.

Although of course it would be *infra dig* (and misleading) to suggest that Richardson's plans were at all inspired by Cass, it is remarkable how closely OUP's changes followed those at CUP. New staff were brought in from commercial houses, most notably the gifted editorial director from Hodder and Stoughton, Robin Denniston, and bright young editors such as Andrew Schuller, Richard Charkin (formerly at Harrap and Pergamon, and later to run Reed Trade and Macmillan) and Ivon Asquith (who would eventually become Oxford Academic Publisher) were recruited to develop fresh lists in fields such as economics or science. Oxford, too, sought and acquired charitable status in 1978. While its position had been by no means as close to the brink as CUP, and its recovery was not as rapid or spectacular, OUP celebrated its rather synthetic fifth centenary in 1978[240] as a much better run, financially fit and powerful publishing house than it had been ten years before. For both university presses it had taken the rigours of economic uncertainty and then growing recession and inflation to shock them out of their academic complacency, but both did emerge as modern, well-run publishing enterprises.

If the 1970s saw the end of publishing as 'a profession for gentlemen', both in reality and myth, it also saw the beginning of a more literal transformation in the gender balance of its managers. Women had always played an important role in publishing houses as we have seen with Mills and Boon, Cape and Gollancz, but unless they had dynastic connections they mainly occupied lowly-paid support positions in editorial, sales or secretarial roles. Exceptional individuals such as Diana Athill, Kaye Webb, Judy Taylor, Ruth Simon and Eunice Frost had forged significant careers in editorial commissioning previously, but women as heads of publishing houses were virtually unheard-of until the 1970s. Even then, female promotions were slow and hard-won.

Perhaps the most important female publisher of the era was Norah Smallwood. She became Managing Director of Chatto and Windus in 1975 in succession to Ian Parsons, after being a director of the company

240 OUP claimed as its origin that the first book printed in Oxford was dated 1478, but the Press as a publishing operation only really dates from the middle of the eighteenth century. CUP was created by a charter of Henry VIII in 1534, although the first books printed in the name of the university did not appear until fifty years later.

since 1953. She had joined Chatto as a secretary in 1936 and after losing her husband in action in 1943 she was able to devote the remainder of her career and her considerable talents to Chatto and its authors. She worked closely with Parsons, who recognized and supported her editorial talent, and with Leonard Woolf in the rejuvenation of the Hogarth Press as an imprint to foster authors such as Laurie Lee, Laurens van de Post and George Mackay Brown. She cared both about good writing and quality of presentation; many of her books are notable for the fineness of their printing and particularly their illustrations, provided by a clutch of gifted graphic artists like Enid Marx, Reynolds Stone and Edward Ardizzone.

Smallwood had a reputation for a sharp tongue, brusqueness and strict staff management. She was also undoubtedly a shrewd politician in dealing with her male rivals, both in the boardroom and the wider publishing world, to build a highly successful career. Some of this was, one suspects, an act to enable her make her way in a hostile male world, but others saw a warmer side to her personality. Certainly she devoted endless care and attention to the authors she discovered, and was rewarded with loyalty and gratitude. Among many she brought to publication were the actor and raconteur Dirk Bogarde and the philosopher and novelist Iris Murdoch, who recalled Smallwood as a 'combination of comrade, leader, mother, business partner and muse ... strong, clever, wise, practical, loyal and absolutely practical'. Jeremy Lewis, who worked with her, recalls her with affection as a formidable autocrat who once enquired of the Company Secretary 'exactly what *is* a balance sheet?' (Lewis, 2008). Others could find her rude, iconoclastic and inflexible, as well as a little out of touch with the financial reality of the modern world. Nevertheless she saw the necessity for the merger with Cape and Bodley Head, and she was good at supporting and developing new and *avant-garde* writing talent like Toni Morrison, who later won the Nobel prize for literature.

When Smallwood retired in 1982, at the age of 73, her successor was nearly her equal as a mould-breaking female publisher. Carmen Callil was an Australian book publicist who in 1972, in association with Harriet Spicer and Ursula Owen, founded a feminist publishing house called Virago. It began by republishing neglected classics of female writing, but soon took on original books issued in a distinctive green livery that was both stylish and a political statement. Virago exactly hit the mood of the time for 'books for women by women', and its output quickly grew to forty titles per year. Its market was largely metropolitan and

Guardian-reading, but it rapidly built up a loyal constituency, with sales approaching half a million pounds and a respectable profit by the end of the 1970s.

Callil was invited by Graham C. Greene to take over Chatto, and with Smallwood-like directness she insisted that the price of her transfer was the purchase of Virago to be part of the group. She negotiated a shrewd and tough deal, won at the expense of nearly alienating her co-founders, but eventually obtained a price in excess of £250,000, mainly in cash. As we have already seen, there was disharmony within the wider Cape, Bodley Head, Chatto group, but Callil was a skilful boardroom politician and she negotiated the testosterone-fuelled egos and scheming there with considerable aplomb (much more successfully than Max Reinhardt, for whom she developed a genuine affection). Other female entrepreneurs established niche publishers during the decade, for example Frances Pinter (1974), Frances Lincoln (1977) and Judy Piatkus (1978).

Elsewhere, women began to make inroads into the management positions in larger and more established houses. New Zealander Liz Calder, who had begun her career in publicity at Gollancz with Callil, emerged at Cape as one of the decade's most perceptive and commercially aware editorial directors in high-end literary publishing. Anita Brookner, Salman Rushdie and Julian Barnes were among her many prestigious authors, although her style was a little cramped by the egotistical ebullience of Tom Maschler.[241] In another sector Paula Kahn was developing a career trajectory in English as a foreign language (EFL) publishing at Longmans that would eventually take her to the chief executiveship of the venerable company.

In certain areas, women began to dominate senior jobs, most particularly in foreign rights, publicity and sales as well as literary agency. Since Sarah Collins had invented the role of the rights manager in 1960, more and more publishing houses felt the need for specialist executives to negotiate and sell translation rights, and these jobs became largely the province of women. The new profession, created by pioneers like Carole Blake at Gollancz and Lynette Owen at Pitman and Longmans, revolutionized the international status of British books and authors and

241 According to an interview in *The Observer* in July 2005 Calder revealed that she had been 'fed up not being party to what was going on at Cape; the men at the top called the shots'. She was also carefully diplomatic about her relationship with Maschler, whom she admired but admitted to finding 'irritating' with 'the uncomfortable ability to take credit for things not entirely his doing' (Maya Jaggi, *Wizard Talent*, 2 July 2005).

created a lucrative new revenue stream for publishing houses. When Calder co-founded Women in Publishing (WiP) in 1979 as a ginger group to promote women's careers and facilitate networking, the previously male-dominated publishing landscape was in a state of flux. The roles of women, as we saw in the last chapter, were changing dramatically and decisively although there still remained a sizeable imbalance of power between the genders. Women had begun to make assaults on the high ground of publishing, but they had much further to go. Gentlemen might have been in decreasing supply as the 1970s came to an end, but the structures and organizations that they had created in publishing had proved remarkably resilient – or, some would say, stubbornly conservative. Nevertheless the forces of agglomeration and corporatism, as well as social change, had begun to have observable impact. It would, however, take the arrival of a woman with the election of Margaret Thatcher as Prime Minister in 1979 to initiate for good or ill the final transformation of the British publishing industry in the twentieth century.

9 'The End of the Affair'

British publishing deregulated, 1980-95

The election of the radical Right-Wing administration of Margaret Thatcher in 1979, with its ideologically-fired policy agenda of monetarism and free-market capitalism, is often seen in retrospect to mark a swift and dramatic end to the consensual social democratic politics that had prevailed since the Second World War (Marr, 2006). Thatcher certainly arrived with a mandate for change and an appetite for the sacrifice of the sacred cows of state ownership, welfare economics and restrictive practices throughout most if not all areas of British society. Nevertheless, her revolution was in reality much more attenuated and slow to start than her apologists may admit, and her drive towards deregulation and the creation of an individualistic, market-driven, property-owning democracy was never as complete nor as consistent as her vision demanded.

She inherited enormous economic problems from the outgoing Callaghan administration, with high inflation, rising unemployment, industrial unrest and looming recession. Initially her policies sharpened the problems; inflation (and interest rates) accelerated and unemployment exceeded the unprecedented postwar figure of three million. Her popularity quickly fell, and had a sudden election occurred in 1981 there is little doubt that she would have lost. Three events coupled with a divided and ineffectual opposition turned the tide in her favour: the first was the jingoistic public response to the recovery of the Falkland Islands following the Argentine invasion in 1982 which cemented her image as the 'Iron Lady';[242] the second was her bitter and prolonged campaign against the striking miners of 1985-86 which virtually eliminated trades unions

242 Although she first received that name from a critical article published in the Soviet Union which she adroitly turned to her advantage (see Marr, 2006).

as a political force; and the third was the financial 'Big Bang' which deregulated the stock market in 1986.

This last in particular allowed the meteoric growth of the City of London to become a world centre of finance and enabled the successful privatization of state assets. The mass public sale of shares in nationalized companies such as British Gas and British Telecommunications (although it was argued by opponents that the purchasers were buying only what they already owned) – together with the policy of the sale of council houses, thus widening property ownership – seemed to have changed forever the political outlook of the population and looked to have made her social transformations irreversible. If, as Marr (2006) remarks, Thatcher was lucky in her enemies, both at home and abroad, she was also supremely fortunate that her premiership coincided with the peak of revenues from North Sea oil which enabled her to fund her regime of low direct taxation, unrestricted financial markets and divisive social policy. From the perspective of the end of the first decade of the twenty-first century, much of Thatcherism – as it came to be known both approvingly and derisively – can be seen to contain some of the seeds of the economic problems that twenty-five years later beset Britain. However, there is little doubt that she dramatically and often courageously challenged and attacked the institutional lethargy and complacent consensualism that had been the hallmark of much of British society. And this, of course, included publishing.

Publishing as an industry was never directly in Thatcher's sights (she had bigger fish to fry) and despite, as we shall see, a couple of direct confrontations, she never much engaged with the world of British books.[243] Nevertheless her creation of a bracing entrepreneurial economic environment did have direct consequences, for good or ill, on the structure and business aims of publishing firms, as well as their ownership and sources of investment. At first, her arrival and immediate policy changes were beneficial for publishing, albeit in a fortuitous and unintentional way. In its attempts to keep inflation under control, the Callaghan government directly managed prices and wages under the strict control of the

243 The only direct Thatcherite intervention was the privatization of the government publisher HMSO, but this took place after she had departed at the fag-end of the premiership of her successor, John Major, in 1996. The Iron Lady herself did receive a record advance on royalties for her memoirs from Rupert Murdoch's HarperCollins after she left office. Since they sold half a million copies, it might be argued a sound business deal.

Prices and Incomes Board (PIB). The PIB had attempted since the mid 1960s to apply a voluntary policy, but had signally failed to control inflation. This failure led to the creation in 1977 of the Price Commission, which was given statutory powers to regulate and prevent businesses from increasing prices without its prior approval. Irksome bureaucracy for many companies, this became an unworkable nightmare for publishing with its tens of thousands of individual products. Particularly hard-hit were those publishers, especially in the reference, educational and academic areas, with active backlists, where reprints were an essential part of the product mix. As the cost of raw materials rose (paper was largely imported and its price therefore uncontrolled), cover prices needed to be increased to make a book reprint viable. Every single proposal to increase a price had to be submitted to the Commission for approval.[244]

If the Commission refused, then the publisher had either to accept the rapidly eroding margin of the fixed price as a result of inflation, or if the book was out of stock, its replacement cost as a reprint. This often meant that it could only be sold at a loss and therefore its reprint had to be abandoned. The position was made worse since printing was undergoing great technical transformation: books originally printed by hot metal letterpress had to be transferred to film and offset-lithography, generating an additional cost for reprints. The Price Commission was abolished less than two weeks after Thatcher came to power, but its two-year sway had undoubtedly consigned many steady-selling titles to oblivion and cut short the potential success of books of all categories, from education to popular fiction. Its swift execution (the Thatcher government's first major abolition of its predecessor's organs of direct economic manipulation) was thus welcomed by publishers who had seen their costs rising and their revenues flattening.

A second rapid policy shift by the new government brought a completely unintentional but nonetheless substantial benefit. Part of Thatcher's fiscal project was to cut taxes on income and increase those on consumption, which she and her ministers argued would control wage inflation and stimulate the economy. This was economically arguable, but the policy was also part of the ideological commitment of the government

244 At Longmans in Harlow, a motorcycle despatch rider was in constant attendance to rush requests for price increases down the M11 motorway to the Commission's offices. My recollection of this period is that about half the price increase requests I made to the Commission were refused.

to monetarism. Value-added tax (VAT), introduced following Britain's accession to the EEC, was the principal tax on goods and services, and it was speedily almost doubled from 8 per cent to 15 per cent. Books and newspapers were one of the few categories of product on which VAT was applied at a zero-rate.[245] Therefore, while many other tax-bearing retail products suffered a sudden price increase early in the Thatcher government books did not, and with the end of price control this enabled lost margins to recover to a degree while prices to the consumer still looked competitive. There is little evidence, however, that many titles lost in the price control period were resurrected.

For most of the following fifteen years, the threat of VAT imposition remained a real concern to publishers and the book trade. Several of Thatcher's Chancellors of the Exchequer, particularly Nigel Lawson and John Major, made no secret of their desire to apply the tax to books, even at a reduced rate of between 5 and 10 per cent, or selectively on certain 'less deserving' categories of publication. The argument ran that not all books were socially valuable, and therefore zero-rating for VAT gave them an unfair advantage over other forms of paid-for entertainment such as cinema or theatre. The Publishers' Association ran several vociferous campaigns to convince ministers that VAT on books would be culturally crippling and although they claimed success,[246] the real reasons for the tax not being applied to publications appear to be two-fold. The first was Thatcher's famous antipathy to the EEC and its desire to seek fiscal harmonization. VAT was already applied at various rates to books in most EEC member states, and European policy-makers wished to see similar rates applied in Britain. Thatcher instinctively resisted such proposals on principle, and thus incidentally – and probably unintentionally – benefited publishing. The other factor was that zero VAT also applied to newspapers (and particularly the advertising they carried). Thatcher felt an obligation towards the powerful Press interests, especially Rupert Murdoch and the Harmsworth *Daily Mail*, which had supported her

245 Books are not, as is sometimes claimed, exempt from VAT, but the rate applied is 0 per cent. The reason why books receive such a benefit is that it is argued they perform a valuable social function and therefore should be taxed lightly to ensure their widespread distribution. Other categories of product so rated include pharmaceuticals, children's clothing and most foodstuffs.

246 This was an issue particularly close to the heart of the PA chief executive of the period, Clive Bradley. He used his considerable charm and advocacy (he was a barrister) to lobby pro-VAT politicians for the cause of books.

editorially and whose industrial actions, such as the breaking of the Fleet Street print unions, had served her policy agenda.

If publishing in general was below Thatcher's radar, there is little doubt that, like all sectors of British industry, her determined and radical economic liberalization and drive to free up markets had a lasting impact. They created an atmosphere and opportunities that allowed some houses to thrive while others, less responsive to change or able to adapt, floundered or even foundered. New structures emerged, some of which had been developing before her access to power, and in particular new sources of capital became available.

The publisher who might be claimed most attuned to the Thatcherite revolution and who made most of the new opportunities she created was, perhaps surprisingly, Paul Hamlyn. At first sight Hamlyn is a most unlikely figure to bracket with Thatcher – a lifelong Labour supporter and donor who often was publicly critical of her social policies. Yet, as we have seen earlier, he was a man of great contradictions who, despite his social conscience and generous philanthropy, had an instinctive and quite ruthless ability to seize entrepreneurial opportunities and make them work. He could certainly be described as one of the much-lauded business risk-takers whom she so much admired. Despite his close friendship with Rupert Murdoch he was nevertheless far from her inner circle of trusted business leaders, and it is unlikely that he would have wanted to have been any closer. He accepted a CBE from John Major's government in 1993, but it would await the return of a Labour government under Tony Blair to recognize his achievements with a peerage in 1998.[247] Yet if one were to select the most Thatcherite of all publishers of the 1980s – in the sense of making the most of the heady financial freedoms of the era – it would be hard to ignore Hamlyn.

247 Hamlyn only briefly wavered in his attachment to the Labour cause when the party under Michael Foot veered leftwards, making room, in the wake of the disastrous election defeat of 1983 (under an extreme manifesto called by some 'the longest suicide note in history'), for the creation of the centrist Social Democratic Party (SDP) by disaffected moderate Labour politicians and supporters, of whom Hamlyn was one. The SDP looked briefly as if it would successfully challenge Thatcherite hegemony. However, it did not sustain its position and eventually merged with the Liberal Party to form the present Liberal Democrats (although a rump party persisted for a time under the direction of the former Labour Foreign Secretary Dr David Owen). Many Labour refugees stayed with the merged party, but Hamlyn rejoined Labour and was a major influence on the 'New Labour' project of Tony Blair.

As we have seen, Hamlyn had insouciantly sailed through the economically troubled 1970s on the irresistible rise of his Octopus Publishing Group (as it later became). He achieved this by a mixture of shrewd merchandizing and marketing, innovative product development and inspired risk-taking in new markets. The results were impressive. In 1972 his turnover was less than £2 million, with an operating profit of just over a quarter of a million pounds. By 1980, revenue had increased twelve-fold to just under £23 million. Margin at £1.5 million, or 6.7 per cent, was less than Hamlyn and his investors would have liked, but was still above many other publishers (de Bellaigue, 2006, p.98). Even allowing for the impact of inflation, growth had been steady and impressive, and seemingly impervious to market downturns.

Hamlyn was not totally unique in his successful commitment to new markets in hard times by creating new types of books for a new public. Although by no means a copy of his formula, one new company emerged in the 1980s as a powerful challenger for the illustrated non-fiction sector that he had pioneered. This was Dorling Kindersley (DK), founded in 1975 as a book packager by refugees from Marshall Cavendish and headed by a publishing genius who shared Hamlyn's flair, drive and innovative sense, the irascible, infuriating and quixotic Peter Kindersley.[248] DK was design-driven and its initial image was set by Kindersley's rather dreamy and hippyish partner and book artist Christopher Dorling. (He would eventually find Peter's tantrums and driven manner too much and retired to raise rare breeds on a Sussex farm.) By 1980, DK was publishing on its own account and had made its mark with a number of iconic and highly profitable publishing projects, such as Alex Comfort's *The Joy of Sex* (with its famously hairy male protagonist) and Miriam Stoppard's *Complete Child and Baby Care*. Its stock in trade was beautifully illustrated, authoritatively written and keenly priced practical reference books on subjects from cookery and first aid to photography, horticulture and that very 1980s preoccupation, 'relationships'.

There is no doubt that DK seized the *Zeitgeist* in a most Hamlyn-like way and, in a similar fashion, broke all the rules. It employed a large

248 Kindersley, although he could be as charming and good company as Hamlyn, was autocratic, impatient and did not suffer fools gladly. I recall meeting him in his chaotic Henrietta Street office where he placed his chair in a doorway, waved me to a seat beside him and proceeded to carry on two conversations, one with me and the other with a group of designers and editors in the room behind him. I had no idea what was going on, but he could clearly manage two complicated discourses simultaneously.

in-house design and photographic staff (creating a distinctive 'look' for its products) and employed unorthodox sales channels, including direct sale via 'party plan' clubs, sometimes dismissively called 'Tupperware' publishing. DK forged alliances and partnerships with American, European and other international publishers that absorbed hundreds of thousands of books and generated high profits. Kindersley was always restless, always seeking new markets and ideas which took him into software and multi-media publishing, probably too far ahead of its time to be commercially viable.

Initially his approach worked very well. DK became a publishing phenomenon and by 1992, with sales approaching £50 million, it was enthusiastically floated on the Stock Exchange with the kinds of glowing financial predictions that recalled the share launches of Penguin and indeed Pergamon. Despite the prevailing economic downturn, shares were over-subscribed six times. Kindersley and his partners became millionaires, and were free to pursue their vision of books and CD-ROMs for all with as much money as they needed. And then, as so often happens, things began to go wrong, although not immediately. Some have argued that Kindersley, famously hands-on, allowed his eye to slip off the ball and became remote from the creative process his energetic intelligence had instigated. Others say that the demands of satisfying rapacious institutional shareholders blunted his judgment while leading to overconfidence. Whatever the truth, his entropic, individualistic, energetic and chaotic publishing house became noticeably more bureaucratic, corporate and – fatally – too cocky. This was to lead to a disastrous publishing venture that destroyed the firm's independence.

In the 1970s and 1980s George Lucas's *Star Wars* films had been all the rage, spinning off all sorts of merchandizing opportunities from action figurines to foodstuffs. A new film in the sequence was planned to be released towards the end of the 1990s, and DK decided that this would produce millions of new fans who would buy undreamed-of quantities of 'tie-in' publications. In 1998 an expensive licence was signed with Lucas's studios for DK to produce these exclusively around the world. DK's turnover was now close to £200 million, but within two years they confidently expected it to grow to £500 million, largely on the back of *Star Wars.*

It is easy to see in retrospect that this was an impossible dream. However, at the time Kindersley and his colleagues really believed they could do it, and they proceeded to print many millions more *Star Wars* books than the market could ever absorb. By any sensible standard the books sold well, but after the dust had settled there remained over thirteen million copies in the warehouse that ultimately would become just so much waste paper. DK was not the first publishing company to be destroyed by overstocks, but it was certainly the most spectacular casualty. By 2000 it had become clear that the crippling quantity of unsold *Star Wars* stock had become, appropriately, a black hole into which vast cascades of money were disappearing. Kindersley had no choice. He sold his beloved company to what had by then become Pearson Education (now a very different place from the old Pearson Longmans from which it had grown) at a knock-down price of £4.50 a share, and saw almost half his workforce of 1500 made redundant; his own restless creativity and original vision was also lost to publishing as he was obliged to retire. DK was incorporated into Penguin and its encyclopedias and practical reference guides continue to be developed there. It has never seemed to be totally comfortable in the Penguin environment, however, despite the best efforts of a sympathetic and supportive director Andrew Welham. He now, in a curious twist of irony, directs Octopus – which brings us neatly back to Hamlyn.[249]

By 1982 Hamlyn was ready to take his company to the next stage of public flotation. He was well aware that previous publishing stock-market share launches, for example Collins, Penguin and Pergamon, had to a greater or lesser extent rebounded unfortunately on their promoters. Hamlyn, however, was determined as ever to break the mould. Well-connected in the world of finance, he recruited experienced and clever advisers and directors such as Sir Claus Moser, the LSE statistics professor who later championed the cause of literacy (the Moser Report, 1998), and Robert Gavron, creator of the highly successful printing group St Ives. They knew both the publishing business and the ways of the stock market.

As de Bellaigue (2004, p.97) queries, the unresolved question is why he wanted to float the company in the first place? Octopus was not short of capital nor seemed to need outside investment. Hamlyn was in his prime and his company, run from its north-west London base in unfashionable (but cheap) Feltham, was tightly and well managed under his control. He was also already wealthy and influential. The suggestion has been made that he needed the approbation of the City to underline his achievements

249 An entertaining and indiscreet account of the rise and fall of DK is provided by one of its founders, Christopher Davis (2009), although some might remark that he understandably underplays his own role in the *Star Wars* fiasco.

(which I find a bit unlikely) or that he wanted to make the point that his approach to publishing was still that of the outsider, determined to do things differently from the dynastic gentlemen of the family firms. Given that many of them still sneered at his 'barrow-boy' origins and methods,[250] I find this rather more convincing. De Bellaigue (2004, pp. 98-9) suggests that one of his prime motivations was to reward his loyal employees with shares that were worth real money. Whatever the reason, his timing was, as always, impeccable.

In spring 1983 the stock market was experiencing what turned out to be a short-term boom. Hamlyn and his colleagues prepared an enticing prospectus. He joked that it was the most expensive book he had ever produced. It offered 3.1 million shares (of which 2.4 million came from Hamlyn and his family, the remainder the property of employees including, characteristically, Hamlyn's chauffeur). Results from the year just ended noted turnover of just over £30 million with over £4 million operating profit, a return to the double-digit margins of the early 1970s (in fact, 13.1 per cent). The offer caused great excitement and a stock market feeding frenzy. Shares were five times oversubscribed and the striking price was £3.50 which valued the company at £55 million, a multiple of almost twice revenue. But Hamlyn had cannily retained control of 67 per cent of Octopus's capital. He was now both tremendously wealthy (he personally made over £7 million on the deal) and had ensured that the new investors could not initiate boardroom battles nor unseat him. It was a coup that was both daring and well thought through. What Hamlyn could not know was that the market for shares had just peaked, and would within months fall steeply. His legendary luck and flair had produced a spectacular result.

Nevertheless, Octopus shares did better than most others in the difficult market that quickly ensued, and his new investors (many of whom were institutions and major equity funds who had never before looked at publishing) stuck with him. He was emboldened to invest in new ventures and make acquisitions. In October 1983 he set up a joint-venture with the designer and retail innovator Terence Conran, who had

250 Hamlyn loved to *épater les bourgeois* by making outrageous statements that he knew would irritate the publishing establishment. He refused to join the Publishers' Association ('waste of money'), declined to sign up to or support the Net Book Agreement ('dead in the water') and thought the Frankfurt Book Fair 'mainly a waste of time' (although he was always there). Many in the industry today would disagree with the first and third of these views, but subsequent events vindicated his second.

created the emblematic store chains Mothercare and Habitat, to produce books on home furnishings, style, parenthood and fashion that mobilized those iconic brands. It did well, achieving sales of almost £3.5 million in two years.

A month later he purchased for £4 million cash (almost small change) Brimax, the Newmarket-based publisher of books for young children. Hamlyn left the Brimax founder, George Rogers and his family, in charge and it operated semi-autonomously, including retaining its own distribution facility. A less original entrepreneur would have attempted to 'rationalize' Brimax and seek 'synergy' (a great buzzword of the Thatecherite age) with his existing lists. It speaks much of Hamlyn's maverick wisdom that he left a successful business alone and allowed it to continue to prosper without (much) interference.

His next venture took an uncharacteristic false step. Perhaps seeking to build on the success of Tigerprint stationery, he offered £3.90 a share for a substantial minority in a Yorkshire-based greetings card publisher, W.N. Sharpe. The Sharpe board saw this as a hostile act, but this action put Sharpe into play and for once the stock market did not play in Hamlyn's favour. The shares rapidly rose well above what he and his advisers considered a sensible valuation. Sharpe was quickly sold to the American card combine Hallmark for £36 million at £5 a share. Hamlyn retired with a handy £1 million profit on the shares Octopus had bought in Sharpe, but nevertheless a trifle disillusioned. This may have been the reason that he concentrated his future acquisitions and investments exclusively in the books sector that he knew so well. He may have ruefully concluded that even the most gifted business buccaneer should know his limits.

So he returned to familiar territory. At the end of 1984 he took over the distributor Webster with whom he had collaborated to launch Bounty Books. Webster was a huge and sprawling concern with turnover half as large again as Octopus and almost five times as many employees, but it was inefficient and barely profitable. Hamlyn got a good deal, offering one Octopus share for ten Webster shares, plus cash of £5.45 per share. This effectively valued the wholesaler at only £21 million against annual turnover of £52 million.

Unlike Brimax, Hamlyn and his team did intervene in Webster's management. Unprofitable operations were disposed of, systems were sharpened and emphasis laid on the core business of sales and fulfilment of orders to booksellers and the 'non-traditional' outlets. Webster had unique expertise and effectiveness in many of these through its Bookwise facility, particularly the distribution of mass market paperbacks to the CTN (confectionery, tobacconist and newsagent) trade – then a major sales channel for cheap books.[251] As de Bellaigue (2004, p.101) observes, the acquisition also gave Octopus 100 per cent of Bounty profits, which must have contributed to the deal's attractiveness.[252] These actions met with stock market approval and Octopus shares climbed to £8 each in late 1984. By the time Webster's retail arm and its Books for Students division were sold in spring 1985, the newly enlarged Octopus was trading at £10.25 per share, valuing the company at £176 million. Hamlyn was now poised for what at the time was thought to be his most establishment-shaking sally (although as we shall see he had even more audacious and surprising tricks up his sleeve for later) – the purchase of William Heinemann.

Heinemann had experienced considerable disruption and change during the early 1980s. Alan Hill had retired, proposing as his legacy a streamlined and logical structure which allowed the educational and trade publishing companies to operate separately while jointly owning the service and distribution facility at Kingswood. Hill's elegant and eminently sensible proposal was not implemented. His memories of the succeeding débâcle are characteristically gentle, generous and uncensorious (Hill, 1988, pp.369-71), but without his guidance Heinemann management descended into chaos and farce.[253] Charles Pick succeeded Hill as Chairman, but he did not have a seat on any of the publishing company boards (St John, 1990, p.613). Hamish MacGibbon, a charismatic and volatile character who could be both brilliant and obtuse,

251 And now almost invisible. This is ascribable to the growth of supermarkets in this sector, the increase in high street retail rents and the decline in the sale of tobacco products due to health concerns (Stevenson, 2006, p.319).
252 For most of the detail concerning Octopus and Hamlyn's subsequent adventures I am heavily indebted to de Bellaigue's elegant and entertaining accounts in Chapters 6 and 7 of his excellent book. As a former stockbroker and long-time observer of the publishing business scene, de Bellaigue has witnessed and carefully charted the financial history of British publishing since the 1960s. The interpretations applied to his facts and observations are, however, mine, and he may not agree with them.
253 Hill had retained his chairmanship of HEB in Nigeria, overseeing a difficult period (which also affected other publishers with large interests in that market such as Longmans and Evans Brothers) when over-ambitious expansion of educational publishing floated on oil revenues came to an abrupt end, causing considerable losses to British companies operating there. He was invited back in 1986 to help rescue HEB, but many of the key staff had gone. He certainly found much that had changed and, although he was too polite to say so, probably not to his taste (Hill, 1988, pp.375-7).

became Managing Director of HEB in 1980 and Tony Beal, a gifted salesman with a broad and instinctive feel for overseas markets, took over the running of HEB's international companies. Both found their plans and proposals mired in a corporate maze between Heinemann and their owners Tilling.

On the trade side, Tom Rosenthal probably spread himself too thinly by trying to run both Heinemann and Secker and Warburg at home and Heinemann's non-educational businesses overseas. He also was involved in a dispiriting wrangle with Tilling about giving up his Secker shares which, although it was eventually resolved in his favour, was distracting and indicative of a new, petty and mean-minded attitude in the company. He also found Pick increasingly uncongenial and difficult, and the former good colleagues were often at loggerheads (St John, 1990, p.613). With recession at home and problems emerging in overseas markets, this was not the time for the company's management to take their eyes off the ball.

As so often happens, unhappiness led to departures both voluntary and involuntary. MacGibbon and Beal left, as did a whole band of talented editorial and sales executives such as Paul Richardson, Graham Taylor, Keith Nettle and Nigel Hollis. Profits by 1982, despite some good acquisitions like the 'Teach Yourself' series and successful new educational textbooks, were slipping and relations between Pick and Rosenthal grew worse and worse. However, a greater nemesis was about to descend to discomfit the unhappy Heinemann further.

The Tilling Group had grown flabby and unfocussed, and its laid-back management style, once a strength, had become a distinct weakness in the new entrepreneurial age. Among its diverse and sprawling interests, it had bought an American oil-services company in 1977. This had initially given good returns, but through a combination of poor management and the cyclical fortunes that affect resource-based companies, it began to make losses, which amounted to £40 million by 1982. Tilling's directors seemed uncertain about what to do, but the position was not lost on a predatory combine BTR,[254] whose rapacious instincts were much more in tune with

254 BTR, was originally a rubber growing and manufacturing company, but was taken over in 1956 and thereafter run by Sir Owen Green. An aristocratic ex-naval officer, he built it up to be an aggressive industrial conglomerate whose unrelenting focus on 'shareholder value' and 'sweating the assets' was very much in tune with Thatcher's vision. Green is often bracketed with Lord Hanson as emblematic of the new ruthless entrepreneur of the 1980s. Although Hanson was probably more favoured by Thatcher, Green was perhaps truer to her vision.

the times. Sensing that Tilling was fatally weakened and its shareholders would welcome its intervention, BTR launched an unfriendly 'dawn raid' on Tilling in April 1983 to acquire it at a relatively knock-down price of £573 million. Tilling reacted with panic and horror, describing the bid as 'unwelcome, unacceptable and inadequate', and promised shareholders a record year of profits and dynamic (although unspecified) new initiatives. The battle quickly became a *cause célèbre* and was one of the first takeover battles to be fought out in the news as well as the financial pages of the newspapers. Both sides took large and dramatic press advertisements to convince shareholders one way or the other, but Tilling always had the weaker case if judged on their performance. Inevitably they lost the argument, and in June BTR succeeded by offering over £660 million for Tilling – at that point the largest-ever takeover bid in British history.

The Heinemann managers forgot their bickering in the drama of bigger events. Although they had been assured that they would be welcome in the new organization (provided they made a good profit), they quickly found the hard-nosed values and relentless drive for growth and returns at all costs unnerving and frightening. Rosenthal resigned the following September to take up a much less weighty but more congenial role at André Deutsch as partner, eventually buying the company completely on Deutsch's retirement in 1987. Pick, who had retired, came back to fill Rosenthal's vacant chair, but was succeeded by Nicolas Thompson from Weidenfeld in February 1985. For their part BTR probably never wanted to hold on to Heinemann, and only a few weeks after Thompson arrived, Hamlyn offered to acquire Heinemann from BTR and merge it with Octopus.

It was probably Pick who suggested to Hamlyn that Owen Green was ready to dispose of the troublesome publisher, but in the event the deal was actually a true merger rather than a sale. Hamlyn again displayed his happy knack of generating respect, admiration and genuine friendship with the most unlikely partners. Temperamentally he was poles apart from Green, yet both liked what they saw in the other and decided that they could do business together. They quickly agreed an arrangement whereby in return for 35 per cent of the new merged Octopus and Heinemann, which valued Heinemann at £100 million, BTR would grant Hamlyn control and management of the new company – but with BTR non-executive directors (including Green himself) to ensure their requirements on financial return of the share they retained were met. It was a good deal for both parties. Hamlyn got relatively unrestricted executive control and gained access to new markets such as education and literary fiction, as well as a dominant market share in fields like children's books and the mass market when the two company's lists were brought together. Green got the flair, marketing nous and drive of Octopus, and could retain the benefits of Heinemann's successful publishing without having to manage it directly.

As de Bellaigue remarks, the association neatly solved the problem of the orphan publisher within BTR's largely industrial portfolio as an illiquid asset and had turned it into a liquid one with great potential (de Bellaigue, 2004, p.102). The stock market clearly acknowledged the scope offered. When the merger was announced, Octopus shares quickly reached £5.85 each valuing the new company at £311 million or nearly six times what Octopus had been floated at two years previously.

Green and BTR, while not directly exercising executive responsibility, brought much-needed discipline and structure to the new company, an area where Hamlyn was not particularly effective or interested. A divisional structure was introduced and clear lines of report and responsibility established. The picturesque and bucolic Heinemann printing works and warehouse at Kingswood, now hopelessly outmoded if much-loved, was abruptly closed, the site sold and warehousing and distribution logistics (printing was abandoned) transferred to a utilitarian concrete box at Rushden in Northamptonshire.[255] There were still clashes of culture between the brash Octopus approach and the more refined and staid Heinemann ways, but the merger did successfully create a powerful new publishing group with clear objectives and effective systems. Hamlyn recognized, with Green's advice, that he had to step back from the day-to-day management of such a large new organization and a group Chief

255 Kingswood was a romantic survival from a gentler, less profit-obsessed age. Built in 1928 in an 'Arts and Crafts' style from designs by Lord Gerald Wellesley and Trenwith Wills, it was more reminiscent of an Edwardian country house than a book manufactory and storehouse. Set in woodland, with rolling lawns, flowerbeds and cricket pitches, it offered the kind of paternalistic and protected working environment that Thatcher and her neo-liberals despised. It even included a fully equipped dispensary and hospital. Mere mention of its name can still make ex-Heinemann employees of a certain age misty-eyed. A book about Kingswood, privately published in 1930, perfectly expresses the utopian values that underlay its design and organization and explicitly links its design to the famous Country Life Press built by Doubleday at Garden City New Jersey in 1910 (*Homes of Doubleday-Doran and Company Incorporated*, privately printed, Garden City NJ, 1930). An aerial view of Kingswood extracted from this rare book is reproduced as figure 17.

Executive, Ian Irvine, recruited from the world of newspapers, brought a different perspective and an energetic, if occasionally peremptory, management style.

As attitudes and ideas transformed, some key people returned, such as Paul Richardson to the then unique post of Director of Publishing Development.[256] Acquisitions were made, including – in what must have been a sweet moment – the purchase of Paul Hamlyn Limited back from Reed and Mitchell Beazley, the part-work and reference specialist. The most symbolic gesture was the gathering in and relocation of all the publishing departments from a motley collection of Bloomsbury and Mayfair terraces and rackety Soho cellars to the glamorous Art Deco Michelin House in Kensington which included Bibendum, a noted restaurant.[257] Hamlyn had come a long way from draughty converted workshops in Camden Town and Feltham.

But there was even more to come. Hamlyn's ability to surprise surpassed all his earlier coups when it was announced, in July 1987, that Octopus was to be taken over by Reed – the lineal descendant of IPC whom Hamlyn had forsaken almost two decades before. The prodigal had come home with a vengeance. Reed valued the company he had built at £535 million, yielding him a personal fortune of £200 million and sparking a stock market frenzy for publishing assets. Publishing companies were in demand; they had suddenly become glamorous investments and, as we shall see, magnets for venture capital. The frowsty, down-at-heel image of book companies had at last been shattered, and it is arguable that Hamlyn had been the catalyst in making publishing the sexiest of investments. And, once again, his timing was almost eerily perfect. Less than three months after he concluded the sale, the first major reverse in the Thatcherite dream of endless prosperity from a bullish stock market occurred. Over £50 billion was wiped off share values in the great collapse known as 'Black Monday', which also nearly derailed one of the largest planned sales of state assets in British Petroleum.

256 Richardson would later become the first Professor of Publishing in the UK at Oxford Brookes University. Here he created a vibrant School of Publishing which provided me with inspiration when I established similar programmes at City University and University College London.

257 The building was actually owned by Hamlyn and Conran, with the Bibendum restaurant being operated by the latter. It was ill-suited to be a publishing office, however, and it famously lacked sufficient sturdy bookshelves. Office walls were flimsily constructed and prone to collapse.

While all this was going on, a book was being published in a remote outpost of the Octopus empire that would precipitate one of the oddest episodes in publishing history. It caused a stand-off with the Thatcher government that still defies analysis and continues to provoke controversy. In 1976 Peter Wright, who had been an Assistant Director of the British security and intelligence service MI5, retired and emigrated to Australia. He began writing his memoirs which, rewritten with the help of journalist Paul Greengrass, were published as *Spycatcher* by Heinemann Australia in 1987. Although promoted as containing sensational revelations, the book is in reality a turgid and self-serving account of a not very distinguished career in counter-espionage, interspersed with prolonged whingeing about Civil Service pension arrangements. It does contain some allegations of illegal domestic activities by security officers and some, perhaps fanciful, claims of actions to destabilize the Wilson government by elements within the intelligence community as well as suggestions of treasonable behaviour already made elsewhere against the erstwhile head of the service, Sir Roger Hollis. Nothing in the book was either particularly new or surprising.[258]

What was surprising was the vehement and hysterical reaction of the Thatcher administration to the book's publication. Citing Wright's duty under the Official Secrets Act to maintain confidence, the British government – apparently under the Prime Minister's direct instructions – sued the author and publisher in the Australian courts and obtained an injunction to suspend publication. The Australian public, outraged by this intervention by a foreign administration in their affairs, bought the book in enormous quantities and it sustained a lively underground sale. Wright and his publisher maintained high-profile legal challenges to the British action which kept the case in the public eye, and the aged spy with his incongruous bush hat, complete with swinging corks, became a familiar figure on world-wide news broadcasts. In Britain, newspapers which planned to reprint extracts were also constrained by Injunction.

Heinemann cannily licensed Penguin (with perhaps a conscious echo of Chatterley) to publish the book in the United States, where publication

258 I was on a business trip in Australia when the *Spycatcher* storm broke, so I bought a copy of the offending volume to read on a three day train journey between Perth and Adelaide. Halfway across 'the long straight' I grew so irritated by the author's self-righteous and whining tone, as well as his inability to write in an interesting way, that I threw the book out of the train's window on to the Nullarbor Plain. Here presumably – in the driest and most isolated section of the continent – it still lies.

would be protected from attempted British suppression by the first amendment to the Constitution and the newly-minted Freedom of Information Act. There were informal and rather crass attempts by British government representatives to lean on Pearson as Penguin's parent to prevent the Penguin edition, which to their credit the publisher resisted. The constant exposure of the case in the news media, aided by the uncompromising attitude of Thatcher's law officers (which suggested that the book did indeed contain sensational secrets), helped to sell half a million copies in a few months. Many in due course ended up in Britain, mailed by outraged American friends of freedom of publication. Heinemann also quietly exported thousands of copies to Ireland and the Netherlands where the book could be published legally, and from where they could not be prevented under EEC rules from being imported into Britain. This doubtless further enraged the eurosceptic Prime Minister.

In June 1988 the Australian courts lifted the injunction and the book was freely republished. Despite an expensive and increasingly desperate legal campaign from British government lawyers, their case was looking more and more threadbare. In September 1988 the British law lords declared that publication of the book and newspaper extracts was 'in the public interest', and the last barrier to *Spycatcher*'s sale in Britain evaporated. The government's humiliation was compounded when the courts awarded costs of over £2 million to the publisher and author, to be paid from public funds. The book was eventually published in Britain on 13 October 1988; it immediately entered the bestseller lists, where it remained for many months. When Peter Wright died in 1995 he had handily supplemented the meagre Civil Service pension that he had excoriated in the book by many millions in royalties courtesy of the intransigence of Margaret Thatcher and her government.

The real mystery of the *Spycatcher* episode is why this particular dull and worthless book was singled out for such draconian and out-of-proportion attention. Had it been ignored it would have doubtless sunk without trace, and might never even have been published in the UK. There was certainly an obsession with secrecy and security in the Thatcher administration, with an almost fetishist value placed on the duty of confidence demanded of public servants by the Official Secrets Act, but this does not totally explain why Wright and Heinemann were pursued with such single-minded venom. The myth of the story maintains that Thatcher herself insisted that the book must be kept out of the public domain at all costs and at any expense. Even if that is untrue or an exaggeration, exactly why Wright was singled out for such vindictive attention is an intriguing puzzle. This will only be resolved when the public records of the case are released in 2018, unless they are held back for security reasons.

It is not without significance that the publisher who bought the United States rights of *Spycatcher* was Penguin, which during the 1980s recaptured their old verve, energy and taste for controversy under the guidance of a mercurial, visionary and determinedly energetic new Chief Executive, Peter Mayer, who had joined Penguin in 1979. Born in New York in 1936, he came from a publishing family and had founded with his father a boutique imprint called Overlook Press, but he made his reputation with the American mass-market paperback house Avon where he pioneered new formats, pricing structures and marketing styles. When Pearson sought a new head of the ailing Penguin, Mayer was not perhaps an obvious choice, but his selection proved inspired. He had much of Lane's originality, drive and mischievousness (which occasionally spilled over into maliciousness) coupled with an original lateral mind, understanding the value of tradition but not being enslaved to it. To survive, let alone grow, Penguin urgently needed an injection of new ideas, fresh approaches and courageous radical restructuring. Mayer would provide this, not always with total success – sometimes his editorial enthusiasm could be badly misplaced – but his impact was swift and dramatic and his achievement lasting.

When he arrived in 1979 Penguin turned over less than £30 million and was loss-making after tax, with a tiny operating margin of 2.5 per cent. By 1987, when he returned more or less full time to the USA to nurture Penguin's American operations, he left the UK company in the secure care of his trusted deputy Trevor Glover. By then turnover was nudging £135 million, and the percentage operating margin had tripled.

When Mayer was appointed, concern was expressed that such an iconically British publishing institution should be entrusted to an American, but he was very sensitive to some of the cultural issues he would encounter. He had been educated at Oxford[259] and was cosmopolitan is his tastes, so he knew what Penguin meant to British *literati*. He also knew that it was dying. No matter how sensitively he expressed it, he understood that the old Lane model of cheap reprints of other people's copyrights in mass quantities and uniform formats was no longer

259 When in the mid 1980s I invited him to address a publishing conference at Christ Church I was struck by his genuine delight to be 'back in his old college'.

sustainable. Penguin needed, he believed, to become an integrated hardback and paperback publisher with a variety of product types and price ranges, but most of all a strong portfolio of its own copyrights that could be exploited in multiple forms. The structure which later became known as 'vertical publishing' – in which rights are acquired for hardback publication, then published in paperback in various formats within the same publishing organization, rather than hardback houses being separate from paperback houses – was his chosen solution. This approach, combined with the retention and recruitment of some of the best publishing talent available, including Peter Carson, Philippa Harrison, Andrew Welham, Tony Lacey and Glover, among several others, enabled him to deliver his spectacular results and to save Penguin's life without sacrificing its soul. It may have looked effortless, but in fact it was a hard balancing act, and not without its false steps.

Indeed Mayer's first demonstration of his new ideas did not look particularly promising. M.M. Kaye's *The Far Pavilions* was a sentimental and rather old-fashioned tale of British India whose author had been inherited from the Longmans list; her earlier books had been published there to no great impact in the 1950s. Mayer selected this rather unpromising title to demonstrate his new vertical publishing concept and how it could work. *The Far Pavilions* was published as a hardback by Allen Lane in 1979, and then produced in paperback by Penguin a year later. But it did not look or feel like a Penguin. It was over 900 pages even in the larger 'B' format, taller and broader than the familiar, pocket-sized 'A' format that was classic Penguin currency. It was also 'aggressively priced' (a euphemism for well above standard Penguin levels) and was accompanied by elaborate point of sale material and a multi-media promotion campaign, paid for in part by the author agreeing to a reduced royalty.

Booksellers at first hated the innovation, but their disgust turned to delight when they saw the title's sales escalate out of sight. Over 400,000 copies sold in a few months with unheard-of reprints, and spin-off special editions, including a collection of related Raj-era pictures, were added to the range. Mayer had proved his point and showed that vertical publishing not only worked but could bring really substantial results.

The next logical step was to make acquisitions that would contribute their copyrights to the model. The first of these was Frederick Warne in 1983, attractive mainly because of their under-exploited Beatrix Potter titles. As well as refurbishing the famous books by making new plates directly from the original artwork (the illustrations had grown muddy over the decades as the old plates had deteriorated) to allow the anthropomorphic characters to glow with renewed vigour, Penguin were also able to license the newly vibrant artwork as 'properties'. They featured on a host of products from bed-linen to crockery and soft toys, creating a completely new and extremely lucrative revenue stream.[260] Two years later, Penguin acquired the trade publishing companies from the Thomson organization, to general surprise. They comprised the literary hardback houses of Hamish Hamilton and Michael Joseph, the paperback publisher Sphere and the packager George Rainbird. None of these imprints were very profitable and Penguin were criticized for paying too much for them, but Mayer argued that in his vertical publishing model their backlists were enormously valuable and they would deliver excellent long-term results.

The heads of the hardback houses, Christopher Sinclair-Stevenson of Hamish Hamilton and Alan Brooke of Michael Joseph, at first identified positively with Mayer's concept. However, they came to find its demands irksome and alien to their ideas of publishing and left in 1989 to set up or join more traditionally organized companies.[261] With its rather downmarket image, Sphere never really successfully integrated into Penguin and was sold to Maxwell in 1990, while Rainbird simply faded away. Nevertheless, Mayer had successfully demonstrated his conviction that vertical publishing was an effective new model for the new conditions of the time and had nursed the sick Penguin through a difficult convalescence to renewed vigour. And it was just at this point that yet another controversial book showed that in the process Penguin had lost none of its essential character, nor taste for valiant support of literary freedom.

In 1989 Penguin published Salman Rushdie's *The Satanic Verses* – a challenging and many layered work of magic realism. Despite its implied criticisms of Islamic orthodoxy neither its author nor publisher foresaw the level of hatred, fear and tragedy that its publication would cause. Rushdie came from a Westernized Indian family with a Muslim heritage. Cambridge-educated, he had worked as an advertising copywriter and

260 Peter Rabbit is particularly and inexplicably popular among young women in Japan. Anthony Forbes Watson, a later Penguin Chief Executive, recalls with glee the profitability of licensing 'bed linen for Japanese secretaries' (source: personal conversation).

261 Sinclair-Stevenson set up an eponymous imprint, but it did not long survive as an independent publisher, eventually being acquired by Random House. It no longer publishes.

had published a string of well-regarded novels and he had gained a reputation of being a clever if rather acerbic member of London's literary set. His novel *Midnight's Children* had won the Booker prize in 1981, and would later be voted the best Booker prize winner since the prize had begun.

When *The Satanic Verses* was published it was respectfully reviewed and sold reasonably well, but suddenly a storm of controversy erupted over the book's alleged insults to Islam in relation to the wife of the Prophet and its parody of certain verses of the Qur'an. In India, and later in Pakistan, Rushdie was accused of apostasy and riots broke out with copies of the book being burned. Outrage quickly spread throughout the Islamic world and Rushdie was the subject of mounting condemnation from mullahs and believers, many of whom never read his book. He was particularly criticized for having traduced his faith and heritage, although he was not a practising Muslim. Indeed many of his accusers found his obvious Westernization and his taste for alcohol and the British literary life particularly offensive.

The anti-Rushdie movement begun to take on an overtly political air and quickly became a co-ordinated campaign by Islamic fundamentalists against Western values and culture. In 1979 a revolution in Iran had replaced the secular, modernizing and corrupt regime of the Shah with a clericalist Islamic state. Its spiritual head was the aged and hard-line Ayatollah Khomeini, whose word was law for many millions of faithful Muslims in Iran and elsewhere. There is no evidence that Khomeini ever read the book or even knew much about its content but on 14 February 1989 he issued a *fatwa* (a religious decree). This imposed a duty on every Islamic believer to kill the blasphemous author and anyone associated with the production and distribution of his book. Rushdie took the threat seriously and immediately went into hiding under the protection of the British security services. He was not a universally popular figure among the literary community and some other writers, such as Germaine Greer and Roald Dahl, criticized his refusal to withdraw the book and denied him their support.

Four days after the *fatwa* Rushdie did in fact issue a qualified apology, which was at first accepted in Iran, and then later rejected. Riots and violence spread, and significantly among the Muslim community in Britain there were violent demonstrations and calls for Rushdie to be delivered up and punished. These translated into riots in towns with sizeable Islamic communities such as Bradford. Bookshops like the Left-

Wing specialist Collets were fire-bombed, and the London university bookseller Dillons received an explosive device in the mail. In August a British Muslim named Mahmoud Mazeh blew himself up in a hotel room in west London while apparently priming a bomb he intended to use to kill Rushdie.

For Penguin the possible consequences of being Rushdie's publisher were threatening. The book had become a bestseller in Britain and the United States, and since Penguin was (as a consequence of Mayer's vertical strategy) its global publisher, everyone who worked for them or was associated with the company throughout the world became targets. Trevor Glover and Rushdie were under pressure from inside and outside the company to withdraw the book and apologize unreservedly. The popular thriller writer John Le Carré was unequivocal:

> Again and again it has been within his [referring to Rushdie] power to save the faces of his publishers and, with dignity, withdraw the book until a calmer time has come ... it seems to me he has nothing more to prove except his own insensitivity. (Quoted in Anthony, 2008, p.7)

The critic John Berger added:

> I suspect that Salman Rushdie, if he is not caught in a chain of events of which he has completely lost control, might, by now, be ready to consider asking his world publishers to stop producing more or new editions of *The Satanic Verses.* Not because of the threat to his own life, but because of the threat to the lives of those who are innocent of either writing or reading the book. (*loc. cit.*)

This was the dilemma that confronted Glover and his senior colleagues in spring 1989. He later told me that it was the hardest decision he ever had to make, but after consulting widely he announced that the book would not be withdrawn under threats and blackmail, and that Penguin would continue to promote and sell the title globally. He was well aware of how serious the consequences might be. Every Penguin employee, agent or associate, every customer and every publisher who produced a translation was at risk of violent attack. Penguin's headquarters at Wright's Lane in Kensington became a virtual fortress, with strict and oppressive security.[262] The cost of the first year's protection amounted to almost £2 million (de Bellaigue, 2004, p.50).

262 I visited the Penguin building in late 1989 and it took almost twenty-five minutes to

Nor was protecting Penguin's headquarters the only expense. Surveillance and guards had to be extended to the cars and homes of Penguin employees. This was not over-reaction – the threat was real. Penguin staff received daily messages of hate and several editors took disturbing and threatening telephone messages at home. Arson attacks were made on Penguin's own branded bookshops. The campaign of disruption escalated to tragedy when the Japanese translator of the book, Hitoshi Igarashi, was stabbed to death by an unknown assailant in 1991. Ettore Capriole, who had produced the Italian translation, was also knifed but survived. Two years later, the hotel in which the Turkish translator Asin Nesin was staying was attacked by a mob, and although he survived 37 other people died in the resulting blaze. William Nygard, the book's Norwegian publisher, was shot and badly injured by an unknown (but presumed Muslim) and un-apprehended attacker.

Rushdie was to remain in hiding for almost a decade, and was in no doubt that if he emerged he was in real danger of being killed. His writing suffered, his marriage collapsed under the strain and he came close to despair. Eventually a change in regime in Iran enabled the campaign against him to die away, although the *fatwa* remained in place. It was not until 2000 that Rushdie felt confident enough to appear in public and the shadow of attack, although diminished, remains with him still. Penguin moved to new offices in 1995, but security measures continued – and to an extent continue to be applied to visitors and deliveries.

With the Rushdie affair, Penguin showed that under Mayer and Glover it had both kept faith with its past and had adapted to the needs of the present. Their regime was by no means perfect: some accused Penguin of moving down-market and not fully exploiting its backlist, and it certainly did publish some undistinguished but enormously lucrative 'bodice-rippers', such as Shirley Conran's *Lace* and Celia Brayfield's *Pearls*.[263] It also possessed a corporate culture that, not unlike the BBC, could be

—

get through the security screen to reach Reception. The blanket seriously hampered Penguin's normal business while it lasted.

263 Some ideas like *Penguin 60s* – a series of short books to be sold at only sixty pence each to celebrate the company's sixtieth anniversary in 1995, although innovative, were not commercially sensible. They were wildly popular with the reading public and sold tens of thousands of copies, but they actually cost more to ship from the warehouse than they returned in sales revenue. Many booksellers thought them far more trouble than they were worth.

smug and condescending.[264] Yet, between 1980 and 1995 Penguin authors won six Booker Prizes, and three became Nobel Laureates for literature.

Although the company was re-organized again following Mayer's departure in 1997, regaining as a consequence some of its more traditional strengths, including the rebirth of the classics list, there is little doubt that Mayer's strategy and Pearson's investment muscle[265] saved the famous imprint from a lingering deathbed. Like so many British institutions, it found the Thatcherite climate both bracing and enervating, but it adapted better than some and Mayer was the essential catalyst. As Campbell-Smith remarks:

> He physically relocated the creative departments from Harmondsworth to offices in Central London, and he also set about relocating the focus of the firm's creative mindset. Instead of relying on its unparalleled backlist and narrow range of frontlist titles that might (or might not) throw up an occasional bestseller, Peter decreed that Penguin should put all the power of its brand behind its frontlist marketing, which would ensure a dozen or two big titles every year. (Campbell-Smith, 2009, p.21)

Once again, an individual who personally would have hated to be identified with Thatcher had seized the spirit of her times to turn round the fortunes of a proud, if sclerotic survivor from a former age. Like Hamlyn, Mayer certainly was never in her famous phrase 'one of us', but he got the point that change was necessary and the market was king.

While Octopus and Penguin were the great publishing success stories of the deregulating decade of Thatcherism no publishing company, large or small, remained untouched. Some, it must be admitted, adapted more successfully than others to the new emphasis on unfettered markets, takeovers, venture capitalism and swashbuckling free enterprise. Others changed their character dramatically. Allen and Unwin had already come a long way from their pious Ruskinesque roots and, following the death

264 Forbes Watson told me that the attitude among Penguin reps was that they would graciously allocate their titles to booksellers, rather than powerfully merchandizing them in the fashion of, say, the Collins sales force.

265 Although Pearson is British-owned it is best described as an 'Anglo-American' company which has adopted aggressive American business practices in its operation. Many of its British executives spend formative parts of their careers at its American companies and its British operations are often guided by American managers, like Mayer and the long-serving CEO of Pearson Education, Marjorie Scardino.

of Sir Stanley and the re-organization under management consultant Geoffrey Cass, the company was a tempting takeover target. Its strong educational and professional business was attractive, but even more so were the copyrights of J.R.R. Tolkien and his *Lord of the Rings* fantasies which were experiencing a great vogue. They caught the eye of Robin Hyman, a publisher cast in much the same mould as Paul Hamlyn who had learned the trade with Evans Brothers. In 1977 he had taken over and revolutionized the fusty but highly profitable schools and university publisher George Bell, which also owned the perennial bestseller Pepys's *Diary*. The new company duly became Bell and Hyman. Dusty Dickensian offices in Lincoln's Inn were disposed of, and the new company moved to cheap and comfortable accommodation in Wapping. Hyman then added the substantial non-fiction list of Mills and Boon, which included some long-established textbooks, to his portfolio.

When Philip Unwin (Stanley's nephew and a very shrewd editor with a keen business sense) died in 1981 (he had retired in 1970 and had written a penetrating memoir in 1972, significantly published by Heinemann, not Allen and Unwin), the direction of the firm was left to Stanley's charming but rather effete and indecisive son Rayner.[266] The first recession of the 1980s hit Allen and Unwin hard; they faltered, despite their solid academic publishing, and redundancies were made. Senior management (there were now only three board directors) seemed at a loss what to do, but Rayner admired Hyman for his transformation of Bell and decided that he could do the same for his family firm. Bell and Hyman and Allen and Unwin were merged in 1985. Hyman had very good City connections and an excellent business reputation, so was able to obtain the necessary finance from merchant bank Hambro. The bank acquired 35 per cent of the equity of the new Unwin Hyman firm.

Hyman had talent and vision, and had his health not faltered he could have become a major publishing force. In the event a debilitating illness (which he happily survived) sapped his energy, denying him the brilliant trajectory of which he was certainly capable. Eventually, his firm was taken over, as we shall see shortly, by a newly-formed HarperCollins.[267]

266 It was Rayner Unwin who as a schoolboy in about 1936 had read and reported on the first of Tolkien's saga, *The Hobbit*, thus substantially enhancing the firm's revenues for the next three decades. He was also a steam railway enthusiast, which accounts for the firm's sizeable list of train-related titles.

267 The lack of a space in the orthography of the firm's name is deliberate, and a lamentable vestige of late 1980s branding pretension.

Before we trace that development, we must look at the events that created that company – essentially the resolution of Rupert Murdoch's long-term stalking of Collins which had begun in 1981 (see Chapter 8) and its subsequent merger with American book publisher Harper & Row. Murdoch had acquired a half-stake of Harper & Row in March 1987, and the final *dénouement* of his determined plan to acquire Collins began shortly afterwards. Ironically Murdoch had called on Collins to act with him as equal partners in the Harper & Row acquisition, and when it was complete Collins directors George Craig and Ian Chapman were appointed its joint Managing Directors. By all accounts, relations between News Corporation (the holding company of News International) and Collins were at this time 'happy and trusting' (de Bellaigue, 2004, p.173). This harmony did not last long, however. Craig resigned from Collins in early 1988 citing 'differences of approach' and soon re-emerged as Murdoch's apparent vicar on earth to become President and Chief Executive of Harper & Row, much to Chapman's chagrin. Although Collins owned 50 per cent of Harper & Row, he had been unaware that this was going to happen.

Murdoch then struck swiftly and with venom. On 17 November 1988 News International, as a subsidiary of News Corporation, announced that it sought to acquire all the shares of William Collins and Son that it did not already own (see the account of Murdoch's earlier attempt to acquire Collins in Chapter 8). At the time financial observers thought this move surprising since Collins had actually recovered quite well from its trading position at the earlier Murdoch foray, much of which was due to the Harper & Row acquisition. Some, however, acknowledged that Murdoch's predatory instincts would not be denied, and he famously hated to be bested.

Murdoch's acquisition document contained brutal criticisms of Collins. It cited executive departures (some of which – like that of Craig, of course – it conveniently forgot to mention it had instigated), low staff morale, poor strategic planning and declining profits. It also mysteriously omitted to recall that Murdoch had owned 41 per cent of Collins since 1981, and had already had several directors on the Collins board who might reasonably have been expected to correct these problems. No matter. Murdoch was relentlessly moving in for the kill, and he chose a formidable huntress in the person of Sonia Land – a Singapore-born publisher who had acquired a reputation for abrasive negotiation.[268] She

268 Land would later become a literary agent at Sheil Land associates where her skills would be well deployed.

also had inside knowledge since she had only recently left the post of Collins financial director.

Land ran the acquisition campaign with *brio* and confidence. Chapman thought her initial offer a 'lousy one for William Collins', even though it valued the whole company at £293 million, and strongly resisted the proposal. He sought refuge with the French publisher Groupe de la Cité, with whom Collins had a good publishing relationship with bilingual dictionaries, as a preferred takeover partner. The French publisher had itself only been formed earlier in 1988 from a consolidation of several famous but variably successful companies such as Larousse, Nathan, Plon and France Loisirs. It possessed reasonable financial resources through one of its major shareholders, the media group Havas and various banks, but in reality it was not yet fully integrated and was probably too weak to be an effective white knight, especially against such a powerful and determined adversary as Murdoch.[269]

Its counter-bid to Land was weak, and within hours was contemptuously dismissed. News International announced it would not sell its shares to anyone else and would match the competing offer price. It is also understood that Rupert Murdoch personally telephoned the President of the French publisher, advising him in pithy terms – readily understood even by one with a limited command of English – to 'back off' (or perhaps more likely expressed in more colourful antipodean language). In any event, Groupe de la Cité did so on the first day of trading in January 1989, and just two days later Chapman wearily threw in the towel. He and his board recommended that all Collins shares be sold to News International and he resigned, leaving Land and Craig to claim the prize for their Australian master. And so, in something of an anti-climax, Murdoch eventually became sole owner of both William Collins and Harper & Row, quickly merged as HarperCollins.

As a News Corporation company within Murdoch's global multimedia empire, HarperCollins's corporate strategy was to make acquisitions to be exploited throughout all its various channels of films, TV, licensing and computer networks. Such a remit made Unwin Hyman, holder of the Tolkien franchise, highly attractive. In fact, this was all that HarperCollins were interested in, and Unwin Hyman's carefully constructed and actually quite profitable educational, academic and

269 The counter-bid was made a few days before Christmas 1988. Although it was not officially revealed who the counter-bidder was, it was at the time described as a 'major French media company'.

serious non-fiction lists (they had rather good publishing on crafts and chess, for example) were brutally disposed of piecemeal or consigned to oblivion. While not necessarily the first or largest publishing conglomerate, HarperCollins provided a perhaps ominous model for the future, announcing its new corporate values brashly and unequivocally. It was multi-national, profit-driven, hard-nosed and ambitious, with the clout of a major international media organization that some thought placed commerce before culture. This may be an unfairly harsh judgment since Collins before Murdoch had been nothing if not a fierce and sharp bookselling machine, but the arrival of Murdochian culture in publishing unsettled not a few of the old guard. The shareholders and investors, however, applauded.

Elsewhere the heady financial atmosphere, fuelled by the new venture capital firms seduced by what they saw as the unrealized assets of publishing companies (and not a little by a totally unrealistic assessment of their glamour and value), saw many sleepy and genteel firms shocked out of their composure and pitched into a money-soused new world. One such was Associated Book Publishers (ABP), formed in 1958 when Methuen had been amalgamated with Eyre and Spottiswoode, the Queen's Printer and holder of one of the letters patent to publish the King James Bible.[270] By the 1980s, under the benign and undemanding stewardship of the Crosthwaite Eyre family, the group had grown into an untidy (if generally well-run) parcel of trade and specialist publishers. It had notable concentrations in academic and professional areas, including law where it was second only to Butterworths. ABP also owned substantial companies in the 'old' Commonwealth, particularly Canada and Australia (see Duffy, 1989, Chapter 8). It was also one of the few publishers to possess substantial publishing in drama, particularly play scripts.

Then ABP awoke from its semi-recumbent posture and embarked on a breakneck round of acquisitions. It began quite modestly by acquiring New Zealand's leading publisher Reed (no relation) for a modest cash payment of £540,000 in 1983, but this proved only a prelude to an almost manic burst of activity that saw it take over the venerable house of Routledge and Kegan Paul for almost £4.5 million in 1983. Routledge had a strong academic profile and, unlike many other publishers with similar lists, had built a good, directly-owned business in America. Its majority

270 The other holders of the right (which is effectively a perpetual copyright) to publish 'The Authorised Version' are Collins, CUP and OUP.

shareholder Norman Franklin, grandson of a banker who had bought the business out of bankruptcy in 1902, was a serious-minded yet affable and clubbable publishing gentleman of the old school, with an iconoclastic streak.[271]

Routledge undoubtedly made a good fit for ABP and particularly its Methuen academic imprint. The acquisition was not straightforward, however, since a large minority of its shares were controlled by a Canadian investment company Camellia, whose main other interests were in tea growing. Routledge had slipped into loss in the early 1980s and Camellia wanted to get out and realize its assets. The arrival of Philip Sturrock – an energetic entrepreneur who would later successfully transform what remained of Cassell and other languishing imprints – as Chief Executive from Pitman did effect some improvements, and although there was recovery Camellia were not mollified. Although Franklin would have preferred to keep his company independent, he bowed to the pressure from the outside investors and agreed to sell to ABP, which he felt would be a safe home.

ABP's next acquisition was the young and energetic academic publisher Croom Helm. Founded in 1972 by two refugees from Macmillan, David Croom and Christopher Helm, it had benefited from the enormous growth in higher education markets at home and abroad during the 1970s and even into the 1980s (although Thatcherite cuts in public expenditure had begun to shrink the domestic market). Croom Helm had been particularly successful in academic libraries, which absorbed enormous amounts of monographs and higher-level textbooks. The company's simple formula was based on the model pioneered by the Macmillan Press, the academic division of Macmillan. They commissioned large numbers of highly specialized books from academics far more interested in being published than in receiving royalties. Print runs were short, production standards (generally) mediocre and marketing generic. Often they asked their authors to produce typewritten 'camera-ready copy' – inelegant but very cheap since it avoided any typesetting

271 His son, Andrew Franklin, has inherited some of his father's strengths and is a notable contemporary publisher. After a career with Hamish Hamilton and Penguin he went on to found Profile Books, one of today's most successful and distinctive independent publishers. He has created a string of successful bestsellers such as Lynne Truss' *Eats, Shoots and Leaves* (on the unlikely subject of correct punctuation) and is steadfastly committed to remaining independent.

bills.[272] They enhanced their cash-flow by selling co-editions to American academic publishers and university presses at long discount but on firm sale. They employed energetic editors such as Peter Sowden to scour universities and polytechnics for often highly esoteric manuscripts rejected by more choosy publishers.

Among the run-of-the-mill, Croom Helm occasionally acquired real gems by this method, including several academic bestsellers and highly influential treatises, mainly in the humanities and social sciences. This approach enabled rapid growth, but already by 1984 it was beginning to become unstuck as competitors such as Dawson Publishing (a short-lived venture by the well-known library supplier), Harvester Press, Pinter, Berg, and Edward Elgar were stealing many of their publishing clothes. Croom Helm's sales had tripled from £1million in 1980 to over £3 million in 1985, but as their cost base expanded their profits came under pressure and began to decline. An ill-advised purchase of an American publishing company, Auburn House, ended acrimoniously, although they did not lose money on the transaction. The two partners found that their interests were diverging with Helm, a keen bird watcher, wanting to expand to produce ornithological books to a much higher standard than the imprint normally adopted.[273]

Croom, a perspicacious if somewhat misanthropic character, clearly saw the writing on the wall and decided the time had come to sell while their luck held. He and Helm made use of a fairly recent style of consultant on the publishing scene, a company broker (Monroe Pofcher), to place their company on the market in late 1985. There was wide interest among larger academic publishers but ABP always led the bidding. Since Croom Helm, like many smaller publishers of the period, had been invested in by the venture capital company Investors in Industry (3i), who wished to realize their stake quickly, the deal was swiftly completed. The consideration was partly in shares, but both founders took a substantial cash payment and doubtless breathed a heartfelt sigh of relief at their new

272 Many academic books published by Croom Helm (and other academic publishers of the period) simply photographed the author's typewritten manuscript to produce the printing plates. This was called 'Author's CRC' and has thankfully become obsolete in an age where typesetters can capture the author's keystrokes from their computer disks (as has happened with the book you are currently reading).

273 Helm later created a superb ornithology list for A&C Black. He ended his career before his untimely death in 2007 by producing from his own resources a series of handsome books on country themes under the imprint Pica Press.

owner's generous settlement. Many observers thought the £3.5 million paid against a declining turnover of £2.7 million and profits of only £277,000 too much, although Pofcher had wanted more. Croom joined ABP to manage their entire academic publishing, while Helm set off in pursuit of bird books.

ABP next rather oddly added the publisher of guidebooks Pitkin Pictorials to its burgeoning empire for just over £1 million in cash a few months later. This was a type of publishing that bore no resemblance to anything else they did in editorial or marketing style.[274] All that could be said in favour of Pitkin Pictorials was that they were cheap and relatively cheerful. This frenetic burst of activity had increased ABP's debt and, in the prevailing mood of limitless funds from financial manipulation, they announced in spring 1987 that they were making a rights issue of shares to raise £11 million to reduce their borrowings and fund further acquisitions. What they did not anticipate was that this action would put them in the firing line to be acquired themselves. Dick Snyder, the swashbuckling head of the American publisher Simon and Schuster, owned by the oil and media conglomerate Gulf and Western, put the company into play and offered the Crosthwaite Eyre family trust and other major shareholders £5 per share – well above the quoted value. Snyder was mainly interested in ABP's trade publishing, but his interest alerted other predators who were much more attracted by the academic and professional lists.

The first 'shark to circle' was Tim Rix, Chief Executive of Longmans. He was interested in the law business of Sweet and Maxwell and the Scottish law publisher W. Green, as well as the scientific, technical and medical lists of Chapman & Hall – particularly its scientific journals where Longmans was weak apart from medicine. The trade and children's publishing, Rix thought, could be neatly fitted into Penguin (although Mayer apparently was not keen). Next on the scene was the Canadian behemoth International Thomson, seeking to add the academic and professional publishing to its rapidly growing 'information universe'; it, too, had no time for the 'frothy' trade lists.

Initially it looked as if Longmans would win since they could easily absorb the whole group, and they did in fact offer a higher price – but it was partly in shares of its parent company S. Pearson. Thomson offered

274 Pitkin Pictorials published cheap, full-colour guides to historic sites such as cathedrals, castles or historic towns mainly sold at the attractions themselves or in souvenir or confectionery shops. Normal bookshops rarely stocked them.

less, but totally in cash. The ABP directors and management stood by apprehensively (several of them told me at the time they would have much preferred to be bought by Longmans, to whom they felt much closer in culture) while the shareholders made up their minds. In the end cash won, and in June 1987 ABP became part of International Thomson. And in the narrow terms of liquidity, events were to prove the shareholders right. Just three months later the stock market crashed, and the Pearson shares that Longmans had offered in part payment dived. Whether ABP would have done better under a British rather than a Canadian owner still remains a matter of opinion.

While all this was going on, a number of new publishing start-ups took advantage of the fashionability of publishing among the venture capitalists and the freeing up of skills through the restructuring and amalgamations among conglomerate publishers. The year 1986 was an *annus mirabilis* for the creation of new publishing companies, most set up by refugees from corporate publishing. The founders saw and grasped the opportunity to strike out on their own with the easy availability of funding from keen merchant bankers. Paul Chapman, for example, who had fled the British end of Harper & Row on its acquisition by Murdoch, set up his own academic company, as did Jessica Kingsley who had been unhappily treading water at distributor Eurospan. David Fulton emerged from the technical publisher Crosby, Staples to set up an innovative publishing house specializing in books for teachers and educational professionals, while Colin Whurr created a successful imprint in health care and psychology. Iain Stevenson, who had joined Pinter Publishers from Macmillan the previous year, anticipated an emerging trend that would come to central importance in the succeeding decade by establishing Belhaven Press from within the framework of Pinter Publishers. This imprint, along with Earthscan, was among the first to publish extensively in environmental science, conservation and increasingly sustainable development and climate change. A year later, he even made an acquisition by purchasing Leicester University Press for Pinter for, as he recalled, 'the price of a small suburban semi'.[275]

275 The model for many of these new start ups was Kogan Page, founded by the ebullient and innovative publishing entrepreneur Philip Kogan in 1967. Kogan pioneered many of the editorial and marketing approaches that the newer companies adopted and he, as I can gratefully testify, was generous with advice, guidance and (occasionally) acerbic criticism. His company, despite many overtures from potential purchasers who would like to acquire his list of business books, continues as one of the largest and most

Remarkably, all these new companies began within a few weeks of each other. They were mostly small, owner-managed enterprises – albeit all with injections of venture capital from merchant banks, noisily vying with each other to give new publishers money.[276] There were, however, two significantly large new publishing companies set up in 1986 which would, in very different ways, change the face of British publishing.

The first of these was Bloomsbury Publishing Ltd, created as a mould-breaking general publisher by Nigel Newton, David Reynolds, Alan Wherry and Liz Calder. Newton had first had the idea for 'a new, independent, medium-sized publisher of books of editorial excellence and originality with high standards of design and production (aiming to) … publish literary authors of the highest quality and sales potential' in 1983 (Newton, unpublished memoir, p.1). He was working at the small, rather idiosyncratic company of Sidgwick and Jackson, and when it fell under the sway of Macmillan he decided to make his move. He wrote a business plan with Reynolds (who was a partner in a small packager) in spring 1986 and secretly canvassed venture capitalist investors to supply starting funding of £1.75 million. Once he had obtained promises from three merchant banks he completed his dream team by recruiting Wherry from Penguin as sales director and Calder from Cape as fiction editorial director, knowing both to be unhappy with the changes overtaking their respective houses. Reynolds would commission non-fiction.

Because of the high profile of the protagonists and the relatively large sums involved, it was necessary to keep the venture secret – which was a challenge since Calder lived with the editor of the trade paper *The Bookseller*, Louis Baum. Nevertheless, since Liz and Louis were both people of the highest integrity discretion was maintained, and there was widespread surprise when all four founders dramatically resigned from their corporate positions on the same morning in September 1986,

---

successful independent publishers. Headquartered in a rabbit warren of offices in Pentonville, it has branches in the USA, Europe, India and elsewhere, now directed by his daughter (although Philip remains chairman).

276 The venture capitalists, of course, wanted their money to grow and the new companies they helped fund eventually to be sold to their profit. The failure rate among the general range of companies funded in the period was quite high (often over 70 per cent), but it is notable that most new publishers created in the 1980s throve and were in fact successfully sold over the next fifteen years. Of the 1986 group only Jessica Kingsley survives as an independent, and is now probably the world's leading publisher on books on autism and related conditions.

announcing in the afternoon their launch of a new publishing house. Their initial plans were idealistic and perhaps a little impractical. One of their innovative ideas was an author's trust which gave 5 per cent of the shares to current and future authors. Their first books were truly beautiful, with flourishes that the trade had generally forgotten such as coloured tops and silk head-and-tail bands. A colophon of Diana the Huntress and an exclusive script typeface were further trademark features, as were silk place markers which became standard on all their hardbacks.

The choice of the name Bloomsbury was inspired since it conjured up literary seriousness, the gentlemanly values of yore and an association with Virginia Woolf and her coterie. Newton recalls that '[a]n intimation of the Bloomsbury Group was not the idea, but did no harm' (Newton, unpublished memoir, p.1). In fact the house was not, and never has been, located in Bloomsbury. Its first offices were in distinctly unliterary Putney, above a Chinese restaurant. The company later moved to Soho Square, occupying the offices that had once housed Rupert Hart-Davis. The substantial funding they had obtained enabled them quickly to recruit a talented staff including Kathy Rooney from Longmans to develop reference publishing, Caroline Michel to manage publicity and Nigel Batt to look after finance. They also created an energetic national and international sales team. One helpful anomaly was that when News International scooped up Unwin Hyman, they overlooked the fact that the Australian company trading as Allen and Unwin Pty was not part of the deal. Its independent-minded director, Patrick Gallagher, offered to act as Antipodean distributor, which later brought him great success.[277] The only false step they made in their early years was establishing a subsidiary, Chancery Law, under Andrew Prideaux. Specializing in law publishing, it did not perform as expected and was later disposed of to Wiley.[278]

Bloomsbury scored great literary successes and won Booker and other prizes. It also built solid lists in non-fiction and reference, and by 1994 was ready to float itself on the stock market. Its shares were popular and the market valued the company at £9 million, which amply repaid the initial investors and provided the author's trust (which was wound up on flotation) with a substantial nest-egg. Pre-tax profits were however only

277 A patio at the firm's Sydney office is known as 'The Harry Potter Terrace'.

278 When my Belhaven Press was sold to Wiley in 1993 I inherited the Chancery offices in Eastcastle Street in London's garment district. They were totally unsuitable as publishing offices, but did boast a rather glamorous roof terrace with sweeping views over Fitzrovia.

£0.75 million, and Bloomsbury had a few anxious years as a public company until in 1997 the company stumbled upon perhaps the greatest publishing stroke of luck of the twentieth century. An unknown (and much rejected) author called Joanne K. Rowling sent them the manuscript of a children's fantasy novel, *Harry Potter and the Philosopher's Stone*. The unprecedented success of this and the subsequent volumes propelled Bloomsbury to become Britain's sixth largest publisher and secured its future as an independent (Stevenson, 2008). Had this not happened it is debatable whether Bloomsbury would have survived unmolested by corporate takeover.

While Bloomsbury was showing what could be done at the high end the same remarkable year of 1986 saw the arrival of a brash new mass-market house aiming to transform the way in which popular fiction was published and sold. This was Headline, set up by an ex-Macmillan graduate trainee Tim Hely Hutchinson. At first sight, the younger son of the eighth Earl of Donoughmore, educated at Eton and Oxford where he had edited the University newspaper *Isis*, was a rather unlikely champion of downmarket popular taste. However, he had served a tough and highly commercial publishing apprenticeship, joining Robert Maxwell after Macmillan in 1982. In return for a very large salary (reputed to be £200,000 a year) Hely Hutchinson ran the sales side of the quixotic and egregious tycoon's book business. By 1985, at the age of 32, he felt he was ready to set up on his own.

Hely Hutchinson raised over £1 million as starting capital and swiftly built an impressive list including highly popular fiction authors such as Danielle Steele. He quickly became renowned for aggressive marketing and brash, even vulgar, presentation, with his books known – not always approvingly – as 'Headline Braille' after the lavish use of foil embossing on their covers. Publicity posters blossomed in unlikely locations such as bus shelters and railway platforms. High energy and attention-grabbing events accompanied book launches. His aim was simple: 'I thought we could turn it completely on its head and be the people's publisher' (quoted in an interview in *The Daily Telegraph*, 11 February 2006). Publishing greybeards were scandalized, but it was a highly successful approach. By 1992 Headline had expanded from three founding employees to 118, and in seven years had grown to a turnover of almost £16 million, with a pre-tax margin of 13 per cent, well above the industry standard which was normally closer to 5 per cent. They had over one thousand titles in print.

Then Hely Hutchinson mounted a takeover whose scale and audacity surprised even his admirers. His target, Hodder & Stoughton, was a long established and rather ramshackle general publisher owned by the Attenborough family and its employees. For decades it had pursued an unobtrusive course and was complacent and self-satisfied. Its owners had discussed the possibility of amalgamation or new investors, and had staved off a cash crisis in 1991 by selling its famous and venerable medical newspaper *The Lancet* to Elsevier for £11 million. Hodder's finances continued audibly to creak, however, and its paternalistic and ineffectual values felt increasingly out of touch with the times. A failed reconstruction and redundancies (which deeply shocked a loyal and stable workforce) did not improve the situation. Hodder's profit margin at under 2 per cent was minuscule, but it possessed a large network of overseas branches and a formidable backlist (which contributed almost half its sales). The company was almost seven times larger than Headline, but Hely Hutchinson was not daunted.

The smaller but much livelier newcomer effectively backed itself into the larger but ailing older publisher. Hely Hutchinson mobilized funds of almost £50 million to acquire Hodder which, although it was gratefully received by Philip Attenborough and his board, looked and still looks cheap considering the assets that were being gained. Some predicted that even an entrepreneur as energetic and visionary as Hely Hutchinson could not successfully merge two very different organizations in scale, culture and ambitions. However, it is undeniable that he did so with great success and panache, and to his credit without much bloodshed or bad feeling on either side. When he was ready to sell out to the retailer W.H. Smith in 1999 the combined company realized £189 million, yielding him in the circumstances a relatively modest personal profit of £4 million.[279]

A number of other publishing conglomerations occurred during the 1980s and early 1990s. They were smaller in scale but followed a similar model to Headline, with new dynamic foundations acquiring larger established houses which generally had fallen on hard times. Anthony Cheetham, who had founded Century in 1981 with his then-wife Rosie, bought Hutchinson in 1985 from its languishing imprisonment within London Weekend Television (LWT) who had acquired the publisher in

279 Hodder Headline was only briefly owned by W.H. Smith and was then sold to the French group Hachette Livre. In 2008 it had become the largest British publisher, having absorbed venerable imprints such as John Murray, Edward Arnold and Robert Gibson (see Stevenson, 2007a).

1978. Century Hutchinson was subsequently bought in 1989 (by a then recent entrant to British publishing, the American literary publisher Random House) for £64 million – almost double its turnover.[280]

Cheetham remarkably pulled off the same manoeuvre in 1991 when his newly created imprint Orion bought George Weidenfeld and Nicolson, which had itself just acquired the remnants of J.M. Dent. Weidenfeld gave up his 80 per cent holding of his company, but received a small shareholding in Orion. This enabled him to continue to work as a publisher in the company that bore his name.

In 1991, one publisher who had left his mark for good and ill on the publishing world for four decades left the scene in a dramatic and even now not wholly explicable fashion. Robert Maxwell would not rest content with the secure and rather dull – although highly lucrative – income that Pergamon Press brought him. He had begun to diversify into other more exciting but less predictable areas, especially newspapers (which had an ominous ring, given the history of earlier press proprietors such as Northcliffe or Cecil King), as well as football clubs and other leisure interests. After he bought the *Daily Mirror* stable of titles in 1984 he was invariably spoken of as a 'media mogul', often in the same breath as Rupert Murdoch with whom he shared a mutually returned dislike (dating back to their acrimonious battle to acquire the *News of the World* in 1969).

But Maxwell's legendary sureness of touch began to desert him. An ill-advised attempt to create a mould-breaking '24 Hour Newspaper' for London in 1987 was derailed by a bitter circulation war with Rothermere's Associated Newspapers; it folded after five months, losing him many millions and denting his credibility. As ever, his dealings were tinged with suspicions of less than scrupulous behaviour, but the banks nevertheless continued to lend him large sums to pursue his increasingly erratic business ventures, including an attempt to buy Manchester United FC. He created a complex network of interlinked companies in various jurisdictions, including the tiny and highly secretive middle European principality of Liechtenstein, and he increasingly involved his two sons, Ian and Kevin, in the operation of his deliberately opaque business

280 Random House, eventually bought by German private media group Bertelsmann, quickly grew to become a major British publisher by absorbing many famous imprints including Cape, Harvill, Heinemann and Transworld. They are currently the second largest British publisher (see Stevenson, 2007a).

empire.[281] The Maxwell of popular memory, grossly obese with a bullying manner and a cavalier disregard for honesty and propriety, emerged into full view in this period. He lost all sense of proportion and caution and, with his often bizarre and laughable personal intervention in the editorial line of the the *Daily Mirror*, probably all grasp on reality. His tangled financial structure spiralled out of control and, in a desperate effort to keep his unstable operations going, he moved enormous sums frenetically around the hotchpotch of businesses that operated as the grandiose Maxwell Communications Corporation – in the process plundering the pension funds of the *Mirror's* workforce. Finally, in desperation, he sold his beloved Pergamon Press to Reed Elsevier for £440 million in February 1991, although many observers thought that it was worth at least half a billion pounds. Ominously, the conservative, careful and righteous Anglo-Dutch conglomerate, then as now the world's largest publisher by value and volume, did not (or could not) perform the usual 'due diligence' search of Maxwell's company. They could only justify their acquisition to their shareholders by creating a complex financial model of the Pergamon business using data that could be verified externally (number of titles, volume of sales, pricing history) to derive its value (de Bellaigue, 2004, p.8). With Netherlandish candour, they were implying they could not believe a word that Maxwell and his advisors were telling them.

A few months later in November 1991, with his creditors closing in, his pension fund thefts becoming impossible to hide and his erstwhile friends and partners deserting him, he took a few days holiday and stepped off the deck of his luxury yacht near the Canary Islands off the coast of Africa, to be drowned in an apparent suicide. There have been suggestions that his death may have been more sinister which have implicated the Israeli secret service or business rivals in a carefully staged murder, but I find this hard to credit. Maxwell at least possessed as much courage as he lacked scruple (he had, after all, been decorated with the Military Cross for his wartime exploits) and I think he just realized that he had finally reached the end of the financial road. After almost forty-five years of dubious dealings, duplicity, fraud and sharp practice (along with, let it be

281 Both Ian and Kevin Maxwell later faced trials for financial irregularities, but were acquitted. At various times they both fell out with their father and were unceremoniously sacked by him. Kevin Maxwell ran for a short period the American educational publisher Holt-Saunders, where I met him during the final interview for the post, since I was the other candidate on the short list. I remain unsure whether I was lucky or unfortunate not to be selected.

said, brilliant publishing and tremendous vision and entrepreneurship), he quite simply had nowhere else to go – and took what must have seemed to have been the only course open to him.[282]

One aspect of the easy money culture of Thatcher's Britain was the rising financial importance of literary agents in the publishing process. Agents, dominated by long-established companies such as Curtis Brown, A.P. Watt and A.M. Heath, had been an important part of the publishing economy for many decades, but their influence had been mainly confined to ensuring publishers' contracts and royalty rates were reasonably fair to their author clients. Stanley Unwin was famously dismissive of their role and most of the publishing memoirs of the era up to the 1980s, like those of Lusty, Cape, Reinhardt and Warburg, barely mention them. During the 1980s their position dramatically shifted as competition between the newly forming conglomerates sharpened, and money – and lots of it – flowed into the literary business. A new breed of agent recognized that authors who could feed the voracious hunger of the venture capital-fired publishers could now command serious money in advances on royalties. Previously a miserly sum, and often not provided at all, advances were only intended to prevent an author from starving while writing. Stanley Unwin insisted that they should never exceed one-third of an author's potential earnings over three years. The 1980s saw an overt shift of power and expectations between publishers and at least certain of their authors that changed all that, with agents as the catalyst.

Agents now knew that they held the whip hand as publishers clamoured to acquire the scarce resource of bestsellers from popular authors. Advances steadily climbed so that they soon bore no relation to what the books would earn in royalties, but were an exorbitant price tag on the work of good authors and (perhaps more importantly) an expensive insurance policy to exclude competitors. New devices such as floor auctions, three-book contracts and 'sweetheart deals'[283] enabled crafty

282 Maxwell's career continues to fascinate, and not only for its publishing impact. Had he not embarked on the last chaotic decade of swindling and unreality (which was at least in part enabled by the regulatory laxity and *laissez-faire* financial and fiscal environment of the Thatcher years) and remained content to be the owner of the world's second-largest (after Elsevier) scientific and academic publisher, I suspect that had he lived he would now be garlanded with honours. To do it justice, his story deserves the creative attention of a great operatic composer.

283 A 'sweetheart deal' is where an agent offers a book to a group of publishers in an

agents to push advances for even quite modest projects well into six figures: for major established authors such as Jeffrey Archer, seven-figure advances were offered and seized. Agents like Deborah Owen (who represented Archer), Ed Victor and Andrew Wylie – who rejoiced in the sobriquet 'the jackal' – exercised enormous influence and became famous for driving the hardest of bargains. Others, such as Carole Blake and Giles Gordon, who had formerly been publishers, jumped the divide to set up their own agencies, benefiting from the newly enhanced status that a once-downtrodden and neglected profession had attained.

The only problem was that not all projects 'earned out'. Although exact figures are understandably not available, it is generally understood that only a tiny proportion, probably less than 10 per cent, of these huge advances ever recouped against actual sales. Certainly during the period many contracts were heavily over-inflated in value, with authors and agents receiving great monetary benefit but leaving publishers to lick their financial wounds as un-recovered advances were written off their balance sheets. The easy availability of funds and the heady financial atmosphere of the period certainly contributed to the reckless expenditure on authors' advances, and publishers must take much of the blame for agreeing to such spendthrift speculation. It was not sustainable for long, and although advances on certain projects remained high into the twenty-first century, some of the completely ludicrous over-ramping of payments typical of the 1980s and 1990s has to an extent been moderated.

What has lasted, however, is the transformed role of the literary agent as an intermediary, now much more important and indeed essential to the economics and business structure of publishing. Many major publishers will not now even consider any new publishing project unless it has been submitted to them by an agent. This is an entire – and not particularly benign – legacy of the roaring market in literary property encouraged by the Thatcherite free market. Indeed for many authors, the agent is now much more important than the editor in their creative lives. Many editors have little hands-on input into authors' works and through lack of time, lack of training and, sadly, lack of inclination have abdicated the key roles of shaping text and cultivating good writing to agents, many of whom admittedly fill these roles well. It is, however, a long way from

open first round auction, but accepts no offer. To prevent a second round, a desperate publisher will offer a large advance directly to the agent on condition that a second auction does not take place.

the exhaustive editorial involvement of Richard Garnett, Diana Athill, T.S. Eliot or Grant Richards.

While virtually every other aspect of the publishing business was rocked to its foundations and transformed profoundly by the economic liberalism of the period, one restrictive practice of an earlier age of interventionism and control survived almost to its end. This was the Net Book Agreement which since its turbulent introduction in 1900 had regulated the retail price at which books could be sold to the public (see Chapter 1). Despite a couple of legal challenges (the last in 1962) that had been robustly dispatched by the massed forces of the book trade, the Agreement remained firmly in place. Publishers fixed the price at which a net book could be sold and, apart from a few trivial exceptions, no exceptional discounts could be offered, no matter the size of the bookseller nor their financial clout. The argument ran that this regulatory regime encouraged retailers to hold a wide diversity of stock and ensured a level playing field. Such restrictions, known as 'resale price maintenance' (RPM), had existed on many categories of goods during the century, but as the new orthodoxy of letting markets rip took hold they faded away, leaving only books and proprietary medicines with legally sanctioned price regulation. The NBA had last been renewed in 1957 and legally validated in 1962 and 'enforceable prices' were applied to the vast majority of British books. Most publishers, if not all, had signed the NBA and applied 'net' prices to their books. Apart from refuseniks such as Hamlyn, the major exceptions continued to be school books which were supplied via educational contractors at 'non-net' terms.

It is remarkable that such a restrictive practice should have survived the ravages of Thatcherite restructuring so long, but although the book trade groused, it was generally content to leave it in place. By 1995, however, the arrangement came under full-frontal attack. Supermarkets, led by ASDA, had begun to stock books, and they were not accustomed to their suppliers dictating the prices they charged to customers. Bookselling was undergoing change and a new retailer, the Pentos group, led by a noisy and belligerent newcomer, Terry Maher, took the NBA as a personal affront and swore to see it abolished. Publishers at the time might have paid him more heed had he paid his invoices on time – Pentos was notorious for withholding payment to its suppliers.

Nevertheless, the clamour increased steadily and although the Booksellers' Association in general (along with many publishers) wished to see the arrangement continue, its days were clearly numbered. The NBA was referred to the Restrictive Practice Court in the spring of 1995, and before its case could be heard a pitched battle of words broke out between its opponents and supporters. In one corner were ranged Pentos, the supermarkets and several radically inclined publishers, confident that their market share and influence would ensure them growth in a post-NBA world; in the other were the majority of the bookselling trade, most medium and small publishers and businesses such as book clubs and library suppliers who depended on an orderly market with predictable and even pricing. The ring was uneasily held by the Council of the Publishers' Association as custodians of the NBA, led by Nick Chapman, publishing director of BBC Books.[284]

TABLE FIVE: Members of the Publishers' Association Council in September 1995

Nicholas Chapman (President) (BBC Books)
Simon Master (Vice President) (Random House)
Colin Whurr (Vice President) (Whurr Publishers)
Jeff Andrew (Pearson Education)
Mark Barty-King (Transworld)
Eddie Bell (HarperCollins)
Iain Burns (Octopus)
Jane Carr (British Library Publishing)
John Clement (HarperCollins)
Trevor Glover (Penguin)
Philippa Harrison (Macmillan)
Christopher Hurst (C. Hurst & Co)
David Kewley (Scholastic)
Robert Kiernan (International Thomson)
Philip Kogan (Kogan Page)
Anthony Pearce (Institute of Physics Publishing)
Fred Perkins (McGraw-Hill)
Iain Stevenson (John Wiley and Sons)
Simon Wratten (Oxford University Press)

Source: PA minutes in personal collection augmented by memory

284 It should be recalled that the Publishers' Association is primarily a trade organization whose main mission is to pursue collective action that will favour the businesses of all its members without benefiting one over the others. All publishing companies (it does not allow individual memberships) are eligible to join, but in reality

As Table Five shows, the Council comprised a mix of representatives of large and small trade publishers, with a sprinkling of educational and academic publishers and a few from the British ends of American multinationals. To the latter two categories, the NBA did not matter a great deal in their markets and some were actively opposed to it. Opinion among the trade publishers was fiercely divided. Some wanted it abolished immediately, others had both a sentimental and practical attachment to it. In truth Nick Chapman did not care much for it, even though as he recalled 'it flowed like the Suez Canal through my drawing room' (personal reminiscence). He kept an admirable impartiality while the debate raged. His Chief Executive, Clive Bradley, was by contrast fiercely attached to the NBA and argued passionately that it needed to be preserved at all costs. All members of the Council were deluged with advice, advocacy, supplications and the occasional veiled threat from all corners of the book business during the summer and early autumn of 1995.

When the NBA actually came before the Restrictive Practices Court in 1996, it was struck down and its legal force ended. In the event, its formal legal demise was an unnecessary ritual since the Council of the Publishers' Association had, more or less meekly, voted no longer to enforce it almost a year before. The key mover in this was the Executive Chairman of HarperCollins, Eddie Bell, who had become convinced that the end of the NBA would bring his aggressive marketing machine commercial advantage, and who in any case was temperamentally disinclined to support cosy gentlemen's agreements. He made it clear to his fellow PA Council members that if they did not vote for the end of the NBA, he would take his company out of PA membership and 'go it alone' by de-netting all his company's books.[285] The loss of such a large subscription would have crippled the organization, and the threat convinced some members to shift their vote. In the event, a special meeting was called for

the cost of the membership fees (which are banded according to size of company turnover) exclude very small companies which tend to join the Independent Publishers Guild (IPG) instead. In fact, the PA has always done a good job representing the interests of smaller publishers and many of its initiatives such as the anti-VAT campaign and the creation of the Copyright Licencing Agency (CLA), which distributes many millions of pounds annually to publishers for copying permissions fees, have been of tremendous financial benefit to the industry.

285 His iconoclastic attitude did him no harm with his boss Rupert Murdoch who relished destroying any protectionist sacred cows which strayed into his path – provided, of course, their disposal did not harm his own businesses.

28 September. Those who attended voted not to abolish the NBA but rather to cease to enforce its terms, a subtle distinction lost on most who read the announcement.[286] It noted that individual publishers could, if they wish, continue to publish books on net terms, but none in fact ever did. Although it expressed regret that an arrangement that had served the book industry well for nearly a century was no longer sustainable, it thereby effectively washed its hands of book pricing policy. Eddie Bell, having made his point forcibly at earlier meetings, did not trouble to attend the NBA's final obsequies.

Neither for that matter, did I. I was an *ex-officio* member of the Council in my capacity as chair of the Council of Academic and Professional Publishers (a division of the PA) and was under instruction from my board that if it came to the vote I was to vote against continuing the NBA, although several of my members disagreed. In the event, I decided that it was good politics to avoid the meeting and keep both opinions happy. I still rather regret missing out on what transpired to have been an historic moment for the book business.

Meanwhile, as a rather poignant coda, it was announced almost simultaneously that arguably the most British of publishers, Macmillan – the company that had produced Britain's only publishing Prime Minister – had agreed to sell itself to a German media combine, Holtzbrinck.[287] Thus in that chill autumn of 1995 both the last vestige of a form of publishing that had come in with the twentieth century disappeared and the publishing house of its architect, Sir Frederick Macmillan, fell into foreign hands. It both felt like, and truly was, the end of an era.

286 The announcement was written by Bradley and he used all his barrister's skill to make crystal clear his own point of view that the decision was a lamentable mistake.
287 Holtzbrinck had actually acquired a majority interest in Macmillan in April 1995, although it left a substantial minority holding with the Macmillan family trust and its actual assumption of control did not occur until later that year. It eventually purchased all the shares four years later.

Conclusion

The ending of the Net Book Agreement fundamentally altered the British publishing landscape, but not necessarily in the ways that its defenders and detractors envisioned. Its immediate consequence was a drop in the number of titles published, but not in the number of books sold nor their value (Stevenson, 2007a). Bookselling chains such as Pentos who had noisily agitated for the change rather failed to take advantage of their desired deregulation and devoted their energies in an eventually toxic war of expansion with their rivals Waterstones,[288] leading to an over-expansion of retail space that was not sustainable. Neither survived the century as free-standing enterprises, and in 1999 the two were amalgamated under the management of the music retailer HMV. Here the Waterstones brand survived while Dillons (the Pentos brand) did not. Some smaller independent booksellers did succumb to a deregulated market, and the long-established provincial retailers such as Hudsons of Birmingham, Georges of Bristol, Austicks of Leeds, Thornes of Newcastle and Thins of Edinburgh, which had by and large been sclerotic for decades, were one by one absorbed by chains.

So far so gloomy, as presaged by the supporters of the NBA. But then, as so often, the portents did not run as predicted. The book market, rather unexpectedly, began to expand. New retailers appeared such as Ottakars[289]

288 Waterstones was founded in 1984 by Tim Waterstone, an entrepreneurial bookseller who envisaged 'a new type of bookshop' with a wide stock, informed booksellers and a rather clubby atmosphere. It is now the largest bookselling chain in the UK although its brief history has been very chequered with numerous changes of ownership and repeated attempts by its erstwhile founder to buy it back. For fuller details see Stevenson (2007a).

289 Ottakars, named for a character in the Tintin comic books of Belgian artist Hergé

and Borders, which had imported the 'destination store' concept from the United States and attracted a new clientele. Their success would be brief, Ottakars being absorbed by Waterstones and Borders eventually retiring back to the United States,[290] but they pioneered new methods of merchandizing that others copied. The Oxford university bookseller Blackwell, long immured in the dreaming spires, began a dramatic expansion elsewhere, opening a branch in Charing Cross Road in London and in 1999 acquiring its ancient Cambridge rival Heffers, as well as opening branches on many new campuses throughout the UK. Foyles, which for almost a quarter of a century had been wracked by fraud and suffered from poor management and unattractive premises – presided over by its idiosyncratic and despotic owner Christina Foyle – underwent a remarkable resurrection following her death in 1999. It was refurbished and welcomed franchised retailers of music and feminist literature, among others, and became once again the leading independent bookseller in Britain. It too expanded by opening new branches.

Some venerable bookselling models did suffer irretrievable decline after the NBA's collapse. Book clubs which had sales of over £210 million in 1995 suffered from an ageing of their clientele which was not replaced. They were unable to compete with the vigorous new discounting of retail booksellers and, increasingly, of the internet bookseller, Amazon – which now has a market share of almost 15 per cent of books sold in Britain (and occupies a virtually monopolistic position as an internet retailer). It is one of the ironies of publishing history that a form of book merchandizing that was once opposed by both booksellers and publishers as undermining the NBA became probably the greatest casualty of its demise. Book club sales had halved by 2005, and have continued to decline precipitously since. Much of their market has been taken by 'party plan' retailers such as The Book People, founded in 1988 to sell large quantities of a restricted list of titles at a high discount to customers at their workplaces, schools and through the mail. Their sales were approaching £100 million towards the end of the first decade of the twentieth-first century.

—

(in a characteristically quirky gesture by its founder James Heanage) also dates from 1984, but its nationwide expansion from a few West Country branches only came after, and as a consequence of, the end of the NBA.

290 They continued to operate as a management buyout, but at the end of 2009 they collapsed leaving Waterstones the sole national bookselling chain, although W.H. Smith had increased their bookselling range.

For publishers the ten years since the NBA disappeared was something of a 'golden decade' – although it would be wrong to claim that the end of price control was the only factor here, as growing prosperity certainly made for an easier market. Nevertheless, after an initial stutter, publishing output steadily increased. Almost 120,000 new titles were published in 2001, nearly two and a half times the number published ten years before. By 2005 title output had increased to over 160,000. Challenges from other media such as computer games, multi-channel television and the internet did not seem to have much competitive impact on traditional leisure reading. Fiction books sold £281 million in 2004, while other important trade categories such as biography, cookery and sport enjoyed notable increases. Entire new genres like 'chick-lit' (fiction aimed at young women who wished they were married), 'yummy mummies' (what happened to them when they were) and 'misery memoirs' (gloomy tales of unrelieved childhood and adolescent deprivation and neglect) were created, and enjoyed a sometimes transitory success. Literary prize-givings such as the (Man) Booker, Whitbread and Orange evolved from being small congratulatory gatherings for literati into major media events, televised live, with red carpets and bookmakers quoting odds on the outcomes. New forms of book appreciation like 'book groups' and broadcast programmes such as the BBC 'Big Read' and, most of all, the 'Richard and Judy Book Club' on Channel 4 created significant new markets for books, albeit mainly for fiction and popular memoirs. They did, however, champion and achieve unprecedented sales for quite literary authors like Joseph O'Connor and Victoria Hislop. And overall there was the impact of seven books featuring the adventures of a boy wizard which confounded the book world by selling over 400 million copies worldwide and making its author, JK Rowling, one of the world's richest women, Her fortunate publisher, Bloomsbury, was projected from its humble beginnings in 1986 to become Britain's sixth largest publisher by 2006, just behind Oxford University Press (Stevenson, 2008).

Publishing houses changed, of course. The French-owned Hachette[291] decided to concentrate on becoming a major player in the English language and acquired a whole string of famous companies, including

291 Hachette also owns most of French trade publishing which it acquired after a disastrous attempt to create an international publishing conglomerate (which included the American publisher Houghton Mifflin) by the utilities company Vivendi Universal went disastrously wrong. Hachette itself is ultimately owned by the French industrial conglomerate Lagardère, which is, among other things, a major arms manufacturer.

Hodder Headline, Little Brown, Orion, Edward Arnold, Robert Gibson and John Murray. For most of the first decade of the twenty-first century it disputed the position of Britain's largest publisher with the German Bertelsmann group, owners of Random House which federates imprints such as Ebury, Vermillion, Chatto, Cape, Virago, Secker and Warburg and the major mass-market paperbacker Transworld. HarperCollins retains echoes of its monolithic past but has shed all vestiges of manufacturing, keeping only a small rump operation in Glasgow producing maps and dictionaries. Penguin expanded its interests by acquiring, as we have seen, the innovative illustrated reference publisher Dorling Kindersley (although it has not been an unrelieved star in its success) and the travel publisher Rough Guides. Within Pearson Education (which grew out of the old Pearson Longmans companies), Penguin operates with renewed self-confidence in a global market and – despite a disastrous experience with an attempt to open a computerized warehouse in 2005 (having sold its revered but hoary Harmondsworth base to allow for the expansion of Heathrow airport) – it retains a 12 per cent share of the British book market. Macmillan, under its German owners Holtzbrinck, continues with its eclectic mix of trade, academic, scientific and overseas education publishing with success. A common feature among these foreign-owned conglomerates (Anglo-American in Pearson's case) is that their ultimate shareholders by and large leave their British management to get on with the publishing.

The post-NBA period also saw, rather unexpectedly, the creation of small independent publishers – probably in greater numbers than at any time since the 1930s. Companies such as Profile Books, Serpent's Tail, Martin Woodhead, Persephone, Canongate and Polygon were established and won literary prizes[292] and high esteem. Publishing still remains a relatively low-cost entry business, and recent technical developments like print-on-demand, digital typesetting and internet selling enable very small publishers to compete in the market, although their access to traditional retail outlets is proving less easy. Nevertheless there are probably still over ten thousand active publishing imprints in the United Kingdom. They are producing more books than ever and participating in an industry which, with a turnover approaching £4 billion, secures for

292 Even if, in Martin Woodhead's case, it was for the Diagram oddest title of the year 2008 – for *Your Cheese Problems Solved.* Woodhead's company, based in a period country house outside Cambridge, produces an admired list of titles in engineering, environmental management and, of course, food science.

this small, off-shore island its position as the world's leading publishing nation in creativity, diversity, influence and reach.[293]

So what does the future hold? Most of this history was written before the sudden shock of the credit crunch and banking crisis of late 2008 threw Britain and the world into recession. British publishing, as we have seen in the 1930s and 1980s, has actually done rather well during previous recessions, and some of its most inventive and lasting innovations (such as Penguins and Pickles) have emerged at times of financial stringency. Thus far, although there have been restructures and downsizing, mainly at trade publishing houses, the British book business seems to be weathering the recession much better than in the United States – and very much better than its near-cousin, the printed newspaper industry, which seems to be in terminal decline.

There are, of course, enormous challenges and problems to overcome. The indiscriminate, across-the-board discounting that is practised by retail chains and internet sellers benefits the customer, but can hardly continue without causing real structural harm to publishing. There have even been calls for a reinstatement of the NBA, or at least a selective measure of price control, such as still exists in other countries such as France. The much-vaunted e-book has yet to make its promised impact, and both publishers and readers seem uncertain about whether digital formats offer an attractive alternative to print on paper. Many publishing functions such as copy-editing or design are being outsourced to less-expensive economies such as India, a trend that is likely to increase.

Despite all these uncertainties and constraints British publishing has, I am convinced, a strong and secure future. The last century has demonstrated conclusively that publishing success depends on talented, thoughtful, creative, inspired, innovative, brave, visionary, risk-taking people – even if some are also occasionally stupid, villainous, selfish, greedy and grandiose. Fortunately they are people who care about what others read and need for pleasure, education and knowledge and feed those needs by print on paper. From Heinemann through Cape, Lane, Deutsch, Hamlyn, Hill, Newton, Hely Hutchinson, even Maxwell, and the thousands who have worked with them to realize their vision, Britain has been exceptionally fortunate in possessing a cultural milieu that has

293 Although they are not representative of anything more than a small part of the industry, it is instructive to study the bestsellers lists in Germany, Italy, Scandinavia, the United States, and even France, to see how many of the books featured there are of British origin.

enabled great publishing to flourish. Their successors are already in the making, and I am convinced that they will inherit that tradition and mould it to the future.

Acknowledgements

I am very grateful to a large number of friends and colleagues who have assisted me during the course of research and writing this book although of course the usual disclaimers apply to the final result responsibility for which lies with me alone. Andrew MacLennan, Gordon Graham and Robert and Edwina Welham read more or less the entire text in draft and made very many useful comments and observations. Jeremy Lewis, whose contribution to modern publishing history is unexcelled, commented on the post-war chapters and added his inimitable gloss to people and events although he still declines to reveal the identity of the girl in the purple woolly hat.

Individual chapters were read and commented on by Rosemary Ashton, Simon Eliot, Valerie Holman, Andrew Nash, Jane Potter and Ian Willison, all of whom generously shared their expertise and research on specific areas and periods. My great friend Ron Costley who has made his own enormous contribution to twentieth-century British book design has for over thirty years been a constant source of anecdote, conversation and insight as well as regular pints of Young's IPA since I had the great good fortune to move next-door to him in 1977. His design of the book is a testament to his consummate skill. Hugh Clout advised me on the publishing history of the Admiralty handbooks and many other areas, adding to a research collaboration between us which has now lasted some thirty-five years. David Way has been an exemplary publisher, not only reading the text and offering constructive criticism but also providing insights from his own publishing career and Catherine Britton has been an enthusiastic and supportive editor. My copy-editor Catherine Bradley not only thoroughly prepared the text but also provided me with a detailed critical read which caused me to rewrite and occasionally rethink many passages. While I have not taken up all her suggestions, her experience and sharp eye for phrase, detail and contradiction has saved me from many solecisms, and from her own extensive background in publishing she provided me with many useful insights. Eric de Bellaigue has provided me with unpublished material from his research and made several useful suggestions. Kate Pool of the Society of Authors donated to me for safe keeping the books on publishing and bookselling the Society has accumulated over the last century allowing me to access several very rare and obscure sources.

In the course of stimulating conversations with Asa Briggs, Tim Rix, Adrian Higham, Ian Jacobs, Dominic Knight, Carole Blake, Andrew Franklin, Norman Franklin, Richard Charkin, Henry Reece, Stephen Bourne, the late Bob Kiernan, Philip Kogan, Jessica Kingsley, Sarah-Jane Coxon, Pam Fulton, Robert MacKay, Martin Woodhead, Colin Walsh, Martin Nield, Simon Littlewood, Gail Rebuck and Graham Taylor, I was provided with intriguing and interesting personal insights and was thereby able to avoid several egregious errors of fact and interpretation. Gloria Bailey of the Publishers' Association kindly searched their records and provided me with documents. Helen Fraser of Penguin provided access to photograph Rodrigo Moynihan's painting 'After the Conference' which graces the wall of their staff canteen and granted permission to reproduce it. My photographer David Clark spent a long day doing justice to this iconic image and providing much technical advice elsewhere. My colleagues David Nicholas, Ian Rowlands, Nick Canty and Anthony Watkinson have provided a congenial working environment in the UCL Centre for Publishing and my students of MA Publishing (and earlier on the MA Publishing Studies course at City University) have been a constant source of enthusiastic comment and reaction as well as providing intellectual stimulation. Their commitment, dedication, originality and professionalism convinces me that the future of publishing is in the best possible hands. My family, Jane, Christine, Miriam, Isabella, Peter and John have stoically put up with houses full of books and endless detours to visit promising second-hand bookshops or obscure publishing locations and have returned my bibliographic obsessions with unstinting love, support and only occasional censure.

To all of these (and anyone I may have inadvertently forgotten) I express my profound gratitude and hope that they will enjoy the final product.

Bibliography

N.B. Where the author is known but is not credited on the title page of the publication, their name is given in parentheses thus – (Allsop, P.).

Acton (Lord) (1969), *Longitude 30 West: a confidential report to the Syndics of Cambridge University Press*, New York, Cambridge University Press.

Adamson, J. (2009), *Max Reinhardt: a life in publishing*, Basingstoke, Palgrave.

Aldis, H.C. revised by J. Carter and E.A. Crutchley (1941), *The Printed Book*, Cambridge, The University Press.

(Allsop, P.) (1974), *Then and Now, 1799-1974*, London, Sweet and Maxwell.

Anon. (1926), *Some Account of the Oxford University Press, 1468-1926*, Oxford, Clarendon Press.

Anon. (1930), *Homes of Doubleday-Doren and Company*, Garden City, N.J., privately printed.

Anon. (1930), *John Murray, 50 Albemarle Street*, London, privately printed.

Anon. (1953), *Gordon & Gotch London, 1853-1953*, London, Gordon & Gotch.

Anon. (1956), *A Brief History of the Cambridge University Press*, Cambridge, The University Press.

Anon. (1957), *Adam and Charles Black, 1807-1957*, London, A & C Black.

Anon. (1975), *The Menzies Group*, Edinburgh, Menzies.

Anon. (1977), *Two Hundred and Twenty-five Years*, Edinburgh, Waterston.

Anon. (1980), *Jamie. An 80th Birthday Tribute from his Friends* [Hamish Hamilton], London, privately printed.

Anon. (1986), *At the Sign of the Mermaid. Fifty Years of Michael Joseph*, London, Michael Joseph.

Anon. (2005), *Life in Books. Friends of Tom Rosenthal celebrate his seventieth birthday*, London, privately printed.

Anthony, A. (2009), 'How one book ignited a culture war', *The Observer Review*, 11 January, pp.6-8.

Ashton, R. (2006), *142 Strand. A radical address in Victorian London*, London, Chatto & Windus.

Athill, D. (2000), *Stet. A Memoir*, London, Granta.

Attenborough, J. (1975), *A Living Memory. Hodder & Stoughton Publishers 1868-1975*, London, Hodder.

Baker, J. (1958), *The Low Cost of Bookselling. An account of the first twenty years of Readers Union*, London, Readers Union.

Barker, R. *et al.* (1966), *Books are Different. An account of the defence of the Net Book Agreement before the Restrictive Practices Court in 1962*, London, Macmillan.

Barty-King, H. (1986), *Her Majesty's Stationery Office. The story of first 200 years, 1786-1986*, London, HMSO.

Batsford, B.C. (1987), *The Britain of Brian Cook*, London, Batsford.

Beavon, J. (2004), 'Cecil Harmsworth King (1901-1987), publisher', *Oxford Dictionary of National Biography*, Oxford Scholarship Online (accessed 9 December 2008).

Bell. E. (1924), *George Bell, Publisher*, London, privately printed.

Bellaigue, E. de (2004), *British Book Publishing as a Business since the 1960s*, London, The British Library.

Bennett, B., and A. Hamilton (1990) *Edward Arnold: A hundred years of publishing*, London, Edward Arnold.

Bingley, C. (1972), *The Business of Book Publishing*, Oxford, Pergamon.

Birkett, N. *et al.* (1951), *Books are Essential*, London, Deutsch.

Black, G. (2008), *Frank's Way: Frank Cass and fifty years of publishing*, London, Valentine Mitchell.

Black, M.H. (1984), *Cambridge University Press, 1584-1984*, Cambridge, Cambridge University Press.

Black, M.H. (1992), *A Short History of Cambridge University Press*, Cambridge, Cambridge University Press.

Blackie, A.A.C. (1959), *Blackie and Son, 1809-1959*, Glasgow, Blackie.

Blackie, W.W. (1933), *John Blackie, Senior*, Glasgow, privately printed.

Blond, A (1985), *The Book Book*, London, Cape.

Bonham-Carter, V. (1978), *Authors by Profession. Volume One from the introduction of printing to the Copyright Act of 1911*, London, Society of Authors.

Bonham-Carter, V. (1984), *Authors by Profession. Volume Two 1911-81*, London, Bodley Head.

Bolitho, H. (1943), *A Batsford Century. A hundred years of publishing and bookselling, 1843-1943*, London, Batsford.

Bourne, R. (1990), *Lords of Fleet Street. The Harmsworth Dynasty*, London, Unwin Hyman.

Bower, T. (1988), *Maxwell: The Outsider*, London, Heinemann.

Bradley, S. (ed.) (2008), *The British Book Trade. An oral history*, London, The British Library.

Briggs, A (1974), *Essays in the History of Publishing*, London, Longman.

Briggs, A. (2008), *A History of Longmans and their Books, 1724-1990*, London, The British Library.

Buckland, E. (1984), *The World of Donald McGill*, Poole, Blandford Press.

Burlinghame, R. (1946), *Of the Making of Many Books. One hundred years of reading, writing and publishing*, New York, Scribners.

(Campbell-Smith, D.) (2008), *The Book of Penguin*, London, Penguin.

Carpenter, H. (2008), *The Seven Lives of John Murray. The story of a publishing dynasty*, London, Murray.
Chainey, G. (1985), *A Literary History of Cambridge*, Cambridge, Pevensey Press.
Clout, H., and C. Gosme (2003), 'The Navel Intelligence Handbooks; a monument in geographical writing', *Progress in Human Geography*, 27, 2, pp.153-73.
Cloutman, B. *et al.* (1929), *Law for Printers and Publishers*, London, Staples Press.
Clowes, W.B. (1953), *Family Business, 1803-1953*, London, Clowes.
Cooper, L. (2005), *All my Friends will buy it*, London, The History Press.
Cox, B. (2002), 'The Pergamon phenomenon 1951-1991. Robert Maxwell and scientific publishing', *Learned Publishing*, 15, 4, pp.273-8.
Cox, H., and J.E. Chandler (1924), *The House of Longman with a record of their bicentenary celebrations*, London, Longmans Green, privately printed.
Craig, A. (1937), *The Banned Books of England*, London, Allen and Unwin.
Crampsey, R. (1988), *The Empire Exhibition of 1938: the last Durbar*, Edinburgh, Mainstream.
Curtis, A. (2004), 'André Deutsch (1917-2000), publisher', *Oxford Dictionary of National Biography*, Oxford Scholarship Online (accessed 9 December 2008).
Davenport-Hines, R. (2004), '(Ian) Robert Maxwell (1923-1991), publisher and swindler', *Oxford Dictionary of National Biography*, Oxford Scholarship Online (accessed 9 November 2008).
Davis, C. (2009), *Eyewitness. The rise and fall of Dorling Kindersley*, Petersfield, Harriman House.
Dent, J.M., and H.M. Dent (1928), *The Memoirs of J.M. Dent, 1849-1926*, London, Dent.
Derricourt, R. (1996), *An Author's Guide to Scholarly Publishing*, Princeton, NJ, Princeton University Press.
Dudley Edwards, R. (1987), *Victor Gollancz. A Biography*, London, Gollancz.
Duffy, M. (1989), *A Thousand Capricious Chances. A history of the Methuen list, 1889-1989*, London, Methuen.
Dutton, G. (1996), *A Rare Bird. Penguin Books in Australia, 1946-1996*, Ringwood, Victoria, Penguin Australia.
Elfick I., and P. Harriss (1998), *T.N. Foulis. The history and bibliography of an Edinburgh publishing house*, New Castle, Delaware, Oak Knoll Press.
Eliot, S. (1994), *Some Patterns and Trends in British Publishing*, London, The Bibliographical Society.
Elliot, D. (1992), *A Trade of Charms*, London, Bellew.
Faber, G. (1934), *A Publisher Speaking*, London, Faber and Faber.
Feather, J. (1988), *A History of British Publishing*, London, Croom Helm.
Feather, J. (1994), *Publishing, Piracy and Politics*, London, Mansell.
Finkelstein, D. (2002), *The House of Blackwood*, University Park, Penn. State University Press.
Finkelstein, D., and A. McLeery (eds) (2007), *The Edinburgh History of the Book in Scotland, Volume 4, 1880-2000, Professionalism and diversity*, Edinburgh, Edinburgh University Press.
Flower, D. (1959), *The Paper Back. Its past, present and future*, London, Arborfield, privately printed.

Flower, D. (1991), *Fellows in Foolscap. Memoirs of a Publisher*, London, Robert Hale.
Franklin, N. (n.d. but 1985), *Routledge and Kegan Paul. 150 years of great publishing*, London, Routledge.
Garnett, R. (2004), *Rupert Hart-Davis Limited. A brief history with a checklist of publications*, London, The British Library.
Gasson, C. (2001), *Who Owns Whom in British Publishing*, London, Bookseller Publications.
Gentleman, D. (2002), *Artwork*, London, Ebury Press.
Gettman, R. (1960), *A Victorian Publisher. A study of the Bentley papers*, Cambridge, Cambridge University Press.
Gloag, J. (1950), *How to Write Technical Books*, London, Allen and Unwin.
Goodman, T. (2004), *The History of Purnell and Sons and the British Printing Corporation*, privately published by the author.
Gordon, G. (1993), *Aren't We Due a Royalty Statement?* London, Chatto and Windus.
Graham, G. (n.d.), *The Literature of the Book*, Marlow, Logos.
Graham, G. (1994), *As I was Saying. Essays in the international book business*, London, Hans Zell.
Graham, G. (2006), *From Trust to Takeover. Butterworths, 1938-1967*, London, Wildy, Simmonds and Hall.
Greenfield, H. (1989), *Books from Writer to Reader (revised edition)*, New York, Crown.
Haight, A.L. (1955), *Banned Books (2nd edition)*, New York, Bowker.
Hampden, J. (1935), *The Book World. A new survey*, London, Nelson.
Hampden J. (1957), *The Book World Today*, London, Allen and Unwin.
Hardwick, D. (1994), *Addicted to Romance. The Life and Adventures of Elinor Glyn*, London, André Deutsch.
Hare, G. (ed.) (1995), *Penguin Portrait. Allen Lane and the Penguin editors*, London, Penguin.
Harte, N. (1986), *The University of London, 1836-1986*, London, Athlone Press.
Hart-Davis, R. (1998), *Halfway to Heaven*, Stroud, Sutton.
Hill, A. (1988), *In pursuit of publishing*, London, John Murray.
Hodges, S. (1978), *Gollancz. The story of a publishing house, 1928-1978*, London, Gollancz.
Hodges, S. (2004), 'Sir Victor Gollancz (1893-1967), publisher and writer', *Oxford Dictionary of National Biography*, Oxford Scholarship Online (accessed 11 December 2008).
Holman, V. (2008), *Print for Victory. Book Publishing in England, 1939-1945*, London, The British Library.
Holmes, H., and D. Finkelstein (2001), *Thomas Nelson and Sons. Memories of an Edinburgh publishing house*, East Linton, Tuckwell Press.
Howard, M. (1971), *Jonathan Cape, Publisher*, London, Cape.
Hurst, C. (1997), *The View from King Street*, London, Thalia Press.
Hurst, C. (2002), *The Invisible Art. The pursuit of book making*, London, Hurst.
Jackson, H. (1938), *The Printing of Books*, London, Cassell.
James, E. (ed.) (2002), *Macmillan. A Publishing Tradition*, Basingstoke, Palgrave.

Jarvis, P., and S. Thompson (2002), 'Paul Hamlyn', *Logos*, 14, 3, pp.120-30.
Jennett, S. (1951), *The Making of Books*, London, Faber and Faber.
Jones, H., and C. Benson (2002), *Publishing Law*, London, Routledge.
Joy, T. (1952), *Bookselling*, London, Pitman.
Jovanovich, W. (1965), *Now Barabbas*, London, Longmans
Joseph, M. (1931), *This Writing Business*, London, Faber and Faber.
Joseph, R. (1986), *Michael Joseph, Master of Words*, Southampton, Ashford Press.
Kay Jones, H. (1980), *Butterworths. History of a Publishing House*, London, Butterworth.
Kegan Paul, C. (1899), *Memories*, London, Kegan Paul.
Keir, D. (1952), *The House of Collins*, London, Collins.
Kennedy, R. (1972), *A Boy at the Hogarth Press*, London, Whittington Press.
King, A., and A.F. Stuart (1965), *The House of Warne. One Hundred Years of Publishing*, London, Warne.
Kingsford, R.J.L. (1970), *The Publishers' Association 1896-1946*, Cambridge, Cambridge University Press.
Kynaston, D. (2007), *Austerity Britain*, London, Bloomsbury.
Lambert, J.W., and M. Ratcliffe (1987), *The Bodley Head, 1887-1987*, London, Bodley Head.
Latham, H.S. (1965), *My Life in Publishing*, New York, Dutton.
Lawrence, D.H. (1961), *Lady Chatterley's Lover*, London, Penguin.
Legat, M. (1982), *An Author's Guide to Publishing*, London, Robert Hale.
(Lehmann, J.) (1943), *New Writing and Daylight*, London, Hogarth Press.
Lewis, J. (1995), *Kindred Spirits*, London, HarperCollins.
Lewis, J. (2005), *King Penguin. The Life and Times of Allen Lane*, London, Viking.
Lewis, J. (2008a), *Grub Street Irregular*, London, Harper Press.
Lewis, J. (2008b), 'Hatching a Penguin. The start of paperback populism', *Logos*, 19, 1, pp.20-25.
Leventhal, L. (2002), *On Publishing. A Professional Memoir*, London, Greenhill.
Liveing, E. (1954), *Adventure in Publishing. The House of Ward Lock, 1854-1954*, London, Ward Lock.
Low, D.M. (1955), *A Century of Writers. A Centenary Volume*, London, Chatto and Windus.
Lusty, R. (1975), *Bound to be Read*, London, Cape.
MacLean, A. (1997), *No, I tell a Lie, it was the Tuesday…*, London, Kyle Cathie.
MacLehose, J. (1931), *The Glasgow University Press 1638-1931*, Glasgow, MacLehose
Macmillan, F. (1924), *The Net Book Agreement 1899 and the Book War 1906-1908*, Glasgow, privately printed.
Mann, P.H. (1971), *Books: Buyers and Borrowers*, London, André Deutsch.
Marr, A. (2006), *A History of Modern Britain*, London, Macmillan.
Marren, P. (1995), *The New Naturalists; a complete history*, London, HarperCollins.
Martin, D. (1989), *An Outline of Book Design*, London, Blueprint.
Maschler, T. (2005), *Publisher*, London, Picador.
(Maxwell, E., ed.) (1988), *Robert Maxwell & Pergamon Press. 40 Years' Service to Science, Technology and Education*, Oxford, Pergamon.

McAleer, J. (1999), *Passion's Fortune. The Story of Mills and Boon*, Oxford, Oxford University Press.

McLean, R. (1951), *Modern Book Design*, London, Longmans, Green for the British Council.

McLean, R. (2000), *True to Type*, London, Werner Shaw.

McLeery, A. (ed.) (1991), *Imprint in Time. The History of Scottish Publishers Past and Present*, Edinburgh, Merchiston Press.

McLeery, A. (2002), 'The Return of the Publisher to Book History: the case of Allen Lane', *Book History*, 5, pp.161-85.

McMurtrie, D.C. (1938), *The Book. The Story of Printing and Bookmaking*, London, Pitman.

Milne, J. (1948), *Printer's Devil or How Books Happen*, London, Epworth Press.

Morgan, C. (1943), *The House of Macmillan, 1843-1943*, London, Macmillan.

Montgomery Hyde, H. (1964), *A History of Pornography*, London, Heinemann.

Morpurgo, J.E. (1974), *Allen Lane King Penguin*, London, Hutchinson.

Mountain, P., and C. Foyle (2002), *Foyles A Celebration*, London, Foyles.

Mumby, F. (1930), *Publishing and Bookselling*, London, Cape.

Mumby, F.A. (1954), *Publishing and Bookselling. A History from earliest times to the present day*, London, Cape.

Mumby, F.A., and Norrie, I. (1974), *Publishing and Bookselling*, London, Cape.

Mumby, F.A., and S.H.S. Stallybrass (1955), *From Swan Sonnenschein to George Allen and Unwin*, London, Allen and Unwin.

Myers, R. (1973), *The British Book Trade from Caxton to the Present Day*, London, André Deutsch.

Nelson, J.G. (1989), *Elkin Matthews: Publisher to Yeats, Joyce, Pound*, Madison, University of Wisconsin Press.

Newton, N. (n.d.), *The Founding of Bloomsbury*, unpublished.

Norrie, I. (1982), *Mumby's Publishing and Bookselling in the Twentieth Century*, London, Bell and Hyman.

Norrie, I. (n.d.), *Mentors and Friends. Short Lives of Prominent Publishers and Booksellers I have known*, London, Elliott & Thompson, printed for subscribers only.

Nowell-Smith, S. (1958), *The House of Cassell 1848-1958*, London, Cassell.

Nowell-Smith, S. (1967), *Letters to Macmillan*, London, Macmillan.

Odhams, W.J.B. (1935), *The Business and I*, London, Martin Secker.

Owen, L. (2006), *Selling Rights. 6th edition*, London, Routledge.

Page, W.H. (1923), *A Publisher's Confession*, Garden City NJ, Doubleday.

Preece, D.M. and H.R.B. Wood (1946), *Modern Geography of the British Isles*, Cambridge, University Tutorial Press.

Pregnall, J. (2001), *Faber, Cape and Gollancz*, unpublished MA Thesis, City University London.

Rainbird, G. (1985), *The Rainbird Archive. An Autobiographical Bibliography*, London, Rainbird.

Raymond, H. (1938), *Publishing and Bookselling. J.M. Dent Memorial Lecture*, London, Dent.

Reinhardt, M. (1998), *Memories*, London, privately printed.

Richards, G. (1932), *Memories of a Misspent Youth*, London, Heinemann.
Richards, G. (1934), *Author Hunting. Memories of an old literary Sportsman*, London, Hamish Hamilton.
Rix, T. (2004), 'Paul Hamlyn (1926-2001), formerly Hamburger, Baron Hamlyn, publisher, businessman and philanthropist', *Oxford Dictionary of National Biography*, Oxford Scholarship Online (accessed 9 December 2008).
Roberts, S.C. (1956), *The Evolution of Cambridge Publishing*, Cambridge, Cambridge University Press.
Roberts, S.C. (1966), *Adventures with Authors*, Cambridge, Cambridge University Press.
Rolph, C.H. (1961), *The Trial of Lady Chatterley. Regina v. Penguin Books Ltd*, London, privately printed.
Rolph, C.H. (2005), *The Trial of Lady Chatterley*, London, Penguin.
Rose, J., and P.J. Anderson (eds) (1991), *British Literary Publishing Houses*, Detroit, MI, Gale Research.
Rosenthal, T.G. (2004), 'Max Reinhardt (1915-2002), publisher', *Oxford Dictionary of National Biography*, Oxford Scholarship Online (accessed 8 December 2008).
Rylance, R. (2005), 'Reading with a mission: the public sphere of Penguin Books', *Critical Quarterly*, 44, 4, pp.48-66.
Sheehan, D. (1952), *This was Publishing*, Bloomington IN, Indiana University Press.
Simner, G., and B. Tonkin (2001), *Post Cards and related Collectibles of the Festival of Britain*, West Wickham, Exhibition Study Group.
Smith, B. (1961), *Industrial Editing*, London, Pitman.
St John, J. (1990), *William Heinemann. A Century of Publishing*, London, Heinemann.
Stevenson, I. (2007a), 'The Book Trade' in Bowman, J., *British Library and Information Work, 2001-2005*, Aldershot, Ashgate, pp.328-49.
Stevenson I. (2007b), 'The Business of Publishing' in Finkelstein, D., and A. McLeery, *loc. cit.*, pp.54-70.
Stevenson, I. (2007c), 'Scientific, Technical and Medical Publishing', in Finkelstein, D., and A. McLeery, *loc. cit.*, pp.330-45.
Stevenson, I. (2008), 'Harry Potter, Riding the Bullet and the Future of Books. Key Issues for the Anglophone Book Business', *Publishing Research Quarterly*, 24, 4, pp.277-84.
Sutherland, J. (1981), *Bestsellers. Popular Fiction in the 1970s*, London, Routledge and Kegan Paul.
Swinnerton, F. (1932), *Authors and the Book Trade*, London, Howe.
Thomson, G.M. (1986), *Martin Secker and Warburg. The first fifty years*, London, Secker and Warburg.
Thornston, J. (1935), *A Tour of the Temple Press*, London, Dent.
Travis, A. (2000), *Bound and Gagged. The Secret History of Obscenity in Britain*, London, Profile.
Tredrey, F.D. (1954), *The House of Blackwood, 1804-1954*, Edinburgh, Blackwood.
Trevitt, J. (2004) 'Martin Secker (formerly Percy Martin Secker Klingender) (1882-1972), publisher', *Oxford Dictionary of National Biography*, Oxford Scholarship Online (accessed 6 November 2008).
Trevitt, J. (2004), 'The Collins Family, publishers', *Oxford Dictionary of National Biography*, Oxford Scholarship Online (accessed 6 November 2008).

Unwin, P. (1972), *The Publishing Unwins*, London, Heinemann.
Unwin, S. (1926), *The Truth about Publishing*, London, Allen and Unwin.
Unwin, S. (1980), *The Truth about a Publisher*, London, Allen and Unwin.
Walford, R. (2001), *Geography in British Schools 1885-2000*, London, Routledge.
Wallis, P. (1974), *At the Sign of the Ship, 1724-1974*, Harlow, Longman, privately printed.
Warburg, F. (1959), *An Occupation for Gentlemen*, London, Hutchinson.
Warburg, F. (1973), *All Authors are Equal*, London, Hutchinson.
Warner, O. (1973), *Chatto and Windus. A Brief History of the Firm's Origins, History and Development*, London, Chatto and Windus.
Waugh, A. (1930), *A Hundred Years of Publishing being the Story of Chapman and Hall Ltd*, London, Chapman and Hall.
Waugh, A. (1931), *One Man's Road*, London, Chapman and Hall.
Whyte, F. (1928), *William Heinemann*, London, Cape.
(Williams, W.E.) (1956), *The Penguin Story, 1935-1956*, Harmondsworth, Penguin.
Williams, W.E. (1973), *Allen Lane, a personal portrait*, London, Bodley Head.
Williamson, H. (1956), *Methods of Book Design*, Oxford at the University Press.
Winchester, S. (1998), *The Surgeon of Crowthorne. A tale of Murder, Madness and the Oxford English Dictionary*, London, Viking.
Woolf, L., and V.Woolf (1927), *Books and the Public*, London, Hogarth Press.
Young, J.L. (1929), *Books from the MS to the Bookseller*, London, Pitman.

Index